Edward Burbidge

Liturgies and Offices of the Church for the Use of English Readers

In Illustration of the Book of Common Prayer

Edward Burbidge

Liturgies and Offices of the Church for the Use of English Readers
In Illustration of the Book of Common Prayer

ISBN/EAN: 9783337161705

Printed in Europe, USA, Canada, Australia, Japan

Cover: Foto ©Lupo / pixelio.de

More available books at **www.hansebooks.com**

LITURGIES AND OFFICES OF

THE CHURCH

FOR THE USE OF ENGLISH READERS,

IN ILLUSTRATION OF

The Book of Common Prayer.

TH A CATALOGUE OF THE REMAINS OF THE LIBRARY

OF

ARCHBISHOP CRANMER.

BY

EDWARD BURBIDGE, M.A.,

RECTOR OF BACKWELL, SOMERSET.

LONDON: GEORGE BELL AND SONS,

YORK STREET, COVENT GARDEN.

1885.

CHISWICK PRESS :—C. WHITTINGHAM AND CO., TOOKS COURT.
CHANCERY LANE.

PREFACE.

AN attempt is made in the following pages to simplify the study of the original sources of the Church Services, by setting forth in an English translation the earliest forms of Christian worship, both of the Eastern and Western Church, by pointing out how these were developed in mediæval Service Books, and by tracing the return to primitive models in the revisions of the sixteenth century.

Notwithstanding that many books have been written, both in former and modern times, upon the Rites of the Church, and the history and contents of the Book of Common Prayer, English students have found a difficulty in gaining such a knowledge of the ancient Liturgies and Offices as would enable them to compare the English Services with those from which they were derived. For an acquaintance with the original forms of separate prayers gives no true idea of the Service to which they belonged. The Service itself must be studied as a whole before its character can be understood. And here has been the difficulty. For to do this, it has been necessary to investigate many books, not only difficult of access, but extremely puzzling to anyone not accustomed to use them; and the result has been that Liturgy, Canon,

Sacramentary, Missal, and Breviary have been names, rather than realities, to all but the few who have taken up Liturgies as their special study.

It has been also thought that the study of the gradual development of acts of Christian worship, if it could be brought within the reach of English students in general, would raise the estimate of the devotional value of the English Services. For it is well known that the omission from the Book of Common Prayer of various devotions and ceremonies which belonged to the Mediæval Services is viewed with regret by many. And the conviction that some of these belong to the very essence of Christian worship has led to results which are much deplored. But the importance of practices and modes of thought which are sometimes spoken of as Catholic assumes very different proportions, if it is discovered that they had their origin, not in ancient, but in mediæval times, and that they have been local, not universal, and changing instead of being fixed.

It appears to the author that the common practice of regarding the forms which were in use in England at the beginning of the sixteenth century, as if they were the original sources of the Prayer Book, is fruitful in mischief. For in this way the origin of the English Services is traced to a collection of devotions more deeply affected by mediæval developments of ritual and doctrine than those of any other country. He has endeavoured, therefore, to open the way for pushing the investigation farther back, and studying the originals upon which the Mediæval Offices were constructed ; so that the successive changes by means of which they reached the form familiar to our reformers may be clearly seen, and the

true and original sources of our Services may be discovered
as near as possible to their rise in Apostolic times.

Accordingly the Eastern form of Liturgy has been
traced up from the first century, by the help of such hints
as may be gathered out of the recently discovered "Doctrine of the Twelve Apostles," and other ancient writings,
to the earliest type of Service—the so-called Clementine
Liturgy of the Apostolical Constitutions—which is set
forth with illustrations from the Catechetical Lectures of
S. Cyril, delivered A.D. 347. To this is added an English
translation of the Liturgy in most common use at the
present day in the Greek Church, viz., the Liturgy of
S. Chrysostom. The translation is made from a copy
belonging to the eleventh century, by means of which
some of the more modern additions can be detected.
And this is illustrated by a Latin version, which is of
special interest to English Churchmen, having been made
for Fisher, Bishop of Rochester, by his friend Erasmus,
in the days when Greek was known only to a few, and
having served, in all probability, as the means of introducing the Eastern Service, if not to Archbishop Cranmer,
at least to his fellow reformers.

Similarly, the Western or Roman Liturgy has been set
out, as far as the existing uncertainty will allow, according to the form in which it was used about the time of
Pope Gregory the Great, at the end of the sixth century.
By this means the ancient prayer, which is known by the
name of "the Canon," is discovered standing free from
the mediæval rubrics which afterwards accompanied it;
and English readers are enabled to study its original
meaning from a devotional, instead of a merely ritualistic,
point of view. This ancient example of the Western

Liturgy is followed by the Mediæval Service of the "Mass," according to the rites used in England, under the fullest development of the Use of Sarum; and by a comparison of the two Services, the difference between practices and doctrines which may be rightly called "Catholic," and those which are strictly speaking "mediæval," can be clearly discovered.

For the purpose of tracing out the manner in which our English Services were compiled, extracts are given from other services and documents, which seem to have served as guides to our Reformers in their work of revision. Amongst these are included specimens of the writings of Dionysius, the (so-called) Areopagite; Archbishop Herman's suggestions, published in Latin in 1535, and in English in 1547; the Mozarabic Missal, which was rescued from oblivion by Cardinal Ximenes, and published to the world in 1500; and Cardinal Quignon's Reformed Breviary, which was published in 1535. This has led to a more careful consideration of the influence of the Protestant divines upon the second revision of the Book of Common Prayer in 1552; and it will be observed that the conclusion has been formed that the traces of this influence are less important than is commonly supposed. It is suggested that the likeness, which has been often observed to exist, between our English Communion Service and the ancient Gallican Liturgy may point to an influence of the opposite kind, and be accepted as a sign that Archbishop Cranmer and his fellow commissioners acted diplomatically in adopting a form of service which accorded with a primitive model, whilst it satisfied the intense desire for change, and the demand for a Communion Service formed upon Scriptural lines, which then prevailed. And attention is called to a treatise upon the Spanish form of Gallican Liturgy belonging to the seventh century, which became well known to English divines, through an edition published in 1534, and which may have helped in producing the hitherto unexplained resemblance between these Liturgies.

The work of tracing out the original forms of Christian Services is like the recovering of antiquities buried beneath successive layers of ruins which are themselves ancient. For the effect of mediæval additions has been not only to conceal the original simplicity of these Services, but also to lead to the supposition that the modes of thought which have been thus expressed are presented to us with all the authority of antiquity. And when the accumulations are stripped away, and the true foundations are discovered, the result is like a new revelation. The closest agreement is found to exist between the original forms of Christian worship and the teaching of Holy Scripture; and the catholicity of our English devotional system is established by its resemblance to primitive models.

The author has no intention of representing the English Services as if they were perfect, or as if they were so sacred that to criticize them is a crime, and to examine into their origin is an act of disloyalty. But he desires to treat them as set forth with the authority of the Church for the reverent use of English Churchmen; and he would discourage the habit of thoughtlessly adopting accusations against them, without considering whether they are reasonable or not; for many of the modern objections are as frivolous as those made in the days of Hooker. He has therefore endeavoured to help the reader to form an opinion for himself respecting such charges, as the occasion may arise, by means of the materials which have been gathered in the notes; and he believes that the conclusion will follow, that whilst it is abundantly evident that our reformers were not free from human infirmities, yet the more their work is examined, the more clearly it appears that they were directed by the good Providence of God in such a way that our English forms of worship are " agreeable to the Word of God, and the primitive Church."

It is well known that Archbishop Cranmer took the leading part in the revision of the English Services; and there is no doubt that he must have been greatly influenced in this work by the books which were before the world at that time. It follows, therefore, that in investigating this subject the attention of students is necessarily directed to such books as can be proved to have been within reach of the archbishop. In the course of the present work the author, having been thus led to search for books upon the services of the Church printed previously to 1549, was induced to inquire for copies of them containing the autograph of Cranmer; and it has been his good fortune to meet with unexpected evidence respecting the studies of Archbishop Cranmer, by means of the recovery of a large portion of his library. Strype (" Memorials of Cranmer," vol. i., p. 630) bears testimony both to the learning of the archbishop, and also to the extensive character of his library; and the subsequent history of his books has been well known to librarians. At the time of the archbishop's death the greater part of them fell into the hands of Henry Fitz-Alan, Earl of Arundel, from whom they passed into the keeping of his son-in-law, Lord Lumley, a great collector of books, and tutor to Prince Henry, eldest son of James I. ; and since both of these noblemen, as well as the archbishop himself, diligently inserted their signatures, most of the Cranmer books contain one or both of their names, in addition to "Thomas Cantuarien." on the title-page. At the death of Lord Lumley his library was acquired by Prince Henry, and the Cranmer books passed into the royal collection, which was begun by Henry VIII., and was at last given to the nation by George II. as the foundation of the library of the British Museum. The Cranmer books are consequently found in many bindings. A few are still in the original covers; some were bound either by Cranmer himself or Lord Lumley, with mitres on the backs; others in Prince Henry's binding, with his arms on the covers ; but the greater number have been re-bound in modern days with alternate Tudor rose and mitre on the backs, or, still more recently, with T. C. stamped below; and the effect of re-binding is shown in many cases by the mutilation or complete cutting away of Cranmer's autograph.

The archbishop's library thus formed one of the rills from which the sources of our great national library were derived. But a large number of his books were scattered throughout England. This may be explained in various ways. It is probable that some. were in the hands of friends at the time of Cranmer's death. It is known also that Lord Lumley gave a considerable number of his books, evidently for the most part duplicates, to the Bodleian Library at Oxford, and the University Library at Cambridge ; and amongst these are several which bear Cranmer's autograph. Other gifts were probably made in a similar way to the archiepiscopal library at Lambeth, and to other collections. And Cranmer books have been dispersed more recently from time to time amongst the duplicates sold by the British Museum.

But whilst the general history of Cranmer's library has been well known, it does not appear that much attention has been hitherto given to his books as evidences of the works which were actually in the hands of our reformers, and which, consequently, may be supposed to have guided them in their revision of the Services. Dean Hook led the way in this inquiry, by mentioning the existence of Archbishop Cranmer's copy of Herman's " Simplex ac pia Deliberatio " ("Lives of the Archbishops," vol. vii., p. 289). And it has been generally accepted as undoubted that the archbishop made use of Cardinal Quignon's reformed Breviary, though no reference to it has been found in his works. But it has been now discovered that more than three hundred volumes are in existence with the autograph " Thomas Cantuarien." upon the title-page. Consequently it becomes evident that the subject opens out into wide dimensions, and that conclusions of no little importance may follow its investigation.

For instance, when the archbishop's copies of the texts of such works as Eusebius' Ecclesiastical History, and Epiphanius adversus Hæreses, are found to be carefully annotated in his own handwriting, no doubt remains as to his familiarity with Greek. And in a similar manner his Hebrew studies can be traced, from his first books of Elementary Grammar, to his own Latin version of the Psalms and other parts of Scripture interleaved in his Hebrew Bible.

It has been thought, therefore, that a catalogue of the remains of this once famous library will not only be interesting to the general reader, but may open the way for more careful study of the literary history of the Reformation period.

In these days of little leisure it is nothing less than astonishing to find how wide was the range of Cranmer's Biblical studies. The diligence with which he collected the works not only of the "Doctors" of scholastic theology, but of their commentators also, proves that at some period of his life he must have deeply imbibed the learning of "The Sentences." Next the texts of Holy Scripture itself engaged his time; and one splendid edition after another was acquired to enable him to investigate them thoroughly. Then the more modern ideas respecting the spiritual teaching of the New Testament, contained in the works of Erasmus and Melancthon, were brought within his reach.

His library of Patristic Theology was equally complete, including the whole range of the "Fathers;" and the various copies, in manuscript and in print, which he possessed of the works of the same author, prove his anxiety to obtain them in the best edition.

Above all, his MS. collections of extracts from Scripture, Councils, Fathers, and theologians, testify to his diligence as a student, and to the thoroughness with which he entered into all the questions of the day.

It is reasonable to suppose that there are still very many of Cranmer's books which have hitherto escaped discovery, but which may be brought into the light when attention has been called to their importance. Notably, such books as the "Greek Text of the Liturgy of S. Chrysostom," from which the archbishop appears to make extracts, according to his own running translation in Latin; Quignon's Breviary; Isidore's De Officiis Ecclesiasticis; Ximenes' Mozarabic Missal. But a singularly clear answer to the supposition not unfrequently entertained, that he was ~~not~~ well informed about liturgical order and ritual propriety, may be given by putting into the hands of his critics his copy of " Gemma Animæ," or " Directorium Sacerdotum secundum usum Sarum," or Erasmus's version of " The Liturgy of S. Chrysostom;" and by offering them a choice of his editions of Durandus' " Rationale Divinorum Officiorum."

The number of books which have appeared of late years in connection with liturgical studies is so great, that it is difficult for the author to express his acknowledgments fully; but he has endeavoured in every case, where information has not been due to independent study, to refer in the notes to the works from which it has been derived.

Quotations which may be found in Bingham's "Antiquities," or in works easy of access, are not as a rule given in full. But the greatest care has been taken not only to verify the references, but to give the true sense of the passages quoted; and information about the books referred to has been added, so as to assist students in pursuing the study farther.

The author desires to express his hearty thanks both to those who have allowed him to give extracts from their works, and to those who have answered his inquiries about Cranmer's library; as well as to the many friends whose kind criticisms and advice have aided him in the completion of this book. His thanks are specially due to the Rev. Prebendary E. C. S. Gibson, Principal of Wells Theological College, for repeated assistance in revising the work; to the Rev. S. S. Lewis, Librarian of Corpus Christi College, Cambridge, for much valuable information, as well as for the loan of books; and to the librarians of the British Museum for the courtesy with which they have assisted him in searching for evidence respecting Archbishop Cranmer's books and MSS.

E. B.

Backwell, August, 1885.

STRYPE'S ACCOUNT OF ARCHBISHOP CRANMER'S
LIBRARY.

" He was a most profound learned man in divinity, as also in civil and canon laws. As appeared by those many voluminous writings and common-places, by him devised or collected out of all the Fathers and Church writings; which Peter Martyr reported he himself saw; and were indeed communicated to him by the Archbishop, while he harboured him at Lambeth. And there was no book either of the ancient or modern writers, especially upon the point of the Eucharist, which he had not noted with his own hand in the most remarkable places: no councils, canons, decrees of Popes, which he had not read and well considered. . . . So that his library was the storehouse of ecclesiastical writers of all ages; and which was open for the use of learned men. Here old Latimer spent many an hour; and found some books so remarkable that once he thought fit to mention one in a sermon before the king. And when Ascham of Cambridge, a great student of politer learning and of Greek authors, wanted Gregory Nyssen in Greek (not the Latin translation of him), and which it seems the University could not afford, he earnestly entreated Poynet, his grace's chaplain, to borrow it in his name and for his use, for some months of the Archbishop. For in those times it was rare to meet with those Greek Fathers in their own language and not spoiled by some ill Latin translation. Another of his books I will mention, because it is now in the possession of a reverend friend of mine near Canterbury; in which book the Archbishop's name is yet to be seen, written thus with his own hand, *Thomas Cantuariensis;* and a remarkable book it is, which we may conclude the Archbishop often perused, viz., *Epistolæ et Historia Joannis Hus:* printed at Wittemberg 1537."—Memorials of Cranmer, vol. i., p. 630.

CATALOGUE

ARCHBISHOP CRANMER'S LIBRARY.

Volumes not otherwise described are in the British Museum.

LIST OF MSS.[1]

PATRISTIC.

Ambrose. De Fide, lib. ix.
6 C. iii.
—— Expositio super Lucam,
lib. x. 6 E. ii. 1.
—— Hexæmeron. 6 A. ix. 1.
Athanasius. De Trinitate, &c.
6.B. xiii. 2.
Augustine. Confessiones, lib.
xiii. 5 B. xiv.
·—— De abusivis. 6 B. xiii. 2.
—— De civitate Dei, lib. xxii.
5 D. vii.
—— Epistolæ. 5 D. vi.
—— Excerpta de anima.
6 A. ix. 3.
—— Expositio in Psalmos. 3
Vols. 5 D. iii-v.
Basil the Great. Admonitio ad
filium spiritualem. 8 F. v. 5.

Basil the Great. Oratio.
10 B. ix. 7.
Cæsarius Arelatensis et Ephraen
Syrus. Ammonitiones de tribus generibus Elemosynarum.
8 F. v. 6.
Ephraen Syrus. De judicio,
Resurrectione, &c., lib. vi.
8 F. v. 4.
Gregory the Great. Homiliæ
xxii. in Ezekiel. 6 B. i.
Jerome. Commentarius in Psalmos 100 priores. 2 vols.
2 E. xiii, xiv.
—— Epistolæ, cxxiii. 6 C. xi.
—— Explanatio in Jeremiæ pro-
phetiam, lib. vi. 3 B. xvi.
Isidorus Hispalensis. Rhetorica.
10 B. ix. 3. •

[1] With a few exceptions these belong to the Collection of Royal MSS. in the British Museum.

b

BIBLICAL.

Chaldee Paraphrase. Joshua, cap.
i-vi., Latinè.   3 B. xviii.
Concordantiæ materiarum
Bibliæ.   5 C. iii. 3.
Four Gospels in Anglo-Saxon.
   1 A. xiv.
Reductorium morale Bibliæ Petri
Berchorii.   3 D. iii.
Translationum præcipuarum Ve-
teris Testamenti collatio; viz.
Heb., Chald., Græc. et Lat.,
Pauli Fagii [Bucklein]. Gene-
sis—Exod. ii., in print; con-
tinued in MS. to end of Exodus
by Matt. Negelin. ·
   Addit. 18987.

Bede.   Expositio in Cantica
Canticorum.   6 A. ix. 4.

Cassiodorus, M. Aur.   Expo-
sitio in Psalmos.   2 F. v.
Petrus Comestor.   Commen-
tarius in S. Pauli Epistolas.
   2 C. ii.
—— Expositiones in Vet. et
Nov. Testamenti.   7 F. iii.
—— Historia Scholastica in Vet.
et Nov. Testamentum.
   7 F. iii.
Petrus Pictavensis.   Allegoriæ
S. Scripturæ.   2 D. xii.
Radulphus Flaviacensis.   Com-
ment. in Leviticum, lib. xx.
   2 F. iii.
Rhabanus Maurus. Expositio in
Matthæum, lib. viii.   4 B. ix.

THEOLOGICAL.

Anselm.   Cur Deus Homo, &c.
   5 E. xxi. 4-12.
—— Homilia.   6 E. ii. 2.
Aquinas, Thomas. Compendium
Theologiæ.   5 C. iii. 8.
Bede.   De Tabernaculo, lib. iii.
   5 F. vi. 1.
—— De Trinitate.   5 F. vi. 2.
Bernard.   Sermones xxxii., in
Cantica Canticorum.
   5 C. iii. 24.
—— Sermones lxxxvi.   6 C. ix.
Cassiodorus, M. Aur. De Anima.
   6 A. ix. 2.
Franciscus Clusinus Episc.   De

quarta parte bonorum monas-
teriis donatorum Episcopi esse.
   10 B. ix. 16.
Homilia in Exodus, xvii.
   6 E. ii. 5.
Jacob de Voragine.   Sermones
quadragesimales.   8 D. xi.
Innocentius Papa III.   De con-
temptu mundi.   5 E. xxi. 3.
Johannes Calderinus. De ecclesiastico interdicto.
   10 B. ix. 15.
Matthæus de Cracovia.   Tract.
ad sciendum quando peccatum
sit mortale.   10 B. ix. 14.

Petrus Remensis. Sermones.
7 D. vii.
Prosper. Liber sententiarum ex operibus Augustini. 5 C. iii. 6.

Sermo (dicitur) S. Edmundi.
5 C. iii. 23.

LITURGICAL AND DEVOTIONAL.

Amalarius. De concordia Officiorum. 6 E. ii. 4.
Anselm. Meditatio.
5 C. iii. 16.
Bonaventura. Meditationes de Passione Christi. 5 C. iii. 13.
—— Meditatio de miseria animæ. 5 C. iii. 19.
Borough, Johannes. Pupilla oculi. 7 B. x.
—— (Another copy.) 7 E. v.
De observationibus Romanæ Ecclesiæ. 6 E. ii. 4.
Excerpta varia. 12 E. xxi.
Gemma animæ. (Honorii Augustodunensis.) 6 E. ii. 3.
Horologium divinæ sapientiæ. Excerpta. 5 C. iii. 14.
Hymnus ad Christum.
5 E. xxi. 2.
Johannes Peckham, Archiepisc.

Cantuar. Officium divinæ Trinitatis. 10 B. ix. 5.
Laurentius Ratholdus Hungarensis. Visitatio Purgatorii S. Patricii. 10 B. ix. 2.
Oratio ad Christum. 5 E. xxi. 1.
Pharetra, lib. iv. 8 E. vi.
Psalter, Canticles, Athanasian Creed, Collects, interlined with Anglo-Saxon version. 2 B. v.
Richard Rolle, Heremita de Hampole. De incendio amoris.
5 C. iii. 21.
—— Forma predicandi.
5 C. iii. 22.
Roger Fretoum. De stauro decanatus Cicestriæ. 5 C. iii. 17.
Simon de Gandavo, Episc. Sarum. Meditatio. 5 C. iii. 15.
Tractatus de elemosyna.
5 C. iii. 20.

VARIOUS.

Aquinas, Thomas. Commentarius in Ethicam Aristotelis.
9 E. i.
Articuli xii. pro divortio inter Henr. VIII. et Katherinam.
Vesp. B. v.
[The pleadings urged in court.]

Aristotle. Problemata et Propositiones metaphysicæ.
5 C. iii. 3, 4.
Ars versificandi. 10 B. ix. 4.
Bartholomæus de Saxoferrato. De Testimoniis.
10 B. ix. 17.

Boethius. Comment. in Consolationem Philosophicam.
5 C. iii. 11.

Chicheley, Archiep. Cantuar. De ponderibus.   7 B. ix. 2.

Cicero. Rhetorica, lib. ii.
15 A. xxvi.

Dictionarium Juridicum.
10 B. ix. 13.

Formulæ testamentorum, præsentationum, &c., dio. Cantuar.
10 B. ix. 1.

Guarinus Veronensis. De assentatoris et amici differentia.
10 B. ix. 10.

Henricus VI., Rex Angliæ. Miraculorum liber.   13 C. viii.

Johannes, Alexandriæ Patriarch. Vitæ residuum.   8 F. v. 8.

Isocrates. Orationes.
10 B. ix. 9.

Leontius Aretinus. Invectiva contra hypocritas.
10 B. ix. 10.

Licentia Papæ concessa R. Angliæ, pro Collegio. 5 C. iii. 18.

Miracula tria.   8 F. v. 1.

Œgidius Romanus. De regimine principum.   5 C. iii. 2.

Plutarch. De ingenuorum educatione.   10 B. ix. 12.

Robert Grostete, Episc. Lincoln. Excerpta ex operibus.
5 C. iii. 9, 10.

Silvi, S. Vita.   8 F. v. 7.

Socrates. Tractatus de morte contemnenda.   10 B. ix. 8.

Virgil. Liber I. Æneidos in linguam Græcam translatus.
16 C. viii.

Xenophon. Tyrannus.
10 B. ix. 6.

The following MSS. are wholly or in part in Archbishop Cranmer's own handwriting.

Collections from Holy Scripture, the Councils, and the Fathers, upon all the Questions of the day.[1] 2 vols.   7 B. xi, xii.
Collections from the Canon Law; with various articles on the Sacraments, in Latin and English.   Lambeth MSS. 1107.

Reformatio Legum Ecclesiasticarum.   Harleian MSS. 426.
Things touching the Sentence of Queen Catherine's divorce, pronounced by Byshop Cranmer at Dunstable, 1533.
Arundel MSS. 151, fol. 342.

---

[1] There is a letter from Archbishop Parker to Sir W. Cecil respecting these volumes, praying for aid to recover them.—Lansdowne MSS. vi. 70. Quoted by Strype, Life of Parker, book ii., ch. xv.; Mem. of Cranmer, Append. num. xc.

LIST OF PRINTED BOOKS.

GRAMMATICAL.

Rudimenta linguæ Hebraicæ. Paganinus. 8vo. Lyons, 1528. 621. d. 10.

Grammatica Hebraica. Sebast. Munster. 8vo. Basle, 1531. 621. d. 10.

De punctis Hebraicis, cum libro Tobit, Hebraicè. 4to. Basle, 1542. 621. g. 5.

Dictionarium, Græco Latinum et Latino Græcum. By Curio Valentinus. Fol. Basle, 1519. 623. l. 6.

Dictionarium Græcum. By Phavorinus. Fol. Rome, 1523. 624. k. 4.

Vocabularius Nebrissensis. Latin and French, by Anton. Œlius de Lebrixa. 4to. Paris, 1500. 625. f. 3.

PATRISTIC.

Ambrose. Opera. 3 vols. Fol. Basle, 1516. 1014. f. 9.

Arnobius. Adversus Gentes. Fol. Rome, 1542. 469. c. 5.

—— Commentarius in Psalmos. Cura Erasmi. Fol. Basle, 1522. 469. c. 5.

Athanasius. Opera. Accessit Erasmi Paraclesis. Fol. Strasbourg, 1522. 1014. e. 3.

Augustine. Opera. 10 vols. Large fol. Paris, 1532. 475. h. 1.

Basil the Great. Opera, Græcè, cura Erasmi. Fol. Basle, 1532. 1014. f. 12.

—— Opera quædam, Græcè. Fol. Venice, 1535. 1014. e. 6.

—— Opera, Latinè. Fol. Basle, 1540. 1013. f. 10.

Cassianus, Johannes. See THEOLOGICAL, Dionysius Carthus.

Chrysostom. Opera, Latinè. 5 vols. Fol. Basle, 1539.[1] Sidney Sussex Coll., Camb.

—— Opera, Latinè. 5 vols. Fol. Basle, 1547.[1] 1013. h. 3.

Cyprian. Opera, cura Erasmi. Fol. Basle, 1523. 1013. f. 3.

Cyril of Alexandria. Ad Nestorium. See THEOLOGICAL, Sichardus, Antidotum.

Damascenus, Johannes. Opera, Latinè. Fol. Paris, 1512. Wells Cathedral Library.

Dionysius Areopagita. Opera, Latinè. Fol. Paris, 1515. Wells Cathedral Library.

Epiphanius. Opera, Græcè.[2] Fol. Basle, 1544. 690. g. 7.

[1] Both of these editions contain the Latin Version of the Liturgy by Erasmus.

[2] Cranmer's autograph has been torn off, but the notes are in his handwriting.

Epiphanius. Opera, Latinè. Fol. Basle, 1543. Camb. Univ. Lib.
—— Contra Hæreses, Latinè. Fol. Antw. 1545. 476. f. 7.
Eusebius Pamphilus. Præparatio Evangelii, Græcè. Fol. Paris, 1544. 476. f. 10.
—— Historia Ecclesiastica, Græcè.[1] Bound with the histories of Socrates, Theodoret, Sozomen, Evagrius. Fol. Paris, 1544. 483. f. 1.
Gelasius. Adversus Eutychen et Nestorium. See THEOLOGICAL, Sichardus, Antidotum.
Gregory Nazianzen. Orationes novem, Græcè. 8vo. Venice, 1536. Durham Univ. Lib.
—— Nyssen. Liber de homine, Græcè.[2] 8vo. Venice, 1516. Durham Univ. Lib.
—— the Great. Opera. Fol. Paris, 1518. 476. g. 3.
—— —— Opera. Fol. Paris, 1533. 1014. h. 5.
—— —— Opera.[3] 2 vols. Fol. Paris, 1542. 1014. h. 6.
Hermas. Pastor. (Under the title, Liber trium virorum et trium spiritualium virginum.) Fol. Paris, 1513.
Bristol Baptist Coll. Lib.

Hilary of Poictiers. Opera. Fol. Basle, 1523. 1009. e. 1.
Jerome. Opera, cura Erasmi. 9 vols. Fol. Basle, 1516. Lambeth Lib.
—— Opera, cura Erasmi. 9 vols. Paris, 1534. 476. g. 10.
Ignatius. Epistolæ xi, Latinè. Fol. Paris, 1515. Wells Cathedral Lib.
Justin Martyr. Admonitorium Gentium. See THEOLOGICAL, Sichardus, Antidotum.
Origen. Opera, Latinè. 4 vols. Fol. Paris, 1519. 689. h. 7.
Polycarp. Epistola. Fol. Paris, 1515. Wells Cathedral Lib.
Proclus. Adversus Nestorium. Græcè. See THEOLOGICAL, Sichardus, Antidotum.
Prosper Aquitanicus. De libero arbitrio. *Ibid.*
Tertullian. Opera. Fol. Basle, 1528.
Ince Blundell Lib. Southport.
Theophilus. Liber Paschalis. See THEOLOGICAL, Sichardus, Antidotum.
Vincentius Lirinensis. Adversus profanas novationes. *Ibid.*

---

[1] Numerous notes in Cranmer's handwriting.

[2] This book seems to be referred to by Strype (Memor. of Cranmer, vol. i., p. 630), who mentions that Ascham of Cambridge wrote to borrow it from Cranmer.

[3] Two volumes in one; no autograph; T. C. on cover only.

SCHOLASTIC.

Albertus Magnus. In quatuor libros Sententiarum. 4 vols. Fol. Basle, 1507. 469. b. 7.

Ales, Alexander de (Doctor irrefragabilis). Summa Theologica. 4 vols. Fol. Lyons, 1516. 470. c. 1.

Aquinas, Thomas (Doctor angelicus). Summa Theologiæ. 2 vols. Fol. Hagen. 1512. 472. c. 3.

Bonaventura (Doctor seraphicus). In quatuor libros Sententiarum; cum Indice Alphabetico, Johannis Beckenhaub. 2 vols. Fol. Lyons, 1515. 472. d. 5, 6.

Duns Scotus (Doctor subtilis). In quatuor libros Sententiarum. 2 vols. Fol. Venice, 1477. 472. d. 1.

—— Super quatuor libris Sententiarum. 4 vols. Fol. Paris, 1513. 472. c. 13.

Ockam, Gulielmus de (Doctor invincibilis). De Sententiis. Fol. 1483. Lambeth Lib.

—— Opera. Fol. Paris, 1487. 476. a. 1.

Antoninus Florentinus. Summa. 4 vols. Fol. 1485. 473. e. 1.

Arboreus, Johannes. Theosophia, Expositiones in sacras

Scripturas ex sententiis. Fol. Paris, 1540. Lambeth Lib.

Astensis. Summa.[1] Fol. Lyons, 1519. 473. b. 8.

Beckenhaub, Joannes. See Bonaventura.

Bovillus, Carolus Samarobinius. Conclusiones.[2] Fol. Paris, 1513. 472. c. 16.

Dionysius Cisterciensis. In Sententiis. Fol. Paris, 1500. Lambeth Lib.

Durandus. In Sententias. Fol. Paris, 1508. 469. b. 11.

Gabrielis. In Sententias.[1] Fol. Basle, 1512. 470. b. 1.

Gulielmus Altissiodorensis. In Sententias.[1] Fol. Paris, 1500. 472. c. 15.

Labienus. Summa summarum. 4to. Bonn, 1517. 854. h. 8.

Lychetus de Brixia. Comment. in Duns Scoti opera. Fol. 1517. Lambeth Lib.

Leuchettus de Brixia. Comment. in lib. sentent. Duns Scoti. Fol. Milan, 1519. Lambeth Lib.

Major, Joannes. In quatuor libros sententiarum. Fol. Paris, 1519. Lambeth Lib.

Pelbartus de Themeswar. Aureum Rosarium ad libros sententiarum. Fol. Hagen, 1503. Lambeth Lib.

---

[1] No autograph; but T. C. on cover.
[2] Autograph cut off in binding.

Petrus de Palude. Quartus liber Sententiarum a Vincentio de Haerlem recognitus. (Title-page only.) 4to. Paris, 1514. Egerton MS. 2603.
Picardus. Thesauri theologorum. 2 vols. 8vo. Paris, 1511. 476. a. 4.
Ricardus Mediavillensis. In

Sententias. 4 vols. Fol. Venice, 1509. 472. d. 3.
Sirectus, Anton. Trombeta. Aureæ Scoticarum lucubrationes in Academ. Patavina. Fol. Venice, 1517. 477. e. 4.
Turrecremata. Questiones.[1] Fol. Davent. 1484. 473. b. 1.
—— Summa de Ecclesia. Fol. Lyons, 1496. 1012. d.

BIBLICAL.

Hebrew Bible, with MS. Latin Version, for the most part in Cranmer's handwriting, including Joshua, Psalms, Proverbs, Job, Daniel, Ezra, Nehemiah. Fol. Soncino, 1488. c. 23. c. 10.
Hebrew Bible. 4to. Venice, 1525. 1942. f. 3.
Biblia Polyglott. Hebrew, Greek, Chaldee, Latin; with Hebrew and Chaldee vocabulary, and Greek vocabulary. 6 vols. Fol. Complutum, 1514-1517. 1277. e.
Biblia Latina, cum postillis Cardin. Hugonis. 6 vols. Fol. Basle, 1504. 465. g. 2.
—— cum glosa ordinaria Nich. de Lyra. 6 vols. Fol. Basle, 1508. 465. g. 8.

Compendium Sacrarum Scripturarum, Mamotrecti. 4to. Strasbourg, 1496. 1010. b. 5.

Concordantiæ Sacræ Bibliæ. 4to. Paris, 1526. 1010. c. 2.
Dictionarium in Sac. Scripturas Petri Berchorii. Repertorium morale perutile prædicatoribus cum indice Joh. Beckenhaub. 3 vols. Fol. Lyons, 1516. 695. i. 2.
De Translatione Bibliæ, Petri Sutor. Fol. Paris, 1525. 1011. a. 22.

Albinus, Diaconus Anglicus. Comment. in S. Johan. 8vo. Strasbourg, 1527. 1016. d. 12.
Aquinas, Thomas. Aurea Catena in Evang. Fol. Paris, 1532. 1008. f. 5.
—— —— (Another copy.) Camb. Univ. Lib.
—— In Epistolas S. Pauli. Fol. Paris, 1526. 1009. e. 13.
—— —— Fol. Paris, 1529. Camb. Univ. Lib.

[1] Autograph cut off in binding. Quoted in "Articuli xii. pro divortio," see List of MSS.

Aquinas, Thomas. In Epistolas S. Pauli. Fol. Paris, 1538. 1009. g. 14.

Arboreus, Johannes. Comment. in Evangelia. Fol. Paris, 1551. Lambeth Lib.

Broikwus. In Evangelia. Fol. Cologne, 1539. 1008. f. 8.

Bruno Carthusianus. Opera. Fol. Paris, 1524. 1009. e. 3.

Bucer, Martin. Metaphrases et enarrationes in Epist. ad Romanos. (Dedicated to Cranmer.) Fol. Strasbourg, 1536.
Colfe Grammar School.

Cajetan, Cardinal Thomas de Vio. Comment. in quinque Mosaicos libros, cum Aug. Eugubini cosmopœia. Fol. Paris, 1539. 1008. e. 12.

—— Novum Testamentum cum Comment. 2 vols. Fol. Paris, 1532. 1277. d. 1.

Cassia, Simon de. In Evangelia. Fol. 1533. 1008. f. 6.

Chromatius, Episc. Romanus. Dissertatio in S. Matt., cap. v, vi. 8vo. Basle, 1528. 1016. c. 16.

Dionysius Carthusianus, de Leuwis. Comment. in Vetus et Novum Testamentum. 14 vols. Fol. Cologne, 1534-1540. 1008. e. 1.

Erasmus, Desid. Annotationes in Novum Testamentum. Fol. Basle, 1527.
Colfe Grammar School.

Erasmus, Desid. Paraphrases in Novum Testamentum. 2 vols. Fol. Basle, 1524. 1277. b.

Eucherius. Comment. in sacras Scripturas. Fol. Basle, 1531. Lambeth Lib.

Euthymius. Comment. in Psalmos. Fol. 1530.
Lambeth Lib.

Faber, Isaac. Comment. in Evangelia. Fol. 1522. Camb. Univ. Lib.

—— —— Fol. Cologne, 1541. 1008. f. 4.

—— Comment. in Epistolas. Fol. Paris, 1531. 1008. f. 10.

Folengius. Comment. in Psalmos. Fol. Basle, 1540. 1008. f. 2.

Gorranus. Comment. in Evangelia. Fol. Cologne, 1537. 1008. f. 7.

Hesychius, Presbyter. Comment. in Leviticum. Fol. Basle, 1527. 467. d. 3.

Holkot, Robertus. Comment. in Sapientiæ libros. Fol. Hagen. 1494. 1010. f. 9.

Hugo, Cardinal. Expositio Evangeliorum. Fol. 1508.
Lampeter Coll. Lib.

Kimchi. In decem primos Psalmos. Hebraicè et Latinè. Fol. Coutances, 1544.
Camb. Univ. Lib.

Lombardus, Petrus. Comment. in Epistolas S. Pauli. Fol. Paris, 1537. 1009. g. 14.

Ludolfus Carthusiensis de Saxo-
niæ. Comment. in Psalmos.
4to. Paris, 1520.
1013. d. 15.
Major, Joannes, Hadingtonianus.
Expositio in Evangelia. Fol.
Paris, 1529. Lambeth Lib.
Melancthon, Philip. Solomonis
Sententiæ, cum Annotationi-
bus. 8vo. Hagen. 1525.
Leigh Grammar School.
Œcumenius. Comment. in Evan-
gelia, ex operibus Chrysos-
tomi. Fol. Lovan. 1543.
1009. e. 12.
—— —— (Another copy.)
Camb. Univ. Lib.

Primacius Uticensis. Comment.
in Apocalypsin. 8vo. Basle,
1544. 1016. e. 11.
Prosper. Expositiones in Sacras
Scripturas. Fol. Lyons, 1539.
1014. e. 12.
Radulphus Flaviacensis. Comment. in Leviticum. Fol.
Cologne, 1536. · 467. d. 3.
Sedulius Scotus. Comment. in
Epistolas S. Pauli. Fol. Basle,
1528. 1009. e. 13.
Titelman. Elucidationes in Psalmos. Fol. Paris, 1545.
1009. f. 10.

THEOLOGICAL.

Albertus Pius. In Erasmum.
Fol. Paris, 1531. 1012. f. 3.
Alexander Anglus. Destructio
vitiorum. Fol. Paris, 1495.
477. e. 3.
Alvarenus. Homiliæ in Cantica
Canticorum. 8vo. Paris, 1515.
852. k. 13.
Alphabetum Theologicum, sive
Tropi Veteris et Novi Testamenti, e Dionysii Areopagitæ
operibus collecti. 4to. Hagen.
1531. 469. a. 21.
Angelus de Clavas. Summa An-
gelica. Fol. Strasbourg, 1494.
1011. b. 9.
Barbatia, Andreus. De Præs-
tantia Cardinalium. 1518.
Trinity Hall Lib., Camb.

Bernardus. Opera. Fol. Paris
(no date). 475. f. 2.
Clichtoveus. De Conceptione,
Passione et Assumptione S.
Mariæ Virginis. 4to. Paris,
1513. 1010. b. 6.
Cusa, Nicholas de. Opera. 2
vols. Fol. Paris, 1514.
1012. d. 16.
Dionysius Carthusianus, de Leuwis. Minor works, including
Joh. Cassian, de cœnobiorum
institutis, &c. Fol. Cologne,
1540. 1008. e. 11.
—— Comment. in Dionysii Areopagitæ libros. Fol. Cologne,
1536. 1014. e. 7.
—— De Trinitate. 4 vols.
Fol. Cologne, 1535. 1015. f. 1.

Dormus Securus. Sermones. 8vo. Lyons, 1495. 852. k. 7.

Driedonius, Johannes. De Ecclesiasticis Scripturis, lib. iv. Fol. Lovan. 1533. Lambeth Lib.

—— ——[1] Fol. Lovan. 1543. Camb. Univ. Lib.

Erasmus, Desiderius. Christiani Matrimonii institutio. 8vo. Basle, 1526. 697. b. 7.

—— Christiani Principis institutio. 4to. Basle, 1519. 526. k. 4.

—— Enchiridion. 8vo. Strasbourg, 1524. 697. b. 9.

—— Paraclesis. 8vo. Basle, 1530. 697. b. 9.

—— Ratio, seu Methodus Theologiæ. 8vo. Basle, 1520. 697. b. 9.

Faber, Episc. Viennensis. Homiliæ. 3 vols. Fol. Cologne, 1541. 473. d. 1.

Fredericus Nausea Blanci-campiani. Homiliæ. Fol. Cologne, 1532. 692. g. 7.

Galatinus, Petrus. De arcanis Catholicæ Veritatis, ex Talmud. Fol. 1518. Camb. Univ. Lib.

Gerson, Johannes Charlier de.

Opera. 4 vols. Fol. Paris, 1521. 472. f. 3.

Gregory Nazianzen. Carmina.[2] 4to. Venice, 1504. 481. c. 3.

—— De Theologia.[3] Fol. Basle, 1523. 586. i. 1.

Haymo, Episc. Halberstallensis. Homiliæ. 8vo. Cologne, 1531. 846. k. 7.

Herolt. Sermones. Fol. Strasbourg, 1503. 474. e. 11.

Hus, Johannes. De Ecclesia. 4to. 1520. Durham Univ. Lib.

Justinianus, Laurentius, Protopatriarch Venet. Opera. Fol. Paris, 1524. 473. f. 6.

Lanspergius. Postilla. Fol. Cologne, 1548. Camb. Univ. Lib.

Ludolphus Saxo. Vita Christi.[1] Fol. Paris, 1517. 691. h. 9.

Maphæus Vegius. De perseverantia Religionis.[4] 4to. Hagen. 1531. 469. a. 21.

Michael Hungarensis. Sermones. 8vo. Antwerp, 1487. 851. i. 2.

Pagninus. Isagoga ad sacras literas. Fol. Lyons, 1536. 689. i. 10.

—— —— ad mysticos sensus S. Scripturæ. Fol. Lyons, 1536. 689. i. 10.

---

[1] Autograph cut off in binding.
[2] Autograph apparently torn out, but doubtful.
[3] Doubtful; bound in one volume with other works, the first of which alone bears the autograph of Cranmer.
[4] Autograph cut off, but known by MS. notes.

Pighius, Albertus. Hierarchiæ ecclesiasticæ assertio. Fol. Cologne. 1538. 1010. f. 22.
Ricardus de S. Victor. Opera. Fol. Paris, 1518. 472. f. 11.
Rusbrochius, Johannes. Tractatus. Fol. Cologne, 1552.
Lambeth Library.
Sichardus, Johannes. Antidotum. (Tracts by various Fathers and Theologians.) Fol. Basle, 1528. Bodleian.

Sichardus, Johannes. Antidotum. (Another copy.)
Lambeth Library.
Speculum, seu Le Mirouer de la Redemption humane. 4to. Lyons, 1493. 1009. f. 17.
Wicelius. Postilla. Fol. Cologne, 1545. 1008. f. 12.
Wiclefus, Johannes. Dialogus, libri quattuor. (Commonly called, Trialogus.) 4to. 1525.
Durham Univ. Lib.

LITURGICAL.

Directorium Sacerdotum, secundum Usum Sarum. 8vo. London, 1501. C. 35. f. 7.
Durandus. Rationale divinorum officiorum. 4to. Lyons, 1506. 468. a. 13

Durandus. Rationale divinorum officiorum. 4to. Lyons. 1508. 468. a. 14.
Herman, Archiepiscopus Colon. Simplex ac pia Deliberatio. Bonn, 1535.
Chichester Cathedral Lib.

LEGAL.

Brunellus, Johannes. Tractatus de sponsalibus et matrimoniis. 4to. Paris, 1521. 498. b. 2.
Brunus, Conrad. De Legationibus. De Cærimoniis. De Imaginibus, lib. iii. Fol. Mayence, 1548. 521. m. 2.
Budæus, Gulielmus. Annota-

tiones in Pandectas. Fol. Paris, 1530. Camb. Univ. Lib.
Durandus de S. Porciano. De jurisdictione Ecclesiæ. 8vo. Paris, 1506. 476. a. 2.
Gratianus. Decretales, sive Concordia discordantium Canonum. Fol. Paris, 1528.
Camb. Univ. Lib.

HISTORICAL.

Annius, Johannes. Antiquitates, lib. xvii. Fol. Paris, 1512. 588. i. 11.

Chronici varii. 3 vols. Fol. Berne, 1540. 580. i. 4.

Chronica, a Nauclero. 2 vols. Fol. Tubingæ, 1516. 580. l. 2.

Chronicon, a Johanne Sichardo. (Including Eusebius, Hieronymus, Prosper, &c.) Fol. Basle, 1529. 581. i. 3.

Chronicorum Supplementum. Fol. Basle, 1538. 583. k. 2.

Chronica (in German), a S. Franck. Fol. Strasbourg, 1531. 580. i. 1.

Dionysius Halicarnassus. Antiquitates Romanæ. Fol. Basle, 1532. Camb. Univ. Lib.

Ecclesiastical Historians. See PATRISTIC, Eusebius.

Eutropius. Historia Romana. Fol. Basle, 1532. 588. i. 9.

Florus, Lucius. De gestis Romanorum. Fol. Basle, 1532. Lambeth Lib.

Hus, Johannes. Epistolæ et Historia. Wittemb. 1537. Mentioned by Strype, Cranmer, vol. i., p. 630.

Justinus Historicus. Epitome in historias Trogi Pompeii, Lucii Flori, Sexti Ruffi. Fol. Paris, 1519. 586. i. 1.

Maximus, C. Valerius. Opera. Fol. 1513. Camb. Univ. Lib.

Orosius. Historiarum Liber.[1] Fol. Paris, 1524. 586. i. 1.

Otto. Rerum Gestarum ab origine mundi.[2] Fol. Strasbourg, 1515. 592. f. 1.

Polybius. De Bello Punico.[1] Fol. Paris, 1512. 586. i. 1.

Rhenanus Selestadiensis. Rerum Germanicarum, lib. iii. Fol. Basle, 1531. Lambeth Lib.

Saxo Grammaticus. Historia, lib. xvi. Basle, 1534. Private Library.

Solinus, Julius. Polyhistor. Fol. Vienne, 1520. 570. g. 7.

Suetonius. Historia, studio Erasmi. Fol. Basle, 1533. Camb. Univ. Lib.

Vergil, Polydore. Historia Anglica. (Presentation copy to Cranmer from the publisher, J. Bebelius.) Fol. Basle, 1534. Camb. Univ. Lib.

[1] Doubtful; bound in one volume with other works, the first of which alone bears the autograph of Cranmer.

[2] Autograph cut off in binding.

ON THE PROTESTANT CONTROVERSY.

Castro, Alfonsus de. Adversus Hæreses. Fol. Cologne, 1539. 474. d. 5.

Clichtovens. Anti-Lutherus. Fol. Paris, 1516. 474. d. 8.

Cochlæus, Johannes. Scopa. (In reply to Apomaxis Calumniarum Joh. Cochlæi in Henricum VIII., by Rich. Morysine.) 8vo. Leipsic, 1538. Lambeth Lib.

Confutatio Assertionis Lutheranæ. Fol. Antwerp, 1523. 474. d. 7.

Eckius, Johannes. Apologia adversus Bucerum. 4to. 1542. Bodleian.

—— Contra Lutherum. Fol. Augsburg, 1530. 474. d. 9.

—— Homiliæ contra Lutherum. 4 vols. Fol. Augsburg, 1533 to 1536. 474. d. 10.

Erasmus, Desiderius. Hyperaspistes Diatribæ, adversus servum arbitrium M. Lutheri. 8vo. Antw. 1526. 697. b. 3.

Haner, Johannes. Prophetia vetus ac nova, de sincera cognitione Christi, de que recta in Illum fide. 4to. Leipsic, 1534. 479. a. 1.

King Henry VIII. Assertio septem Sacramentorum, adversus M. Lutherum. London, 1521. Private Library.

Perbonus, Hieronymus, Marchionis Oviliarum. Thesaurus Philosophiæ, adversus Lutherum, lib. xxvi. Fol. Milan, 1533. 1012. e. 1.

Pighius, Albertus. Apologia adversus M. Bucerum. 4to. Mayence, 1543. 477. a. 3.

Sacræ Cæsareæ Majestatis declaratio. 4to. Bodleian.

Wicelius, Georgius. Confutatio Jodochi Koch, cum assertione bonorum operum. 4to. Leipsic, 1533. 479. a. 1.

—— Syllabus locorum ex utroque testamento de bonis operibus. 4to. Leipsic, 1534. 479. a. 1.

CLASSICAL.

Aristotle. De historia animalium. Fol. Basle, 1534. 520. i. 1.

—— Metaphysica. Fol. Paris, 1520. 520. g. 5.

—— De generatione: cum comment. Themistii. Fol. Venice, 1520. 519. i. 19.

Aristotle. Questiones Johannis Buridani. Fol. Paris, 1513. 519. i. 11.

—— Comment. Joachimi Perionii, in Aristotelem. 8vo. Basle, 1540. 520. b. 18.

—— Comment. Roberti Lincoln. Fol. 1501. 520. h. 4.

Aristotle. Questiones Scoti in Metaphysicam. Fol. Venice, 1491. 520. h. 3.
—— Opuscula Petri Tatareti in Aristotelem. Fol. 1500. 519. g. 16.
Astronomici veteres. Latinè. Fol. Venice, 1493. Bodleian.
Cicero. De Officiis. De Amicitia. De Senectute, cura Erasmi. 4to. Basle, 1528. 525. i. 4.
—— Comment. in Oratorem Ciceronis. Fol. Venice, 1477. 525, k. 31.
Euclid. Latinè. Fol. Paris. Bodleian.

Herodotus. Græcè. Fol. Basle, 1541. Trin. Coll. Lib., Camb.
Mela, Pomponius. De orbis situ. Fol. Basle, 1542. 570. g. 7.
Quintilian. Institutiones oratoriæ. Fol. Paris, 1516. 836. l. 7.
Strabo. Geographicorum, lib. xvii. Fol. Basle, 1523. 569. h. 7.
Theophrastus. De historia plantarum. Fol. Basle, 1534. 520. i. 1.
Thucydides. Græcè. Fol. Basle, 1540. Trin. Coll. Lib., Camb.
Virgil. Opera cum Commentariis. Fol. 1528. Camb. Univ. Lib.

MEDICAL.

Dioscorides. Opera. Græcè et Latinè. Fol. Cologne, 1529. Camb. Univ. Lib.
Galen. Opera. Latinè. 6 vols. Fol. Basle, 1542. Worcester Coll. Lib., Oxford.

Paulus Ægineta. Opera. Græcè. Fol. Basle, 1538. Camb. Univ. Lib.

GENERAL.

Alexander ab Alexandria. Opera.[1] Fol. Paris, 1532. 630. l. 2.
Badius Ascensius. Annotationes doctorum virorum in Grammaticos, Oratores, &c. Fol. Paris, 1511. 631. k. 1.

Bartholomæus. De proprietate rerum. Fol. Harlem. 1485. Camb. Univ. Lib.
—— —— Fol. Strasbourg, 1505. 525. l. 10.
Bayfius. De re navali. Private Library.

[1] Doubtful; bound with another book which alone bears Cranmer's autograph.

Bocatius, Johannes. Genealogia deorum. Fol. Basle, 1532.
696. m. 19.

Boethius, Anicius Manlius. De consolatione Philosophiæ, &c. Fol. Venice, 1499.
524. i. 12.

Budæus, Gulielmus. Epistolæ.[1] 4to. Basle, 1521.
1084. m. 6.

Erasmus, Desiderius. Apologia, qua respondet duabus invectivis Edwardi Lei. 8vo. Antwerp, 1520.   697. d. 6.

Legenda Sanctorum ; vel speculum exemplorum. Fol. Hagen. 1505.   488. h. 5.

—— vel hagiologium. Fol. Mayence, 1541.   488. h. 13.

Œcolampadius. Græcæ literaturæ dragmata. 8vo. Basle, 1523.   622. d. 3.

Petrus Crinitus. Opera. Fol. Paris, 1525.   630. l. 2.

Philelphus. Epistolæ. Fol. Brescia, 1485.   635. l. 3.

Pogius Florentinus. Opera. Fol. Basle, 1538.   632. l. 6.

Richerius, Lod. Cælius, Rhodiginus. Lectionum Antiquarum, lib. xv.[2] Fol. Basle, 1517.   632. l. 5.

Textor, Ravisius. Officina. Fol. Paris, 1520.
Camb. Univ. Lib.

Vergerius, Petrus Paulus. De ingenuis moribus. (Including Hieronymus, De Officiis, and Quintilianus, De Officiis.) 4to. Paris, 1510.   526. k. 1.

₎ *Much labour has been spent in making this List as correct as possible, and the Author will be glad to be informed of any volumes which have escaped discovery, and of any errors which have been made.*

[1] Autograph torn off.

[2] Autograph crossed out; " Si non hodie quando " written over it.

CONTENTS.

CHAPTER I. INTRODUCTION.

Two kinds of Jewish worship. Temple Service sacrificial. Synagogue Services non-sacrificial. Jewish Services the patterns of Christian Services. Sacrifices pointed to Christ. The Christian Sacrifice. Sacrifices not always propitiatory. Eucharist instituted in place of the old sacrifices. All the ideas connected with the sacrifices transferred to the Eucharist. The Sacrifice of the Cross perfect and sufficient. The Christian Sacrifice altogether superior to Jewish sacrifices. The Common Prayers supplementary to the Eucharist, as the Synagogue services to the Temple sacrifices. References to them in Holy Scripture; in early Christian writings. Praise, Hearing, and Prayer their main divisions. Plan of the work described. Antiquity of existing Services. Subject to be treated under two divisions, according to the two classes of Service Books . . . . . . Page 1

CHAPTER II. EASTERN LITURGIES.

Services not committed to writing in the first ages. The Apostolic model variously adapted in different Churches. Liturgy a technical name. Form of Service in " DOCTRINE OF THE TWELVE APOSTLES." Service described by JUSTIN MARTYR. The CLEMENTINE LITURGY. Its resemblance to the Liturgy of S. James. Liturgy referred to in the Homilies of S. Chrysostom. Changes in the Liturgy of S. Chrysostom. Latin Version by Erasmus. LITURGY OF S. CHRYSOSTOM in English and Latin . Page 19

CHAPTER III. THE ROMAN LITURGY.

Sacramentaries. Uncertainty about the Roman Liturgy until the ninth century. Revision of the Services by Gregory the Great. ROMAN LITURGY

. c

LITURGIES AND OFFICES OF THE CHURCH.

CHAPTER I.

INTRODUCTION.

"Ab ortu enim solis usque ad occasum, magnum est nomen meum in gentibus, et in omni loco sacrificatur, et offertur nomini meo oblatio munda."
—*Mal.* i. 11.

A T the time of our Lord's earthly ministry two distinct methods of worship prevailed amongst the
Jews, namely, the Temple worship at Jerusalem, and the
Synagogue worship in every town inhabited by Jews,
whether in Palestine or in heathen lands. The Temple
worship had been founded upon the Ordinances of the
Law, received from God by Moses. The Synagogue
worship had grown up gradually amongst the Lord's
People, partly as a help to keep up their remembrance
of God during the intervals between their visits to the
Holy City, and partly as a means for preserving or im-
parting the knowledge of God amongst those who could
not attend the Feasts.[1]

[1] The origin of such services may be traced back probably as far as to
the days of Samuel; though the regular institution of the Synagogues seems
to have arisen in the time of Ezra, after the return from the captivity,

B

The Temple Services consisted mainly of various kinds of public and private sacrifices, viz., (1) the daily Burnt Offering, morning and evening, which may be regarded as representing the desire of the Lord's People to ascend in heart to Him and praise Him ;[1] (2) the frequent Peace Offerings, which were acts of thanksgiving for mercies received, and varied according to the circumstances of the worshipper;[2] (3) the Sin Offerings on stated occasions, which illustrated the need of cleansing to enable sinful men to approach God.[3]   In addition to these sacrifices the Incense was daily offered, morning and evening; prayers were said; psalms were sung according to the musical arrangements appointed by David and Solomon, and the blessing was given by the Priest in the form pre-scribed by God through Moses.[4]

The Synagogue Services consisted of certain solemn prayers, followed by Lessons from Holy Scripture—from the Law and the Prophets according to a fixed order—with

when it was found to be necessary not only to read the Law to the people, but also " to give the sense, and cause them to understand the meaning " (Nehem. viii. 1-8). Synagogue worship was so extended through the settle-ment of Jews in all parts of the Roman Empire, that S. James could say, " Moses hath in every city those that preach him " (Acts xv. 21).   For a full account of the various uses of the word Synagogue, see Schleusner, Lexicon Vet. et Novi Testam.

[1] Exod. xxix. 38-42.   The word commonly used for Burnt Offering is from the root *alah*, to go up.

[2] Levit. vii. 11-16 ; Joshua viii. 31 ; 1 Kings iii. 15, viii. 63.

[3] Exodus xxix. 35-37 ; Levit. iv. 2-35, xvi. 5, 6 ; 2 Chron. xxix. 21.

[4] Numb. vi. 24-26.   Reference is made to this part of the service in the account given by S. Luke of the angel appearing to Zacharias : " The people were praying without," whilst Zacharias was offering the incense within the Temple, and they " waited for Zacharias, and marvelled that he tarried so long in the Temple.   And when he came out he could not speak unto them " (S. Luke i. 10-22).   See Dict. of the Bible,—" Incense."

addresses of explanation and exhortation.[1] It is said that these prayers were composed by Ezra. They consisted originally of eighteen forms, including acts of Confession, Praise, Supplication, and Thanksgiving; and to these a nineteenth prayer was added in later times, apparently imprecating God's wrath upon the followers of Christ.[2] At all events, it is certain that, with this one exception, they are very ancient; and there is no doubt that they were used in the time of our Lord, and that He must have joined in them with the rest of the Jews as often as He went into their synagogues.

The existence of these two classes of services amongst the Jews is known to all, through the frequent references in Holy Scripture to the Temple and the Synagogues;

[1] For a description of the Synagogue Services, see Prideaux's "Connection," book vi. vol. i. p. 297.

[2] Amongst these prayers are the following:—

"1. Blessed be Thou, O Lord our God . . . who rememberest the good deeds of our fathers, and in Thy love sendest a Redeemer to those who are descended from them, &c.

"2. Thou, O Lord, art powerful for ever. Thou raisest the dead to life, and art mighty to save . . . Blessed art Thou, &c.

"3. Thou art Holy, and Thy saints do praise Thee every day, &c. Blessed art Thou, &c.

"6. Be Thou merciful unto us, O our Father, for we have sinned; pardon us, O our King, for we have transgressed against Thee, &c. Blessed art Thou, &c.

"7. Look, we beseech Thee, upon our afflictions. Be Thou on our side, &c.

"8. Heal us, &c.

"18. We will give thanks unto Thee with praise . . . our Rock. To all generations will we give thanks unto Thee, &c."

The additional prayer is now numbered 12. "Let there be no hope to them who apostatize from the true religion; and let heretics how many soever they be all perish as in a moment. Blessed be Thou who destroyest the wicked, &c."—Prideaux's "Connection," *ut supra.*

but in a general way they probably receive little attention, because they are supposed to contain no very useful lessons for Christians. If, however, they are considered with the object of seeking for the sources out of which Christian Services grew, they are recognized at once as the patterns by which Jews, when they became Christians, learned to fashion the worship of God, in accordance with their additional knowledge of Him.

It has been often said, and universally acknowledged, that the Temple Sacrifices pointed to the Messiah, the Christ, who was to come. With our knowledge of the work of Christ we can see Him prefigured in all the ordinances of the Law, and realize that He alone could fulfil the ideas connected with them, and that He did fulfil them. Accordingly we find, as we might naturally expect, that from the earliest days of Christianity the sacrificial teaching of the Old Testament was referred to as prefiguring the more perfect worship of Christians. Under the guidance of the Holy Spirit the Epistle to the Hebrews led up the thoughts of Christians from the patterns set forth in the Law to the realities worked out by the Sacrifice and Ascension of our Blessed Lord. And this example was followed in the writings and practices of the ages which followed. The early Christians transferred to the Office of the Holy Communion the sacrificial terms and teaching to which they, or their fathers, had been accustomed in times past.[1] They regarded it as the means provided by Christ Himself for keeping up their connection with His One Perfect Sacrifice of the Cross, and for pleading the merits of His Death. And therefore they did not hesitate to refer to the Eucharist

---

[1] Freeman, " Principles of Divine Service," part ii. chap. i. sect. 1.

as the Christian Sacrifice, and they called it "The Sacrifice without Blood."[1]

[1] Illustrations of the transference of sacrificial terms to Christian services
may be given from almost every Christian author. Clemens Romanus, *circa*
A.D. 97, exhorting the Corinthian Church to preserve due order and unity,
makes mention of the Jewish system of priests and sacrifices as furnishing
patterns for Christians to follow, saying, "Those, therefore, who present their
offerings at the appointed times are accepted and blessed; for inasmuch as
they follow the laws of the Master, they sin not. For his own peculiar services are assigned to the High Priest; and their own proper place is ascribed
to the Priests; and their own special ministrations devolve on the Levites.
The layman is bound by the laws that pertain to the laymen."—Clemens
Rom., Epist. i. ad Corinth., cap. 40.

Justin Martyr, *circa* A.D. 139, arguing with Trypho, a Jew, declares that
God had taught in the Old Testament that the services of Christians would
take the place of the Jewish sacrifices, saying, "We are the true high-
priestly race of God, as even God Himself bears witness, saying that in every
place amongst the Gentiles sacrifices are to be offered, well pleasing to Him
and pure. . . . So then God referring beforehand to the Sacrifices which
we offer through this Name—even those which Jesus the Christ instituted,
that is to say, through the Eucharist of the Bread and the Cup—and which
are presented by Christians in all places throughout the world, bears witness that they are well pleasing to Him. But He utterly rejects those which
are presented by those priests of yours, saying, Neither will I accept an
offering at your hand. For from the rising of the sun my Name shall be great
among the Gentiles."—Justin Martyr, Dial. cum Trypho, cap. cxvi., cxvii.

Irenæus, *circa* A.D. 177, says: "Our Lord was giving counsel to His disciples to offer to God the first-fruits of His creatures, not as if He was in
need of them, but in order that they should be neither unfruitful nor un-
grateful; and He took that which as a part of His creation was bread, and
gave thanks, saying, 'This is My Body,' and similarly the cup, saying,
'This is My Blood.' And thus He taught them the new offering of the
New Testament, which the Church has received from the Apostles and offers
through the whole world to God." He then quotes Mal. i. 10-12, as describing what has come to pass, that the Jews have ceased to offer, but
that in every place sacrifice is offered to God, and His Name is glorified
amongst the nations.—Iren. adv. Heres., lib. iv. cap. xxx.

Tertullian, *circa* A.D. 200, uses such expressions as this, "We sacrifice
for the safety of the Emperor . . . in simple prayer."—Tertull. ad Scap., cap. ii.

Cyprian, *circa* A.D. 250, makes very frequent reference to Christian services under sacrificial terms. Speaking of his continual remembrance of

The use of such terms in all the known forms of early Christian worship is so frequent, that it is necessary to refer to it at once. But the mention of Sacrifice in connection with the Eucharist is known to be very distasteful in a general way to the minds of English Churchmen. Some explanation seems, therefore, to be needed to remove objections, and to make the intentions of the early Christian writers clear.

It is probable that the word sacrifice is commonly understood to express the idea of an offering for sin. But it is far from the truth to suppose that the Sacrifices of the Law consisted only of Sin Offerings. On the contrary, it was the exception rather than the rule for a

certain men, he says, he has them in his mind, " both when in the sacrifices I offer prayer with many, and when in retirement I pray with private petitions."—Cyprian, Epist. xxxvii., *aliter* xv., ad Moysen et Maxim. Speaking of God's ministers administering the Eucharist to those in danger of persecution, he says, " It is the great honour and glory of our Episcopate, to have granted peace to martyrs, so that as priests who daily celebrate the sacrifices of God we may prepare offerings and victims to God."—Epist. lvii., *aliter* liii., ad Cornelium, de lapsis. These illustrations from Cyprian's writings might be greatly multiplied.

In the sermons of S. John Chrysostom, *circa* A.D. 387, similar references occur continually. Thus he says, " The sacrifices of the Law were not well pleasing to God, nor according to His intention, but only permitted by Him ; and He attached to the acts of sacrificing a type and image of the coming dispensation of Christ, so that, though not acceptable of themselves, yet on account of their representing Him they might become well pleasing. Throughout them all He gives the image of Christ, and shadows forth things to come. And whether a sheep, or an ox, or a dove were offered, all referred to the Saviour."—Chrysost., Homil., 166, tom. v., p. 986 (Eton, 1612). Moreover, he continually refers to the Eucharist under the name " Sacrifice," which he is careful to connect with the Sacrifice of Christ, by way of memorial. For instance, he uses such expressions as this, " Many receive of this Sacrifice but once in the year ; " and he describes it as, " the holy Sacrifice," " the spiritual Sacrifice," " the fearful and tremendous Sacrifice," and " the reasonable Sacrifice." Quoted by Suicer, Thesaurus, under the word θυσία.

sacrifice to be in this sense propitiatory. For as has been already mentioned, the Burnt Offering expressed the idea of Praise rather than of propitiation for sin ; and the Peace Offerings were acts of Thanksgiving. In considering the meaning of Sacrifice, it is well to recall Jonah's words : " But I will Sacrifice unto Thee with the voice of Thanksgiving ; "[1] or the happy exclamation of the Psalmist, " Now shall mine head be lifted up . . . therefore will I offer in His Tabernacle sacrifices of joy ; "[2] or his cry, " O that men would praise the Lord for His goodness . . . let them sacrifice the sacrifices of Thanksgiving."[3]

There is need of caution in speaking of the propitiatory power of the ancient sacrifices. The truth is, One Sacrifice alone has been able to atone for sin. The sacrifices of the Law could do no more than point to this One Perfect Sacrifice under different aspects. They represented different sides of the truth respecting " the Lamb of God which taketh away the sin of the world ; " but they could not be of themselves propitiatory. For " it is not possible that the blood of bulls and of goats should take away sin."[4] They served the purpose assigned to them ; but they did this only by being figures of the Sacrifice that was to come. By them the pious Jew was drawn near to God, because his faith was excited, and his service became acceptable through Him to whom they pointed.

When " the Lamb of God " had been offered upon the Cross, the sacrifices, which as figures had pointed men

---

[1] Jonah ii. 10. " Ego autem in voce laudis immolabo tibi."—*Vulgate.*
[2] Psalm xxvi. 6. " Immolavi in tabernaculo ejus hostiam vociferationis." —*Ibid.*
[3] Psalm cvi. 21, 22. " Sacrificent sacrificium laudis."—*Ibid.*
[4] Hebrews x. 4.

forwards to the true Sacrifice, were no longer wanted. Our Blessed Lord had declared that a new Covenant was made between God and man, not now in the blood of beasts, but in His Own Blood, saying, " This is My Blood of the Covenant which is shed for many unto remission of sins."[1]   Henceforth, in place of the sacrifices which had prefigured the One Perfect Sacrifice, an Ordinance was appointed which should be a Memorial of it.   And He added, " This do in remembrance of Me."[2]

The sacrifices of the Law having fulfilled their purpose passed away.   But the ideas connected with those ancient acts of worship were of perpetual importance. Thanksgiving, Praise, and Prayer for pardon were still as necessary for man as ever.   And when all the sacrifices of old time were replaced by the one Sacrament of the Eucharist, all the ideas which had been connected with them naturally found a place in the Ordinance of Christ. But there was this difference.   The various aspects of the coming Sacrifice had been kept distinct in the Jewish ceremonies; they were combined in the Christian service. The name "Eucharist" (Thanksgiving) proves that the main idea in the minds of the early Christians with respect to this service, was that which had been connected in previous times with the Peace Offerings.   The Feast which followed the Peace Offerings was replaced

[1] S. Matt. xxvi. 28 (Revised Version).

[2] S. Luke xxii. 19.   It should be noticed that the word " Me " is emphatic; literally the words are, " This do (or offer) for the Memorial that is Mine."   Very emphatic use of this pronoun occurs frequently throughout the last discourses of our Blessed Lord, wherein He calls attention to the contrast between the world and His Service; *e.g.*, " the commandments that are Mine " (S. John xiv. 15); " the peace that is Mine " (ch. xiv. 27); " the love that is Mine " (ch. xv. 9); " the joy that is Mine " (ch. xvii. 13); " the glory that is Mine " (ch. xvii. 24).

amongst Christians by the Feast of Holy Communion; and the thanksgiving for the blessings enjoyed by Jews, as the chosen people of God, was expanded into thanksgiving for Redemption through the Son of God. But this did not exhaust the sacrificial efficacy of the Sacrament of the Body and Blood of Christ. As the Burnt Offerings had expressed the desire to ascend in heart to God, and find acceptance with Him, so in a similar, but much more vivid manner, the Eucharistic Memorial or representation of the Sacrifice of the Lamb of God was regarded as drawing men into communion with their Heavenly Father. And as the Jew by the Sin Offering not only made acknowledgment of guilt before God, but also received ceremonial cleansing; so, only in a far higher sense, the Christian felt that, by means of this Holy Sacrament, he could come as a sinner before God acknowledging his guilt and unworthiness, and plead the Sacrifice which avails for all the sins of the whole world.[1]

In all these senses, therefore, the Eucharist is the Christian Sacrifice, inasmuch as by the Ordinance of Christ it has taken the place of the sacrifices of every kind under the Law. It is the great Thanksgiving; the great offering of Praise; the great act of Communion;

---

[1] It will appear in the course of this work, that the changes which grew up in mediæval times were connected with a completely altered view of this pleading for remission of sin. The mediæval services, instead of leading the worshipper to plead the work of Christ in the way which He appointed, set forth the act of celebrating this holy ordinance as the ground for remission of sin and acceptance with God. There were in all ages many spiritually minded men who took a higher view of the spiritual character of the Christian Sacrifice; and, as will be shown in later chapters, corresponding devotions were provided for the laity to use during the service; but the lower and materialistic view was that which chiefly prevailed in the times preceding the Reformation.

the great means of pleading the merits of Christ for the remission of sin, and for all human needs. But the Sacrifice of Christ upon the Cross stands altogether by itself, inasmuch as it alone was worthy to atone, and able to make satisfaction for sin. To speak as if that Sacrifice had not been perfect and sufficient is nothing less than blasphemy, because it is to make light of the unutterable work of the Son of God. This was clearly recognized by the ancient Christian authors. They were carefully on their guard that no such interpretation should be placed upon their words. One of the ordinary accusations brought by the heathen against the Christians was that they had no sacrifices, and, therefore, that their religion was immoral. It remained for a very much later age to bring in the belief that the Sacrament of the Body and Blood of Christ was a means of making atonement, as if it could be offered continually as a fresh Sacrifice.[1] The ancient authors themselves ex-

---

[1] It is held by some that such a view of the Eucharist was only the popular misconception of the words of the mediæval Service Books, which do not necessarily imply any such meaning; and that it would now be rejected by all theologians, Romanist as well as Anglican. But that it was once commonly held is clear from our Article XXXI., *Of the one oblation of Christ finished upon the Cross :*—"Wherefore the sacrifices of Masses in which it was commonly said that the Priest did offer Christ for the quick and the dead, to have remission of pain or guilt, were blasphemous fables and dangerous deceits."

It has been pointed out to me by the Rev. Preb. Gibson, Principal of Wells Theological College, that the language used in the Augsburg Confession is another proof of the reality of the corruption in the doctrine of the Eucharistic Sacrifice :—"Accessit opinio quæ auxit privatas missas in infinitum, videlicet, quod Christus sua passione satisfecerit pro peccato originis et instituerit missam in qua fieret oblatio pro quotidianis delictis, mortalibus et venialibus " (Syllog. Confess., p. 139)—and that the words of our own Article II. :—"Christ . . . truly suffered . . . to be a sacrifice not only for

pressed no such idea. They regarded the Christian Sacrifice as a pleading of the merits of Christ, in the way that He had appointed. They considered that this sacred Service led directly to the Cross of Christ; pointing men back to the One Perfect Sacrifice, as the sacrifices of old had pointed men forwards to it. And if there are some passages in which they appear to speak differently, yet the general scope of their teaching shows clearly that they did not regard the Eucharist as being itself a propitiatory offering, and overthrows any number of quotations which seem to imply the contrary.[1]

Whilst the early Christian writers were thus guarded in their references to the idea of Propitiation in connection with the word sacrifice, they seized every opportunity to assert that the Christian Sacrifice was altogether

original guilt, but also for all actual sins of men," may be interpreted as based upon the same foundation.

The following Prayer before Service from the Sarum Missal confirms this: "Concede propitius ut in hoc altari ad quod indignus accedo, hostias acceptabiles atque placabiles offeram pietati tuæ pro peccatis et offensis meis, et innumeris quotidianisque excessibus meis atque cunctorum Christianorum culpis abluendis; et per eum sit tibi votum meum acceptabile qui se tibi Deo Patri pro nobis obtulit sacrificium."

[1] To take one instance out of many, the testimony of Chrysostom, A.D. 387-403, is clear and certain, though expressions which he uses are sometimes referred to in the opposite sense. He connects the Eucharist with the Sacrifice of Christ, by way of memorial, and, assigning its whole force and efficacy to the pleading of the Cross, he says, "There is one Sacrifice. We offer not another sacrifice but always the same; or rather we make a memorial of the Sacrifice."—Epistle to Hebrews, Hom. xvii., tom. iv., p. 523. He is careful to raise the thoughts of his hearers above the material form of worship to the heavenly reality of which it is a representation, saying, "Our Sacrificial Victim is above; our Priest is above; our Sacrifice is above. Therefore such sacrifices only do we offer as can be offered on that heavenly altar."—Epistle to Hebrews, Hom. xi., tom. iv., p. 492. For other similar quotations, see Suicer, Thesaurus, under the word θυσία.

superior to the Jewish sacrifices which had passed away. Almost every early writer refers with this intention to the words, "for from the rising of the sun even unto the going down of the same My Name shall be great among the Gentiles; and in every place incense shall be offered unto My Name, and a pure offering: for My Name shall be great among the heathen, saith the Lord of Hosts."[1] The inferior position which the sacrifices of the Law held in comparison with the commemorative Christian rite was thus brought clearly into view, and the higher privileges and blessings of Christians were made manifest.

In other words, the Eucharist has not only superseded all the sacrifices of former ages, it has in every sense surpassed them.

But devout Jews could join only at long intervals in the Temple Sacrifices; and by degrees the system of the Synagogue services grew up, accustoming them to the idea of worship by other means, not independent of the sacrificial system, but in addition to it, and in place of it.

In a similar way a system of Common Prayer, in addition to the Office of Holy Communion, seems to have been established amongst Christians. We find mention of such

---

[1] Mal. i. 11. "In omni loco sacrificatur, et offertur nomini meo oblatio munda."—*Vulgate.* See Justin Martyr, Dial. with Trypho, chap. cxvi., cxvii., quoted above, page 5; Tertullian adv. Marcion, lib. iii., cap. xxii.; Cyprian adv. Judæos, lib. i., cap. xvi. An interesting passage occurs in the newly discovered "Doctrine of the Twelve Apostles," cap. xiv.:—Κατὰ κυριακὴν δὲ Κυρίου συναχθέντες κλάσατε ἄρτον καὶ εὐχαριστήσατε προσεξομολογησάμενοι τὰ παραπτώματα ὑμῶν, ὅπως καθαρὰ ἡ θυσία ὑμῶν ᾖ. Πᾶς δὲ ἔχων τὴν ἀμφιβολίαν μετὰ τοῦ ἑταίρου αὐτοῦ μὴ συνελθέτω ὑμῖν, ἕως οὗ διαλλαγῶσιν, ἵνα μὴ κοινωθῇ ἡ θυσία ὑμῶν· αὕτη γάρ ἐστιν ἡ ῥηθεῖσα ὑπὸ Κυρίου· Ἐν παντὶ τόπῳ καὶ χρόνῳ προσφέρειν μοι θυσίαν καθαράν· ὅτι βασιλεὺς μέγας εἰμὶ λέγει Κύριος, καὶ τὸ ὄνομά μου θαυμαστὸν ἐν τοῖς ἔθνεσι.

Prayers from the very beginning of the Church of Christ. In the Book of the Acts S. Luke describes the foundation of the Church on the day of Pentecost by the coming of the Holy Ghost, through whose influence three thousand converts were made at one time. He then takes the opportunity to add a description of the general life of the early Christians, and mentions four particulars by which they were distinguished from their fellow Jews. " They continued stedfastly (1) in the Apostles' doctrine, (2) in the Fellowship, (3) in the Breaking of Bread, (4) in the Prayers."[1] From which we gather that the Common Prayers of Christians, in addition to the service of the Holy Communion, date from the very beginning of the Church of Christ.

The notices of the Common Prayers in early Christian writings are less frequent and distinct than those which relate to the Holy Communion. But sufficient mention of them is made to lead to the conclusion that there were other services, which came into regular use, partly in connection with the Office of Holy Communion on the Lord's Day, and partly to keep up throughout the week the Communion of Christians with their Lord. The resemblance also of these services to the synagogue worship can be clearly traced, as might be expected when it is remembered that for many years the Church consisted principally of Jews. The earliest detailed account of these services to which a date can be attached with certainty is given by Basil, Bishop of Cæsarea, *circa* A.D. 370. He says :—

" The customs which now prevail among us agree in all the Churches of God. For very early in the morning, even while

[1] Acts ii. 42.

it is still night, our people resort to the house of Prayer, where they confess unto God their sins, with groans and sorrow and tears of anguish; and lastly rise from their prayers, and betake themselves to Psalmody."[1]

It is also well known that in the times of Chrysostom, Archbishop of Constantinople, and Augustine, Bishop of Hippo in Africa, *circa* A.D. 387-430, the New Testament, as well as the Old Testament, was in regular use in the services; and that courses of sermons were preached by both of these bishops, which form commentaries on whole books of the Bible, and prove both the large use of Holy Scripture which was made, at that early time, in the services, and also the general custom of preaching, even daily at certain periods of the year. We are thus able to detect three main features of the daily worship of Christians in early times, viz., the use of Psalmody; the reading and preaching of God's Word; and prayer mingled with confession. In other words, Praise, Hearing, and Prayer formed the main divisions of the Common Prayers of Christians, as they had done in the Synagogue services of Jews; and these have been handed down to our own times, through the elaborate forms of mediæval daily services, out of which our Morning and Evening Prayer have been formed.

It may be concluded, therefore, that there is abundant evidence to prove that from the earliest days of Christianity two forms of worship prevailed in the Church of Christ; and that these followed, more or less closely, the patterns set by the services previously in use amongst the

---

[1] Basil, Epist. 63 ad Neocæsar; Bingham, Antiquities, book xiii. ch. x. 13. Such services are also referred to by pseudo-Athanasius, De Virgin.; and in the Apostolical Constitutions, as will be shown in Chapter IV.

Jews in their Temple and Synagogues, viz., (1) the Eucharist, or Sacrament of the Body and Blood of Christ, instituted by Him as the perpetual memorial of His Death, and (2) the Common Prayers, or daily worship of Christians.

In the following chapters it is proposed to inquire into the earliest known forms of these services, in order that the sources of the existing acts of worship may be discovered, and the changes which have taken place in them may be traced out. But when we begin to ask, " Where do these services come from," and " By whom were they composed ? " we find that we are entering upon very complicated questions, concerning which a vast number of books have been written, both in ancient and modern times. The general history of the Church Services forms so extensive a subject, and spreads out into so many divisions, that the mass of details belonging to it seems to be overwhelming. Consequently, it is not possible to give much more than an outline of it within the limits of the present work. Yet it is hoped that, whilst very much which may appear to be of great importance will be necessarily omitted, the outline which will be given will furnish the student with a clear idea of the framework of our acts of worship.

It is essential that the reader should be impressed with the fact of the antiquity of the existing services. They date back to the first ages of Christianity. Consequently it is not possible to understand or appreciate the particular form in which they are now presented for our use in the Book of Common Prayer, without some knowledge of the original sources from which they have sprung. It is commonly said that our English Prayer Book is de-

rived from a revision of the Mediæval Services. But
whilst this is true, the statement gives a very wrong im-
pression unless it is known that these were themselves
framed upon older forms still in existence, and that our
English Services are the result of the return to those
more ancient patterns of worship which were used in the
purer days of the first six centuries.[1]

As the Church spread by degrees from the eastern
parts of Europe, where Greek was the language in common use,[2] to the countries where the educated classes
spoke in Latin, the services which had been originally
used in Greek were turned into Latin and altered and
added to in various ways, in different lands and at different times. An illustration may be found in the interesting relic contained in the last prayer but one in our
Morning and Evening Service, which by its heading, "A
Prayer of S. Chrysostom," connects our English services
by name with those most ancient Greek forms of worship.
Nor must we suppose that this is the only tie connecting
us with the East, the cradle-lands of Christianity. For, on
the contrary, the general plan of the Greek services, both
for the Holy Communion, and for the Common Prayers,

---

[1] For instance, Dean Hook says, "The reader who would do justice to
the historical facts to be brought under his notice must bear in mind that
our Prayer Book dates not from the era of the Reformation, but from the
year 1085."—Lives of the Archbishops, vol. vii., page 255. In being
content to trace our Liturgy to the Use of Sarum, Dr. Hook has made it
appear that our service is derived from a source which is farther removed
from the simplicity of Apostolic worship than any form of any church in
Christendom. See the Sarum Use compared with other Uses in Maskell,
"Liturgy of the Church of England."

[2] Even in Rome it is probable that the services were originally used in
Greek, the language in which S. Paul wrote his Epistle to the Christians
at Rome.

can be clearly traced as the basis on which the services of our own and other Western Churches have been framed.[1]

The services which were thus brought from the East, were, by degrees, enlarged and improved for the use of various branches of the Western Church, until a rich treasury of devotion was compiled, of prayers, hymns, psalms, lessons, and anthems. It is true that these were mixed up with a multitude of ceremonies, responses, and legendary readings, which would appear to us in these days frivolous and wearisome. But the deep religious sense of the ancient authors of our Service Books becomes clearer the more we dig into the mine of wealth which they have left us. And the fact that a large proportion of the most popular of our modern hymns are translations or adaptations of those which are found in the ancient Offices, may be taken as an illustration of their deep spiritual character.

The two divisions of the subject must now be treated separately. For as the Services were of two distinct kinds, so the Service Books were divided into two classes; and, however much they were altered or enlarged in the course of centuries, they always remained distinct. They are found in the West under two general names : " The Missal," containing the Services for the Holy Communion throughout the year; and " The Breviary," containing the Services for " The Hours " of the day, commonly called " The Common Prayers." [2]

[1] See Palmer's " Origines Liturgicæ," in which the details of the originals of the various prayers of our services are very carefully traced; also, " Principles of Divine Service," by the late Archdeacon Freeman, in which their general agreement with ancient forms is very ably shown. See also Comparative Table of Liturgies, facing the title-page.

[2] The earliest collections of Services for the Holy Communion were called

A beginning will be made in the following chapter by
tracing out, as briefly and simply as so complicated a subject will allow, the original sources of the Eucharistic
Service according to the Eastern Liturgies.

"Sacramentaries," and each service in these collections was named *Missa.*
In course of time, as the services were arranged in a more orderly manner,
the book containing the services for the various days of the year was called
in consequence " The Missal."

Both Missal and Breviary were commonly divided into various volumes,
containing certain parts of each service, and named accordingly; such as
the *Gradual*, containing the verses to be sung after the Epistle, together
with musical settings of the " Kyrie " and " Gloria in excelsis;" the *Anti-
phonarium*, containing the anthems and hymns; the *Psalter* containing the Psalms according to the order in which they were appointed to be
used.   The Breviary was also divided into two portions for summer and
winter; and in the Roman Church into four, according to the four seasons.

CHAPTER II.

"Quod nunc agimus multiplici orationum, lectionum, cantilenarum et consecrationum officio, totum hoc Apostoli et post ipsos proximi, ut creditur, orationibus et commemoratione passionis Dominicæ, sicut Ipse præcepit, agebant simpliciter."—*Walafridus Strabo.* (Ninth Century.)

AS long as persecution lasted great care was taken to preserve the mysteries of the faith from the mockery and contempt of unbelievers; and, consequently, it is probable that many years passed before the more solemn parts of the Communion Service were committed to writing. There is no doubt that at first the ministers of Christ were directly guided by the Holy Spirit in their choice of words in acts of worship. S. Paul evidently refers to this when he supposes the case of the man praying in an unknown tongue, and asks, " When thou shalt bless with the Spirit, how shall he that occupieth the room of the unlearned say Amen at thy Eucharist? "[1]

[1] 1 Cor. xiv. 16. S. Chrysostom, preaching upon this passage, refers the common salutation, " The Lord be with you," and the answer, " And with thy spirit," to this cause ; regarding them as relics of a higher condition of spiritual life, at a time when those who spoke in church spoke as they were moved by the Holy Ghost.—Chrysost. in 1 Cor., Hom. xxxvi., page 487.

Justin Martyr, A.D. 137, also describes the Eucharistic prayers and thanksgivings as offered in the minister's own words, saying, " Bread is offered and wine and water, and he who takes the lead puts up prayers likewise and

But whilst the words were left to the inspired utterance
of the minister, no doubt a general plan was followed as
closely as possible.   It is reasonable to suppose that the
service originally used in an Apostolically founded
Church would remain stored up in the memories of its
members ; and that this service, whilst agreeing with the
model which had been used amongst the Apostles from
the beginning, would be expressed in such varying words
as the Holy Spirit suggested.   Consequently it might be
expected that certain types of service having a general
agreement, yet with variations of expression and arrangement, would be found in different countries.   And this
expectation is confirmed by what has been discovered.
All existing services may be traced back to certain distinct types belonging to certain great Churches ; and
amidst many diversities one plan runs through them
all.¹

To these types of service the name " Liturgies " has
been given.   The word " Liturgy," meaning " a solemn
service," has become the technical name for the fixed
order of the Service of Holy Communion, irrespective of
the parts which vary with the seasons.   The Greek Services were almost entirely unvarying, consequently every

thanksgivings according to his ability, and the people give their assent,
saying, Amen."—Justin Martyr, Apol. I., cap. 67.
    This is confirmed by the lately discovered " Doctrine of the Twelve
Apostles," belonging apparently to the first century, in which, after a short
outline of a service, it is added, " But permit the prophets to give thanks in
what terms they will," cap. x.   Bryennius, Metropolitan of Nicomedia, who
discovered this MS., well remarks upon this, that the expressions used in
these passages need not be understood as describing *extempore* prayers,
uttered on the spur of the moment ; but rather, on the contrary, as referring
to prayers composed with all possible care and study.
    ¹ See the Comparative Table of Liturgies facing the title-page.

distinct service in use in the churches of the East was called a Liturgy. But in the Western Churches, where every service was more or less different according to the day, the volume containing these varying services was named at first a " Sacramentary," and at a later time a " Missal; " and the word Liturgy is correctly applied only to that peculiar type and order of service to which these variable parts were attached.

As the object of this chapter is to simplify a very complicated subject, for the use of general readers, all lesser differences between these services will be passed over, and the attention will be confined to the main points only. It seems to be sufficient, in approaching the devotional study of the Church's forms of worship for the Holy Communion, to fix the mind upon the fact that there were three great families of ancient Liturgies, from which all existing Offices have been derived. *First,* there was the Eastern or Greek family of Liturgies, in which the service was almost, if not quite unvarying through-out the year. *Secondly,* there was the Gallican family of France and Spain, in which almost the whole service varied every day. *Thirdly,* there was the Roman family, in which the main part, named the Canon, was unvarying, but which admitted of endless varieties in other respects according to the season and the day.[1]

[1] These may be subdivided as follows :—I. The Eastern family included at least four groups ; viz., the Liturgies of (1) S. James, (2) S. Basil and S. Chrysostom, (3) S. Mark, (4) Eastern Syria. These are found in different forms, having been translated into various languages and adapted to the habits of various nations. Amidst much diversity there is a great resemblance between them all ; and those named after S. Basil and S. Chrysostom, which are to this day in regular use in Russia and Eastern Europe, follow exactly the same plan. II. The Gallican included (1) the ancient form of French

Our knowledge of the original character of the Liturgical Service in use in the early Church, has been greatly advanced by the recent discovery of the manuscript of a treatise, entitled "The Doctrine of the Twelve Apostles." There is no doubt that this describes the condition of the Church before the end of the first century. Amongst other information it contains an outline of a Service for the Eucharist, as follows : [1]—

"Chapter ix.   Respecting the Eucharist; thus give ye thanks.   First for the Cup ; 'We give thanks to Thee, our Father, for the holy Vine of David Thy servant, which Thou didst make known to us through Jesus Thy servant.   To

---

Liturgy in use before the eighth century, and (2) the Mozarabic, or ancient Spanish Liturgy, the use of which has lingered on to the present day in one chapel at Toledo.   It also considerably influenced the form of the ancient Celtic Liturgy, in use in Ireland and Britain before Saxon times.   III. The Roman included (1) the Roman ; (2) the Ambrosian, or Liturgy of Milan, which still survives ; and (3) the English Pre-Reformation Liturgy.   It also largely influenced the form of the French Liturgy, which was built up in the eighth or ninth century, and which in part followed the older Gallican services, but in the main conformed to the Roman type.   At the present day, with the few exceptions here mentioned, the Roman Service has stifled all local peculiarities ; the use of one uniform plan having been established in all European countries which acknowledge the Papal supremacy.

[1] Διδαχὴ τῶν Δώδεκα 'Αποστόλων, Constantinople, 1883 ; it is edited by Bryennius, Metropolitan of Nicomedia, by whom the MS. was discovered in 1875, in a library at Constantinople.   Cap. ix. Περὶ δὲ τῆς εὐχαριστίας, οὕτως εὐχαριστήσατε· πρῶτον περὶ τοῦ ποτηρίου· Εὐχαριστοῦμέν σοι Πάτερ ἡμῶν, ὑπὲρ τῆς ἁγίας ἀμπέλου Δαβὶδ τοῦ παιδός σου, ἧς ἐγνώρισας ἡμῖν διὰ 'Ιησοῦ τοῦ παιδός σου· σοὶ ἡ δόξα εἰς τοὺς αἰῶνας.   Περὶ δὲ τοῦ κλάσματος· Εὐχαριστοῦμέν σοι, Πάτερ ἡμῶν, ὑπὲρ τῆς ζωῆς καὶ γνώσεως, ἧς ἐγνώρισας ἡμῖν διὰ 'Ιησοῦ τοῦ παιδός σου· σοὶ ἡ δόξα εἰς τοὺς αἰῶνας. "Ωσπερ ἦν τοῦτο κλάσμα διεσκορπισμένον ἐπάνω τῶν ὀρέων καὶ συναχθὲν ἐγένετο ἕν, οὕτω συναχθήτω σου ἡ ἐκκλησία ἀπὸ τῶν περάτων τῆς γῆς εἰς τὴν σὴν βασιλείαν· ὅτι σοῦ ἐστιν ἡ δόξα καὶ ἡ δύναμις διὰ 'Ιησοῦ Χριστοῦ εἰς τοὺς αἰῶνας. Μηδεὶς δὲ φαγέτω μηδὲ πιέτω ἀπὸ τῆς εὐχαριστίας ὑμῶν, ἀλλ' οἱ βαπτισθέντες εἰς,

Thee be the glory for ever.' And for the broken bread; 'We give thanks to Thee, our Father, for the life and knowledge which Thou didst make known to us through Jesus Thy servant. To Thee be the glory for ever. As this broken bread had been scattered over the mountains, and when brought together became one, so let Thy Church be brought together from the ends of the earth into Thy Kingdom. For

ὄνομα Κυρίου· καὶ γὰρ περὶ τούτου εἴρηκεν ὁ Κύριος· Μὴ δῶτε τὸ ἅγιον τοῖς κυσί.

Cap. x. Μετὰ δὲ τὸ ἐμπλησθῆναι οὕτως εὐχαριστήσατε· Εὐχαριστοῦμέν σοι Πάτερ ἅγιε, ὑπὲρ τοῦ ἁγίου ὀνόματός σου, οὗ κατεσκήνωσας ἐν ταῖς καρδίαις ἡμῶν, καὶ ὑπὲρ τῆς γνώσεως καὶ πίστεως καὶ ἀθανασίας, ἧς ἐγνώρισας ἡμῖν διὰ Ἰησοῦ τοῦ παιδός σου· σοὶ ἡ δόξα εἰς τοὺς αἰῶνας. Σύ, δέσποτα παντοκράτορ, ἔκτισας τὰ πάντα ἕνεκεν τοῦ ὀνόματός σου, τροφήν τε καὶ ποτὸν ἔδωκας τοῖς ἀνθρώποις εἰς ἀπόλαυσιν ἵνα σοι εὐχαριστήσωσιν, ἡμῖν δὲ ἐχαρίσω πνευματικὴν τροφὴν καὶ ποτὸν καὶ ζωὴν αἰώνιον διὰ τοῦ παιδός σου. Πρὸ πάντων εὐχαριστοῦμέν σοι ὅτι δυνατὸς εἶ· σοὶ ἡ δόξα εἰς τοὺς αἰῶνας. Μνήσθητι, Κύριε, τῆς ἐκκλησίας σου τοῦ ῥύσασθαι αὐτὴν ἀπὸ παντὸς πονηροῦ καὶ τελειῶσαι αὐτὴν ἐν τῇ ἀγάπῃ σου, καὶ σύναξον αὐτὴν ἀπὸ τῶν τεσσάρων ἀνέμων, τὴν ἁγιασθεῖσαν εἰς τὴν σὴν βασιλείαν, ἣν ἡτοίμασας αὐτῇ· ὅτι σοῦ ἐστιν ἡ δύναμις καὶ ἡ δόξα εἰς τοὺς αἰῶνας. Ἐλθέτω χάρις καὶ παρελθέτω ὁ κόσμος οὗτος. Ὡσαννὰ τῷ υἱῷ Δαβίδ. Εἴ τις ἅγιός ἐστιν, ἐρχέσθω· εἴ τις οὐκ ἔστι, μετανοείτω· μαραναθά. Ἀμήν. Τοῖς δὲ προφήταις ἐπιτρέπετε εὐχαριστεῖν ὅσα θέλουσιν.

It has been well remarked with respect to this passage :—" The ἀγάπη seems to be not yet disjoined from the Eucharist, if indeed every meal has not somewhat of an Eucharistic character."—" Teaching of the Twelve Apostles," by H. de Romestin, p. 5. Compare Acts xxvii. 35. But it is difficult to believe that the latter of these forms was a grace after meat at an ordinary meal, as has been suggested. (Church Quarterly Review, July, 1884, page 474.) A passage in Pseudo-Athanasius, which has been appealed to as proving that it is a grace, is worthy of being given at length, as an evidence of the mode of thought in early days; but it resembles the former rather than the latter of the above thanksgivings. " When you sit at table and begin to break bread, sign it thrice with the cross and give thanks thus, We give thanks to Thee, our Father, for Thy holy resurrection ; for Thou hast made it known to us through Jesus Thy Servant; and according as the bread which is upon this table was once dispersed in many seeds and is now collected into one, so let Thy Church be congregated from

Thine is the glory and the power through Jesus Christ for ever.' But let no one eat or drink of your Eucharist, except those baptized into the name of the Lord. For about this also spake the Lord, 'Give not that which is holy to the dogs.'

"Chapter x. And after being filled, give thanks thus ; ' We give thanks to Thee, Holy Father, for Thy holy Name which Thou didst enshrine in our hearts, and for the knowledge and faith and immortality which Thou didst make known to us through Jesus Thy servant. To Thee be the glory for ever. Thou, Lord Almighty, didst create all things for Thy Name's sake, and didst give meat and drink unto men to enjoy, in order that they might give thanks to Thee; and to us Thou didst grant spiritual food, and drink, and life eternal through Thy servant. Before all things we give thanks to Thee because Thou art mighty. To Thee be the glory for ever. Remember, O Lord, Thy Church to deliver it from all evil, and to perfect it in Thy love ; and bring it together from the four winds, even that which is sanctified unto Thy Kingdom, which Thou didst prepare for it. For Thine is the power and the glory for ever. Let grace come, and this world pass away. Hosanna to the Son of David. If any one is holy, let him come. If any one is not holy, let him repent. Maranatha. Amen.' But permit the prophets to give thanks in what terms they will."

Herein we have a form of words with which some branch of the Church of the first century observed the Commemoration appointed by our Blessed Lord as the distinguishing mark of Christians. A comparison of these thanksgivings with the order of service described

the ends of the earth into Thy Kingdom ; for Thine is the power and the glory for ever. Amen." After meat the Lord's Prayer was to be said throughout.—Athanasii Opera, de Virgin., vol. i., p. 828.

by Justin Martyr, some forty years later, leads to the conclusion that they were supplied for the use of Christians in the absence of a "Prophet," who could "put up prayers and thanksgivings according to his ability." And though it would be rash to assert that we have here a service which may be described as an authorized form of Liturgy, the value of this extract is undoubtedly very great as revealing the character of the Eucharistic Service in the first days. Special attention should be given to the fact that its main purpose is Thanksgiving; and this Thanksgiving is for the Revelation which God has made known to us through "Jesus His servant." The use of this word "servant" carries us back to the first recorded service in the Church of Christ. When the Apostles Peter and John had been released, after their arrest in consequence of the healing of the cripple, the Christian community joined in a service "with one accord," using this expression; first, as in the above extract, with reference to David, and then twice in connection with our Lord.[1] The same expression continued to be in use in later times, when the Service of the Eucharist was more definitely fixed, as will be presently seen in the so-called Clementine Liturgy.

It is interesting to compare this Christian account of the Eucharistic Feast with the brief reference to it made by a heathen about the same period. Pliny, the Roman Proprætor of the province of Pontus and

---

[1] Acts iv. 25, 27, 30 (Revised Version). The same expression ὁ παῖς μου is used in the Septuagint Version of Isai. lii. 13, " My Servant shall deal prudently," immediately preceding the description of the suffering Messiah : and the same Hebrew word *avdi* occurs again ch. liii. 11, " My righteous Servant," and Zech. iii. 8, " My Servant the Branch," though different renderings are given in the Septuagint.

Bithynia, A.D. 103, was accustomed to write to the Emperor Trajan for instructions upon all matters of difficulty, and amongst other details he referred to his dealings with the numerous Christians whom he had found in his district. After describing the course which he had taken to put a stop to what he calls "their obstinate folly," he stated that many had renounced their connection with the Christians,—

"Adored the images and cursed Christ. And yet that they persisted in affirming that the sum and substance of their fault or error had consisted in this—that they had been accustomed on a stated day to assemble before light, and to sing amongst themselves in turn a hymn to Christ as God; and to bind themselves with an oath (*sacramentum*) not to any crime, but that they would not commit theft or robbery or adultery, nor break their word, nor be false in that which was entrusted to them. And that after this it was their custom to separate, and to meet together again to take a meal, but that it was in common and harmless." [1]

The information which is thus given is the more important because it is the testimony of an opponent. It proves the observance of a fixed day in the week— evidently not the Jewish Sabbath with which a Roman governor would be familiar—and it points to a service in commemoration of Christ which was regarded as binding to a holy life. In this case the *Agape* does not seem to have been connected with the Eucharist, but followed at a later hour in the day.

The next account of the Eucharist belongs to *circa* A.D. 139. It is given by Justin Martyr in his "Apology"

---

[1] Pliny, Epist., lib. x., 97.

addressed to the Emperor Antoninus Pius, and is much more full and important than any previous reference to this service. He says :—

" On the day called Sunday a meeting takes place of all who dwell in cities or in the country, and the memoirs of the Apostles or the writings of the Prophets are read as long as time permits. Then when the reader ceases, the one who takes the lead admonishes by word of mouth, and exhorts to the imitation of these good things. Then we all rise together and put up prayers; and, as was said before, when we have ceased from prayer, bread is offered and wine and water, and he who takes the lead puts up prayers likewise, and thanksgivings according to his ability, and the people give their assent, saying Amen. And there is a distribution to each person, and a partaking of the things over which thanks were given, and to those who are absent a portion is sent by the deacons."

He says also :—

" When we have finished the prayers we salute one another with a kiss. Then bread and a cup of water and mixed wine are offered to him who takes the lead amongst the brethren. And when he has taken them he sends up praise and glory to the Father of all, through the Name of the Son and the Holy Ghost, and he gives thanks at considerable length for our being counted worthy to receive these things from Him. . . . And this food is called among us the Eucharist; and no one is allowed to partake of it but the man who believes that the things which are taught among us are true, and who has been washed with the washing which is for remission of sins, and unto regeneration, and who is living as Christ enjoined." [1]

[1] Justin Martyr, Apology I., cap. 67 ; *ibid.*, 65, 66.

From this extract we may gather that before the middle of the second century the Eucharistic Service was approaching to a fixed form. A service consisting of Lessons from Holy Scripture, preaching, and prayers preceded the Communion Service itself. Then the kiss of peace was given; after which the bread and wine and water were brought in, and presented to the minister, who received them in a formal manner as offerings. The offering of praise and glory to God followed, with prayer, and thanksgiving at considerable length, and to the best of the minister's ability. The people took part in the service by responding, " Amen," at the conclusion.[1] Then the distribution was made. It is evident that Thanksgiving was the main idea of the service, giving to it its name, Eucharist; and that the order of the service which was afterwards developed in the Liturgies, was already adopted;[2] as follows :—

Instruction and Preparatory Prayers.

The preparation of the Faithful, and the Kiss of Peace.

The Offertory.

The Praise and Glory in connection with Thanksgiving, as afterwards fixed in the *Sanctus.*

The Great Prayer and Thanksgiving.

The Communion.

The earliest specimen of a fixed order of service which has been preserved to us is that which is commonly called the Clementine Liturgy.[3] It is found in a collection

---

[1] Compare 1 Cor. xiv. 16.

[2] See Comparative Table of Liturgies facing the title-page.

[3] A second and apparently more ancient form of service has been preserved, Apost. Const., book vii., cap. 25, 26, but it is imperfect, con-

of eight books called the "Apostolical Constitutions," containing directions about various religious matters, and compiled not later than the middle of the fourth century from writings and traditions apparently then ancient.[1] Unfortunately the form in which the collection has been made is such as to excite doubts about its contents. The author, according to the fashion common in later times of assigning everything ancient to the Apostles, has been pleased to describe everything which he records as having been appointed by such and such an apostle. Consequently there is a doubt whether the service here given is anything more than an ideal service which the author has ascribed to S. James. But whether the words of the prayers formed the Liturgy of some particular Church or not, there is no doubt that they represent the kind of service which was in use at least as early as the beginning of the fourth century. A translation of the main parts of this service will give an idea of the extreme antiquity of the general form and order of our own and other Communion Services, and prepare the way for studying them more thoroughly. In the accompanying notes an explanation of the various parts of the service is added, which in consequence of its antiquity deserves to be regarded with considerable interest. The words are taken from one of a series of lectures delivered to a class of catechumens in the Church of the Holy Sepulchre, A.D. 347, by Cyril, when

sisting only of a thanksgiving before and after Communion, without any rubrical directions explaining the order of the service; and it has been lately proved to be nothing more than an expansion of the still older form contained in the "Doctrine of the Twelve Apostles." See above, page 22.

[1] Epiphanius, Bishop of Cyprus, A.D. 367-402, frequently refers to passages in the "Apostolical Constitutions," and states that though they were held

a presbyter at Jerusalem, and they prove that the service which was used there at that time agreed in nearly every particular with the order of service here set forth.

THE ANCIENT GREEK LITURGY OF S. CLEMENT, OR, MORE PROBABLY, S. JAMES.[1]

Litany and Prayer for Catechumens, and Dismissal.
Litany and Prayer for Energumens, and Dismissal.[2]
Litany and Prayer for those preparing for Baptism, and Dismissal.
Litany and Prayer for the Penitents, and Dismissal.
Litany and Prayer for the Faithful.

doubtful by many, they were not to be rejected as spurious.—Hæres. 45, num. 5 ; 70, num. 10. But undoubtedly some of these passages have been altered since his time. The Council in Trullo at Constantinople, A.D. 692, canon 2, rejected the Constitutions on the ground that heretical additions had been made to them. We may conclude, therefore, that they were collected before A.D. 367, but altered between that date and A.D. 692. See dissertations in Cotelerius, Patres Apost., vol. i., pp. 190-196, vol. ii., pp. 213-220.

[1] Apostolical Constitutions, book viii., cap. xi.-xv.; see Patres Apostolici, edited by Cotelerius. The Liturgy is quoted in full by Bingham, Antiquities, book xv., chap. iii. It is named after S. Clement because his name is put forward in the title to the " Apostolical Constitutions," as handing on these instructions to other bishops. But in the text itself, the Liturgy is assigned to James, the brother of John. This is confirmed by the fact that Cyril's Lecture refers to an almost identical service, since the Liturgy of Jerusalem is known to have been that which belonged to the Patriarchate of Antioch, and which is now named after S. James; though there is an apparent confusion between the son of Zebedee and James the Less.

[2] " The Energumens are those who are driven and harassed by evil spirits. Under this name are not only those who are hurried away to a demoniac fury, but moreover all men of the deepest guilt, who either disguise their religion, . . . or, though nominally Christians, lead the life of profane heathens."—Dean Colet, " On the Hierarchies of Dionysius," by J. H. Lupton, p. 79.

Deacon. Let us attend.

The Bishop then salutes the Church, saying,

The Peace of God be with you all.

People. And with thy spirit.

Deacon. Greet ye one another with an holy kiss.

Here let the Clergy kiss the Bishop, the laymen the laymen, the women the women.

Here let a subdeacon bring water to the Priests to wash their hands : a sign of the purity of souls consecrated to God.[1]

(And I, James, the brother of John, the son of Zebedee, say that the deacon shall then proclaim :—)

Deacon. No catechumens. No hearers. No unbelievers. No heterodox. Those who have made the former prayer depart. Mothers take the children. No one in malice, nor hypocrisy. Let us stand upright before the Lord in fear and trembling to offer.

Then let the deacons bring the gifts to the Bishop to the altar. . . .

The Bishop [literally, *Chief Priest*] *having said his private prayer together with the Priests, and put on white apparel, stands at the Altar ; and making the sign of the Cross upon his forehead before all, says :—*

[1] Cyril Hierosol., Catech. Lect. xxiii., describes the service as beginning with the washing of the hands of the ministers as a symbol that they all ought to be pure from sinful and unlawful deeds. "Then the deacon invites to the kiss of peace, not as a common kiss, but as a sign that our souls are mingled together, and have banished all remembrance of wrongs; as S. Paul says, Greet ye one another with an holy kiss, and S. Peter, With a kiss of charity."

[One who was formerly a missionary on the Malabar coast informs me, that in the Syrian Church at Malabar the kiss is given to this day, in the following manner :—The bishop, joining his hands together, places his finger-tips to his lips, and the priest receives the kiss by touching with his own finger-tips those of the bishop; he then delivers the kiss to the deacon in the same way, who carries it to the people, the tips of the fingers taking the place of the lips.]

The Grace of Almighty God, and the Love of our Lord Jesus
Christ, and the Communion of the Holy Ghost be with you all.
All answer together. And with thy spirit.
Bishop. Up with the mind.
All. We lift it up unto the Lord.[1]
Bishop. Let us give thanks unto the Lord.
All. It is meet and right.[2]
Bishop. It is truly meet and right before all things to
celebrate Thee, the very God. (Then follows a very long
Preface, making mention of God's mercies to His people of
old ; and ending thus:—) For all things to Thee be glory,
O Lord Almighty. Thee the countless armies of Angels,
Archangels, Thrones . . . worship. The Cherubim and six-
winged Seraphim, which with two do cover their feet, and
with two their heads, and with two do fly, saying with
thousand thousands of Archangels, and ten thousand times
ten thousands of angels, which cry without ceasing and without silence ; [3]

Here all the people say together. Holy, Holy, Holy, Lord of
Sabaoth. Heaven and earth are full of His glory. Blessed
for ever. Amen.

[1] " After which the priest cries aloud, ' Up with your hearts.' For truly
ought we in that most awful hour to have our heart on high with God, and
not below, thinking of earth and earthly things. Let no one come here who
with his lips can say, ' We lift them up unto the Lord,' but in mind employs
his thoughts on worldly business."—Cyril, *ut supra.*

[2] " Then the priest says, ' Let us give thanks to the Lord.' For in good
sooth are we bound to give thanks that He has called us, unworthy as we
are, to so great grace ; that He has reconciled us who were His foes ; that
He hath vouchsafed to us the spirit of adoption."—Cyril, *ut sup.*

[3] " After this we make mention of heaven, and earth, . . . and all crea-
tion, . . . of Angels, Archangels, . . . in effect repeating that call of
David, ' O magnify the Lord with me ' (Ps. xxxiv. 3). We make mention
also of the Seraphim . . . who cried, ' Holy, Holy, Holy, Lord God of
Sabaoth ' (Isa. vi. 3), that we may join in Hymns with the Hosts above."—
Cyril.

Bishop. For holy art Thou in truth . . . and holy is Thine only Begotten Son, our Lord and God, Jesus the Christ who . . . (Then follows a very long Commemoration of the whole work of Redemption.)

Mindful, therefore, of what He endured for us, we give Thanks to Thee, O God Almighty, not as much as we ought, but as much·as we can ; and fulfil His command. For in the night in which He was betrayed, He took bread in His holy and blameless hands, and looking up to Thee, His God and Father, He brake it, and gave it to His disciples, saying, This is the mystery of the new Covenant. Take of it and eat. This is My Body which is broken for many for the remission of sins. Likewise also the cup He mingled of wine and water, and sanctified and gave it to them, saying, Drink ye all of it. This is My Blood which is shed for many for the remission of sins. This do in remembrance of Me. For as often as ye eat this bread, and drink this cup, ye do show forth My death, until I come.

Mindful, therefore, of His Passion, and death, and resurrection, and ascension, and second coming with power and glory to judge the quick and the dead . . . we offer to Thee, our King, and our God, according to His command, this Bread and this Cup, giving thanks to Thee through Him, for that Thou hast vouchsafed unto us to stand before Thee, and be priests to Thee.

And we desire Thee that Thou wilt graciously look upon these gifts, set forth before Thee, O God in want of nought, and be well pleased with them to the honour of Thy Christ, and send down upon this sacrifice Thy Holy Spirit, the witness of the sufferings of the Lord Jesus, that He may make this bread the Body of Thy Christ, and this cup the Blood of Thy Christ, in order that they who partake thereof may be confirmed in piety, may gain remission of sins, . . . and eternal life.[1]

[1] " Then having sanctified ourselves by these spiritual hymns, we call

D

Moreover, we pray Thee, O Lord, for Thy Holy Church, from one end of the earth to the other, which Thou didst purchase with the Precious Blood of Thy Christ . . . and for the whole Episcopate that rightly divideth the word of truth ; moreover, we beseech Thee for my unworthy self who am offering to Thee; and for the whole Presbytery, for the Deacons, and the whole Clergy . . . moreover, we beseech Thee, O Lord, for the King, and those in authority, and the whole army . . . .[1] Moreover, we offer to Thee, also, for all saints who have been pleasing to Thee from the beginning of the world, patriarchs, prophets, righteous men, apostles, martyrs, confessors, bishops, presbyters, deacons, sub-deacons, readers, singers, virgins, widows, lay people, and all whose names Thou knowest.[2] Moreover, we offer to Thee

upon the merciful God to send forth His Holy Spirit upon the gifts lying before Him ; that He may make the bread the Body of Christ, and the wine the Blood of Christ; for whatsoever the Holy Ghost has touched is sanctified and changed."—Cyril.

[1] " Then after the spiritual sacrifice is perfected—the Bloodless Service upon that Sacrifice of Propitiation—we entreat God for the common peace of the Church, for the tranquillity of the world, for kings, soldiers, allies, the sick, the afflicted ; in a word, for all who stand in need of succour, we supplicate and offer this sacrifice."—Cyril.

[2] " Then we commemorate also those who have fallen asleep before us ; first, patriarchs, prophets, apostles, martyrs, that at their prayers and intervention God would receive our petition. Afterwards also on behalf of the holy fathers and bishops, and, in a word, of all who have fallen asleep among us."—Cyril.

[Cyril adds his own opinion of the value of praying for the departed, on the ground that we can never plead Christ in vain. He shows also that a distinction was made at this date between some whose prayers were desired, and others for whom prayers were offered. This Liturgy represents an earlier form of Commemoration of the Blessed Dead. There is no request to God for their intercessions, and there is no distinction like that mentioned by Cyril. In later Liturgies we find both. See additional Note B, on prayers for the departed, at the end of Chapter VII. For an example of the character of the private prayers for the departed in these early days, see Apost. Constit., lib. viii., cap. 41.]

for this people, that Thou mayest set them forth to the praise of Thy Christ a royal priesthood, a holy nation; for the virgins and the widows of the Church; for those in holy marriage . . . for the babes of Thy people . . . Moreover, we desire Thee also for this city and those who inhabit it; for the sick, for those in bitter slavery . . . .for sailors and travellers. Moreover, we beseech Thee also for those who hate and persecute us for Thy Name's sake; for those who are without and have erred, that thou mayest turn them to that which is good and soften their hearts; moreover, we beseech Thee for the catechumens. . . . Moreover, we offer to Thee also for the mildness of the air and the fruitfulness of the crops, that we may receive of Thy good things without fail, and praise Thee unceasingly. . . . Moreover, we beseech Thee for those who are absent for good cause, that Thou mayest keep us all in piety . . . unblameable. For to Thee belongeth all glory, veneration and thanksgiving, honour and worship, the Father, and the Son, and the Holy Ghost, now and for ever, world without end.[1]

Here all the people say, Amen.

Bishop. The peace of God be with you all.

People. And with thy spirit.

---

[1] [It should be noticed that the words "beseech," παρακαλέω, and "offer," προσφέρω, are used alternately in this prayer, as if synonymous. The sacrificial offering in the Eucharist was at first a distinctly spiritual act of pleading, and so similar to praying that the two expressions could be used alternately. The same words are found in the corresponding prayer in the Liturgy of S. Chrysostom, though they are not used there quite in the same manner. It is evident that as time passed a less purely spiritual sense was attached to the idea of the offering made to God in the Eucharist, until in mediæval times it would doubtless have seemed strange to speak as if offering and praying were synonymous; but it is interesting to notice how the word was used at first, and it strengthens the conviction that mediæval ideas were founded upon words which had been formerly used in different senses. Compare Tertull. ad Scap., cap. ii., quoted above, p. 5.]

Here follows a bidding prayer proclaimed by the Deacon.[1]

Bishop. O God . . . the God and Father of Thy holy Servant Jesus our Saviour,[2] look upon us, and upon this Thy flock, . . . and sanctify us in body and soul, and make us worthy . . . to receive the offered blessings; and judge none of us to be unworthy; . . . through Thy Christ, with whom to Thee be all glory, &c. Amen.

Deacon. Attend.

Bishop. Holy things to the[3] holy.

Let the people answer. One holy, one Lord, one Jesus Christ, to the glory of God the Father, blessed for ever. Amen. Glory to God in the highest, and on earth peace, good-will towards men. Hosanna to the Son of David; blessed is He that cometh in the name of the Lord, God the Lord, and He hath been manifested unto us. Hosanna in the Highest.[4]

---

[1] " Then we say that prayer which the Saviour delivered to His disciples, with a pure conscience styling God our Father and saying, Our Father which art in heaven."—Cyril.

[The omission of the Lord's Prayer from the above Liturgy is a singular circumstance, of which no explanation can be given.]

[2] [For this expression, see extract from " The Doctrine of the Twelve Apostles," pp. 22-25.]

[3] " After this the priest says, ' Holy things to holy men.' Holy are the gifts presented, since they have been visited by the Holy Ghost; holy are you also, having been vouchsafed the Holy Ghost; the holy things therefore correspond to the holy persons. Then ye say, ' One is holy, One is the Lord, Jesus Christ.' Truly, for One only is holy by nature; we too are holy, but not by nature, only by participation and discipline and prayer."—Cyril.

[4] [It is interesting to find this hymn of praise towards the end of the Liturgy, because it thus corresponds to some extent with the position into which *Gloria in Excelsis* was brought in the Second Prayer Book of Edward VI., A.D. 1552; and it should be compared with the similar expressions in the Thanksgiving after Communion, in the " Doctrine of the Twelve Apostles," above, p. 24. Another form of this hymn, more closely corresponding to our own, is found in another part of the " Apostolic Constitutions." It is headed, A Morning Prayer. " Glory to God in the highest and on earth peace, good-will towards men. We praise Thee, we sing to

*After this let the Bishop communicate. Then the priests and
the deacons . . . and deaconesses . . . and then all the people in
order with reverence, and attention, without noise.*

And when the Bishop gives the Offering, let him say, The
Body of Christ.

Let the receiver answer, Amen.

And let the Deacon hold the cup, and give it saying, The
Blood of Christ, the cup of life.

And let him who drinketh say, Amen.

Let Psalm XXXIV. *be sung whilst all the rest are receiving.*[1]
*And when all, both men and women, have received, let the
Deacons take what remaineth and carry the same into the
Priest's chamber.*

When the Psalm is finished let the Deacon say,[2] Having

Thee, we bless Thee, we glorify Thee, we worship Thee, through the Great
High Priest; Thee the True God, the One Unbegotten, alone unapproach-
able, for Thy great glory; O Lord, Heavenly King, God the Father
Almighty, O Lord God, the Father of Christ, the blameless Lamb who
taketh away the sin of the world, receive our prayer; who sittest above the
Cherubim; for Thou only art Holy; Thou only the Lord Jesus, the Christ
of the God of all creation, our King; through whom to Thee be glory,
honour, and worship."—Apost. Constit., lib. vii. 47. It should be noticed
that in both cases the reading, "Good-will towards men," is followed.]

[1] "After this ye hear the chanter with a sacred melody inviting you to
the Communion of the Holy Mysteries, saying, 'O taste and see how
gracious the Lord is' (Ps. xxxiv. 8). Trust not the decision to thy bodily
palate, but to faith unfaltering; for when we taste, we are bidden to taste
not bread and wine, but the sign of the Body and Blood of Christ. Approach
therefore not with thy wrists extended, or thy fingers open, but making thy
left hand as it were a throne for thy right, which is about to receive the
King. Then hollowing the palm, receive the Body of Christ, saying after
it, Amen. Then approach also to the cup of His Blood; not stretching forth
thine hands, but bending, and saying in the way of worship and reverence,
Amen, be thou hallowed by partaking also of the Blood of Christ."—Cyril.

[2] "Then wait for the prayer, and give thanks unto God who hath
accounted thee worthy of so great mysteries. Hold fast these traditions
unspotted, and keep yourselves free from offence. Sever not yourselves
from the Communion; deprive not yourselves, by the pollution of sins, of

partaken of the Precious Body and of the Precious Blood of Christ, let us give thanks, &c.

Bishop. O Lord, God Almighty, Father of Thy Christ the blessed Servant, . . . we give thanks to Thee that Thou hast vouchsafed unto us to partake of Thy holy mysteries, &c.

Deacon. Bow down to God through His Christ, and receive the Blessing.

Bishop. O God Almighty . . . be favourable and hear me for Thy Name's sake; and bless those who have bowed down their necks before Thee, and give them the desires of their hearts, as may be expedient for them, &c.

Deacon. Depart in peace.

It cannot be stated with certainty whether the prayers in the above service are copies of a form of Liturgy which was in actual use or not. But however this may be, many signs may be detected which connect this service with the form of Liturgy handed down in the Churches of Palestine and Syria, under the name of the Liturgy of S. James.[1] With this Liturgy S. Chrysostom

these holy and spiritual mysteries. 'And the God of peace sanctify you wholly,' &c. (1 Thess. v. 23), to whom be glory and honour, now and for ever. Amen."—Cyril Hierosol., Lect. xxiii.

[1] Amongst other resemblances may be noticed the form of the Doxology preceding the Anaphora, which mentions God the Father first, instead of beginning as in other Liturgies, and in 2 Cor. xiii., "The grace of our Lord Jesus Christ." The expression "Up with the mind," agrees also with the unusual form in the Liturgy of S. James, referred to by S. Chrysostom in his ninth Homily on Penitence, "Let us lift up our mind and our hearts." The form of Preface also agrees in the mention of sun and moon and earthly powers, though it was much reduced in length in the Liturgy of S. James; and the description of the Cherubim and six-winged Seraphim is almost word for word the same in both. The great Prayer of Consecration begins abruptly with the same form, "Holy art Thou,' &c.; and the character and order of the intercessions after the Consecration are very similar in both. It is interesting to recall to mind in connection with these resemblances that,

was familiar, as a presbyter of Antioch, A.D. 386-397, and he frequently refers in his "Homilies" to various distinctive features of it.[1] These references form an interesting subject of study; but care is necessary in referring to them to avoid confusing this Liturgy of S. James with that which now bears the name of S. Chrysostom.

The Liturgy named after S. Chrysostom belongs to the Church of Constantinople, to the See of which he was elected A.D. 397. At the present day two very similar forms of Liturgy are in use in the Greek Church, named respectively after S. Basil and S. Chrysostom; and since they are found in an ancient MS. which proves that they were in contemporaneous use a thousand years ago, it is very probable that they belong almost to the days of these bishops. This early copy, which is known by the name of the Barberini MS., assigns certain prayers in each to S. Basil and S. Chrysostom as their authors; but as time went on the two services became more and more fused together; and prayers which were once distinctive of the service of S. Basil, are now found in that of S. Chrysostom.[2]

as was mentioned before, the Clementine Liturgy is expressly assigned to one named S. James, as the author of it, and to notice that the references in Cyril's Lecture apply as well to the one as to the other.

[1] These references are given in full in Bingham, Antiq., book xiii., chap. vi.; and in Palmer's Origines Liturgicæ, vol. i., pp. 30-34. Many of them are also mentioned by Dr. Swainson, "The Greek Liturgies," pp. 218-324.

[2] Curious to say, that which is called "A Prayer of S. Chrysostom," and which is now placed at the end of our Matins and Evensong, is found first in the Barberini MS. of the Liturgy of S. Basil. And from this it seems to have been afterwards introduced into the Liturgy of S. Chrysostom. See Dr. Swainson's "Greek Liturgies," pp. 76, 89, 113.

The variation which is found to exist in different copies of the Liturgy of S. Chrysostom has been the cause of much perplexity. There is no doubt that it is due, partly to the gradual adoption of prayers from the originally distinct Liturgy of S. Basil and of new devotions added between the eleventh and sixteenth centuries, but chiefly to the fact that the rubrical directions and the deacon's parts arc inserted in some and omitted in other copies. It is the custom for the deacon to lead the congregation in certain audible devotions whilst the priest prays silently, the concluding ascription of praise being the only part said aloud in each prayer. Many copies contain the priest's parts only, and appear, in consequence, to be much more simple than the others. The apparent confusion of the latter is due to the fact that they contain two distinct sets of devotions, which are appointed to be used simultaneously, namely, the inaudible prayers of the priest, and the petitions of deacon and congregation, which are said aloud.

The modern form of the Liturgy of S. Chrysostom, as it is now used in the Eastern Church, has been often published, containing the additions introduced at various times in the shape of rubrical directions and secret devotions of the ministers, and complicated with the *diaconica* at full length.[1] In the following English translation a specimen is given of the Liturgy of S. Chrysostom, as it was handed down from times preceding the eleventh century; and, though there is no intention

---

[1] It is given by Dr. J. M. Neale, " Liturgies of S. Mark, S. James, S. Chrysostom, and S. Basil ; " by F. Procter, " History of the Book of Common Prayer ; " by C. E. Hammond, " Liturgies Eastern and Western ; " as well as in other works more difficult of access.

to affirm that no ceremonies besides those mentioned in the text were then in use, attention will be called to the proof here afforded that various devotions which now belong to this Liturgy are modern additions to it.[1]

Accompanying this translation a Latin version is given, which has been found in an edition of S. Chrysostom's works of 1536, and is described as a translation made several years before by Erasmus of Rotterdam for the use of the Bishop of Rochester.[2] Fisher, Bishop of Rochester, when Chancellor of the University of Cambridge, gave much encouragement to the study of Greek, and was the great friend and patron of Erasmus, who was Lady Margaret Prbfessor of Divinity, 1511-1514.[3] It is therefore probable that this translation was made during this period; and its importance will at once appear when it is remembered that it is a proof that the Eastern Liturgies were known and studied in England in the times preceding the Reformation. Archbishop Cranmer was himself a Greek scholar, and would not need the assistance of this Version; and, moreover, it is clear that a Greek Text of this Liturgy was known to him, for he quotes from it in an independent Latin version evidently

[1] In " The Greek Liturgies," edited by Dr. C. A. Swainson, copies are given of the Barberini MS. of the Liturgies of S. Basil and S. Chrysostom, which is assigned to the eighth or ninth century, and of a MS. of S. Chrysostom of the eleventh century, belonging to Lady Burdett Coutts, as well as the text of S. Chrysostom from the first printed edition by Demetrius Ducas, 1526. The translation which follows is taken by kind permission of the Syndicate of the University Press, from the copy of the MS. of the eleventh century.

[2] Chrysostomi Opera, by Chevallon, Paris, 1536, tom. v., pp. 350-354, in the Cathedral Library at Wells. The words within brackets are the marginal notes of this edition.

[3] Hook, " Archbishops of Canterbury," vol. vi., p. 429.

translated by himself.[1]   But in those days Greek was known to few, and there is little doubt that the version which was commonly used by our Reformers is here preserved.[2]

[1] Cranmer's " Collections from Scripture and the Fathers," vol. ii., p. 347, under the heading, *Contra purgatorium,*—" Præterea offerimus tibi rationabilem hostiam hanc pro hominibus qui in fide requiescunt, progenitoribus, patribus, patriarchis, prophetis, apostolis, prædicatoribus, evangelistis, martyribus, confessoribus, continentibus, et omni spiritu in fide defuncto. *Notabiliter.*   Præcipue sancta, immaculata, semper benedicta, gloriosa domina nostra, dei genitrice et semper virgine Maria."—Brit. Mus. Royal MSS. 7 B. xii.

[2] Palmer, Origines Liturg., vol. i., p. 75, mentions this translation, and its variation from other copies.   But its existence seems to have been forgotten, or it has escaped discovery of recent years.   The translation was made from some MS. or MSS. not now known, for it differs completely from the copy published in 1526, by Demetrius Ducas, which is supposed to have been the first printed edition, and has points of variation from all other copies which I have met with.   It appears from a marginal note that more than one copy was consulted by Erasmus; see below, page 50.   The work published by Ducas, Rome, 1526, contained the Liturgies of S. Chrysostom, S. Basil, and the Pre-sanctified; and the same text of the Liturgy of S. Chrysostom was published at Venice, in 1528, by Fratres de Sabio, together with a Latin version.   In 1644, a different text of this Liturgy was published at Venice, which is described as being " commonly used in certain monasteries," and a Latin translation accompanies it, which is that above mentioned as made by Erasmus.   This is stated to have been taken from the works of Chrysostom published by Morell at Paris, and to have been previously published in a separate form by Anton. de Sabbio at Venice.   I have not succeeded in finding a copy of the original edition of this Greek text, which was probably published before 1528.   Copies of the editions of 1526, 1528, and 1644, are in the British Museum, as well as an edition of S. Chrysostom's Works in Latin, 5 vols. Basil, 1547, (Press Mark, 1013. h. 3), which contains the version of Erasmus.   This last work belonged to Archbishop Cranmer and bears his autograph.

THE DIVINE LITURGY OF OUR FATHER AMONG THE SAINTS,
JOHN, ARCHBISHOP OF CONSTANTINOPLE, THE GOLDEN-
MOUTHED.[1]

[In later copies other Vestry Prayers occur before the
following, which is said whilst the Elements are placed upon
the *Prothesis,* or Credence Table.]

The Prayer of the Prothesis.

O God, our God, who didst send the Bread from Heaven,
the food of the whole world, our Lord and God Jesus Christ,
Saviour and Redeemer and Benefactor, who blesseth and
sanctifieth us, do Thou bless this oblation (*Prothesis*), and

---

[1] MISSA S. JOANNIS CHRYSOSTOMI SUPRA COMPLURES ANNOS AB ERASMO
ROTERODAMO, IN GRATIAM EPISCOPI ROFFENSIS, VERSA. [Chrysostomi
Opera, Paris, 1536 ; Basil, 1547.]

Oratio quam dicit sacerdos priusquam ingrediatur templum ubi sacrificat.
Domine Deus noster emitte manum tuam de sancto habitaculo tuo et corro-
bora me ad propositum ministerium tuum, ut citra condemnationem assistam
metuendo altari, et immaculatum sacrificium peragam et nunc et semper et
in sæcula sæculorum. Amen.

Oratio quam dicit sacerdos cum ingreditur. Introibo in domum tuam, &c.
(Ps. 5 b).

*Hæc ubi dixit, osculatur mensam quater in figuram crucis, et accipit stecha-
rion, i.e., lineam vestem dextra manu : et osculatur ac benedicit eam.* Exultet
anima mea in Domino, &c. (Esai. 61 d).

In cervicale. Dominus regnavit, &c. (Ps. 92 a).

In cingulum. Accingere gladio tuo, &c. (Ps. 44 a).

Oratio pallii. Sacerdotes tui Domine, &c. (Ps. 131 b et 2 Paral. 6 g).

Ad primam sublationem. Tanquam ovis, &c. (Esai. 53 c).

Ad secundam sublationem. Precibus Domine ejus quæ genuit te deiparæ
et semper virginis Mariæ, sanctarum omnium potestatum spiritualium, preciosi prophetæ precursoris ac Baptistæ Joannis, sanctorum gloriosorum apostolorum et S. Nicolai cujus et memoriam celebramus, miserere et serva nos.

Benedictio tertiæ sublationis. Memento Domine augustissimorum et Dei
observantium regum nostrorum : memento Domine spiritualis nostri patris,

admit it to Thy heavenly altar. Remember according to Thy goodness and kindness those who offered and those for whose sake they brought it, and keep us uncondemned in the ministering of Thy divine mysteries. For Thy honourable and magnificent Name is sanctified and glorified, even of the Father and of the Son and of the Holy Ghost, now and for ever, world without end. Amen. [This prayer is found in the Barberini MS. of S. Basil; but not of S. Chrysostom, where another prayer takes its place.]

Latin Version of Erasmus—continued.

et totius in Christe fraternitatis nostræ, et omnium qui præmigrarunt e vita, patrum et fratrum nostrorum.

Ad infusionem vini. Et unus militum lancea latus ejus aperuit, &c. (Joan. 19 f).

Et addens aquam dicit. Et aqua, &c. (ibid.).

Diaconus. Dominum obsecremus.

Oratio mystica. Domine Deus noster qui obtulisti te ipsum agnum irreprehensibilem pro mundi vita respice ad nos, et ad panem hunc et ad poculum hoc, et fac illum immaculatum et preciosum tuum sanguinem in transsumptionem animarum et corporum; quoniam sanctificatum est et glorificatum preciosissimum et augustum nomen tuum, patris et filii et spiritus sancti.

[This prayer is found in the Barberini MS. of S. Chrysostom; but it seems to have fallen out of all other known MSS., including that above of the eleventh century.]

Oratio thymiamatis. Thymiama offerimus in conspectu tuo Domine, &c.

Ad discum. Operuit cœlos virtus, &c. (Abac. 3 a).

Cum tetigit calicem. Dominus regnavit, &c. (Ps. 92 a).

Cum mittit nebulam. Et nebula lucida obumbravit eos, &c. (Matt. 17 a et Ps. 32 b).

Oratio ad oblationem cum ponuntur sacra,[1] *priusquam inferantur ad altare: qui locus est in sinistra altaris.* Deus Deus noster qui cœlestem panem alimoniam totius mundi Dominum nostrum Jesum Christum et Deum emisisti servatorem et redemptorem et beneficum benedicentem ac sanctificantem nos, ipse benedic oblationem hanc, et accipe eam in supercœleste tuum sacrarium. Memento, quippe bonus, et humanus, eorum qui intulerunt et per quos intulerunt. Nosque sine condemnatione serva in celebratione divinorum tuorum mysteriorum : quoniam benedictum, &c.

---

[1] Edition of 1644. "Oratio ad Propositionem ubi ponuntur sacra," &c.

Deacon. Sir, give a blessing.

Priest. Blessed be the kingdom of the Father and of the Son and of the Holy Ghost, now and for ever, world without end. [The Litany which follows is named, " The Great Collect."] *Deacon.* In peace let us pray to the Lord. (Lord, have mercy.) For the peace from above, and the salvation of our souls, let us pray to the Lord. (Lord, have mercy.) For the peace of the whole world, &c.

*　　*　　*　　*　　*　　*　　*

The Prayer of the First Antiphon.

O Lord our God, whose might is incomparable and glory incomprehensible, whose mercy is measureless and love

Latin Version of Erasmus—continued.

Deinde venit diaconus et accipit benedictionem a sacerdote et sacerdos dicit : Angelus Domini dirigit viam tuam et una nobiscum sacra peraget.

Primum benedicit sacerdos populum. Gratia sanctissimi et boni et vivificantis spiritus sit vobiscum.

Sacerdos autem cum diacono faciunt ascensiones tres in sanctum sacrarium, et accipit benedictionem sacerdotis diaconus, et sacerdos benedicit caput illius dicens : Angelus Domini dirigit viam tuam, &c.

Diaconus autem egressus sacrarium dicit : Benedic Domine.

Et sacerdos. Ecphonesis. Benedictam regnum patris et filii, &c.

Tunc diaconus exclamat : In pace Dominum obsecremus. *Populus.* Domine miserere.

Diaconus. Pro superna pace, et salute animarum nostrarum, Dominum rogemus. *Populus.* Domine miserere.

*　　*　　*　　*　　*　　*　　*

Diaconus. Pro temperie aëris, fertilitate et temporibus pacificis, Dominum, &c.

Diaconus. Pro navigantibus, viatoribus, ægrotantibus, laborantibus, captivis, et pro salute illorum, Dominum, &c.

Diaconus. Ut liberet nos ab omni tribulatione, iræ, et necessitatis [*sic*], Dominum, &c.

Dum Diaconus pronunciat rogationes, sacerdos dicit hanc orationem secretè : Domine Deus noster, cujus robur inæstimabile et gloria incomprehensibilis,

ineffable, do Thou, O Lord, according to Thy tender love, look down upon us and upon this holy house, and enrich us and those who pray with us, with Thy mercy and pity.

Deacon. Defend, save, have mercy upon us, and guard us, O God, by Thy grace.

Commemorating our all holy, undefiled, most blessed Lady, Theotokos, and ever virgin Mary, with all the Saints, let us commend ourselves and one another, and our whole life to Christ our God.

Aloud. For to Thee belongeth all glory, honour, and worship, the Father and the Son and the Holy Ghost, now and for ever, world without end. [This and the two following prayers are found in the Barberini MS. of S. Basil, but not of S. Chrysostom. The Antiphon follows each prayer.]

Latin Version of Erasmus—continued.

cujus misericordia immensurabilis et humanitas ineffabilis, ipse Domine secundum clementiam tuam respice in nos, et ad sanctam domum hanc, et fac nobiscum, cunque his qui nobiscum vota faciunt, divites misericordias tuas et miserationes tuas.

Populus. Domine miserere.

Diaconus. Defende, serva, miserere, custodi nos Deus tua gratia. Sanctissimæ, incontaminatæ, super omnes benedictæ gloriosæ dominæ nostræ, deiparæ, et semper virginis Mariæ, cum omnibus sanctis memoriam agentes, nos ipsos, et invicem, et omnem vitam nostram Christo Deo nostro commendemus. *Populus.* Domine miserere.

Exclamatio sacerdotis. Quoniam decet te omnis gloria, &c.

Antiphonum primum. Chorus unus canit: Bonum confiteri, &c. (Ps. 91 a, &c.). *Hoc idem in altera chori parte canitur :* Precibus sanctissimæ deiparæ, servator, serva nos. Ad annuntiandum mane misericordiam tuam, et veritatem tuam omnibus diebus nostris. Precibus deiparæ, servator, serva nos. Quoniam rectus Dominus Deus noster, et nunc est in justitia vultus illius. Precibus deiparæ, &c.

Oratio. Domine Deus serva populum tuum et benedic hæreditati tuæ, plenitudinem ecclesiæ tuæ serva, sanctifica diligentes decorem domus tuæ. Tu eos vicissim glorifica divina tua virtute, et ne deseras nos sperantes in te. *Diaconus.* Defende, &c. [Ending as former prayer.]

Prayer of the Second Antiphon.

O Lord, our God, save Thy people, and bless Thine inheritance; guard the fulness of Thy Church, &c.

Prayer of the Third Antiphon.

O Thou who hast given us grace with one accord to make our common supplications unto Thee; and hast promised that when two or three are gathered together in Thy Name Thou wilt grant their requests, do Thou Thyself fulfil now the petitions of Thy servants as may be expedient for them; granting us in this world knowledge of Thy truth, and in the world to come life everlasting.

Deacon. Defend, save, &c. Commemorating our all holy, &c.

Aloud. For Thou art a good and loving God, and to Thee we ascribe glory, the Father and the Son, &c.

[The Gospels are now brought in. This is the Iittle Entrance.]

Prayer of the Entrance.

O Master, Lord, our God, who hast ordained in heaven hosts and armies of angels and archangels for the service of

Latin Version of Erasmus—continued.

Antiphonum secundum. Dominus regnavit, &c. (Ps. 92). Gloria Patri, &c. *Oratio.* Qui communes has et concordes preces largitus es, quique quando duo aut tres concordant in nomine tuo petitiones præstaturum te promisisti (Matt. 18 c); ipse nunc quoque Domine servorum tuorum postulationes ad eorum utilitatem imple, concedens nobis in præsenti seculo cognitionem veritatis, et in futuro vitam æternam largiaris. *Diaconus.* Etiam atque etiam, in pace Dominum rogemus. *Populus.* Domine miserere. Sanctissimæ incontaminatæ, &c. *Exclamatio sacerdotis.* Quoniam bonus et humanus Deus es et tibi gloria, &c.

Antiphonum tertium. Venite exultemus Domino, &c. (Ps. 94 a). *Canuntur hæc ab utroque choro alternatim. Sacerdos autem egreditur e parvo ostio, portans evangelium, præcedente ministro cum lucerna. Et conversus ad Christi imaginem inter duo ostia inflexo capite, cum exclamatione dicit hanc orationem primum secretè:* Here Domine Deus noster, qui constituisti in cœlis ordines, et exercitus angelorum et archangelorum in minis-

Thy glory, grant that with our entrance there may be an
entrance of holy angels ministering together with us, and
with us glorifying Thy goodness.

For to Thee belongeth all glory, &c.

Deacon. Wisdom.   Stand up.

*And after the entrance, and the Troparion, and the Kontakion
of the day, the Priest says:*

For Holy art Thou, our God, and to Thee we ascribe glory,
the Father and the Son and the Holy Ghost, now and for ever.

Deacon. World without end.

*The people sing the Trisagion Hymn ("*Holy God, Holy
Mighty, Holy and Immortal*"), and the Priest says the Prayer.*

Prayer of the Trisagion.

O God the Holy, who restest in the Holy, who art hymned
by the Seraphim with the sound of the Trisagion, and glorified
by the Cherubim, and worshipped by all Heavenly powers ;
who out of nothing didst bring all things into being ; who didst
create man after Thine image, &c.   Do Thou, O Lord, receive
even from the mouth of us sinners the Thrice Holy Hymn, and
visit us in Thy goodness.   Forgive us every offence, voluntary
and involuntary ; sanctify our souls and bodies, and grant
that we may serve Thee in holiness all the days of our life,

Latin Version of Erasmus—continued.
terium tuæ gloriæ fac ut cum nostro ingressu, fiat ingressus sanctorum
angelorum nobiscum sacra celebrantium et pariter glorificantium tuam
bonitatem.   *Tunc addit sacerdos:* Benedictus sit ingressus sanctorum tuorum,
nunc et, &c.

   Et tollens in altum evangelium in imaginem Crucis, magna voce dicit: Sapientia recta.

   Chorus. Venite adoremus, &c.

   Cantor. Sanctus Deus, sanctus fortis, &c.   Gloria Patri et filio, &c.

   Dum hæc canuntur sacerdos dicit tacitè hanc orationem: Deus sancte, qui
in sanctis requiescis ; qui ter sancta voce a Seraphim laudaris, et a Cherubim glorificaris, et ab omni supercœlesti potestate adoraris ; qui a non ente
ad esse producis universa, &c.

through the intercessions of the holy Theotokos, and all Saints who have been well pleasing to Thee from the beginning. (*Aloud.*) For holy art Thou, &c. *Deacon.* Attend. *Priest.* Peace to all. *Deacon.* Wisdom. *And after the Apostle and the Alleluia, then a Psalm. The Priest says the Prayer of the Gospel.*

Cause, O Loving Master, the pure light of the knowledge of Thee our God to shine in our hearts, and open the eyes of our understanding to comprehend the Gospel messages, &c. [This is omitted in modern copies.]

After the Gospel the Deacon says :

Let us all say, with our whole soul and with our whole heart let us say :

(Lord have mercy.) .

Lord Almighty, God of our fathers, we pray Thee hear and have mercy.

(Lord have mercy.)

Latin Version of Erasmus—continued.

Sacerdos. Attendamus. Pax omnibus. Sapientia recta.

Cantor. Psalmus David, &c.

Tunc dicit epistolam ad Hebræos. Epistola Pauli. Fratres, si enim per angelos dictus sermo fuit firmus, &c. (Hebr. 2 a).

Post epistolam sacerdos dicit : Pax omnibus. *Cantor.* Sapientia recta. Psalmus David. et Alleluia. *Tunc venit diaconus ad sacerdotem flexo capite, sacerdos autem orat super eum ;* Dominus dabit verbum evangelizantibus virtute multa per preces dominæ nostræ deiparæ et semper virginis Mariæ, sancti et gloriosi apostoli et evangelistæ hujus.

Sacerdos. Sapientia recta. Audiamus sanctum evangelium. *Diaconus.* Ex Lucæ evangelio. *Et populus,* Gloria tibi Domine. *Et sacerdos,* Attendamus. *Diaconus.* Dixit Dominus discipulis suis, Qui vos audit, &c. (Luc. 10 c).

Post evangelium Diaconus. Dicamus omnes ex tota anima et ex tota mente dicamus.

Sacerdotis exclamatio. Domine omnipotens Deus patrum nostrorum, dives in misericordia et bonus in miserationibus, qui non vis mortem peccatoris sed expectas conversionem et pœnitentiam, ut convertatur et vivat.

Diaconus. Pro sancta domo hac et iis qui, &c. [Short Litany follows; then prayers for catechumens, and dismissal.]

E

[*A brief Litany follows, varying in different copies, ending with " The Prayer of earnest supplication."*
Then follow the prayers for the Catechumens, and their dismissal.]

First Prayer of the Faithful, after the unfolding of the Corporal.

We thank Thee, O Lord God of hosts, that Thou hast deemed us worthy to stand at this present time at Thy holy Altar and to throw ourselves upon Thy compassion for our own sins and the ignorances of Thy people. Accept, O God, our prayer. Make us to become worthy to offer to Thee prayers and supplications and sacrifices without shedding of blood for all Thy people ; and enable us whom Thou hast placed in this ministry, by the power of Thy holy Spirit, to call upon Thee blamelessly and without offence, with the clear testimony of our conscience in every time and place ; that Thou mayest attend and be merciful unto us in the abundance of Thy goodness.

Deacon. Defend, save, &c. Wisdom.

Aloud. For to Thee belongeth all glory, &c.

Latin Version of Erasmus—continued.

Oratio fidelium prima. Gratias agimus tibi Domine Deus virtutum qui dignatus es nos ut assistamus et nunc tuo sancto sacrario, et ut provolvamur tuis miserationibus pro nostris peccatis et populi ignorantiis, suscipe Deus deprecationem nostram : fac nos dignos ut offeramus tibi deprecationes et supplicationes et sacrificia immaculata[1] pro populo tuo; et idoneos nos redde quos posuisti in ministerio tuo hoc, in virtute spiritus tui sancti, sine condemnatione, et offensa in puro testimonio conscientiæ nostræ ut invocemus te in omni tempore et loco, ut exaudiens nos propitius nobis sis in multitudine bonitatis tuæ. *Diaconus.* Defende serva, &c. *Populus.* Domine miserere et custodi nos Deus. Sapientia. Quoniam te decet, &c. (*Note in margin.* In exemplari quodam Græco desunt, et custodi nos Deus. Et post Sapientia, ponit ἐκφώνησις τοῦ ἱερέως.)

Diaconus autem dicit litanias.

[1] It should be noticed that here and in other places *immaculatum* is used as the translation of ἀναίμακτος. In the edition of 1644 this is altered to *incruentum.*

The Second Prayer of the Faithful.

Again and oftentimes we fall down before Thee, and pray Thee of Thy goodness and kindness to look upon our prayer, and to cleanse our souls and bodies from all pollution of flesh and spirit . . . and vouchsafe, O God, to those who pray with us advance in life, faith, and spiritual understanding. Give to them who always serve Thee with fear and love to partake without blame and condemnation of Thy holy mysteries, and to be counted worthy of Thy heavenly Kingdom.

Deacon. Defend, save, &c. Wisdom.

Aloud. That being always, guarded by Thy might we may ascribe glory to Thee, &c.

Prayer which the Priest makes by himself whilst the Cherubic Hymn ("We, who in a mystery represent the Cherubim and sing the Ter-sanctus," &c.) *is sung.*

None is worthy among them that are bound with fleshly desires and pleasures to approach or draw near or minister unto Thee, O King of Glory. For to serve Thee is great and terrible even to the heavenly hosts. Yet through Thine unspeakable and boundless love for man Thou becamest Man unchangeably and unalterably, and didst take the title of our High Priest and commit to us the ministration of this act of worship, this Sacrifice without shedding of blood. . . . Look upon

Latin Version of Erasmus—continued.

Oratio fidelium secunda. Iterum et sæpius tibi provolvimur et te rogamus, &c. *Exclamatio sacerdotis:* Ut a tua virtute semper servati, &c.

Oratio cherubici a sacerdote prolata. Nullus dignus est implicitus carnalibus desideriis et voluptatibus accedere . . . . Sacrificiorum ritum instituisti, ac solennis hujus et immaculati sacrificii celebrationem nobis tradidisti, &c.

Et cum sacerdos dicit hanc orationem cantores canunt hæc : Qui cherubim mysticè representamus et vivificanti trinitati ter sanctum hymnum canimus, et omnem vitæ deponimus solicitudinem, tanquam regem omnium suscipientes, et angelicis invisibiliter stipati agminibus, Alleluia.

me a sinner, Thine unprofitable servant, and purify my soul and heart from an evil conscience, and enable me, who am endued with the grace of Priesthood, by the power of Thy holy Spirit to stand before this Thy holy table, and administer Thy holy and undefiled Body and Thy precious Blood, &c.

[The Elements are here brought in. THE GREAT ENTRANCE.]

Prayer of Oblation after the placing of the divine gifts upon the holy table.

O Lord God Almighty, the only Holy, who receivest the sacrifice of praise from those who call upon Thee with their whole heart, receive also the prayer of us sinners, and bring it to Thy holy Altar, and enable us to offer Thee gifts and spiritual sacrifices for our own sins and the ignorances of Thy people; and make us meet to find grace before Thee, that our sacrifice may be acceptable unto Thee, and that the good Spirit of Thy grace may rest upon us and upon these presented gifts, and upon all Thy people. [Many ceremonies are now appointed here, with varying devotions. In the Barberini MS. this

Latin Version of Erasmus—continued.

Sacerdos vero post orationem sequitur diaconum et vadit ad oblationem. Et inclinatis capitibus ter in terram, sumunt, diaconus quidem corpus, sacerdos vero sanguinem, et exeunt ex parvo ostio, dicente sacerdote paululum egresso. Meminerit tui Dominus Deus in regno suo, nunc, &c. [A short Litany follows.]

Oratio post depositionem sanctorum donorum a sacerdote. Dominus Deus noster, qui omnipotens es, qui solus sanctus, qui accipis sacrificium laudis ab iis, qui invocant te in toto corde, accipe et nostram peccatorum deprecationem, et adducito in sanctum tuum sacrarium. Et idoneos nos redde ad inferenda tibi dona et sacrificia spiritualia pro nostris peccatis, et populi ignorantiis, et dignos nos fac; ut inveniamus gratiam in conspectu tuo, ut acceptabile fiat sacrificium nostrum, et ut obumbret spiritus gratiæ tuæ bonus super nos, et super proposita dona hæc, et omnem populum tuum. *Populus.* Præsta Domine. [A short Litany follows.]

prayer is headed, "Prayer of oblation of the holy John the Golden-mouthed, after the holy gifts are placed upon the holy Table and the people have finished the mystic hymn."]

Deacon. Defend, save, have mercy. (Lord, have mercy.)

That the whole day may be perfect, holy, peaceful, and sinless, let us ask of the Lord. (Grant, Lord.)

Pardon and forgiveness of our sins and transgressions, let us ask of the Lord. (Grant, Lord.)

*   *   *   *   *   *   *

Priest. Peace to all.

Deacon. Let us love one another that with one mind we may confess.

(*Choir.* Father, Son, and Holy Ghost, the consubstantial and indivisible Triuity.)

And after the KISS *is given the deacon says :*

The doors, the doors. In wisdom let us attend.

People. I believe in one God, &c.

Deacon. Let us stand well, stand with fear : let us attend to the holy Anaphora that we may offer in peace.

[The ANAPHORA, or Liturgy Proper, begins here.]

Latin Version of Erasmus—continued.

Sacerdos. Pax omnibus. *Populus.* Et cum spiritu tuo.

Diaconus. Diligamus invicem, ut in concordia confiteamur. *Populus.* Patrem, filium et Spiritum sanctum, trinitatem unius essentiœ et insepara-bilem.

Tunc osculatur sacerdos operculum quater et dicit : Hostia, Hostia,[1] in sapientia attendamus.

Lector autem dicit : Credo in unum Deum, &c.

Post symbolum autem dicit sacerdos : Stemus honestè. Stemus cum timore Dei. Attendamus sacram sublationem in pace offerre. *Chorus.* Miseri-cordiam pacis. Laudis hymnum.

---

[1] This singular misprint for *Ostia, Ostia,* should be noticed. It is the same in Cranmer's copy of 1547, but it is corrected in the edition of 1644.

Aloud. The grace of our Lord Jesus Christ, and the love of God the Father, and the Communion of the Holy Ghost be with you all. (And with thy spirit.)
Let us lift up our hearts.
(Let us lift them up unto the Lord.)
Let us give thanks unto the Lord.
(It is meet and right.)

The Priest bends forward and prays.

It is meet and right to hymn Thee, to bless Thee, to praise Thee, to give thanks to Thee, to worship Thee in every place of Thy dominion. For Thou art God indescribable, inconceivable, invisible, incomprehensible, I AM for ever the same, Thou and Thine Only-begotten Son, and Thy Holy Spirit. Thou out of nothing didst bring us into being, and when we were fallen Thou didst raise us again, and didst not cease doing all things for us until Thou broughtest us unto Heaven, and gavest us the Kingdom that is to come. For all these things we give thanks to Thee, and Thine Only-begotten Son, and Thy Holy Spirit, for all things known and unknown, Thine open and hidden favours bestowed upon us. We give Thee thanks also for this Service which Thou hast vouchsafed to receive at our hands, although there stand by Thee thousands of Archangels, and ten thousands of Angels, the Cherubim and the six-winged Seraphim, full of eyes, floating in air, winged ;

Latin Version of Erasmus—continued.

Exclamatio sacerdotis. Gratia Domini nostri Jesu Christi, et dilectio Dei patris, et communio sancti spiritus cum omnibus vobis. *Populus.* Amen.
Diaconus. Sursum habeamus corda. *Populus.* Habemus ad Dominum.
Diaconus. Gratias agamus Domino. *Populus.* Dignum et justum.
Sacerdos secretè. Dignum et justum te canere te benedicere te laudare, tibi gratias agere, &c.
Exclamatio sacerdotis. Victorialem hymnum canentia, vociferantia, clamau-

Aloud. Singing the triumphal hymn, shouting, crying out and saying,

People. Holy, Holy, Holy Lord of Sabaoth (Heaven and earth are full of Thy glory ; Hosanna in the highest ; blessed is He that cometh in the name of the Lord.)

The Priest bends forward and prays.

With these blessed powers do we also, O loving Master, cry out and say, Holy art Thou and all-Holy, Thou and Thy Only-begotten Son, and Thy Holy Spirit. Holy art Thou and all-Holy, and high is Thy glory : who. didst so love the world as to give Thine Only-begotten Son, that whosoever believeth in Him should not perish, but have everlasting life.

Who, when He came and fulfilled all the dispensation for us, in the night in which He was betrayed, or, rather, gave Himself up for the life of the world, took bread in His holy and undefiled and blameless Hands, and gave thanks, and blessed, sanctified, brake, and gave to His holy disciples and apostles, saying,

Aloud. Take, eat. This is My Body, which is broken for you, for the remission of sins. (Amen.)

Latin Version of Erasmus—continued.

tia et dicentia; *Populus*, Sanctus, sanctus, sanctus Dominus Sabaoth. Pleni sunt cœli et terra gloria tua; osanna in excelsissimis. Benedictus qui venit in nomine Domini.

Sacerdos autem inclinato capite dicit : Cum his et nos beatis potestatibus Domine hominum amator clamamus et dicimus, Sanctus es et totus sanctus ; tu et unigenitus filius tuus ac spiritus sanctus, sanctus es et totus sanctus, et magnifica gloria tua, qui mundum tuum sic dilexisti, ut filium tuum unigenitum dares, ut omnis credens in illum non pereat, sed habeat vitam æternam (Joan. 3 b): qui veniens et omnem pro nobis dispensationem adimplens, nocte qua traditus est, magis autem seipsum tradidit pro mundi vita, accipiens panem in sanctis suis et immaculatis et incontaminatis manibus, gratias agens, benedicens, sanctificans, frangens dedit sanctis suis discipulis et apostolis dicens : Accipite, comedite, Hoc est corpus meum, quod pro vobis frangitur in remissionem peccatorum, Amen. (Matt. 26 et Marc. 14 c, et Lucæ 22 b).

Silently. Likewise also the cup after supper, saying,
Aloud. Drink ye all of it. For this is My Blood, of the New Testament, which is shed for you and for many for the remission of sins. (Amen.)

The Priest bending forward prays.

Mindful then of this saving command, and of all that happened for us, the Cross, the Tomb, the Resurrection on the third day, the Ascension into Heaven, the Session at the Right Hand, the Second and glorious Coming again,

Aloud. Offering Thee Thine own of Thine own in respect of all things and for all things,

People. We hymn Thee, we bless Thee, (we give thanks to Thee, O Lord, and pray to Thee our God).

The Priest bends forward and prays.

Moreover, we offer to Thee this our reasonable Service, without shedding of blood, and we beseech, and pray, and intreat, Send down Thy Holy Spirit upon us, and upon these presented gifts.

And, rising up, he signs with the Cross three times the holy gifts, saying :

Latin Version of Erasmus—continued.

Similiter postquam cœnatum est, accipiens calicem, et benedicens, dicit, Bibite ex eo omnes. Hic est sanguis meus novi testamenti, qui pro vobis et multis effunditur in remissionem peccatorum.

Secreta oratio. Memoriam igitur agentes salutaris hujus mandati, et omnium pro nobis factorum, crucis, sepulchri, triduanæ resurrectionis, in cœlos ascensionis, ad dexteram consessus, secundi et gloriosi rursum adventus.

Exclamatio sacerdotis: Tua ex tuis tibi offerentes et omnia et per omnia.
Chorus. Te laudamus, tibi benedicimus, tibi gratias agimus.

Rursum inclinato capite dicit sacerdos: Propter hoc tibi offerimus rationalem hunc et immaculatum cultum, et invocamus, et rogamus, et supplicamus. Emitte spiritum tuum sanctum super nos, et super proposita dona hæc, Amen. *Et surgens obsignat sacra dona, et dicit:* Et fac panem quidem hunc

And make this bread the precious Body of Thy Christ.
Deacon. Amen.
Priest. And that which is in this cup the precious Blood of
Thy Christ.
Deacon. Amen.
Priest. Changing them by Thy Holy Spirit.
Deacon. Amen. [This seems to have been an addition
made by S. Chrysostom to the older service. It is now found
in modern copies of S. Basil; but in place of it, in copies of
the eighth and eleventh centuries, these words occur, "That
was shed for the life of the world."]

The Priest bending forward, prays.

That they may be to them that partake, for soberness of
soul, for remission of sins, for Communion of Thy Holy
Spirit, for fulfilment of the Kingdom of Heaven, for boldness
towards Thee, and not for judgment, nor for condemnation.

Moreover, we offer to thee this reasonable Service for those
who have fallen asleep in faith, our forefathers, fathers,
patriarchs, prophets, apostles, preachers, evangelists, martyrs,
confessors, those who have lived in continence, and every
just one made perfect in the faith.

Aloud. Especially our all-holy, undefiled, most blessed
Lady, Theotokos, and ever-virgin Mary. [In later copies a

Latin Version of Erasmus—continued.

preciosum corpus Christi tui, Amen. *Et in calice dicit:* In calice vero hoc
preciosum sanguinem Christi tui, transmutans spiritu tuo sancto.

Sacerdos orat. Ut fiat assumentibus in lotionem animarum, in remissionem peccatorum, in communionem sancti spiritus, in regni cœlorum im-
pletionem, in fiduciam apud te, non in judicium, non in condemnationem.

Præterea offerimus tibi rationalem hunc cultum, pro in fide requiescentibus
majoribus, patribus, patriarchis, prophetis, et apostolis, præconibus et evangelistis, martyribus, confessoribus, continentibus, et omni spiritu in fide
initiato: præcipue pro sanctissima, immaculata, super omnes benedicta,
domina nostra deipara, et semper Virgine Maria.

Theotokion is inserted here, as below, or, "It is very meet to bless Thee, the Theotokos," &c.]

Deacon. The diptychs of them that sleep.

The Priest, bending forward, prays.

Also the holy John, the Prophet, Forerunner, and Baptist; the holy and renowned Apostles, and holy (such an one), whose memory also we celebrate, and all Thy Saints, at whose intercession look down upon us, O God; and remember all who sleep in hope of the resurrection of life eternal.

Remember, O Lord, the souls of Thy servants, who have fallen asleep before us (*here he commemorates whom he will*), and give them rest where the light of Thy countenance shines upon them.

Moreover, we beseech Thee, remember, O Lord, the whole Episcopate of the orthodox, &c.

Moreover, we offer to Thee this reasonable Service for the whole world, the holy Catholic and Apostolic Church, &c.

Latin Version of Erasmus—continued.

Ut verè dignum et justum est, glorificare te deiparam et semper beatissimam, et penitus incontaminatam matrem Dei nostri, honoratiorem Cherubim, et gloriosiorem incomparabiliter Seraphim, quæ citra corruptionem Deum peperit: verè deiparam te magnificamus.

Hæc canente choro sacerdos dicit: Ave gratia plena Maria, dominus tecum, &c.

Oratio. Honorabilium, incorporalium, supercœlestium, sancti Joannis prophetæ precursoris et Baptistæ, sanctorum gloriosorum et omnino celebrium Apostolorum, sancti hujus cujus et memoriam agimus, et omnium sanctorum tuorum, quorum supplicationibus respice nos Deus, et memento omnium qui dormierunt in spe resurrectionis et vitæ æternæ, et requiescere eos facito, ubi videtur lumen vultus tui.

Adhuc te invocamus, In primis memento Domine omnis episcopatus orthodoxorum, recte interpretantium verbum tuæ veritatis, totius sacerdotii, in Christo diaconatus, et omnis sacerdotalis ordinis.

Etiam offerimus tibi rationale hoc obsequium pro orbe terrarum, pro sancta Catholica et apostolica Ecclesia, pro iis quoque qui in pura et casta vita degunt. Pro fidelissimis et Christum amantibus nostris regibus, omni

Aloud. Amongst the first remember, O Lord, our Bishop
——, &c. *Deacon.* The diptychs of the living.

The Priest, bending forward, prays.

Remember, O Lord, the city in which we dwell, &c., &c.

Remember, O Lord, those who travel by sea or land, the
sick, &c.

Remember, O Lord, those who bear fruit and do good work
in Thy holy churches, &c.

Aloud. And grant them with one mouth and one heart to
glorify and praise Thy glorious Name, &c.

*   *   *   *   *   *   *

The Priest, bending forward, prays.

To Thee we commit our whole life and hope, O loving
Lord, and we beseech Thee and pray and entreat; make
us meet to partake of Thy heavenly and fearful mysteries
of this holy and spiritual table, with a pure conscience, unto
remission of sins, and pardon of transgressions, unto Communion of the Holy Spirit, and inheritance of the Kingdom
of Heaven, not for judgment, nor for condemnation.

Deacon. Defend, save, have mercy, &c. (followed by a short
Litany).

Latin Version of Erasmus—continued.

palatio et exercitu illorum. Da illis Domine pacificum robur, ut et nos in
tranquillitate illorum pacatam et quietam vitam agamus in omni pietate et
religione.

Exclamatio. In primis memento domine omnis episcopatus orthodoxorum
et rectè interpretantium verbum tuæ veritatis.

Chorus. Et quos quisque in animo cogitat.

Diaconus. Et da nobis uno ore et uno corde glorificare et celebrare
preciosum et augustum nomen tuum, &c. [A short Litany follows.]

Sacerdos inclinans orat: Tibi commendamus vitam nostram omnem et
spem Domine amator hominum, et invocamus te, et rogamus, et supplicamus:
Dignos nos facito ut participes simus supercœlestium tuorum et tremendorum
mysteriorum hujus sacræ et spiritualis mensæ, &c.

Diaconus. Defende, serva, &c. [A short Litany follows.]

Aloud. And make us meet, O Lord, with boldness and uncondemned to venture to call upon Thee, the Heavenly God, our Father, and to say:

People. Our Father, which art in Heaven, &c.

Priest aloud. For Thine is the kingdom, and the power, and the glory, the Father, the Son, and the Holy Ghost, now and for ever, world without end.

Peace to all. (And with thy spirit.)

Deacon. Let us bow our heads to the Lord. (To Thee, O Lord.)

The Priest bends forward and prays.

We thank Thee, King invisible, who with Thy boundless might madest all things . . . Do Thou, O Lord, look down from Heaven on those who have bowed their heads to Thee; for they bowed not to flesh and blood but to Thee, the terrible God. Equalize then, O Lord, the presented gifts unto us all for good, according to everyone's own need: sail with those who sail; travel with the travellers; heal the sick, O Physician of souls and bodies.

Aloud. Through the grace, &c.

Latin Version of Erasmus—continued.

Exclamatio sacerdotis. Et dignos fac nos Domine, ut cum fiducia et sine condemnatione audeamus invocare te supercœlestem Deum, et dicere. *Populus.* Pater noster qui es, &c. *Exclamatio.* Quoniam tuum est regnum et potestas et gloria, patris et filii et sancti spiritus, nunc et semper et in sæcula sæculorum. Amen.

Sacerdos. Pax omnibus.

Diaconus. Capita vestra Deo inclinate.

Sacerdos dicit orationem hanc: Gratias agimus tibi rex invisibilis qui immensa tua virtute omnia condidisti, et multitudine misericordiæ tuæ a nihilo ad esse universa produxisti, ipse Domine cœlitus respice ad servos tuos inclinantes tibi sua capita. Non enim inclinarunt carni et sanguini, sed tibi metuendo et humano Deo. Tu igitur Domine proposita dona omnibus nobis in bonum exæques juxta propriam cujusque indigentiam; cum navigantibus naviga, cum viatoribus viam ambula, ægrotos sana, medicus animarum et corporum. Gratia et miserationibus, &c.

The Priest bends forward and prays.

Attend, O Lord Jesus Christ, our God, from Thy holy dwelling-place ... and come to sanctify us, Thou who sittest above with the Father, and art here invisibly present with us ; and by Thy mighty hand vouchsafe to give to us a share of Thy spotless Body and of Thy precious Blood, and through us to all the people.

Deacon. Let us attend.

Priest. Holy things to the holy.

(One Holy, One Lord Jesus Christ, to the glory of God the Father. Amen.)

Deacon. Fulfil, Master.

The Priest takes a portion of the Bread and puts it into the holy Cup, saying,

The fulness of the Holy Ghost.

Latin Version of Erasmus—continued.

Sacerdos orat. Attende Domine Jesu Christe Deus noster de sancto habitaculo tuo, et de throno gloriæ regni tui et veni ad sanctificandum nos, qui in excelsis una cum patre sedes, et hic nobiscum invisibiliter ades, et dignos nos redde potente manu tua, ut participes simus immaculati tui corporis et preciosi tui sanguinis et per nos omnis populus.

Sacerdos autem spargit fumum incensi sacris. Exclamatio : Attendamus.

Sacerdos elevans sanctum panem dicit : Sancta sanctis. *Chorus dicit :* Unus sanctus, unus Dominus Jesus Christus in gloria Dei patris.

Sacerdos autem elevat panem dicens : Super cœlos Deus, et super omnem terram gloria ejus effusa est.

Divisurus sacerdos panem dicit : Dividitur agr.us Dei qui tollit peccatum mundi.

Et accipiens sacerdos ex pane particulam mittit in calicem dicens : Plenitudo spiritus sancti, nunc et semper et in sæcula sæculorum. Amen.

Et tunc sacerdos assumit et populus canit et sacerdos potitus particula divini corporis dicit : Convivii tui mystici hodie fili Dei communionem assumpsi, non tamen hostibus tuis dixi mysterium. Neque osculum tibi dabo quemadmodum Judas, sed veluti latro ille confitebor tibi, Memento mei Domine, cùm veneris in regnum tuum (Lucæ 23 e).

Deacon. Amen. [Modern copies direct hot water to be added to the holy cup; and various devotions are used. The cup is then shown to the people, they are bidden to approach, and a blessing is given. Incense is used and the Discos (Paten) is shown to the people. Then follows the Thanksgiving. Mention of the communion of the people is omitted.]

Then : With fear of God and faith approach.

Then, when the partaking is finished, and the holy remains have been taken from the holy Table, the Priest prays :

We thank Thee, O loving Lord, Benefactor of our souls, that Thou hast this day vouchsafed unto us to receive of Thy heavenly and immortal mysteries. Make straight our way, establish us all in Thy fear, guard our life, make safe our steps, through the prayers and intercessions of the glorious Theotokos, and ever-virgin Mary, and all Thy saints.

As the holy gifts are removed the deacon censes them thrice, and the Priest says privately :

Be Thou exalted, O God, above the heavens, and Thy glory above all the earth. *Aloud.* Always, now and for ever, world without end. (Amen.)

Latin Version of Erasmus—continued.

Hunc orationem dicunt duo priusquam assumant divina : Deus remitte, dimitte, ignosce mihi peccatori peccata mea et voluntaria et involuntaria, &c.

Oratio. Fiat mihi Domine Jesu Christe corpus tuum sanctum in remissionem peccatorum meorum, et sanguis tuus preciosus in vitam æternam. Et in secundo tuo adventu annumera me justis tuis et electis ovibus.

Oratio. Gratias agimus tibi Domine humane benefactor animarum nostrarum quoniam et hodierno die dignatus es nos supercœlestibus tuis et immortalibus mysteriis : dirige nostram viam, confirma nos in timore tuo omnes, custodi vitam nostram, stabili nostros gressus, precibus et supplicationibus sanctæ deiparæ et semper virginis Mariæ et omnium sanctorum.

Tunc aperitur magnum ostium suspensis lucernis. Et sacerdos ostendit calicem populo dicens : Cum timore Dei et fide et dilectione accedite. *Chorus dicit :* Benedictus qui venit in nomine Domini. *Sacerdos dicit :* Benedictus Deus noster nunc, et semper, et in sæcula sæculorum. Amen.

Deacon. Stand up. Having᾿ partaken of the Divine . . .
mysteries, let us give thanks worthily unto the Lord. Defend,
save, &c.

Aloud. For Thou art our sanctification, and to Thee we
ascribe glory, the Father, &c.

Deacon. In peace let us depart.

[Vestry prayers follow and various devotions are added in
modern copies.]

Latin Version of Erasmus—continued.

Diaconus egressus e sancto altari, dicit post depositionem sanctorum donorum.
Recti qui participes fuimus divinorum, immaculatorum, immortalium, supercœlestium, vivificantium, tremendorum mysteriorum dignè in omnibus gratias
agamus Domino. Defende serva, &c.

Omnem diem perfectum, sanctum, pacatum, et peccati expertem postu-
lantes nos ipsos et invicem, &c. *Exclamatio.* Quoniam tu sanctificatio
nostra, et tibi gloriam referimus, Patri et Filio et Spiritui sancto.

Diaconus. In pace accedite.[1] *Populus.* In nomine Domini.

Diaconus. Dominum rogemus. *Populus.* Domine miserere.

Oratio post ambonem. (Ἄμβων locus æditus, ascensus.) Qui benedicis
benedicentibus tibi Domine, &c.

Tunc populus dicit. Sit nomen Domini benedictum, ex hoc, nunc et
usque in sæculum.

Benedicam Dominum in omni tempore *et reliqua* (Ps. 33 a).

Sacerdos autem benedicit sancta et exuit. Qui ipse es impletio legis et pro-
phetarum Christe Deus noster, qui implesti omnem paternam dispensationem,
imple gaudio et exultatione corda nostra nunc, &c. Deo gratias.

Missa divini Joannis Chrysostomi finis.

---

[1] This seems to be a mistake for *discedite*. It is the same in Cranmer's copy of 1547,
but corrected in the edition of 1644.

CHAPTER III.

> "Tho worthyest thing, most of godnesse,
> In al this world hit is tho messe.
> In alle tho bokes of holy kyre,
> Thate holy men that tyme con wyre (*theme did work*)
> Tho messe is praysed monyfolde;
> Tho vertus might neuer be tolde."
>
> *Lay Folk's Mass Book.* (Twelfth century.)

THE earliest record of the form of the ancient Liturgy of Rome dates from the middle of the fifth century. What the Services were like before this is uncertain; but three collections of Latin Services are in existence, called "Sacramentaries," which have been named respectively after Pope Leo the Great (A.D. 440-461), Pope Gelasius (A.D. 492-496), and Pope Gregory the Great (A.D. 590-604).

The earliest is the so-called "Sacramentarium Leonianum." Pope Leo is known to have given attention to the compilation of additional services to meet the needs of the day; and a Sacramentary in an imperfect condition has been conjecturally named after him, having been evidently compiled out of services composed or used by him.[1]

---

[1] The ravages of Attila, King of the Huns, and of Genseric, King of the Vandals, befell the Empire during the episcopate of Leo. The clemency of Attila in sparing the city of Rome, A.D. 451, at the intercession of Leo is well known. Genseric sacked the city for fourteen days, A.D. 455. Both events seem to be referred to in this Sacramentary:—"Magnificentiam

It contains a large number of Collects furnishing the variable portions of the Service of Holy Communion for the greater part of the year, from which a general idea of the services in use at Rome in the fifth century may be formed.

In the course of the next generation a second Sacramentary was compiled, to which the name " Sacramentarium Gelasianum " has been given. In this "The Canon" first appears. Its use spread through the countries of the west of Europe, as far as to Ireland;[1] and it was not wholly replaced by the Gregorian Liturgy until the time of Charlemagne, in the early part of the ninth century.

At the end of the sixth century the Roman Services were again revised by Pope Gregory the Great; and they were brought nearly if not exactly into the form in which they appear in the Sacramentary which bears his name.

tuam, Domine, prædicamus, suppliciter implorantes, ut qui nos imminentibus periculis exuisti, a peccatis quoque benignus absolvas, &c.

Munera nomini tuo, Domine, cum gratiarum actione deferimus, qui nos ab infestis hostibus liberatos Paschale Sacramentum placida tribuis mente suscipere. Per, &c.

Vere dignum . . . deprecantes ut sic vitia nostra depellas, sicut corporum ferales extinguis inimicos ; nec captivitatem, quam extrinsecus summovisti, sustinere nos patiaris internam."—Muratori, Liturgia Romana vetus, vol. i., p. 371; cf. also pp. 320, 322, where the attacks of the Arian Genseric seem to be described under the petition, " Sic hostes Romani nominis et inimicos Catholicæ professionis expugna."

Further proof of its connection with the age of Leo may be found in the fact that various passages in his Sermons agree word for word with Prefaces belonging to corresponding Festivals in this Sacramentary.—Muratori, vol. i., pp. 20-22.

[1] The Stowe Missal ; " Liturgy and Ritual of Celtic Church," by F. E. Warren.

F

These three so-called Sacramentaries may be regarded as Missals of the early Roman Church, which, in their original forms, replaced each other in that Church before the seventh century. The Gregorian Sacramentary only gradually asserted its superiority; but by degrees it displaced the older services in other Churches besides the Roman, and became the recognized Service Book for the Western Church. And as it contains almost the whole of the Collects which were handed down in the English Church in the Sarum and other Missals and Breviaries, it may be regarded as one of the direct ancestors of the Book of Common Prayer.

Much uncertainty about the exact form of the Roman Liturgy prevails down to the seventh century; for, since the use of the older Sacramentaries continued contemporaneously with the Gregorian, it is difficult to say whether the form in which they have survived belongs strictly to the age when they were originally compiled. There is some doubt also respecting the original form of even the Gregorian Sacramentary; for, whilst there are several MSS. in existence, the oldest belong to the ninth century, and, in the course of the two centuries since the age of its author, many additions had been introduced which caused considerable variation in the different copies.[1] These variations increased as the centuries passed, until the whole of the varying Missals of the west of Europe were elaborated out of the Gregorian

[1] The simplest and probably the oldest form of this Sacramentary is that contained in the Vatican MS., published by Muratori, Liturgia Romana vetus. The edition by Menard contains a later form. But both of these MSS. are assigned to the ninth century. Another very interesting form of it is contained in the Leofric Missal of Exeter, which belongs to the tenth century; lately edited by F. E. Warren.

ho , not exactly

Service Book, with the exception of the Ambrosian Missal of Milan, which belongs to a great extent to an older date, and has been only slightly modified by the Gregorian, and the Mozarabic Missal of Spain, which in the main is contemporary with the Gregorian, but wholly independent of it.

Pope Gregory the Great took much pains in perfecting the Service, by collecting Anthems for various purposes, by shortening the Prefaces which had been excessively lengthened in the older Sacramentaries, and by replacing many of the old Collects and adding fresh ones. He described the Canon, or more solemn part of the Service containing the act of Consecration and the great Prayer for the Church, as being already ancient in his day, "having been composed by some unknown Scholastic." This he left as he found it, except that he added a few words and placed the Lord's Prayer at the end. And it has continued unchanged to the present day. Upon this the ceremonies of the Mediæval Mass were built, partly by devotions prefixed to it, partly by the insertion of rubrics which gave, as will presently appear, a completely changed character to its ancient words.[1]

---

[1] The ancient Roman Liturgy may be best studied in Muratori, Liturgia Romana vetus, which contains the three Sacramentaries above described, all the ancient Gallican Missals which have been discovered, and the earliest forms of the *Ordo Romanus,* or directory for the various services.

The MS. of the Sacramentary which has been assigned to Pope Leo (belonging to about A.D. 700) contains Collects for a considerable number of days in every month, except January, February, and March, the services for which are wanting. The common form of service consists of one or more Collects for the day, a Collect of Oblation, a Preface beginning with the words, " Vere dignum," and one or more post-Communion Collects. Unfortunately no form of Canon or Consecration Prayer is to be found in it, though there are occasionally additional prayers, as, for instance, for Pente-

The form of Service for the Festival of the Epiphany is here given. Special attention should be paid to the simplicity of this ancient Liturgy, with the view of comparing it with the elaborate Mediæval Service according to the Use of Sarum, which follows it.[1]

cost, beginning with the words of parts of the Canon, " Hanc igitur oblationem," &c., and " Communicantes et diem," &c., which seem to point to a Canon similar to, though perhaps not identical with, that of later times.

The Sacramentary of Gelasius is much more elaborate in character. It is divided into three books. The first contains services for the various seasons and festivals ; the second for saints' days ; the third for ordinary Sundays and various occasions. Each service consists of one or more Collects for the day, a Prayer of Oblation named " Secreta," a Preface beginning with a sign representing " Vere dignum," with occasional additions to the Canon, headed " Infra actionem," and " Infra canonem ; " also a post-Communion Collect, and a Prayer headed " Ad populum." In the third book the Canon named after Pope Gelasius is found, followed by several post-Communion Collects, and " Benedictiones super populum post communionem." The MS. belongs to about A.D. 750.

The Vatican MS. of the Sacramentary of Gregory (belonging to about A.D. 800) begins with a rubric describing the order of the service, followed by " Sursum corda," and a Preface for ordinary use, ending with the " Sanctus." Then the Canon is given ; after which a number of services follow for the various days and festivals of the year. Each service consists of one Collect for the day, a Prayer " Super oblata," a short Preface, a post-Communion Prayer named " Ad complendum," ending frequently with a Prayer " Super populum." The services are much shorter and fewer in number than in the Gelasian Sacramentary. A vast number of Benedictions, Collects for Sundays and various occasions, and Ordination and other services are added. The MS. edited by Menard is from the Library of Corbey in Picardy, and is said to have belonged to Eligius, Bishop of Noyon, A.D. 640-659, but it is more probably a copy taken from his Missal, with later additions. In this we find various rubrics which are not found in the Vatican MS. edited by Muratori, and which seem to have been introduced from the First *Ordo Romanus*, or certainly to have been added later than the date of the copy from which the Vatican MS. was transcribed.

[1] Attention has been called to the fact that " we know from the *Ordines Romani* that a very elaborate ritual admitted of being engrafted upon . . . the dry bones of the Sacramentary."—" Church Quarterly," July, 1884,

The Ancient Roman Liturgy.[1]
The Service began with an Introit, *according to the Festival or the day; then—*
Kyrie eleison.
Kyrie eleison.

p. 471. But it would be a mistake to suppose that this ritual brings the ancient Roman service into agreement with the mediæval forms. The ritual of the earliest *Ordo Romanus* includes elaborate directions for the order of processions and explanations of various points in the service, but it contains none of the distinctly mediæval devotions, to which attention will be presently called.

[1] The Vatican MS. of the Sacramentary of Gregory begins with this rubric :—

" In nomine Domini. Incipit liber sacramentorum de circulo Anni, ex-positum a Sancto Gregorio Papa Romano, editum ex authentico Libro Bib-liothecæ Cubiculi, scriptum : Qualiter Missa Romana celebratur.

Hoc est in primis Introitus qualis fuerit statutis temporibus, seu diebus festis sive quotidianis. Deinde *Kyrie Eleison.* Item dicitur *Gloria in excelsis Deo,* si Episcopus fuerit, tantummodo die Dominico, sive diebus festis. A Presbyteris autem minime dicitur, nisi solo in Pascha. Quando vero Letania agitur, neque *Gloria in excelsis Deo* neque *Alleluja* canitur. Postmodum dicitur Oratio ; deinde sequitur Apostolus. Item Grada-lis, seu *Alleluja.* Postmodum legitur Evangelium, deinde Offertorium, et dicitur Oratio super Oblatam. Inde dicit Sacerdos excelsa voce :

Per omnia Sæcula sæculorum.
Amen.
Dominus vobiscum :
Et cum spiritu tuo.
Sursum corda :
Habemus ad Dominum.
Gratias agamus Domino Deo nostro :
Dignum et justum est.

Vere dignum et justum est, æquum et salutare, nos tibi semper et ubique gratias agere, Domine sancte, Pater omnipotens, æterne Deus, per Christum Dominum nostrum, per quem Majestatem tuam laudant Angeli, adorant Dominationes, tremunt Potestates, Cœli Cœlorumque Virtutes ac beata Sera-phim socia exultatione concelebrant. Cum quibus et nostras voces ut admitti jubeas, deprecamur, supplici confessione dicentes : Sanctus, Sanctus Sanctus, Dominus Deus Sabaoth."—Muratori, vol. ii., p. 1.

Christe eleison.

Christe eleison.[1]

Then is said, if the Bishop be present, on Sundays and Festivals, and if the Litany be not performed,[2] Gloria in excelsis Deo.

Glory be to God on high, and on earth peace, &c.

THE COLLECT.

O God, who by the leading of a star didst manifest, &c. (Collect for Festival of the Epiphany.)

THE EPISTLE.

Then followed the Gradual, i.e. one or more verses of Holy Scripture sung as an Anthem ; or, Alleluia.

THE GOSPEL.[3]

Then followed the Homily or Sermon.

The Offertory *was then sung, during which the oblation of the Elements was made, followed by* THE PRAYER OF THE OBLATION, *which varied daily.*

We beseech Thee, O God, mercifully to look upon the gifts

---

[1] That this was the Roman method of saying these words is proved by the words of Gregory the Great, in answer to an inquiry why *Kyrie eleison* was said in the Roman Liturgy, " Kyrie autem nos neque diximus, neque dicimus sicut a Græcis dicitur ; quia in Græcis simul omnes dicunt, apud nos autem a clericis dicitur, a populo respondetur, et totidem vocibus etiam *Christe eleison* dicitur, quod apud Græcos nullo modo dicitur."— Gregory, Epist. vii. 64, to John, Bishop of Syracuse.

[2] This rubric is an interesting proof that on certain days the Litany was used here, after the pattern set by Eastern Liturgies. For the various forms of ancient Liturgical Litanies,' see Chap. IX., LITANIES AND INVOCATIONS.

[3] In the ancient exposition of the Mass, named " Gemma Animæ," assigned to Honorius, surnamed the Solitary, priest of Autun, *circa* A.D. 1120, the following account is given of this part of the service : " Anastasius Papa (A.D. 398-410) decrevit ut dum *Evangelium* legitur nullus sedeat. *Credo in unum Deum* Constantinopolitana Synodus composuit, sed

of Thy Church, wherein are no longer offered gold, frankin-
cense and myrrh, but that which is signified by these gifts is
sacrificed and received ; through our Lord Jesus Christ.

After which the Priest says, aloud,
World without end. Amen.
The Lord be with you.
Answer. And with thy spirit.
Lift up your hearts.
Answer. We lift them up unto the Lord.
Let us give thanks unto our Lord God.
Answer. It is meet and right.

It is very meet, right, just, and salutary that we should at
all times and in all places give thanks unto Thee, holy Lord,
Father Almighty, everlasting God ; because when Thine only-
begotten Son appeared in substance of our mortal flesh, He
renewed us after the new Light of His own immortality;
   And therefore with Angels and Archangels . . . saying,

Holy, Holy, Holy, Lord God of Sabaoth.   Heaven and
Earth are full of Thy Glory. Hosanna in the highest. Blessed
is He that cometh in the name of the Lord. Hosanna in the
highest.

THE CANON.[1]

Thee therefore, most merciful Father, through Jesus Christ
Thy Son our Lord, we humbly beg and pray ; that Thou wilt

Damasus Papa (A.D. 366-384) ad Missam cantari instituit. *Offertorium*
Gregorius Papa (A.D. 590-604) composuit et ad Missam cantari statuit."
—Gemma Animæ, cap. 88.   See Catalogue of MSS. in Archbishop
Cranmer's Library.

[1] With the exception of the addition of a very few words, the Roman
Canon has remained unaltered from the days of Gregory to the present time,
so far as the text is concerned. The alterations in the sense and spirit of
the words through the additions of the mediæval rubrics will be shown
presently, under the Sarum Use. See also Additional Note A, ON THE
CANON, at the end of this chapter.

   The Latin text is taken from the Canon in the Sacramentary of Pope

accept and bless these gifts, these presents, these holy sacrifices of a pure kind; which first of all we offer to Thee for
Thy holy Catholic Church, which do Thou vouchsafe to bring
into a state of peace, to guard, unite, and govern, throughout
the whole world; together with Thy servant, our Pope N.,
and our Bishop N. [and our King N., and all the orthodox
and maintainers of the Catholic and Apostolic faith].

[*Commemoration of the Living.*]

Remember, O Lord, Thy servants and handmaidens N., and
all here present, [and all faithful Christians] whose faith is
seen and whose devotion is known by Thee; [for whom we
offer to Thee, or] who are offering to Thee this Sacrifice of
Praise, for themselves and all belonging to them, for the redemption of their souls, for the hope of their salvation and
security; and are rendering their vows unto Thee, the Eternal
God, living and true.

(*Commemoration of the Departed.*)

In communion with (and celebrating the most sacred day,
&c.   *A special commemoration of the Festival was introduced*

Gelasius, because that probably represents the most ancient form of it
which is now in existence.—Muratori, vol. i., page 695. The English
version shows the additions made in the age of Gregory, or later, inclosed
in brackets [   ].

CANON MISS.E. Te igitur, clementissime Pater, per Jesum Christum
Filium tuum Dominum nostrum supplices rogamus et petimus: uti accepta
habeas et † benedicas hæc † dona, hæc † munera, hæc † sancta Sacrificia †
inlibata. In primis quæ tibi offerimus pro Ecclesia tua Sancta Catholica: quam
pacificare, custodire, adunare, et regere digneris toto orbe terrarum unà
cum famulo tuo Papa nostro *illo*, et Antistite nostro *illo* Episcopo. Memento,
Domine, famulorum famularumque tuarum et omnium circumadstantium.
Quorum tibi fides cognita est, et nota devotio: qui tibi offerunt hoc Sacrificium laudis pro se, suisque omnibus, pro redemptione animarum suarum,
pro spe salutis et incolumitatis suæ; tibi reddunt vota sua æterno Deo vivo
et vero.

Communicantes et memoriam venerantes; in primis gloriosæ semper

here on certain days), and venerating the memory of, first of all, the glorious and ever-Virgin Mary, Mother of God and our Lord Jesus Christ, as also of Thy blessed Apostles and Martyrs Peter, Paul, Andrew, &c., and of all Thy saints; for whose sake and prayers grant that in all things we may be defended by Thy most mighty protection; through [the same] Christ our Lord.

This oblation therefore of our service, as well as of Thy whole family, we beseech Thee, O Lord, graciously to accept; and to dispose our days in Thy peace, and direct us to be delivered from eternal damnation and numbered amongst the flock of Thine Elect; through Christ our Lord. Amen.

Which oblation do Thou, we beseech Thee, O [Almighty] God, vouchsafe to render in all respects blessed, accounted, valid, reasonable, and acceptable, that it may be made unto us the Body and Blood of Thy most dearly beloved Son, our Lord Jesus Christ.

Who, the day before He suffered, took bread into His holy and most honoured hands, and lifting up His eyes to heaven

Canon Missæ—continued.

Virginis Mariæ, Genitricis Dei et Domini nostri Jesu Christi, sed et Beatorum Apostolorum ac Martyrum tuorum, Petri, Pauli, Andreæ, Jacobi, Johannis, Thomæ, Jacobi, Philippi, Bartholomæi, Matthæi, Simonis et Taddei, Lini, Cleti, Clementis, Xysti, Corneli, Cypriani, Laurenti, Grisogoni, Johannis et Pauli, Cosmæ et Damiani, et Eleutherii, et omnium sanctorum tuorum : quorum meritis precibusque concedas : ut in omnibus protectionis tuæ muniamur auxilio. Per Christum Dominum nostrum.

Hanc igitur oblationem Servitutis nostræ, sed et cunctæ Familiæ tuæ, quæsumus, Domine, ut placatus accipias : diesque nostros in tua pace disponas : atque ab æterna damnatione nos eripi ; et in Electorum tuorum jubeas grege numerari. Per Christum Dominum nostrum.

Quam oblationem tu Deus in omnibus quæsumus benedictam, adscriptam, ratam, rationabilem, acceptabilemque facere digneris : ut nobis Corpus et Sanguis fiat dilectissimi Filii tui Domini Dei nostri Jesu Christi.

Qui pridie quàm pateretur, accepit panem in sanctas ac venerabiles manus

to Thee, O God, His Father Almighty, and, giving thanks to Thee, He blessed, and brake, and gave it to His disciples, saying: Take and eat ye all of this; for This is My Body. Likewise after supper taking also this most excellent cup into His holy and most honoured hands, and after the same manner giving thanks to Thee, He blessed, and gave it to His disciples, saying: Take and drink ye all of this, for This is the cup of My Blood, of the new and everlasting covenant, the mystery of faith, which shall be shed for you, and for many for the remission of sins. These things, as often as ye shall do, ye shall do in remembrance of Me.

Wherefore also, O Lord, we Thy servants, as well as Thy holy people, are mindful of the so blessed passion of [the same] Christ Thy Son our Lord (God), and likewise of His resurrection from the dead, as also of His glorious Ascension into Heaven ; we offer unto Thine excellent Majesty of Thy gifts and bounties, a pure Offering, a holy Offering, an undefiled Offering, the holy bread of Life Eternal, and the cup of everlasting salvation.

Upon which do Thou vouchsafe to look with favourable and

Canon Missæ—continued.

suas: elevatis oculis in cœlum ad te Deum Patrem suum omnipotentem, tibi gratias agens, benedixit, fregit, deditque discipulis suis, dicens : Accipite, et manducate ex hoc omnes : Hoc est enim Corpus meum. Simili modo posteaquàm cœnatum est, accipiens et hunc præclarum Calicem in sanctas ac venerabiles manus suas, item tibi gratias agens, benedixit, dedit Discipulis suis dicens : Accipite, et bibite ex eo omnes : Hic est enim Calix Sanguinis mei, novi et æterni testamenti, mysterium fidei : qui pro vobis et pro multis effundetur in remissionem peccatorum. Hæc quotiescunque feceritis, in Mei memoriam facietis.

Unde et memores sumus, Domine, nos tui servi, sed et plebs tua sancta Christi Filii tui Domini Dei nostri tam beatæ Passionis, necnon et ab inferis Resurrectionis, sed et in cœlos gloriosæ Ascensionis : offerimus præclaræ Majestati tuæ de tuis donis ac datis Hostiam puram, Hostiam sanctam, Hostiam immaculatam, Panem sanctum vitæ æternæ, et Calicem salutis perpetuæ.

gracious countenance, and hold them accepted, as Thou didst vouchsafe to hold accepted the presents of Thy righteous servant Abel, and the sacrifice of our Patriarch Abraham, and that holy sacrifice, that undefiled offering, which Thy high Priest Melchisedech offered unto Thee.

We humbly beseech Thee, Almighty God, direct these things to be carried by the hands of Thy [holy] Angel to Thine Altar on high in sight of Thy divine Majesty, that all we who are partakers through this holy Communion of the most sacred Body and Blood of Thy Son, may be fulfilled with Thy grace and heavenly benediction; through the same Christ our Lord. Amen.

[Prayer for the Faithful Departed.

Remember also, O Lord, Thy servants and handmaids who have gone before us with the sign of faith, and sleep in the sleep of peace. Grant, we pray Thee, to them and all who rest in Christ, a place of refreshment, light, and peace; through the same Christ our Lord.]

(Prayer for Fellowship with the Departed.)

To us also, Thy sinful servants, who hope according to the

Canon Missæ—continued.

Supra quæ propitio ac sereno vultu respicere digneris, et accepta habere; sicuti accepta habere dignatus es munera pueri tui justi Abel, et sacrificium Patriarchæ nostri Abrahæ, et quod tibi obtulit Summus Sacerdos tuus Melchisedech, sanctum sacrificium, immaculatam hostiam.

Supplices te rogamus, omnipotens Deus, jube hæc perferri per manus angeli tui in sublime Altare tuum, in conspectu divinæ Majestatis tuæ : ut quotquot ex hac Altaris participatione sacrosanctum Filii tui Corpus et Sanguinem sumpserimus, omni benedictione cœlesti et gratia repleamur. Per Christum Dominum nostrum.

[The *Memento* for the Departed is omitted in the copy of the Gelasian Canon edited by Muratori, who states that it was probably left out of the MS. by accident (vol. i., page 62). But it is absent also from the Canon contained in the ancient *Ordo Romanus*, edited by Hittorpius, de Officiis divinis, page 57. Consequently the omission may not have been accidental.]

multitude of Thy mercies, vouchsafe to grant some part and fellowship with Thy holy Apostles and Martyrs (*the names of fifteen martyrs are here mentioned*), and with all Thy saints ; into whose company, not weighing our merits, but pardoning our offences, we pray Thee to admit us ; through Christ our Lord. Through whom Thou ever makest all these things good, and sanctifiest, quickenest, blessest, and bestowest them upon us. Through Him, and with Him, and in Him there is to Thee, God the Father Almighty, in the Unity of the Holy Spirit, all honour and glory, world without end. Amen.

Let us pray.

Admonished by saving precepts, and following the pattern of the Divine institution, we are bold to say,

Our Father which art in Heaven . . . &c.

[Deliver us, we beseech Thee, O Lord, from all evils, past, present, and to come ; and at the intercession of the blessed and glorious ever-Virgin Mary, Mother of God, and Thy blessed Apostles Peter and Paul and also Andrew, graciously give peace in our days, that, assisted by the help of Thy mercy, we may be ever free from sin, and safe from all disturbance ; through, &c.] [1]

Canon Missæ—continued.

Nobis quoque peccatoribus, famulis tuis, de multitudine miserationum tuarum sperantibus, partem aliquam societatis donare digneris cum tuis sanctis Apostolis et Martyribus, cùm Johanne, Stephano, Matthia, Barnaban, Ignatio, Alexandro, Marcellino, Petro, Felicitate, Perpetua, Agatha, Lucia, Agnem, Cæcilia, Anastasia, et cùm omnibus Sanctis tuis ; intra quorum nos consortia non æstimator meriti, sed veniæ, quæsumus, largitor admitte. Per Christum Dom. nostr.

Per quem hæc omnia, Domine, semper bona creas, sanctificas, vivificas, benedicis, et præstas nobis. Per ipsum et cùm ipso, et in ipso est tibi, Deo Patri omnipotenti, in unitate Spiritus sancti omnis honor et gloria per omnia sæcula sæculorum. Amen."

[1] This was a later addition : see Martene, de Eccles. ritibus, lib. i., cap. iv., art. ix. But it occurs in the MS. (*circa* A.D. 750) of the Gelasian Canon, edited by Muratori. At what time it began to be used as the con-clusion of the Lord's Prayer is not known. But in Gregory's time we

An Episcopal Benediction followed, varying daily.

May God, the true light, who was pleased this day by the leading of a star to reveal His Only-begotten Son to the Gentiles, vouchsafe to enrich you with His Blessing. Amen. May you be led by this example of the Magi, to offer mystic gifts to the Lord Jesus Christ, and be enabled to spurn the old enemy and the contagion of sin, and to return to the eternal home by the path of virtue. Amen.

May He who was pleased that the Holy Spirit as a dove should be seen over His Only-begotten Son, grant unto you true innocence of mind; and may your minds be exercised in the understanding of the secrets of the Divine Law by that same mighty power by which in Cana of Galilee the water was turned into wine. Amen.

know that the Lord's Prayer was said as the conclusion of the Canon : see Greg., Epist., lib. vii., ii., 64, quoted by Cranmer, " MS. Collections," vol. ii., p. 175—" Orationem vero Dominicam idcirco mox post precem dicimus, quia mos Apostolorum fuit, ut ad ipsam solummodo orationem hostiam consecrarent. Et valde mihi inconveniens visum est, ut precem quam scholasticus composuerat supra oblationem diceremus, et ipsam traditionem quam redemptor noster composuit, supra ejus corpus et sanguinem non diceremus " —cf. S. August., Epist. lix., ad Paulin. quæst. 5, tom. ii., p. 114. The following account is given in Gemma Animæ: " *Pater noster*, Dominus quidem docuit, sed Matthæus composuit: Gregorius verò Papa ad Missam cantari censuit, sicnt Apostolorum doctrina tradidit ; hic etiam præcedens capitulum *Oremus ; Præceptis salutaribus moniti*, et sequens, *libera nos Domine* addidit." —Gemma Animæ, cap. 90. Such prayer for a blessing through the prayers of the saints was a very ancient Christian practice, arising out of the belief that those who had spent their lives here in prayer for the brethren would not cease to do the same in the world of spirits. One of the prayers in the Sacramentary of Leo is as follows : " O God who, knowing us to be incapable of worthily approaching Thy Majesty in prayer, hast granted us the aid of those who have been well pleasing to Thee ; grant that we may be assisted by the prayers of those whose help Thou hast mercifully provided for us ; through Christ our Lord."—Muratori, vol. i., p. 294.

The Benedictions ended thus :—

Which may He vouchsafe to grant, whose Kingdom and Dominion endureth for ever, world without end. Amen.

The Blessing of God the Father and of the Son and of the Holy Ghost, and the Peace of the Lord be always with you.

Answer. And with thy spirit.[1]

[1] There is some doubt whether these Episcopal Benedictions were ever used in the Roman Church, since few traces of them appear except in MSS. written in France; and, if they were, the practice soon fell into disuse. In the Sacramentary of Gelasius a number of Benedictions " Super populum post-Communionem," are found after the post-Communion prayers at the end of the Canon, which leads to the idea that these Benedictions were given originally at the end of the service. They are in the form of Collects. In the Sacramentary of Gregory a large number of Benedictions are found, both for festivals, and for daily use; they all contain three sentences, after which they end with the same form as above, the last words being always " Pax Domini sit semper vobiscum." But these early MSS. are French.

The Episcopal Benedictions were retained in some Churches long after all traces of them cease in the Roman Church. In a Pontifical of the Church of Chalons directions are found which describe " when and how the solemn Episcopal Benediction should be given," mentioning the Book of Benedictions kept for the purpose. Afterwards these words are added : " But the Roman Church does not make use of these Benedictions, but at the end of the Mass they say, ' Let the Name of the Lord be blessed,' " &c.— Martene, de Eccl. rit., lib. i., cap. iv., art. xii., 23. These Benedictions formed a special feature in the Anglo-Saxon services, as will be presently shown.

In the very ancient *Missa* edited by Mathias Flaccus Illyricus, mention of the Episcopal Benediction is made immediately after the Lord's Prayer ; and, after the mixture of the elements, there follows the kiss of peace, which was directed to be given with the words, " Habete vinculum pacis et charitatis, ut apti sitis sacrosanctis mysteriis ; " and the people were directed to say to one another in turn, " Pax Christi et ecclesiæ abundet in cordibus nostris." The giving of the benediction, " Pax Domini," &c., must not be confused with the practice of giving the kiss of peace, which came afterwards. There is no trace of the kiss in the early Roman Sacramentaries, though it is said to have been introduced by Innocent I. at the beginning of the fifth century, and it is mentioned in the first *Ordo Romanus*, which is assigned to the early part of the seventh century. It was an Eastern practice, and from the East was introduced into the Gallican and

If the Bishop was not present, the Priest said these words only :—

The Peace of the Lord be always with you.

Answer. And with thy spirit.

Then followed the Communion of the Clergy and People in order.[1] *When all had received, the Post-Communion Collects were said.*

CONCLUDING PRAYER, *which varied daily.*

Grant, we beseech Thee, Almighty God, that our hearts may be so cleansed that we may comprehend and at length attain to the things which we commemorate in our solemn service ; through our Lord Jesus Christ.

Other similar Collects followed.

Then the Deacon proclaimed : Ite missa est ; *or,*

Spanish Churches, where it was given at the beginning of the service. See above, page 31, and Chapter VI. for the Gallican practice ; also Comparative Table of Liturgies facing title-page. It was one of the peculiarities of the Sarum Use that the kiss was given by the priest to his assistants at the beginning of the service immediately after the Absolution. See below, page 93. The kissing of the Pax at the time of Communion became the general custom in mediæval times in place of the actual kiss of the faithful. See below, page 102.

[1] " Post hæc communicat Sacerdos cum Ordinibus sacris cum omni populo."—Sacram. Gelas., Muratori, vol. i., p. 698. Very exact directions are given in the ancient *Ordo Romanus* about the Communion of the people :—" Afterwards the bishops communicate the people at a sign from the celebrant, and the deacons confirm (administer the cup) after them. But the presbyters, at the order of the celebrant, communicate the people and also confirm them. For presently, as soon as the celebrant has begun to communicate the people, the choir immediately begins the Anthem for the Communion, and they sing until all the people have been communicated, even on the women's side, and he returns to his seat."—*Ordo Romanus*, Hittorpius, de Eccles. Officiis. Various similar directions were given in successive editions of the *Ordo.* See also the two forms of the *Ordo* in Muratori, vol. ii., pp. 986, 1028.

Sir, give a blessing.

The Bishop answered : The Lord bless us.[1]

The early history of the Church in Britain is too frag-
mentary to enable us to know very much about the condition of religious life here in the centuries preceding the
mission of Augustine, A.D. 594. But the existence of
a British Church in the fourth century is proved by
several independent witnesses. The names of three
British bishops who attended the council of Arles, A.D.
314, have been preserved.[2] Hilary, Bishop of Poictiers,
A.D. 358, in the opening of his book, De Synodis, addresses it " To the Bishops of the Provinces of Germany, Belgica, Lugdunum, Aquitania . . . and Britain."[3]
British bishops attended the council of Ariminum in Italy,
A.D. 359, some of whom are mentioned as being provided
with necessaries at the emperor's charges in consequence
of poverty.[1] In the next century Pelagianism gained
such a hold upon the Church in Britain, that the inhabitants, unable themselves to refute it, begged help from
the Gallican Church in their spiritual conflict ; and, after
a great synod had been held, the Gallican bishops determined to send Germanus, Bishop of Auxerre, and Lupus,

---

[1] The following account of the formation of the last part of the service
is given in Gemma Animæ : " *Pax Domini sit semper vobiscum,* Innocentius Papa (*circa* A.D. 417) dici constituit et pacem dari censuit. *Agnus Dei*
Sergius Papa (A.D. 687-701) composuit, et ad Missam cantari instituit.
Julius Papa (A.D. 337-352) intinctionem corporis Domini in sanguinem
prohibuit; et Gelasius Papa illum excommunicavit qui Corpus Domini
acceperit et sanguinem non sumpserit. *Communionem* Gregorius Papa
composuit."—Gemma Animæ, cap. 90.

[2] Eborius, Restitutus, and Adelfius.—Collier, Eccles. Hist., vol. i., p. 59.

[3] Hilarius Pictavensis, Opera—Migne's Patrol., tom. x., p. 479.

[4] Collier, *ut supra*, p. 85.

Bishop of Troyes, *circa* A.D. 429.[1] Upon the authority of Usher and Stillingfleet, it has been repeatedly asserted that these Gallican bishops introduced the Gallican Liturgy into Britain,[2] but more careful study of the MS. in the Cotton Library, belonging apparently to the eighth century, upon which their opinions were formed, makes it very doubtful if this conclusion can be maintained.[3] It seems far more probable that there had been from the first a close connection between the Liturgies in use in the Gallican and British Churches, and that the author of this document was referring to the improvements introduced by Cassian into the monastic " Hour " services to which these bishops had been accustomed, and which they may possibly have brought with them into this country. Unfortunately, " no relics of any British Liturgy prior to the eighth century are known to exist."[4] That the British Liturgy was different from the Roman is certain ; what it actually was is uncertain.[5] And the difference between the rites and customs of the two · Churches was so considerable, that it was declared by Gildas, *circa* A.D. 570 : " The Britons differ

---

[1] Bede, Hist. Eccles., lib. i., cap. xvii.

[2] Usher, Britannicarum Ecclesiarum Antiquitates, p. 185 (folio, London, 1687) ; Stillingfleet, " Antiquities of British Churches," vol. i., chap. iv., p. 320 (Oxford, 1842).

[3] Haddan and Stubbs' " Councils and Ecclesiastical Documents," vol. i., p. 138 ; Palmer, Origines Liturg., vol. i., Introd., sect. xi., p. 177.

[4] Haddan and Stubbs' " Councils," *ut supra.*

[5] ." Qualis fuerit apud Britones et Hibernos sacrificandi ritus non plane compertum est. Modum tamen illum a Romano diversum exstitisse intelligitur ex Bernardo in libro de vita Malachiæ, cap. 3, 8 ; ubi Malachias barbaras consuetudines Romanis mutasse et canonicum divinæ laudis officium in illas ecclesias invexisse memoratus."—Mabillon, De Liturg. Gallic., lib. i., cap. 2.

G

from the whole world, and are opposed to the Roman customs not only in the Missa, or Service of the Eucharist, but in the Tonsure, or clerical mark, as well." [1]

From the frequent references to these differences in connection with the Celtic missions established in Northumbria in the seventh century, we may conclude that the British and Celtic customs must have been very similar, if not identical. When Paulinus, one of the band of Roman missionaries in Kent, was sent to convert the heathen in the north, A.D. 625, he brought with him to the court of King Edwin at York the Roman customs and services which Augustine had introduced in the south. But after the disastrous battle in which the king was slain by Penda, A.D. 633, Paulinus returned to Kent, and the country relapsed into paganism. Two years later, S. Aidan, the Celtic missionary, came from Iona, and settled the site of his bishopric at Lindisfarne instead of York, and, as the Northumbrians were gradually won over to Christianity, Celtic customs and rites were established amongst them. Consequently the historian Bede, notwithstanding his admiration for S. Aidan, is careful to record his disagreement with the bishop's practice of keeping Easter and his other Celtic customs. [2] S. Aidan died A.D. 651, and his successors in the see of Lindisfarne continued to uphold the Celtic customs until A.D. 664, when Bishop Colman was defeated upon this question at the synod at Whitby. The controversy arose through the dissatisfaction of a monk named Wilfrid with the discipline of the Celtic monastery. He desired to go to

---

[1] Quoted in F. E. Warren's "Liturgy and Ritual of the Celtic Church," p. 76.
[2] Bede, Hist. Eccles., lib. iii., cap. 3, 17.

Rome to learn more perfectly, and on his return brought back with him the Roman customs. The question was then formally raised whether the Celtic or Roman customs should prevail, especially with respect to the observance of Easter; Bishop Colman was overruled, and Wilfrid gained the day.[1] He was then nominated by the king to the see of York, which was revived on purpose, and refusing consecration at the hands of the Celtic bishops, he went to France to seek it from the Gallican Church. But when the king found that Wilfrid lingered long in France, he sent Ceadda (S. Chad) into Kent to be consecrated in his place.[2] Ceadda had been one of the twelve English boys whom S. Aidan had trained and taught, and was a firm upholder of the Celtic customs. Wilfrid, on his return, finding his bishopric filled by another, retired to a monastery at Ripon. But as soon as Theodore became Archbishop of Canterbury, A.D. 669, he held a visitation, and deposed Ceadda, and restored Wilfrid.[3] From which it appears that the British or Celtic Use lingered in Northumbria until A.D. 669. And almost another century passed before the Roman usages were generally adopted throughout the English dioceses. For it was necessary to ordain at the Council of Clovesho, A.D. 747, that "in the Office of Baptism, in the Celebration of the *Missæ*, and in the method of chanting, all things should be done according to the pattern described in writing concerning the Roman Church."[4]

[1] Bede, Hist. Eccles., lib. iii., cap. 25; lib. iv., cap. 4.
[2] *Ibid.*, lib. iii., cap. 28. [3] *Ibid.*, lib. iv., 2, 3.
[4] Haddan and Stubbs' "Councils," vol. iii., p. 367. The monks of Iona maintained their custom in the observance of Easter until A.D. 716; see Bede, Hist. Eccles., lib. v., 22.

The complete independence of the ancient British or
Celtic Churches has been carefully and ably shown in a
recent work on the Liturgy and Ritual of the Celtic
Church, and cannot be better expressed than in the
following extract :—

"The above facts present to our view a vast Celtic communion existing in Great Britain and Ireland, and sending
its missions among the Teutonic tribes on the Continent, and
to distant islands like Iceland ; Catholic in doctrine and
practice, and yet with its claims to Catholicity ignored or
impugned by the Church of Rome; with a long roll of saints
every name of note on which is either that of one like
S. Columbanus, taking a line wholly independent of Rome,
or, like Bishop Colman at the Synod of Whitby, directly in
collision with her ; having its own Liturgy, its own translation of the Bible, its own mode of chanting, its own monastic
rule, its own cycle for the calculation of Easter, and pre-
senting both internal and external evidence of a complete
autonomy." [1]

Unfortunately no relics of the original British or Celtic
Service Books have yet been discovered. The fragments
which are known as the Books of Deer, Dimna, and
Mulling, and the still more important Stowe Missal, all
belong to a later period, when the fusion between Roman
and Celtic usages had taken place. But they show the
Gelasian Canon in conjunction with much which had been
taken from the Gallican Church, "whole passages, in
addition to many isolated phrases from the Gallican
Liturgy," appearing in them, and confirming the conclusion that the British Liturgy must have been originally

[1] "Liturgy and Ritual of the Celtic Church," by F. E. Warren, p. 46.

either identical with, or very like, the ancient Liturgy of Gaul.[1]

The story about Pope Gregory the Great sending Augustine to convert our Saxon forefathers is well known. When Augustine had settled at Canterbury, the arrangement of the Services soon engaged his attention. He wrote to Pope Gregory for advice, having been struck with the variations in the Service of Holy Communion which he had met with in his journey through France. Gregory's answer was to this effect: he desired him to pick out everything that seemed to be particularly pleasing to God in the services which he had met with, and so to form the best possible Service Book for the new Church of the English.[2] What Augustine did for the Saxon Church of Kent and the South of England in respect of a Service Book is not known for certain. Probably this advice was followed

---

[1] "Liturgy and Ritual of the Celtic Church," p. 61. The following books may also be consulted with advantage on the subject of the ancient British Church:—"Life of S. Columba," written by S. Adamnan, by Dr. Wm. Reeves, publ. for Irish Archæol. Soc., Dublin, 1857; Smith's "Dict. of Christian Biography;" Faber's "Life of Wilfrid;" Todd's "Life of St. Patrick."

[2] The question of Augustine was, "Cur cum una sit fides, sunt ecclesiarum consuetudines tam diversæ? et altera consuetudo missarum est in Romana Ecclesia, atque altera in Galliarum Ecclesiis tenetur?"

To which the answer was given: "Novit fraternitas tua Romanæ Ecclesiæ consuetudinem in qua se meminit nutritam. Sed mihi placet ut sive in Romana sive in Gallicanarum seu in qualibet Ecclesia aliquid invenisti quod plus omnipotenti Deo possit placere, sollicite eligas; et in Anglorum Ecclesia quæ adhuc ad fidem nova est, institutione præcipua quæ de multis ecclesiis colligere potuisti, infundas. Non enim pro locis res, sed pro bonis rebus loca amanda sunt. Ex singulis ergo quibusque ecclesiis quæ pia quæ religiosa quæ recta sunt, elige, et hæc quasi in fasciculum collecta apud Anglorum mentes in consuetudinem depone."—Gregory the Great, Epist., lib. xii., indict. vii., 31, tom. iv., p. 464.

with caution; and there is little doubt that the Gregorian Service, with certain variations, was brought into use. But we learn from the historian Bede, that a conference was held between Augustine and the Bishops of the ancient British Church who had survived the invasions of the Saxons, and were settled upon the borders of Wales, and that he endeavoured in vain to persuade them to give up their customs with respect to the keeping of Easter, to administer baptism according to the usages of the Roman Church, and to own the Pope's authority.[1]

But whilst it must not be supposed that any one Service Book was appointed by Augustine for use throughout England, it is probable that very similar usages were adopted as the different dioceses were formed. Relics remain of an Anglo-Saxon Service Book of Durham, as well as the Pontifical of Egbert, Archbishop of York, A.D. 735-766. The former of these MSS. is assigned to the ninth century, and the latter to the tenth, but they are evidently copies of books in use at least two centuries earlier, belonging to the days before the first incursions of the Danes, when Northumbria was famous throughout Christendom as the home of Bede and other great scholars and saints.[2] They agree in showing that the

[1] Bede, Hist. Eccles., lib. ii., c. 2; Collier, Eccles. Hist., vol. i., p. 175-180.

[2] These MSS. have been edited, and published by the Surtees Society. The Durham Ritual is in Latin, interlined with a Saxon translation. It is traditionally regarded as a copy of a book which belonged to King Alfrid, who reigned A.D. 685. It contains a collection of verses from Holy Scripture and Collects for the various seasons and festivals of the year, followed by forms of Benediction of men and virgins upon renouncing the secular life, and the *Missa* used in the Marriage Service. It contains no perfect service with the Prayers and Canon at length, but the *Missæ* for a virgin

Gregorian Services were adopted in England, in the simple form which has been described above; but that variations from the Roman Use were introduced in various particulars, agreeing with the special features of the ancient Gallican Liturgy.

Another more important example of the Anglo-Saxon Services is given by the Leofric Missal. The larger part of this MS. is assigned to the first half of the tenth century. It seems then to have belonged to Leofric, Bishop of Exeter, 1050-1072, and certain addi-

and for a marriage are sufficiently full to show that the Roman form of Liturgy was adopted. The former is the *Missa* which is found in the Gelasian Sacramentary, containing Collect, *secreta*, *infra actio.*, and *ad complend.* The latter is the Gregorian Service, with the addition of the Benedictions with which our Marriage Service is still enriched, and which are found in various Gallican Missals of the twelfth and thirteenth centuries. —Martene, de Antiq. Eccles. Ritibus, lib. i., cap. ix., art. v., ordo 3, 4. The Collection of Collects is mainly that of the Gregorian Sacramentary, only confined to Collects for the Day and *super populum*, or *ad fontes* or *ad vesperas*. But in some cases Collects from the Gelasian Sacramentary are found, which are not in the Gregorian Sacramentary, *e.g.*, S. Stephen's Day and Holy Innocents. And in other respects variations from the Gregorian Services are frequent.

The Pontifical of Egbert also follows in the main the Gregorian Sacramentary, but with many variations, omissions, and additions. See, for instance, *Missa in reconcil. Eccles.* Its connection with the Gallican Use is shown by the large number of Episcopal Benedictions which it contains for use before Communion. Some of these are found in the Gregorian Sacramentary (see above, note 1, p. 78), but the custom was mainly a Gallican one. Amongst others, the Benedictions for Dom. i. post Nativ. Domini; i. ii. iii. iv. post Epiph., lxxma, lxma, are found here for the first time.

Amongst the Royal MSS. in the British Museum is another Anglo-Saxon Service Book of the tenth century (2 B. v.), containing the Psalter, Canticles, Athanasian Creed, and various prayers in Latin, interlined with an Anglo-Saxon version. This formerly belonged to Archbishop Cranmer's library, and bears his autograph. He possessed also an Anglo-Saxon version of the Four Gospels of the twelfth century (1 A. xiv.).

tions were made to it.   It is in the main a copy of the
Gregorian Sacramentary, but with additional services
from the Gelasian Sacramentary and elsewhere, and with
many additional Benedictions, including some but not all
of the Benedictions of the Pontifical of Egbert.[1]   It therefore bears the same testimony as the earlier Anglo-Saxon
Rituals of the Northern Province, to the effect that in
the days before the Conquest the English Church used
Service Books founded mainly upon the Gregorian form
of Liturgy, but that the suggestion of Gregory was followed, and additions were freely admitted from other
sources.

Whilst the Gregorian Liturgy was being followed in
its original form in England, it was undergoing a gradual
but very complete change in other countries, especially
in France and Normandy.[2]   These changes were introduced in two ways; partly by means of devotions preceding the Canon, in addition to the original Collect and
Secreta, or Prayer *Super oblata,* and partly by rubrics
inserted in the Canon.   A great variety was thus admitted according to the will of successive bishops.
Several Missals are in existence belonging to the Gallican
Church of the ninth and tenth centuries, and in these
the changes can be traced by which the original simpli-

---

[1] The Leofric Missal has been edited by Rev. F. E. Warren, with a
very valuable preface, Clarendon Press, Oxford, 1883.

[2] See J. R. Green's "Conquest of England." He shows how, in the
course of the tenth century, the policy of Christianization and civilization
prevailed against the northern customs and tongue of the settlers in Normandy, and how the Normans and Franks were gradually drawn together
under the growth of Church influences, pp. 388-391. He states also that
Norman chaplains were introduced before the Conquest by Edward the
Confessor, as men of special ability in legal and religious matters, p. 545.

city of the Roman Liturgy was overwhelmed beneath a mass of mediæval additions. In the Roman Church itself the alterations were far less extensive than in the Churches of France and Normandy.[1] But in all the Churches of the Empire the services became adapted to a changed view of the Holy Eucharist, which was gradually established, and which has prevailed more or less completely in the Roman Communion from that period to the present day.

After the invasion of William the Conqueror many Norman Bishops were appointed to the English Bishoprics. One of these, Bishop Osmund of Sarum, A.D. 1085, revised the Service Book which he found in use in his diocese with such skill that it became the pattern for the greater part of the country, and under the name of "The Sarum Use" prevailed very generally for nearly five hundred years in the Churches of England. Consequently, in considering the sources of our Communion Service, we may take the Sarum Missal as the best representative of the character of the English Services before the Reformation.

For the sake of clearness, and to avoid the multiplication of details, it seems best to give an outline only of

[1] For examples of the services in these ancient Missals, see Martene, De Antiq. Eccles. Ritibus, lib. i., cap. iv., art. xii., ordo 4, 5, 6. See also Maskell, "Ancient Liturgy of the Church of England," in which the Roman Liturgy is compared with the English Uses. The present Roman Service was revised at the Council of Trent, but a comparison between it and the earlier Roman Missals shows that the alterations then made were few. The Sarum Use is seen to be far more full of mediæval developments than the rest, and its peculiarities can be almost entirely traced to the changes which appear in French and Norman Service Books of the ninth century.—Martene, *ut supra.* The reader will find the gradual growth of these developments traced out in the following notes.

this elaborate form of Western Liturgy. The attention of the reader should be paid especially to the parts preceding the Canon, and to the Rubrics inserted into the Canon, and these should be compared with the previous example of the ancient Roman Liturgy, which may be regarded as prevailing up to the time of the Conquest in England. The special beauties of the Sarum Use will thus be made clear, and at the same time the reader will be able to see for himself how the simple devotion of earlier days was overlaid with new and strange ceremonies.

THE MEDIÆVAL ENGLISH LITURGY, ACCORDING TO THE USE OF SARUM.[1]

In the Vestry, whilst robing, the Priest repeated the hymn, Come, Holy Ghost, our souls inspire,[2] &c.; *followed by the Collect for Purity,* O God, unto whom all hearts be open,[3] &c.; *then Psalm* xliii., Give sentence with me, O God, &c., *with the*

---

[1] The Sarum Use is necessarily mentioned in connection with the Roman Liturgy, because it followed the general plan of the ancient Sacramentaries. But it is a mistake to suppose that the services in use in England previous to the Reformation were the same as those in use in Rome. The Sarum Missal and the Roman Missal were both founded upon the ancient service already described; but they differed in very many ways. The English Service Books have always been distinctly *English.*

[2] The deep spiritual devotion upon which the ceremonial of the Middle Ages was founded is well illustrated by the use of this hymn before the service. It is still more plainly manifested in a very interesting exposition of the service, belonging to about the beginning of the ninth century, which explains every part of the service as it then existed, apart from the innumerable ceremonies which were added in the eleventh century.—Martene, lib. i., cap. iv., art. xi.

[3] This Collect is peculiar to the Sarum Use in this position, and has been well retained in our English Communion Service for the same purpose.

Antiphon, I will go unto the altar of God; *after which was said :*

Kyrie eleison. Christe eleison. Kyrie eleison.

Our Father, which art in Heaven, &c.

Hail, Mary,[1] thou that art highly favoured, the Lord is with thee. Blessed art thou among women; and blessed is the fruit of thy womb, Jesus.

Then was sung the Office *or* Introit.

Meanwhile the Priest and his assistants approached to the step of the Altar, and made confession, thus :

And lead us not into temptation;

Answer. But deliver us from evil.

Let us confess unto the Lord, for He is gracious; for His mercy endureth for ever.[2]

[1] This personal address to the Blessed Virgin Mary became in mediæval times the regular mode of opening the Hour Services, in conjunction with the Lord's Prayer and the Creed. But its position here is peculiar to the Sarum Use. The introduction into Eastern Liturgies of similar devotions addressed to the Blessed Virgin seems to belong to the same period. See Dr. Swainson's "The Greek Liturgies," introd. p. xxxvii.

[2] "Confitemini Domino quoniam bonus" (Ps. cvi. 1). This illustrates the confusion produced by *confiteor* in the Vulgate. *Hodah,* Hiphil of the root *yadah,* "to acknowledge by extending the hand," appears to be used in the Psalms only once in the restricted sense of "confess" (Ps. xxxii. 6) —"I said I will confess my sins unto the Lord"—where the Septuagint has ἐξαγορεύω, and the Vulgate *confiteor.* Yet in only seven of the passages where a derivative from this root occurs (Ps. xxvi. 7; l. 14, 23; lvi. 12; lxix. 30; cvii. 22; cxvi. 17), the Septuagint has αἴνεσις and the Vulgate *laus* or *laudatio;* and in all other cases (Ps. vi. 6; vii. 17; ix. 1; xviii. 49, &c.; xlii. 5; xcv. 2, &c.), the Septuagint has ἐξομολογέομαι or ἐξομολόγησις, and the Vulgate *confiteor* or *confessio.* It is interesting to trace the changes in the translation of these words in the English versions. In the Wyckliffe Bibles *confiteor* is uniformly translated by "knouleche;" *confessio* by "confession" in one version, and by "knoulechyng" in the other; and *laus* by "praising" in one, and by "heriyng" in the other. The expression, "give thanks," occurs in the first printed Bible of 1535 (Coverdale's Bible) as the usual translation of the derivatives of *yadah;* except that in Ps. l. 14, 23, lvi. 12, where the Vulgate has *laus,* the double expression, "thanks and

I confess to God, to Blessed Mary, and all the Saints,[1] and to you; I have sinned exceedingly in thought, word, and deed, through my fault. I pray holy Mary,[2] all God's saints, and you to pray for me.

The Absolution, *to be said by the assistant Ministers.*

Almighty God, have mercy upon you, and forgive you all your sins, deliver you from all evil, preserve and strengthen you in goodness, and bring you to everlasting life. *Amen.*

---

praise," or "praise and thanksgiving," is used; and in Ps. xxvi. 7, "praise;" though in other similar cases where *laus* occurs (Ps. lxix. 30; cvii. 22; cxvi. 17), the English is "thanksgiving." The same expressions were continued in Matthew's Bible, 1537; but in Cranmer's Bible, 1539, from which the English Psalter is taken, the expression, "thanks and praise," was retained only in Ps. l. 23, and "thanksgiving" was used in the other places. The result is that the idea of thanksgiving stands out prominently in the English Psalter, for the word occurs in fifty-four passages, where the Vulgate has *confiteor, confessio,* or *laus.* But it is less marked in the Authorized Version, where "praise" is used indiscriminately with "thanksgiving," which occurs only in thirty places. See Kimchi, In Psalmos, Ps. vi. 6. In the Revised Version "thanksgiving" is restored to its rightful position, occurring in fifty-one places; but there is still some uncertainty about it. For in eight places where the phrase "give thanks" is found in the Psalter (Ps. xxx. 9; xlii. 4, 5, 11; xliii. 4, 6; lxxxvi. 12; xcix. 3), the Revised Version follows the Authorized Version in rendering the Hebrew by "praise;" though in five places, where both the Psalter and Authorized Version have "praise" (Ps. xxxiii. 2; xliv. 8; liv. 6; cxxxviii. 2; cxlv. 10), the Revised Version has "give thanks." In Ps. l. 23, "the sacrifice of thanksgiving" takes the place of "thanks and praise;" and in Ps. lvi. 12, the word "thankofferings" represents the Vulgate rendering *laudationes.* The above references are numbered according to the Authorized Version.

[1] This confession to the saints was a novelty introduced apparently about this time, A.D. 1085, as it is not found in a Missal dated about A.D. 1000. In the older forms confession was made to God alone.—Martene, lib. i., cap. iv., art. xii., ordo 4, 5, 13, 16. ·See below, p. 136.

[2] This appears to be the first introduction into the Western Liturgy of direct prayer to the saints. In the older Liturgical prayers God was entreated to grant that the saints should pray for the worshipper.

The Ministers then made confession as before, and the Priest repeated the Absolution,[1] *adding :*

Almighty and merciful God, grant you absolution and re-mission of all your sins, space for true repentance, and amendment of life, and the grace and consolation of the Holy Spirit. *Amen.*

The Priest then said :

Our help is in the Name of the Lord ;

Answer. Who made Heaven and earth.

Blessed be the name of the Lord ;

Answer. Henceforth and for evermore.

Let us pray.

Then having finished his prayers, the Priest gave the KISS of peace to the deacon and subdeacon,[2] *saying :*

Receive the Kiss of peace and love, that you may be fit to perform the divine offices at the most holy Altar.

[1] The laity were instructed that the Absolution was pronounced for the benefit of all who were willing to confess ; and they were bidden to confess their sins privately, and add other devotions, whilst the priest and ministers were repeating the public forms.

Tho preste assoyles hom there belyue	(*absolves them forthwith*)
lered & lewed that wil hom shryue	(*learned and ignorant confess*)
& knowe to God that thai are ille,	
Whether hit be in loude or stille.	
Therefore knelande on thi knese	
als thou bisyde the other sese	(*as beside seest*)
shryue the there of alle thi synnes	
bigynnande thus when he bigynes.	

"Lay Folks Mass Book," p. 6.

[2] This kiss of peace is not found in other Western Missals, nor was it adopted in other English Service Books. It is repeated again after the Canon, which is the usual position for it in the Roman Liturgy. This Sarum practice seems to be a relic of the ancient Gallican customs, which resembled in many ways the Eastern Liturgies ; for in the Eastern Church the kiss of peace was given at the beginning of the service ; see above, p. 31. See also the Comparative Table of Liturgies facing the title-page.

*The candle-bearers then put down the candles at the altar step;
and the Priest prayed:*

Remove from us, we beseech Thee, O Lord, all our iniquities, that we may be permitted to enter the most holy place
with pure minds; through Christ our Lord.

In the Name of the Father and of the Son and of the Holy
Ghost.

*Then incense was brought, and after a prayer for it to be
blessed, the Altar was censed, and then the Priest.*[1]

*Then the Introit was repeated again, and the elements were
brought in, and a basin and water and a towel. Then was
repeated:*

iii. Kyrie eleison.

iii. Christe eleison.

iii. Kyrie eleison.[2]

Then was sung, Gloria in excelsis Deo.

Glory be to God on high, and in earth peace, good will
towards men. We praise Thee, &c.[3]

---

[1] This use of incense to cense persons and things was novel. According
to the earliest *Ordo Romanus,* incense was merely carried in procession and
burnt before the Altar. According to the Second *Ordo Romanus,* it was
also brought near for men to smell, drawing the smoke towards them with
the hand: " thuribula per altaria portantur et postea ad nares hominum
feruntur et per manum fumus ad os trahitur."—Muratori, tom. ii., pp. 978,
980, 1023.

[2] These words are an interesting relic of the Litany which is still used
at the commencement of the Liturgy in the Eastern Church. See above,
p. 45, and Chap. IX., LITANIES AND INVOCATIONS.

[3] On certain days words in honour of the Blessed Virgin Mary were
introduced in various parts of *Gloria in Excelsis;* " Son of the Father
(first-born of Mary Virgin Mother) . . . receive our prayer (to the glory
of Mary) . . . Thou only art holy (sanctifying Mary), Thou only art the
Lord (ruling Mary), Thou only art most high (crowning Mary)." This
gives an idea of the manner in which the worship of the Middle Ages
became interpolated with novelties. Sarum Graduale, Paris, 1532 (British
Museum), contains this as the Ninth form of " Gloria," for use on all

The Priest then signed himself, and said:

THE COLLECT FOR THE DAY.

THE EPISTLE, *followed by the Gradual.*

Before the reading of the Gospel, many ceremonies were per-formed, including blessing the book and the reader, making sundry crosses, and singing the Sequence or Tract, according to the season.

THE GOSPEL.

THE CREED.[1]

THE OFFERTORY.

The Deacon gave the Chalice and Paten to the Priest, kissing his hand each time. Then the Priest raised the Chalice a little, and offered the Sacrifice[2] to the Lord, saying:

Receive, O Holy Trinity, this oblation which I, an un-worthy sinner, offer in Thy honour, and in honour of blessed

Commemorations of the Blessed Virgin. Similar *farsures* are found in a Roman Missal, Lugd. 1500 (British Museum), for use on the Festival of Purif. B. V. M.

[1] For the use of the Creed here, see Chap. X., THE CREEDS, sect. iv.

[2] In the early Liturgies the sacrifice and offering had been represented as spiritual acts of thanksgiving, praise, and pleading, but at this period the words *sacrificium* and *hostia* were commonly applied to the elements, both before and after consecration. The change had been gradually introduced. At first it appears in expressions used in conjunction with words which implied some spiritual act, as in the prayer "that He who turned the water into wine may turn the oblations and vows of all of us into a *divine sacri-fice.*"—Missale Gothicum, in diem Epiphaniæ ; or, "Mercifully look upon these present *sacrifices*, in which not gold, incense, or myrrh is offered, but that which is signified by such gifts;" or, "We offer to Thee this pure *offering* (hostiam), this reasonable offering, this offering without blood, this holy bread, this cup of salvation."—*Ibid.,* Muratori, vol. ii., p. 542-544. It is true that even in the time of Gregory the Great (A.D. 590), we find signs of more materialistic views of the sacrifice ; for instance, he describes a man saying, "Take this bread, and offer it as a sacrifice for my sins."—Greg., Dial., iv., 55. But such modes of speaking had not previously appeared in the service itself.

Mary,[1] and all Thy Saints, for my sins and offences; for the salvation of the living, and for the rest of all the faithful departed.[2]

In the Name of the Father, and of the Son, and of the Holy Ghost, let this new Sacrifice[3] be acceptable to Almighty God.

Various rubrics followed, describing how the Sacrifice was

---

[1] This placing of God and His saints on the same level illustrates the strange changes in mediæval services. This form of the prayer, " Suscipe Sancta Trinitas," is peculiar to the Sarum Use. The older form in most general use had been " this oblation which I offer in memory of the Passion of our Lord Jesus Christ, and in honour of the blessed Virgin Mary and all the Saints." This had grown out of a form belonging to about the ninth century, following other prayers in which mention was made of God alone, and containing a memorial of "all Thy Saints who have pleased Thee from the beginning of the world." This is another illustration of the need of watching carefully the development of religious ideas which have no certain foundation of Holy Scripture.—Martene, lib. i., cap. iv., art. xii., ordo 4.

[2] Another illustration of the development of doctrines in mediæval times. In the Greek Liturgies the Eucharistic Offering is an offering of praise and thanksgiving for the redemption of the world through Jesus Christ. To this naturally follows a pleading of His merits whose death is being shown forth in the way ordained by Himself. In the ancient Latin Sacramentaries a similar pleading of Christ's merits is found; and the prayers for cleansing and forgiveness are distinct *prayers*, based upon the mercies of God through Jesus Christ. But here the plea for acceptance is the act of oblation offered by a sinner in honour of God.

[3] The word " new " was peculiar to the Sarum Use. It is not clear what was intended by it. Possibly there was a reference to the *New* Covenant. But it was undoubtedly a novelty of mediæval times to regard the oblations of bread and wine as propitiatory offerings in this manner, at the time of the offertory. This addition to the prayer, " Suscipe Sancta Trinitas," is not printed at length in some editions, as if objections had been raised against it in some quarters. It is found in the Sarum Missal of 1500, printed at London, but not in the London editions of 1504 and 1520, nor in the Great Sarum Breviary of 1531. It is found in various foreign editions, 1519 [Rouen]; 1527, Antwerp; 1529, 1531, 1534, 1555, Paris; and again in the London edition in Queen Mary's reign, 1557.

to be censed ; and the sign of the Cross was to be made over it, and round it, and on both sides ; and the Altar was to be kissed.

After this the Priest was directed to wash his hands.

Then he returned to the front of the Altar, and prayed, saying :

In the spirit of humility, and with a contrite heart, may we be accepted by Thee, O Lord ; and may our Sacrifice be so made in Thy sight, that it may be accepted by Thee this day, and be pleasing to Thee, O Lord my God.[1]

The Priest then asked for the prayers of the people, saying :

Pray, brethren and sisters, for me, that my Sacrifice, and your own as well, may be accepted by the Lord our God.

Prayer was then made for him, as follows :

The grace of the Holy Spirit illumine thy heart and thy lips ; and the Lord graciously accept this Sacrifice of Praise at thy hands, for our sins and offences.[2]

Certain secret prayers followed, varying daily, in addition to the ancient Secreta, *or prayer* super oblata ; *these were ended by the Priest saying aloud :*

For ever and ever. Amen.

The Lord be with you.

Answer. And with thy spirit.

Lift up your hearts, &c.

---

[1] This prayer seems to correspond with our " Prayer of Humble Access," which, in the First Prayer Book of Edward VI., was placed after the Consecration, immediately before the Communion, but has now been brought nearer to this position ; the difference being that it now follows, instead of preceding the Preface and Sanctus.

[2] The strange confusion of ideas which appears in these words is peculiar to the Sarum Use. The new idea of a distinct offering being made in the Eucharist, which could atone for sins, is attached to the ancient phrase, *Sacrificium laudis.* The incongruity of the new and old ideas does not seem to have been noticed.

H

THE PREFACE AND SANCTUS.
THE CANON, as above, page 71.[1]

Thee, therefore, most merciful Father, through Jesus Christ Thy Son our Lord, we humbly beg and pray; that Thou wilt accept and bless these gifts, these presents, these holy sacrifices of a pure kind : (*three crosses were here made over the Cup and the Bread*) which first of all we offer to Thee, &c.

Remember, O Lord, Thy servants, &c. (*Directions for the private prayers of the Priest were here given.*)

In communion with, &c. (*Here the Priest was directed to regard the Host with great veneration, saying :*)

This oblation, therefore, of our service, &c. (*Here again the Priest was to regard the Host, saying :*)

Which oblation do Thou, we beseech Thee, &c. (*here he was to make three crosses over both as he said :*) blessed, accounted,

[1] The rubrics which at this period appeared in the Canon according to the Use of Sarum were as follows :—

"Te igitur . . . rogamus (*corpore inclinato donec dicat*) ac petimus, (*hic erigens se sacerdos osculetur altare a dextris sacrificii dicens*) uti accepta habeas et benedicas, (*hic faciat sacerdos tres cruces super calicem et panem dicendo*) hæc dona . . . illibata, (*factis signaculis elevet manus suas, ita dicens*) Inprimis quæ offerimus, &c.   Memento Domine famulorum famularumque tuarum N et N. (*In qua oratione ordo debet attendi propter ordinem charitatis.   Quinquies orat sacerdos.   Primo pro se ipso.   Secundo pro patre et matre, carnali et spirituali; et pro aliis parentibus.   Tertio pro amicis specialibus, parochianis et aliis.   Quarto pro omnibus astantibus.   Quinto pro omni populo Christiano; et potest hic sacerdos omnes suos amicos Deo commendare.   Consulo tamen ut nullus ibidem nimis immoretur; tum propter cordis distractionem; tum propter immissiones quæ possunt fieri per angelos malos; tum propter alia pericula.*)

Communicantes, &c. (*Hic respiciat sacerdos hostiam cum magna veneratione dicens*)

Hanc igiter oblationem, &c. (*Hic iterum respiciat hostiam dicens*)

Quam oblationem . . . quæsumus (*hic faciat tres cruces super utraque, cum dicat*) benedictam, ascriptam, ratam . . . ut nobis (*hic faciat crucem super panem dicens*) corpus (*hic super calicem*) et sanguis (*junctisque manibus, dicens*) fiat . . . Christi. (*Hic erigat sacerdos manus et conjungat; et*)

valid . . . that it may be made unto us (*here a cross over the bread*) the Body, (*here a cross over the cup*) and Blood, &c. (*The words of consecration were to be said in one breath, without pause. Afterwards he was to bow towards the Host, and elevate it for the people to see, and reverently replace it before the cup, making the sign of a cross with it. Then the cup in like manner. After the Consecration, he was to raise his arms in the form of a cross, until the words :*) of Thy gifts and bounties ; (*then five crosses were to be made as he said the words :*) a pure Offering, a holy Offering, an undefiled Offering, the holy Bread . . . . and the Cup . . . .

Upon which, &c. (*Here the Priest was to bow with clasped hands.*)

We humbly beseech Thee, &c. (*Here the Priest was to raise himself, kiss the altar on the right of the Sacrifice, and make the*

Canon Missæ—continued.

ˉ*postea tergat digitos, et elevet hostiam dicens*) Qui pridie . . . cœlum (*hic elevet oculos suos*) ad Te . . . omnipotentem (*hic inclinet se et postea elevet paululum dicens*) tibi gratias agens ; benedixit ; fregit (*hic tangat hostiam dicens*) dcditque . . . corpus meum. (*Et debent ista verba proferri cum uno spiritu et sub una prolatione ; nulla pausatione interposita. Post hæc verba inclinet se sacerdos ad hostiam ; et postea elevet eam supra frontem ut possit a populo videri ; et reverenter illam reponat ante calicem in modum crucis per eandem factæ. Et tunc discooperiat calicem ; et teneat inter manus suas, non disjungendo pollicem ab indice nisi dum facit bencdictiones tantum, ita dicens*) Simili modo . . . item tibi (*hic inclinet se dicens*) gratias agens . . . ex eo omnes (*hic elevet sacerdos parumper calicem, ita dicens*) Hic est enim calix . . . peccatorum. (*Hic elevet calicem usque ad pectus vel ultra caput dicens*) Hæc quotiescunque . . . facietis. (*Hic reponat calicem et fricet digitos suos ultra calicem propter micas, et cooperiat calicem. Deinde elevet brachia sua in modum crucis, junctis digitis, usque ad hæc verba*) . . . de tuis donis ac datis (*Hic quinque cruces fiant ; scd tres primæ cruces super hostiam et calicem dicendo*) hostiam puram . . . immaculatam, (*quarta super panem dicendo*) panem . . . æternæ . . . (*quinta super calicem dicendo*) et calicem salutis perpetuæ.

Supra quæ, &c. (*Hic sacerdos corpore inclinato et cancellatis manibus dicat*) Supplices te rogamus . . . participatione (*et tunc erigat se deos-*

sign of a cross thrice, over the Host and the Cup, and upon his face.)

Remember also, O Lord, Thy servants, &c. (*Here he was to smite his breast once, as he said :*) To us, also, Thy sinful servants, &c. Through whom Thou ever makest, &c. (*Here he was to make the sign of the cross upon the Cup thrice, as he said:*) sanctifiest, quickenest, blessest. (*Then he was to uncover the Cup, and make the sign of the cross five times with the Host, as he said:*) Through Him, and with Him, &c.

After the Lord's Prayer, the following prayer was inserted:

Deliver us, we beseech Thee, O Lord, from all evils, past, present, and to come ; and at the intercession of the blessed and glorious ever-Virgin Mary, Mother of God, and Thy blessed Apostles Peter and Paul, and also Andrew, and all saints, (*here the Priest kissed the Paten, and placed it in front of each eye ; then made the sign of the cross with it above his head, saying :*) graciously give peace in our days; that, assisted by the help of Thy mercy, we may be ever free from sin, and

Canon Missæ—continued.

culans altare a dextris sacrificii, et faciat signum crucis super hostiam et calicem et in facie sua cum dicit) omni benedictione cœlesti.

Memento etiam, &c. (*Hic percutiat pectus suum semel dicens*)

Nobis quoque peccatoribus, &c.

Per quem . . . creas (*hic ter signet calicem dicens*) sanctificas . . . nobis. (*Hic discooperiat calicem et faciat signaculum crucis cum hostia quinquies. Primo ultra calicem ex utraque parte ; secundo calici æquale ; tertio infra calicem ; quarto sicut primo ; quinto ante calicem.*) Per ipsum, &c."

The Canon thus remained unaltered, except by the addition of rubrics; but how great an alteration was thus produced will be seen by comparing the Gregorian with the Sarum Service. The sign of the Cross was made twenty-six times in the course of the Canon ; a twenty-seventh time in the prayer which was added to the Lord's Prayer; and three times more in the giving of the Peace. The multiplication of manual acts gave to the ignorant the idea that a mysterious power belonged to certain ceremonies, irrespective of the spiritual intentions of the hearts of the worshippers ; and there is abundant proof of the low view of holy words and acts which was thus impressed upon the multitude.

safe from all disturbance; (*here the Priest was to uncover the Chalice, and take the Body with an inclination, placing it in the bowl of the Chalice, holding it between his thumbs and forefingers ; and he was to break it into three parts, saying :*) through the same, our Lord Jesus Christ, &c.[1]

The Priest was then directed to make three crosses, saying :
The peace of the Lord be always with you.
Answer. And with thy spirit.
O Lamb of God, which taketh away the sin of the world, Have mercy upon us.
O Lamb of God, which taketh away the sin of the world, Have mercy upon us.
O Lamb of God, which taketh away the sin of the world, Grant us peace.
A portion of the consecrated bread was then mingled with the wine, and the sign of the cross was made, with these words :

[1] " Libera nos quæsumus Domine ab omnibus malis præteritis præsentibus et futuris ; et intercedente beata et gloriosa semperque Virgine Dei genitrice Maria ; et beatis apostolis tuis Petro et Paulo atque Andrea; cum omnibus sanctis, (*hic committat diaconus patenam sacerdoti, deosculans manum ejus dextrâm, et sacerdos deosculetur patenam ; postea ponat ad sinistrum oculum, deinde ad dextrum ; postea faciat crucem cum patena ultra caput ; et tunc reponat eam in locum suum, dicens*) da propitius pacem in diebus nostris ut ope misericordiæ tuæ adjuti; et a peccato simus semper liberi, et ab omni perturbatione securi. (*Hic discooperiat calicem, et sumat corpus cum inclinatione, transponens in concavitate calicis, retinendo inter pollices et indices ; et frangat in tres partes ; prima fractio dum dicitur*) Per eundem Dominum . . . tuum, (*secunda fractio*) qui tecum . . . Deus (*hic teneat duas fracturas in sinistra manu, et tertiam fracturam in dextra manu in summitate calicis ita dicens aperta voce*) per omnia sæcula sæculorum. (*Hic faciat tres cruces infra calicem cum tertia parte hostiæ dicendo*) Pax Domini sit semper vobiscum."
The addition of these manual acts shows the mode of thought of the time. They seem to be hardly distinguishable from an idolatrous veneration of the Elements. The Sarum Rubrics differ from those of all other Missals in the multiplication of the ceremonial acts, being excessively lengthened with minute particulars.

May this most holy mingling of the Body and Blood of our Lord Jesus Christ become to me and to all who receive it salvation of mind and body, and the saving preparation for attaining and receiving life eternal; through the same Christ our Lord.   Amen.

Then, before the Peace was given, the Priest said :

O Lord, Holy Father, Almighty, everlasting God, grant to me so worthily to receive the most holy Body and Blood of Thy Son Jesus Christ, that I may obtain thereby remission of all my sins, and be filled with Thy Holy Spirit, and have Thy peace.   For Thou art God, and there is none other but Thee ; whose glorious kingdom endureth for ever.   Amen.

The KISS of Peace was then given.   The Priest kissed the corporal, and the chalice, and afterwards the deacon, saying :

Peace be unto thee, and unto the Church of God.

Then the Deacon received the PAX (or instrument for the people to kiss), which was handed on in order.[1]

[1] The Kiss of peace was ordered to be given before the Communion by Pope Innocent I. (A.D. 402-417), and was regarded as being closely connected with the act of Communion, so that a doubt existed in the ninth century whether anyone might receive the Kiss unless he communicated at the same time.—Walafrid Strabo, de rebus Eccles., cap. xxii.   "The actual kiss of the faithful was superseded, probably in the thirteenth century, by the kissing of the *Pax*, which was made of wood, metal, ivory, or glass." But so many quarrels for precedence arose from the practice, that it seems to have been given up in the Roman Church in the last century.—Canon Simmons, "Lay Folks Mass Book," p. 296.

By the kindness of the Secretary to the South Kensington Museum, I have been favoured with the information that there are thirteen specimens of the mediæval *Pax*, or *Paxbrede*, in that collection.   The oldest is a French one, belonging to about A.D. 1340.   They are of various materials, enamel, bronze, and silver.   They vary in size from about 4 inches to 10 inches long, and from 2½ inches to 7 inches wide, and are carved or engraved with various subjects.   They are fitted with a handle behind, as shown in an engraving in J. D. Chambers' "Divine Worship in England," p. 383.

It is possible that Shakespeare makes use of an allusion to the use of the

Then various prayers followed; and after the Priest had received the Communion,[1] *the following Thanksgiving was said :*

I give thanks to Thee, O Lord, Holy Father Almighty, everlasting God, who hast refreshed me with the most sacred Body and Blood of Thy Son, our Lord Jesus Christ;[2] and I

Paxbrede when he says : " His kissing is as full of sanctity as the touch of holy bread."—As You Like It, act iii., scene 4.

[1] It will be noticed that no instructions are given for the Communion of the people. The general disuse of Communion in the times preceding the Reformation may be gathered from this. The Sarum Missal does not appear to contain any notice at all about the ordinary Communion of the people. It is said that a custom had grown up of howselling (communicating) the people out of Mass time, at their Easter Communion, or on the rare occasions when it was administered. It appears that the rule for receiving the Communion had been reduced to once a year. We find in Archbishop Thoresby's Catechism, A.D. 1357 :—

       The sacrement of the auter   (*altar*)
    whilk ilk man & woman, that of eld is,
    aught for to resceyve anes in the yhere,
    that is at sai, at Paskes, als hali kirke uses   (*to say, Easter, as holy*)
    when thai er clensed of syn through penaunce
    of payne of doyng out of hali kirke.

But in the " Lay Folks Mass Book," or instructions how to behave during the service (*circa* A.D. 1150), nothing is said about the administration of the Sacrament, which shows that the celebration of the Mass was even then completely dissociated from the Communion of the laity.

[2] This Thanksgiving after Communion is peculiar to the Sarum Use, and is one of its distinguishing beauties. It has been continued in the English Church, in our second Post-Communion Form. There is nothing corresponding to it in the modern Roman Liturgy, nor in ancient Missals connected with the Roman Use. It is one of the relics which have come down to us of the more ancient Celtic form of service, which was evidently allied to the Gallican Liturgy. Such a Thanksgiving is found in the fragments of the ancient Stowe Missal.—Warren, " Liturgy and Ritual of the Celtic Church." Similar forms frequently occur in the ancient Gallican Services; see Muratori, tom. ii., pp. 519, 649, 780, &c. A similar Thanksgiving is found also in a Missal of the Church of Evreux in Normandy.—Martene,

pray that this Sacrament of our salvation, of which I
an unworthy sinner have partaken, turn not to judgment
nor condemnation, according to my deserts, but be profitable for the health of my body and soul unto life eternal.
Amen.

*Then, after many ceremonies for cleansing the sacred vessels,
various Post-Communion Collects were said, varying every day ;
and the service ended thus :*
The Lord be with you.
Then the Deacon said :
Let us bless the Lord.
Answer. Thanks be to God.
Or, on Sundays and Festivals :
Ite missa est (*i.e.* Depart, the service is over).
Answer. Thanks be to God.

There were other Service Books in use in England
during the Middle Ages, besides that of the diocese of
Sarum; they were commonly spoken of as the Hereford
Use, the Bangor Use, and the York Use.[1]   Whilst
they followed the same general plan and order of service as are found in the Sarum Use, they gave far less
prominence to the novelties of faith and practice which
have been pointed out in the preceding notes.[2] The most
peculiar features of the Sarum Use were absent.   But
it is evident that the Sarum Use was the popular form of
service in England.   And consequently it must be understood that, previous to the Reformation, our forefathers

lib. i., cap. iv., art. xii., ordo 28.   Post-Communion Thanksgiving is thoroughly in harmony with the primitive forms of Eastern Liturgies.   See
pp. 24, 38, 62.
    [1] These are referred to in the Preface " Concerning the Service of the
Church " at the beginning of the Book of Common Prayer.
    [2] See these Uses compared in Maskell's " Ancient Liturgy of the Church
of England."

had been accustomed to a service which was farther removed from the simplicity of the Ancient Liturgies than
any other service of ancient or modern times.[1] It retained the ancient form of words in the Canon, which,
from the time of the Emperor Charlemagne, had been in
universal use throughout Europe, but its rubrical additions to this were entirely English, whilst the introductory
parts of the service were unlike any other service in
many important particulars.

[1] The present Roman Service is free from most of these very startling
novelties, though it continues to follow the Mediæval Church in the general
view of the Sacrifice, as being propitiatory rather than eucharistic.

Additional Note, A ; On the Canon. (To page 71.)

THE original simplicity of the ancient Prayer, which bears the name of "The Canon," is brought into view when it is studied apart from the rubrics and ceremonial acts added to it between the ninth and eleventh centuries. Special attention should be given to the following particulars :—

1. Its History.—It is found first under the name of "The Canon of Pope Gelasius," and it occurs almost in its complete form in the Sacramentary named after him. But some parts of it can be traced back to the earlier Sacramentary of Pope Leo, where the opening words of the following portions occur thus : "Hanc igitur oblationem," &c., and "Communicantes . . . sed et memoriam venerantes," &c.—Sacram. Leon., Muratori, vol. i., pp. 314, 316, 318, 321, &c.

Walafridus Strabo (died A.D. 849) calls attention both to the antiquity and the gradual formation of the Canon. In proof that it was composed of parts brought together from various sources, he refers to the two lists of the saints who are commemorated ; the first, in the part beginning, "Communicantes et memoriam venerantes . . . ;" and the second in the part beginning, "Nobis quoque peccatoribus . . . ." He points out that these lists consist of the names of persons belonging to the same times, and that they must have been put together at the discretion of different authors. The order in which the Apostles are mentioned in the first list of names appears to him a sign of the extreme antiquity of the earlier part of the Canon, because it does not accord with any list given in the Gospels. And this view is confirmed by the fact that the prayer in which the names occur is found, as mentioned above, in the most ancient of the Sacramentaries. He mentions also the tradition that Pope Alexander (*circa* A.D. 109), whose name appears in the second list of saints, introduced into the Canon the Commemoration of the Passion of our Lord. And this tradition was maintained in some of the Mediæval Missals ; for in the Canon according to York Use, the words *Alexander Papa instituit* are found preceding "Qui pridie."—Canon from a York Missal, in "Lay Folks Mass Book." This tradition seems to point to the simple original of the Canon, as first used in the Roman Church, and to support the suggestion which Walafrid makes, that "what we now do by the varied means of prayers, lessons, hymns, and consecrations, the Apostles, and those who came next to them, did simply by prayers and the commemoration of the Passion of the Lord."—Walafrid Strabo, de rebus Eccles., cap. xxii.; edited by Hittorpius, de divinis Officiis. Similar traditions are found in the ancient exposition of the Mass named Gemma Animæ, cap. 88, 90, where the dates of all parts of the service are traditionally given.

2. ITS SACRIFICIAL TERMS.—The offering is first described as " hæc dona, hæc munera, hæc sancta sacrificia illibata; " then as " hoc sacrificium laudis; " then the word " oblatio " is found; and after the consecration these words occur, "offerimus . . . hostiam puram, hostiam sanctam, hostiam immaculatam ; " but immediately afterwards the last of these phrases is used in connection with sacrifices of the Old Testament, "munera Abel, sacrificium Abrahæ, et quod obtulit Melchisedech sanctum sacrificium, immaculatam hostiam;" and the prayer follows that " these things may be carried by the hand of God's holy Angel to the Altar on High." It may be remarked here, *first*, that the variety of these expressions may be explained by the suggestion, mentioned before, that the Canon was formed out of separate prayers. *Secondly*, that a comparison of these sacrificial terms thus brought together leads to the conclusion that a spiritual view of the Sacrifice was taken by those who composed the Canon. For the comparison of this offering with the sacrifices of Abel, Abraham, and Melchisedech is intelligible only if the service be regarded as the means of pleading the merits of Christ in a spiritual or sacramental sense. The offering made by Melchisedech was a type of the Body and Blood of Christ only in a figurative way, and it was only by expressing, as by a shadow, the mystery of the Christian Sacrifice, that he became a likeness of Him of whom it is said, " Thou art a priest for ever after the order of Melchisedech." (See Isidore Hispalensis, de Eccles. officiis, lib. i., cap. 18.) *Thirdly*, that the prayer that " these things may be carried," &c., is made in respect of the whole action. For these words cannot be restricted to the material gifts, nor do they apply to the Sacrifice of the Lamb of God Himself; they must therefore refer to the thanksgiving, prayer, and pleading connected with the sacramental acts instituted by Christ, and they imply the necessity of partaking of the Holy Communion in order to receive the benefit.

Various distinctions have been drawn by ancient authors between the words *dona*, *munera*, *sacrificia*, &c. (Amalarius, cap. xxiii., printed in Speculum antiq. devot., by Joh. Cochlæus; Exposition, by pseudo-Isidore Hispal., Migne's Patrol., tom. lxxxiv.; notes to Menard's Sacram. S. Gregorii.) But the verbal criticisms of mediæval writers do not always agree together, and are not very trustworthy. It seems hardly to admit of a doubt that the words came into use through the Latin versions of the Holy Scriptures, and will be best studied by their help. It is generally accepted as certain that the words *dona* and *munera* at the beginning of the Canon refer to the elements of bread and wine; and, if this be so, the following words *sancta sacrificia illibata* seem to express the idea of the superiority of the offerings belonging to the Christian Sacrament over the ancient offerings of blood (Mal. i. 11). Amalarius, Archbishop of Treves in the time of Charlemagne, quotes approvingly from S. Augustine :—" Si quis vult dona Deo offerre se ipsum offerat ; si quis munera, sæpius memoretur beneficiorum ejus ; si quis sacrificia illibata, humilitatem laudemque et charitatem offerat" (Amal., *ut supra*), which shows the importance attached to the spiritual side of such offerings. The general teaching of S. Augustine in De civit. Dei, lib. x., cap. 3-6, and many other places, seems to be here referred to, and is well worthy of study in connection with this.

The phrase *sacrificium laudis*, which comes next, is undoubtedly taken from such passages as " Immola Deo sacrificium laudis, et redde Altissimo vota tua " (Ps. xlix. 14), and may be regarded as the nearest Latin equivalent to the word *Eucharist*.

The word *hostia* demands special attention on account of its modern use under the form " Host." In the Vulgate Version of the Old Testament it is the word commonly used for any offering : " Ait Moses, Hostias quoque et holocausta dabis nobis " (Exod. x. 25 ; cf. xviii. 12). In Leviticus it is used in a similar way for burnt offerings (chap. i.), for peace offerings (chap. iii.), and for sin offerings (chap. iv.). And by the Psalmist it is used in a spiritual sense for the offering of praise and thanksgiving : " Tibi sacrificabo hostiam laudis " (Ps. cxv. 17). In the New Testament, besides being used of the sacrifices of old time (Heb. x. 1, 5 ; xi. 4), it is found in passages which refer to the Sacrifice of Christ, who offered Himself " oblationem et hostiam Deo in odorem suavitatis " (Ephes. v. 2 ; cf. also Hebr. ix. 23, 26). But it is most commonly used to describe the offerings of Christians, who are exhorted to present their bodies, " hostiam viventem, sanctam, Deo placentem, rationabile obsequium " (Rom. xii. 1), and to offer through Christ, " hostiam laudis semper Deo, id est, fructum labiorum confitentium nomini ejus ; " to which is added, " talibus hostiis promeretur Deus " (Hebr. xiii. 15, 16) ; and they are said to be themselves built up to be a holy priesthood, " offerre spirituales hostias acceptabiles Deo per Jesum Christum " (1 Pet. ii. 5). This varied use of the word accounts for its frequent occurrence in the prayers of the Western Church, and shows that there is no reason why we should restrict its application in the Canon in accordance with the modern use of the term " Host."

3. SIGNS OF EUCHARISTIC WORSHIP.—In the days of Gregory the Great it did not seem unusual for a Christian to say, " Take this bread, and offer it as a sacrifice for my sins " (Greg., Dial., lib. iv., cap. 55). But it is

doubtful if any author of the first four centuries would have spoken of offering the elements of bread and wine " for the Holy Catholic Church " in
the sense of making a propitiatory offering for sin. It is necessary,
therefore, to consider in what sense these words would have been used by
them, " In primis quæ tibi offerimus pro ecclesia," &c. *Pro* is often used, as
in the phrase *pro-consule*, to mean " in the name or place of another." For
instance, Cyprian says : " Sacrificia pro eis semper offerimus, quoties martyrum passiones celebramus " (Cyprian, Epist. ad Presb. et Diac., xxxix.,
aliter xxxiii.). Martyrs were least of all men in need of propitiatory offerings on their behalf; in fact S. Augustine draws this distinction between
them and others, saying, " At the Table of the Lord we do not commemorate them as we do others who rest in peace, so as actually to pray for them,
but rather so that they may be praying for us, that we may follow their
steps " (Tract. 84, in Evang. Johan., ad cap. xv.). And in another sermon he
does not hesitate to say, " Injuria est enim pro martyre orare, cujus nos debemus orationibus commendari " (Sermo xviii., ad Rom. vi. 16). We conclude, therefore, that such offerings were made *for* them, in the sense of *in
the name of* those whom the Communion of Saints caused to be present with
the worshippers. (See notes to Cyprian, Epist. i., Oxon., 1682.) Similarly
it is quite possible that the first part of the Canon was originally intended
to express the sense of the Communion of Saints, and to unite the whole
Church in prayer for peace, and in thanksgiving for redemption. This
is confirmed by what follows. For in the next paragraph the offering is
described as " a sacrifice of praise " offered for all " for their redemption,"
qui offerunt hoc sacrificium laudis pro se suisque omnibus pro redemptione.
It is true that a mediæval writer explains this to mean that the sacrifice
is offered first *pro laude Dei*, and afterwards *pro se suisque omnibus*, implying
that the latter is not a thanksgiving for redemption, but a prayer for it
(Pseudo-Isidore, *ut supra*); and a later writer says, " Sacrificium laudis,
quia Deus per illud magnopere laudatur."—Bellarmine, de Missa, lib. ii.,
cap. 21; quoted in " Scottish Communion Office," by J. Dowden, p. 213.
But such interpretations can satisfy few who pay attention to the original
institution of the Eucharist. The more natural conclusion is that the
Canon sets forth the Sacrifice in the form in which it is represented in the
Eastern Liturgies, as the *Eucharist*, or Sacrifice of Thanksgiving for Redemption. It is probable that in the Mediæval Church this act of eucharistic
worship was seldom noticed; but attention was called to it by Archbishop
Herman in his " Enchiridion"; see Canones Concil. Provinc. Colon., 1536,
fol. 109. And it is proved by the ancient metrical instruction named " The Lay
Folks Mass Book," that the people were taught by those who were spiritually
minded, that the intention of the opening part of the Canon was eucharistic.

For at the beginning of the service the worshipper was directed to kneel down and say :—

Lord honourd mot thou be,   (*mayest*)
with al my hert I worship the ;   (*thee*)
I thonk the, Lord, als me wele owe,   (*as well befits me*)
of more gode then I con knowe,   (*For*)
that I haue of the resayued,
syn tho tyme I was consayued ;

*   *   *   *

Al my lyue & al my lyuynge
holly haue I of thi gyuynge ;   (*wholly*)
thou boght me dere with thi blode,
& dyed for me opon tho rede ;

*   *   *   *

Of thes godes and many moo
I thonk the, Lord, I praye als soo.

" Lay Folks Mass Book," pp. 30, 32.

4. THE SACRIFICE OF THE MASS.—It is evident that the idea of *Eucharist*, *i.e.*, thanksgiving, was more prevalent in the Eastern than in the Western Church. The Roman mind turned more naturally to the idea of offering material gifts than to the offering of thanks, and, as has been said before, the Latins had no word for thanksgiving corresponding with the word *Eucharist*. The consequence was that the words denoting material gifts in the Roman prayers lost by degrees the spiritual meanings which had been attached to them at first. The Sacramentaries prove that the idea of gaining something in return for their gifts began, as years passed, to occupy an increasing share of the attention of the worshippers. In the Sacramentary of Leo the idea of propitiation is indeed quite apparent, and is frequently referred to, but it becomes much more prominent in the Sacramentary of Gelasius, and in the Sacramentary of Gregory it commonly holds the chief place in the prayers. The idea of offering *hostia laudis* to the honour of God, gave place to the idea of offering *hostia placationis* for the benefit of the worshipper. Here is an example from the earliest Sacramentary showing the original idea connected with Christian Sacrifice : " Hostias populi tui, quæsumus, Domine miseratus intende ; et ut tibi reddantur acceptæ, conscientias nostras Sancti Spiritus salutaris adventus emendet ; per," &c. This was replaced by another in the Sacramentary of Gregory ; in which such prayers as these are common specimens : " Purificet nos Domine, quæsumus, muneris præsentis oblatio," &c. ; " Hæc hostia Domine, quæsumus, emundet nostra delicta," &c.—Muratori, vol. i., pp. 320, 600 ; vol. ii.,

pp. 87, 92. At length the idea of gaining personal benefit grew to such an extent, that the very phrase "Sacrificium laudis" was used, as has been shown above, p. 97, as if it implied the expectation of a return. The result was that the sacrifice of the Mass assumed in mediæval times a new character, and its main feature, instead of being the memorial of redemption, became the satisfaction for sins.

5. GENERAL PLAN OF THE CANON.—Having traced back the meaning of words, and the ideas respecting the Christian Sacrifice to the times before Pope Leo, when the Canon was formed, it is now possible to consider the general plan which the authors of this ancient Prayer seem to have had in mind. The Preface having led up to the grand idea of universal Thanksgiving and Praise from all created beings, the sacramental gifts are offered with renewed prayer for acceptance, *inprimis* in the name of the whole Church, which under the mystical bond of the Communion of Saints, unites in prayer for Peace, and, in particular, for the bishop, the king, and the faithful of this or that land. *Secondly,* the offering is made in the name of all present, who thus offer their sacrifice of Praise and Thanksgiving for their own redemption and hope of salvation, according as Christ ordained. *Thirdly,* the offering is continued in the name of the holy and great of other days, the mention of whose names calls forth the prayer that God will hear them in their prayers for the worshippers. All sections of the Universal Church having been thus united in the great act of the Church's worship, the offering is now regarded as the oblation of the whole family of God, "servitutis nostræ, sed et cunctæ familiæ tuæ;" and, again, "nos tui servi, sed et plebs tua sancta;" who make the commemoration of the institution of the Holy Sacrament as a memorial of the Death, Resurrection, and Ascension of Christ. Thus the idea of the Preface is continued : "It is meet . . . that we should at all times and in all places give thanks . . . Therefore with angels," &c. Whether present or absent, the faithful have some sort of share in the service, and whether in this life or in paradise, they join their thanksgivings with the ceaseless adoration of the angels, whose ministry is now asked for to bear to Heaven the imperfect worship of earth, to the end that those who now become partakers of the Body and Blood of Christ, according to His institution, may be fulfilled with grace and heavenly benediction. And, lastly, as the thought of the departed is brought to mind, a prayer is added for those who sleep in the sleep of peace, which proves by its simplicity and agreement with similar prayers in Eastern Liturgies the great antiquity of the Canon, beseeching that refreshment, light, and peace may be granted to them, and some fellowship with them to the worshippers.

CHAPTER IV.

THE HOUR OFFICES.

" Libellum de genere officiorum ordinatum misi, ex scriptis vetustissimorum authorum, ut locus obtulit, commentatum. In quo pleraque meo stylo elicui : nonnulla verò ita ut apud ipsos erant admixui, quo facilius lectio de singulis fidei authoritatem teneret. Si quæ tamen ex his displicuerint, erroribus meis paratior venia erit ; quia non sunt referenda ad culpæ meæ titulum, de quibus testificatio adhibetur authorum."—Isidore Hispalensis. (Seventh century.)

FIXED hours of prayer were observed amongst the Jews long before the foundation of the Church of Christ; and the Apostles continued the practice. Thus in the prison at Philippi, " at *Midnight* Paul and Silas prayed and sang praises unto God," and it seems probable that they were joining in some settled form of service from the fact that " the prisoners heard them."[1] It was at " the *Third* Hour of the day " that the Holy Spirit came upon the Apostles, who were assembled together " with one accord in one place."[2] It was "about the *Sixth* Hour" that " Peter went up upon the housetop to pray " at Joppa.[3] And it was " at the *Ninth* Hour " that " Peter and John went up together into the Temple " to pray.[4] The devotional longings which had influenced Old Testament saints were thus maintained amongst the first generation of Christians, who continued to do as David had done, according to his words, " I will bless

[1] Acts xvi. 25.   [2] Acts ii. 1, 4, 15.
[3] Acts x. 9.   [4] Acts iii. 1 ; cf. x. 30.

the Lord at all times, His praise shall continually be in
my mouth;" "Evening, and morning, and at noon will
I pray;" "At midnight I will rise to give thanks unto
Thee;" "Seven times a day do I praise Thee, because
of Thy righteous judgments." They followed Daniel in
his acts of devotion, who "kneeled upon his knees three
times a day, and prayed, and gave thanks before his
God."[1]

The habit of observing stated times in the day for
private devotion, which may thus be traced to the
Apostles, was encouraged amongst Christians as years
went on. But the prevalence of persecution rendered
the practice of meeting together for this purpose not
merely difficult but almost impossible. Consequently,
few references to stated services for the various hours
of the day are found during the first three centuries.
The hours of prayer are mentioned, and various reasons
are given for their observance, but they were evidently
regarded as opportunities for regular private devotion,
rather than for public worship. Thus Cyprian, Bishop
of Carthage in North Africa, A.D. 248-258, speaks of
settled times for prayer having been handed down
amongst Christians, because at the third hour the Holy
Spirit descended upon the Apostles, at the sixth hour
the Lord was crucified, and at the ninth He washed away
our sins in His Blood. And he exhorts that the early
morning should be observed by prayer as a means of celebrating the Lord's Resurrection; and the evening, as re-
minding us of our need that Christ should come to bring

---

[1] Psalm xxxiv. 1; lv. 17; cxix. 62, 164; Daniel vi. 10. Most of these
passages are quoted by Archbishop Cranmer, MS. Collections, De Canon.
Horis, vol. i. p. 88.

us the gift of everlasting light.[1]   The Apostolical Constitutions give similar advice, saying, "Make your prayers at dawn, at the third, at the sixth, at the ninth hour, in the evening, and at cock crowing." Various reasons are added, and the bishop is advised that he should hold the services at home if it is impossible to go out to church in consequence of the unbelievers; or that, if a congregation cannot be collected either at home or at church, every one should be directed to say the Psalms, read, and pray by himself, or two or three together.[2] Similarly, Ambrose, Bishop of Milan, A.D. 374-397, urges that prayer should be said with thanksgiving, (1) when we rise from sleep, (2) when we go forth, (3) when we prepare to take our food, (4) after food, (5) at the hour of lighting, (6) when we go to rest, and he adds, "Yea, in my couch I like to sing psalms mingled frequently with the Lord's Prayer."[3]

At the same time, whilst men were encouraged to observe these various hours for private prayer, special mention was made of the daily meetings for morning and evening worship. In the Apostolic Constitutions the bishop is exhorted to "charge the people to come regularly to church in the early morning and evening of every day . . . and not to think that it was said only of the priests, but to consider that it was said to themselves individually by the Lord, 'He that is not with Me is against Me; and he that assembleth not with Me, scattereth' . . . That in the morning they should say Psalm lxiii., and in the evening Psalm cxli. And that

[1] Cyprian, de Orat. Dominica, *ad finem.*
[2] Apost. Constit., lib. viii., cap. 34.
[3] Ambrose, de Virgin., lib. iii., cap. 4; cf. Jerome, Epist. vii., ad Lætam.

they should meet together with special earnestness on the Sabbath, and on the Lord's Day."¹ In another passage the services which were used at these daily meetings are described at length ; and the description is confirmed by statements of other authors. The Evening Service is first mentioned ; it is as follows : ²

The Evening Service.

The Evening Psalm, i.e. Psalm cxli.

Lord, I call upon Thee, haste Thee unto me: and consider my voice when I cry unto Thee.

Let my prayer be set forth in Thy sight as the incense: and let the lifting up of my hands be an Evening Sacrifice,³ &c.

After this the Deacon recited the Prayers for Catechumens and others, *the same as in the Service of the Eucharist ; and after their dismissal, this* Prayer for the Faithful.

*The Evening Bidding Prayer.*⁴

Save us, and raise us up, O God, through Thy Christ. Let us stand up, and pray to the Lord for His mercies and compassions: for the Angel of Peace ; for what is good and convenient for us ; for a Christian end. Let us pray for the evening and night to be peaceful and free from sin: and for our whole life to be without rebuke. Let us commend ourselves and one another to the living God, through His Christ.

¹ Apost. Constit., lib. ii., cap. 59.
² The practice of counting the services of a festival as beginning with the previous evensong may thus be traced as far back as the fourth century.
³ Chrysost. Hom. in Psalm cxl. mentions that the Fathers appointed this Psalm to be used daily in the Evening Service, not merely on account of this expression, " an evening sacrifice," but as a heavenly medicine for removing daily stains of sins.
⁴ Προσφώνησις ἐπιλύχνιος ; literally, " at the lighting of the lamps."

The Bishop then said the Evening Thanksgiving:

O God, without beginning and without end, the Maker and Preserver of all things, . . . who didst make the day for works of light, and the night to give rest to our weakness: for the day is Thine, and the night is Thine; Thou didst prepare the light and the sun: do Thou now, O Lord, loving and kind, graciously receive this our Evening Thanksgiving. Thou that hast led us through the length of the day, and brought us to the beginning of the night, keep us by Thy Christ; grant that we may pass this evening in peace, and this night without sin; and deem us worthy of eternal life, through, &c.

Deacon. Bow down for the imposition of hands.

Bishop. O God of our fathers, and Lord of mercy, who by Thy wisdom didst make man a rational being, the dearest to Thee of all things upon earth, and gavest him dominion over the earth, and didst appoint in Thy judgment kings and priests, the one for the security of life, and the other for Thy lawful worship; do Thou now bow down, O Lord Almighty, and shew the light of Thy countenance upon Thy servants that bow down the neck of their hearts before Thee, and bless them by Christ, by whom Thou hast enlightened us with the light of knowledge, and revealed Thyself to us: with whom, &c.

Deacon. Depart in peace.[1]

---

[1] Apost. Constit., lib. viii., cap. 35-37.

In another passage the following evening devotions are provided, apparently for private use:

Ps. cxiii. 1. "O praise the Lord, ye servants," &c.

"We praise Thee, we hymn Thee, we bless Thee for Thy great glory; O Lord King, the Father of Christ, the spotless Lamb, that taketh away the sin of the world. To Thee belongeth praise and singing and glory, God the Father, through the Son, in the holy Spirit, world without end. Amen."

S. Luke ii. 29. "Lord, now lettest thou thy servant depart in peace," &c., Apost. Constit., lib. vii., cap. 48.

𝕮𝖍𝖊 𝕸𝖔𝖗𝖓𝖎𝖓𝖌 𝕾𝖊𝖗𝖛𝖎𝖈𝖊.

The Morning Psalm, i.e. Psalm lxiii.

O God, Thou art my God : early will I seek Thee, &c.[1]

Deacon, after the dismissal of the Catechumens :

Save them, O God, and raise them by Thy grace.

Let us pray God for His mercies and compassions; that this morning, and this day, and all the time of our pilgrimage be peaceful, and free from sin ; for the angel of peace ; for a Christian end. Let us commend ourselves to the living God, through His only begotten Son.

Bishop. O God, the God of Spirits, and of all flesh, incomparable, and in want of nothing, who gavest the sun to rule the day, and the moon and the stars to govern the night, do Thou now look down upon us with the eyes of Thy favour, and receive our morning thanksgivings, and have mercy upon us. For we have not stretched out our hands to any strange God. For there is no new God among us, but Thou, the eternal and without end. Do Thou who hast given us our being through Christ, and our well-being also through Him, deem us worthy of eternal life, through Him, with whom, &c. Amen.

Deacon. Bow down for the imposition of hands.

Bishop. O God, faithful and true, that shewest mercy to thousands and ten thousands of them that love Thee ; who art the Friend of the humble and Defender of the poor, of whom all things are in need, because all things serve Thee ; look down upon this Thy people, who bow their heads before Thee, and bless them with all spiritual benediction ; keep them as the apple of Thine eye ; preserve them in piety and righteousness, and deem them worthy of eternal life, in Christ Jesus Thy beloved Son ; with whom, &c. Amen.

[1] The use of this Psalm in the Morning Service is mentioned by Chrysost., Comment. in Psalm cxl. ; Cassian, Instit., lib. iii., cap. 3 ; Athanasius, de Virgin.

Deacon. Depart in peace.[1]

From these simple beginnings the daily services of the Church have sprung. With the rise of the monastic bodies in the latter part of the fourth century, the hours of prayer came into greater prominence. More elaborate services than the above were provided for the morning and evening meetings, and other services for stated times of the day. The brethren who were associated together in these communities devoted themselves to two sets of duties, viz., common labour and common devotion. It was a part of their system to "watch unto prayer," which made it necessary that special attention should be given to provide the Night Services, or "Nocturns," with many Psalms and lengthened devotions. Other shorter services were used at regular intervals through the day, which was brought to a close with a carefully arranged service for Evensong. S. Basil, Bishop of Cæsarea, in Cappadocia, A.D. 370-379, and the founder of the monastic system, describes the character of these services, and urges the importance of observing the

[1] Apost. Constit., lib. viii., 37-39.
Athanasius mentions another form of Morning Service for private use : saying, " In the middle of the night you will rise and praise the Lord Thy God . . . and when you rise, say first, ' At midnight will I rise to give thanks unto Thee because of Thy righteous judgments,' and pray, and say Psalm LI. all through . . . And say as many Psalms as you can : and at each Psalm add prayers, kneeling down and confessing with tears your sins to God, and praying that they may be forgiven. And after three Psalms, say, Alleluia . . . And at dawn say this Psalm : ' O God my God, early will I seek Thee,' &c. (Psalm lxiii.). And when it is light, say, ' O all ye works of the Lord, bless ye the Lord;' and ' Glory to God in the highest,' and the rest."—Athan. de Virgin., tom. i., p. 832. "Gloria in excelsis" is also mentioned as a Morning Prayer in Apost. Constit., lib. vii., cap. 47. See Bingham Antiq., book xiii., ch. x. xi., where the texts of most of these quotations are given.

hours of prayer prescribed by holy men of old ; referring to the words of David, " At midnight will I rise to give thanks unto Thee," and " Evening and morning and at noon day will I pray." [1]

From the East the monastic system was introduced into the West of Europe by Cassian, about the beginning of the fifth century ; and with it the observance of the hours of prayer by means of stated services. Cassian had great opportunities for learning how to perfect these services. In his youth, after studying for several years in a monastery at Bethlehem, he travelled amongst the hermits of Egypt, and became thoroughly acquainted with their life and worship. He then went to Constantinople, where he was ordained by S. Chrysostom ; and shortly afterwards he was sent to Rome. A few years later he settled at Marseilles, where he established two monasteries, and there he laboured and wrote until his death at an advanced age, *circa* A.D. 440. We may therefore consider that we are indebted to Cassian for the introduction of the daily services of the Eastern Church to the Christians of the West. The experience which he had gained in his extensive travels enabled him to open out rich stores of devotion for the Gallican Church ; [2] whence there is no doubt other neighbouring countries, and our own in particular, profited. His account of the services amongst the hermits in Egypt, upon which his own rules

?

[1] Basil, Sermo I., de instit. Monachorum : Epist. lxiii. ad Neocæsar. ; Regul. Major., quæst. xxxvii. See Bingham Antiq., book xiii., chap. ix., 11, 12 ; x., 13, where most of these quotations will be found in full.

[2] The Mozarabic Breviary of the Spanish Church seems to have preserved these ancient devotions in the purest shape. The services are full of resemblances to the present daily offices of the Eastern Church, and are singularly free from mediæval alterations and developments.

were partly founded, is deeply interesting, showing the simple piety which he desired to foster. They met, he says, twice a day for worship, viz., in the evening, which was called " The hour of lighting," when they held the " Vesper Meeting ; " [1] and in the middle of the night, when they held the " Nocturnal Meeting." [2] At both meetings twelve Psalms were repeated. These were read by a reader, whilst the rest sat in silence ; and at the end of every ten or twelve verses a pause was made for a short prayer or meditation. Every Psalm was followed, not by the *Gloria*, but by a prayer; except the last, after which *Alleluia* was sung. After the Psalms two lessons were read, one from the Old Testament, the other from the New Testament, except on Saturdays and Sundays, when both were from the New Testament. Then all knelt down and gave thanks to God ; after which they stood whilst the Abbot brought the service to a close, by collecting as it were the vows and prayers of all the brethren into one, and offering them to God in a public prayer, which was hence named " Collect." The services at the third, sixth, and ninth hours were said privately in their cells, when three Psalms were repeated with a prayer. Cassian remarks upon this, that their reason for stopping at the end of every few verses of the Psalms was, because they delighted, not so much in the number of the verses, as in the understanding of them ; as S. Paul says, " I will sing with the spirit, and I will sing with the understanding also." And he gently rebukes that haste to get to the end of a Psalm, which was apt to take the place of the desire to open out its sense to the listeners. He also

---

[1] Vespertina Solemnitas vel synaxis.
[2] Nocturna Solemnitas vel synaxis.

calls particular attention to the fact that the Morning Service (Mattins, afterwards named Prime) which had become common in the West of Europe at the time he wrote, had been introduced from his old monastery at Bethlehem, where, he says, " Our Lord Jesus Christ vouchsafed to be born, and where by His Grace He strengthened in holy religion the yet tender infancy of His servant." The hours of worship thus established by Cassian included, (1) Night-watches (afterwards named Mattins and Lauds), (2) Mattins (afterwards named Prime), (3) The Third Hour, (4) The Sixth, (5) The Ninth, (6) Vespers.[1]

At some later period the service called " Compline " was added; and the system of services for the seven canonical hours was finally perfected by the celebrated S. Benedict, who founded the great monastery of Monte Casino in Italy, and composed there the Benedictine Rule, *circa* A.D. 530.[2]

The hour services, as they were thus perfected for the use of monastic communities, were soon adopted for general

[1] Cassian, de Cœnob. Instit., lib. ii., cap. 4, &c.; lib. iii., cap. 4. Archbishop Cranmer refers to this account, saying:—" Institutio solemnis officiandi a S. Marco dicitur incepisse in Alexandria, quæ postmodum ad alias defluxit ecclesias; testatur Philo Judæus, renarrat Eusebius cos novos composuisse hymnos (Hist. Eccles., lib. ii., cap. 17), et de nocturnis officiis et psalmorum lectione. Duodecim psalmos ordinatos fuisse testatur Cassianus, et totidem lectiones ex novo et veteri testamento." Respecting the advantage of so many hours of prayer, he quotes from Eckius—" Sub lege erant tertia, sexta, et nona, Ecclesia addidit matutinas, primas, vesperas et completorium, ut sic justitia nostra abundaret," adding, " quod scriberem et Pharisæorum."—MS. Collections, De canon. horis, vol. ii., pp. 88, 89. For his editions of these authors, see Catalogue of Cranmer's Library.

[2] Martene, De Antiq. Eccles. Ritibus, lib. iv. The " Hours " are seven, though the services are eight; Mattins and Lauds counting as one " Hour."

use by the clergy and devout laymen. Frequent references
are found in the lives of saintly bishops and others, to
their attendance at the daily services; and mention is
made of their exhortations to the people to assemble together, rising in the middle of the night for the Nocturns
before daybreak, and seeking the bishop's blessing in the
Evensong.   But when the obligation of saying the daily
offices began to be enforced, it is evident that the burden
of reciting them publicly was found to be more than could
be borne.   The heaviest penalties were attached to their
omission.[1]   All priests were required to sound the bell
of their own church, and celebrate the sacred offices at
the appointed hours of the day and night.[2]   But penalties
and statutes were equally in vain; the attempt to establish them as public services failed; and, at length, private
recitation of the hour services was universally accepted
as sufficient.[3]

But even the private recitation of the eight canonical
offices was more than men could carry out.   Consequently, as years passed, the practical difficulties in the

---

[1] For instance, amongst the rules of Egbert, Archbishop of York,
A.D. 732-766, are the following: " Si quis Clericus aut Monachus, corporis
sanitate consistens, vigiliis et quotidianis officiis defuerit, perdat communionem." " Si quis clericus dato signo non statim ad Ecclesiam properaverit,
correptionibus subjacebit." Pontifical of Egbert.

[2] The Emperor Charlemagne, A.D. 822, sanctioned this statute, "Ut
omnes sacerdotes horis competentibus diei ac noctis suarum sonent signa
Ecclesiarum et sacrata Deo celebrent officia."   Martene, De Antiq. Eccles.
Ritibus, lib. iv., cap. i. ii.

[3] It is stated by the late Archdeacon Freeman that the public use of the
ancient Western offices is nowhere maintained in cathedrals and parish
churches, except under the form of the two daily services in the Church of
England.   In the other churches of the West the hour services are used
only in religious communities, and for private devotion.   A new service
named " Benediction " is the popular evening service amongst Roman
Catholics.   Freeman, " Principles of Divine Service," vol. i., pp. 278-280.

way of arranging for these numerous services, except in monasteries, gave rise to various changes; and at the time of the Reformation, whilst the number of "the Hours" was nominally the same, they really formed only three services. The Nocturn Service of the middle of the night had become an early morning service named "Mattins" and "Lauds," with which "Prime" was united, so as to form a single service. The Third, Sixth, and Ninth Hours formed a second service. And "Vespers" and "Compline" formed together the Even-song. The same practice is followed to this day in the Eastern Church; and the eight corresponding offices become by aggregation three daily services.[1]

Whilst one general plan of daily services was thus uni-versally adopted, a great variety of rules was admitted amongst the various orders of monks, and in the parish churches of different provinces. Consequently there was a corresponding variety of Service Books in the Western Church; and the English Breviaries, though they agreed in the main with the Roman pattern, were distinct from all others. Amongst them the Breviary according to Sarum Use was pre-eminent; and seems to have been generally adopted throughout England in the times immediately preceding the Reformation.[2] It is a noble treasury of devotion; containing not only collects, prayers, and psalms, but hymns of great beauty for all seasons and occasions, and homilies, selected from the

[1] See Neale's "Holy Eastern Church," Introd., vol. ii. "Midnight," "Dawn," and "First Hour" are said together early in the morning; Tierce, Sext, and the Liturgy, later; Nones, Vespers, and Compline in the evening.

[2] The word "Breviary" is found in the eleventh century, as the name of the whole collection of the various parts of the daily services. But it was often divided into separate volumes containing the Psalms, or the Anti-

choicest writings of the Fathers upon the Gospels for all
Sundays and Holy-days.   But it is also the most complicated of all such compilations.   An outline of the
services for a single day will now be given, which will
show how much these differed from the simple forms described by Cassian in the fifth century, and how great
need there was for a thorough revision to render them
practically suitable for congregational use.

THE MEDIÆVAL COMMON PRAYERS ACCORDING TO THE USE
OF SARUM.[1]

The Morning Service.[2]

The Priest first said, secretly: Our Father which art in
Heaven, &c.

Hail, Mary, full of grace, the Lord is with thee; blessed art
thou among women; and blessed is the fruit of thy womb,
Jesus. Holy Mary, mother of God, pray for us sinners now,
and in the hour of death.   Amen.[3]

I believe in God the Father, &c.

phons, &c. It was also in later times divided into portions for summer and
winter; each portion being then called Portiforium, or Portuary.

In 1509 an Aberdeen Breviary was brought out by Bishop Elphinstone
to supersede the Sarum Breviary, which had hitherto been in use; but it
seems doubtful if it was ever publicly used.

[1] Taken from " Breviarium ad usum insignis Ecclesiæ Sarum," edited by
Proctor and Wordsworth; published by the Cambridge University Press,
1879; a copy of the Great Breviary of 1531.

[2] Three offices, named Mattins, Lauds, and Prime, formed the Morning
Service. An outline of a Sunday Service is here given; but as every
service was liable to almost endless variations according to the calendar
date of any particular week, under the rules, called " The Rules of the
Pie," it is hardly possible to give the exact service of any one day.

[3] The use of such addresses to the Blessed Virgin Mary was probably
introduced about the eleventh century. The first part, taken from S Luke
i. 28, 42, was anciently used in certain monasteries in the Commemorations of
the Saints which followed Mattins, as an Antiphon to Psalm xciii.—" The
Lord is King," &c. Martene, De Antiq. Monach. Ritibus, lib. i., cap. iii.

The service then began with these versicles :
O Lord, open Thou my lips ;
And my mouth shall shew forth Thy praise.
O Lord, make speed to save us ;
O Lord,.make haste to help us.
Glory be to the Father, &c.
(Alleluia.)

Then followed PSALM XCV., O, come let us sing unto the
Lord, &c., *with an anthem called the Invitatory, sung before and
after, and intermingled with it.*[1]

Upon the Festival of the Purification, or as it was originally called, " The
Festival of S. Simeon," another form of Antiphon was used as follows :
" Ave gratia plena, Dei genitrix Virgo, ex te enim ortus est sol justitiæ,
illuminans quæ in tenebris sunt. Lætare tu senior juste suscipiens Jesum in
ulnis liberatorem animarum nostrarum donantem nobis et resurrectionem."
Twelfth century Pontifical of the Church of Besancon. Martene, De
Antiq. Eccles. Ritibus, lib. iv., cap. xv., ordo i. 2.

S. Bonaventura, *circa* A.D. 1256, directed the Brethren of the Franciscan
order to exhort the people to salute the Glorious Virgin Mother of Jesus,
when the bell sounded after Compline, by repeating this angelic salutation.
Martene, lib. iv., cap. viii. 11. It was not introduced into England until
A.D. 1237. And the latter part of it is not found except in the Great
Breviary of Sarum of A.D. 1531, until after the English Reformation. See
index to above edition.

[1] The Invitatory was intended to strike, as it were, the key-note of the
services for the day ; but it is doubtful if this excellent intention was equally
good in practice as it seems to be in theory. A different Invitatory was
appointed in the Sarum use for every day of the week ; it varied also for the
Sundays according to the season ; and a proper one was provided for every
saint's day and festival. The number of these Invitatories has been much
reduced in the revised Roman breviary. On Advent Sunday, the Sarum
Invitatory was, " Behold the King cometh ; let us go to meet our Saviour." It
was used as follows :—It was sung, 1, before *Venite* began ; 2, after the
second verse ; 3, after the fourth verse these words only were said : " Let
us go to meet our Saviour ;" 4, after the seventh verse ; 5, after the ninth
verse, " Let us go," &c. ; 6, after the last verse ; 7, after the *Gloria*, " Let
us go," &c., and then the whole repeated again. On Christmas Day the
Invitatory was, " Christ is born to us ; O come let us worship." On the first
Sunday in Lent, " Let it not be in vain to us to rise early before the light ;

HYMN.[1] O, Heavenly Word, eternal Light (Hymns A. and M., 46), followed by a *Versicle* and *response.*

Then followed the three Nocturns,[2] *consisting of Psalms, Benedictions, and Lessons.*

FIRST NOCTURN. Twelve PSALMS, divided into three portions, under three *Glorias* and three *Antiphons.*[3] The Sunday Psalms were Psalms i.-iii. and vi.-xv.[4]

Verse.[5] I have been mindful of Thy Name, O Lord, in the night season.

for the Lord hath promised a crown to them that watch." On Palm Sunday, "But they have not known My ways; unto whom I sware in My wrath that they should not enter into My rest." On Easter Day, "Alleluia, alleluia; Christ is risen to-day, Alleluia." On Ascension Day, "Alleluia, Christ ascending into heaven; O come let us worship, Alleluia." On Whitsunday, "Alleluia; The Spirit of the Lord hath filled the world; O come and worship, Alleluia." On Trinity Sunday, "The true God, one in Trinity, and the Trinity in Unity, O come and worship." The Invitatories were further complicated by being classified as simple, double, and triple. The use above described is of the simple Invitatory. A double Invitatory would be repeated first in part then wholly, after the first word had been intoned by the Chanter, called the Rector of the Choir. See Index to Cambridge edition of Breviary.

[1] Various hymns were provided according to the season, and a different one for every day in the week. The above is the Advent Mattin hymn.

[2] The word Nocturn was a relic of the ancient mode of using these services, which were intended to occupy a considerable part of the night. On week days there was only one Nocturn.

[3] The Antiphons were variable Anthems, which were sung before and after the Psalms in all services. There were three Antiphons provided for each Nocturn on Sundays, and six Antiphons for the one Nocturn on week days.

[4] Twelve Psalms were appointed for every day of the week. It was intended that the Psalter should be read through weekly, in the course of the Services of the Hours. But as the same Psalms would always be used on Sundays, the multitude would hear but these few, often repeated, and would be ignorant of the rest.

[5] The verse and response varied according to the season of the year, the day of the week, and the festival of the saint.

Answer. And have kept Thy Law.

Our Father, &c. Hail, Mary, &c. The *Benediction.*[1]

Three LESSONS, generally taken from Holy Scripture,[2] with certain *Responses.*[3]

[1] These varied according to the books from which the lessons were taken, and also according to the season and the festival. The Reader first said, "Jube Domine benedicere," then the Priest added the proper Benediction. A Table of Benedictions was provided at the beginning of the Breviary. They were generally in rhyme. For instance, " Evangelica lectio, Sit nobis salus et protectio," " Alma virgo virginum ; Intercede pro nobis ad Dominum," " Stella Maria maris Succurre piissima nobis." The number of these Benedictions is reduced in the Roman Breviary, and the rhyming ones are less frequent.

[2] Proper lessons, which were not commonly taken from Holy Scripture, were provided for so many Saints' days, that the ordinary course of the Sunday and week-day lessons must have been continually interrupted. Moreover no regular order of reading the books of the Bible was observed. For instance, lessons were provided from the Book of Isaiah during Advent, as far as to chapter xiv. ; then various proper lessons, until the Second Sunday after Epiphany, when the Epistle to the Romans was begun, and read for a week, as far as to chapter v. Then 1 Corinthians to chapter v. Then 2 Corinthians to chapter vi., followed by parts of Galatians, Philippians, and 1 Thessalonians. Then Genesis was begun on Septuagesima Sunday, and the chapters were read fairly on through Lent as far as Exodus iv. Then came lessons connected with the Passion, &c. After Easter they read the Book of Revelation, and after Trinity they began the Old Testament again with the Books of Samuel. So that the complaint was evidently quite justified, that " commonly when any book of the Bible was begun after three or four chapters were read out, all the rest were unread. And in this sort the Book of Isaiah was begun in Advent and the Book of Genesis in Septuagesima ; but they were only begun, and never read through."—Preface in the book of Common Prayer. Regular series of lessons from the different books of the Bible were provided for certain parts of the year ; and these seasons were known by the first words of the response which followed the first of these readings. Thus Advent was spoken of as *Aspiciens,* and the 1st Sunday after Trinity as *Deus Omnium ;* these being the first words of the first response to the Books of Isaiah and Samuel respectively, which were begun on those days.

[3] These responses were complicated repetitions of words which referred to the contents of the lesson. Thus on Advent Sunday Isaiah i. 1-4 was

SECOND NOCTURN.[1]　PSALMS xvi.-xviii., with three *Antiphons.*

The *Verse.* Our Father, &c.　The *Benediction.*

Three LESSONS, taken from Holy Scripture, or from a sermon of some Father, with *Responses.*

THIRD NOCTURN.　PSALMS xix.-xxi.,[2] with three *Antiphons.*

The *Verse.* Our Father, &c.　The *Benediction.*

Three LESSONS from a Homily,[3] with *Responses.*

read as the first lesson; the reader adding, "Thus saith the Lord God, Turn ye unto Me, and ye shall be saved," which was the proper conclusion of all lessons from the Prophets.　Then followed the response, "Looking from far, behold I see the power of God coming; and a cloud covering the whole earth.　Go to meet him, and say, Tell us if thou art he that shall rule thy people Israel."　Then various verses were said, and parts of this response were repeated again and again, ending with the *Gloria.*　Then followed Isaiah i. 5-9 as the second lesson, and another response, with a verse and repetitions.　Then Isaiah i. 10-15 as the third lesson, with another response and repetitions.　These are well described in the preface to the Book of Common Prayer as a "multitude of responds, verses, vain repetitions."

[1] On ordinary week-days there was only one Nocturn of Psalms and Lessons.　The service would then be called an Office of Three Lessons. The lessons in the second Nocturn were taken on Sundays from Holy Scripture, or from some godly sermon of an ancient bishop.　But on Saints' days they were often taken from "uncertain stories and legends" about the lives and supposed miracles of those who were commemorated.

[2] In the second and third Nocturns three Psalms were appointed for Sundays, but not for the other days of the week.　In the first Nocturn Psalms were appointed for every day in the week, and always twelve in number. But as different Psalms were appointed for Festivals, nine in number, it appears that the daily Psalms were generally omitted.　So that the Preface to the Book of Common Prayer contains the complaint, "Notwithstanding that the ancient Fathers have divided the Psalms into seven portions, whereof every one was called a Nocturn; now of late time a few of them have been daily said and the rest utterly omitted."　The Festival Psalms with their nine Antiphons were either placed together in one Nocturn, or divided between three Nocturns, according as three or nine lessons were appointed.

[3] These homilies were written discourses upon the Gospel of the Day,

Then followed, except in Advent and Lent, and on certain vigils,

TE DEUM LAUDAMUS: We praise Thee, O God, &c.

Verse. The Lord is high above all nations;
Answer. And His glory above the heavens.

The Service of 𝕷𝖆𝖚𝖉𝖘 here began.[1]

O God, make speed to save us, &c.
Glory be to the Father, &c.
Alleluia.

Then followed these PSALMS, *each with an Antiphon, or under one Antiphon on certain days :*

Psalm xciii. The Lord is King, &c. *(Or, on week days,* Psalm li. Have mercy upon me, O God.)

Psalm c. O, be joyful in the Lord, &c. *(On Sundays only ; a variable Psalm on other days.)*

Psalm lxiii. O God, Thou art my God, &c., and Psalm lxvii. God be merciful unto us, &c., under one *Antiphon.*

Psalm. BENEDICITE OMNIA OPERA. O, all ye works of the Lord, &c. *(On Sundays only ; a variable Canticle on other days.[2])*

which was first read in part or wholly ; the three lessons were from the same homily, divided by the usual responses and repetitions.

[1] There was always a verse and response between Mattins and Lauds. The above was the usual Sunday verse. The week-day verse was, "O Lord, let Thy mercy be showed upon us : As we do put our trust in Thee ;" which now follows the *preces* at the end of the Litany. On Saints' days it was generally, "Pray for us holy ——." The union of three Services together involved much repetition. Our modern custom of joining Mattins, Litany, and Communion Service together is very similar.

[2] On Mondays, "O Lord, I will praise Thee," &c. Isaiah xii. 1-6.
On Tuesdays, "I said in the cutting off of my days," &c. Isaiah xxxviii. 10-20.
On Wednesdays, "My heart rejoiceth in the Lord," &c. 1 Sam. ii. 1-10.

K

Psalm cxlviii. O, praise the Lord of Heaven, &c.; Psalm cxlix. O, sing unto the Lord a new song, &c.; and Psalm cl. O, praise God in His holiness, &c., under one *Antiphon.*[1]

A short Lesson.[2] Blessing and glory and wisdom, &c. (Rev. vii. 12.)

Thanks be to God.

HYMN.[3] O Christ, our joy, gone up on high (Hymns A. and M., 145).

Verse. God hath gone up with a merry noise;

Answer. And the Lord with the sound of the trumpet. Alleluia.

Antiphon.[4] When the Comforter shall come whom I will

On Thursdays, "I will sing unto the Lord, for He hath triumphed gloriously," &c. Exodus xv. 1-19.

On Fridays, "O Lord, I have heard Thy speech, and was afraid," &c. Habakkuk iii. 2-19.

On Saturdays, "Give ear O ye heavens," &c. Deut. xxxii. 1-43.

[1] Psalms cxlviii.-cl. gave the name *Laudes* to this service.

[2] The short lesson, or *Capitulum*, on week-days was, "Watch ye, stand fast in the faith, quit you like men" (1 Cor. xvi. 13); and on festivals it varied according to the season and the person commemorated.

[3] The verse varied with the hymn. Two hymns were appointed for Sundays, according to the season, and one for every week-day. Special hymns were provided for festivals. The above is the Ascensiontide hymn and verse. The ordinary Sunday verse was, "The Lord is King: And hath put on glorious apparel. Alleluia."

[4] The Antiphons to *Benedictus* in Lauds, and to *Magnificat* in Vespers, were of peculiar importance. On Sundays and festivals they were commonly taken from the Gospel of the day; and they were frequently selected for the following week-days in such a way as to keep up the teaching of the Gospel throughout the week. The above was the Antiphon for the Sunday after Ascension Day. On the Monday following the Antiphon was, "They therefore went forth and preached everywhere, the Lord working with them, and confirming the word with signs following." On Tuesday, "I will pray the Father, and He will send," &c. On Wednesday, the same as Monday. On Thursday, the same as on Ascension Day, "I ascend unto

send unto you from the Father, even the Spirit of Truth,
which proceedeth from the Father, He shall testify of Me.
BENEDICTUS. S. Luke i. 68.
Blessed be the Lord God of Israel, &c.

Then followed Psalm cxxiii. Unto Thee lift I up mine eyes,
&c. (*On Sundays only.*)
Kyrie eleison.
Christe eleison.
Kyrie eleison.
Our Father, &c.
(*Note that the Priest is directed to stand up on week days
whilst these verses are said.*)
O Lord, arise, help us,
And deliver us for Thy Name's sake.
Turn us again, O Lord God of Hosts,
Show the light of Thy countenance, and we shall be whole.
O Lord, hear my prayer,
And let my cry come unto Thee.[1]

my Father," &c. Similar care was taken during the week after the Epiphany.
And for the weeks after Septuagesima and Sexagesima Sundays, verses
were appointed for the Antiphons out of the Sunday Gospel, or from the
homily upon it. On double feasts this Antiphon was sung through twice,
both before and after the Canticle. On other days it was sung in part only
before and wholly after the Canticle.

[1] On week days these *Preces* were more numerous. From very ancient
times they formed a special feature of Lauds. (See Martene, De Antiq.
Monach. Rit., lib. i., c. iii., for the ancient Benedictine Preces.) The Sarum
week-day *preces* were as follows:—

I said, Lord be merciful unto me,
Heal my soul, for I have sinned against Thee.
O Lord, let Thy mercy be shewed upon us,
As we do put our trust in Thee.
Endue Thy Priests with righteousness,
And make Thy saints joyful.
O Lord, save the king:
And mercifully hear us when we call upon Thee.

The Lord be with you.
And with thy spirit.
Let us pray.

THE COLLECT FOR THE DAY.[1]

Then followed the Memorial of S. Mary.[2]

Antiphon. The angel Gabriel was sent to Mary, a virgin espoused to Joseph.

Verse. There shall come forth a rod out of the stem of Jesse.

Answer. And a branch shall grow out of his roots.

The Collect. O God, who wast pleased that from the womb of the Blessed Mary ever a virgin, according to the message of an angel, Thy Word should take flesh ; grant to us, we beseech Thee, that we who believe her to be truly the Mother of God, may be aided by her intercessions before Thee ; through the same our Lord Jesus Christ.

My God, save Thy servants and Thy handmaids,
　Who put their trust in Thee.
O Lord, save Thy people, and bless Thine heritage ;
　Govern them, and lift them up for ever.
Peace be within Thy walls ;
　And plenteousness within Thy palaces.
Let us pray for the faithful departed.
　Eternal rest grant them, O Lord, and let perpetual light shine upon them.
Hear the voice of my prayer, O Lord, when I cry unto Thee :
　Have mercy upon me, and hear me.

Psalm li. " Have mercy upon me, O God," &c.
Then let the Priest stand up, and go to the choir step (as well in the Morning as in the Evening Prayer), whilst these verses are said :—

　O Lord, arise, help us,
　　And deliver, &c. (*as on Sundays*).

[1] The close agreement of our English services with the ancient Sarum Use may be seen from the fact that no less than forty-five of our Sunday Collects are taken, more or less completely, from the Sarum Collects.

[2] In addition to this Memorial, separate services were said daily, called the Hours of our Lady, either before or after the Hours of the Day.

Then followed the Memorial of Peace.[1]
Antiphon. Give peace in our time, O Lord, because there is none other that fighteth for us, but only Thou, O Lord.
Verse. Peace be within Thy walls, O Lord ;
Answer. And plenteousness within Thy palaces.
The Collect. O God, who art the author of peace, &c. (the Second Collect for Peace).
The Lord be with you.
Let us bless the Lord.

The Service of 𝔓𝔯𝔦𝔪𝔢 here began.

HYMN. Now that the daylight fills the sky (Hymns A. and M., 1).

Then followed these PSALMS, *under one* Antiphon, The Lord is my Shepherd, &c.:[2]
Psalm xxii. My God, my God, look upon me, &c.
Psalm xxiii. The Lord is my Shepherd, &c.
Psalm xxiv. The earth is the Lord's, &c.
Psalm xxv. Unto Thee, O Lord, will I lift up my soul, &c.
Psalm xxvi. Be Thou my judge, O Lord, &c.
Psalm liv. Save me, O God, for Thy Name's sake, &c.

[1] Other Memorials were used on week days in addition to the above, consisting in the same way of Antiphon, Verse, Response, and Collect, viz., Memorial of All Saints. Memorial of the Cross, Memorial of the Holy Spirit, Memorial of the Saint in whose honour the Church is dedicated, and Memorial of Relics.
The Memorial of the Holy Spirit was as follows :—
Antiphon. Come, Holy Ghost, fill the hearts of Thy faithful people, and kindle the fire of Thy love within them.
Verse. Let Thy breath go forth, and they shall be made.
Answer. And Thou shalt renew the face of the earth.
The Collect. God, who didst teach the hearts of Thy faithful people, &c. (Collect for Whitsun Day.)
[2] This was the usual Sunday Antiphon ; on week days it was, " O God, hear my prayer, ponder with Thine ears the words of my mouth."

Psalm cxviii. O give thanks unto the Lord, for He is gracious, &c.

Psalm cxix. 1-32.[1] Blessed are those that are undefiled, &c.

Antiphon.[2] Thee, God the Father, unbegotten; Thee, the Only Begotten Son; Thee, the Holy Ghost, the Comforter; One Holy and Undivided Trinity, with our whole heart and with our mouth, we confess and praise and bless; to Thee be glory for ever.

THE CREED OF ATHANASIUS.

Whosoever will be saved, &c.

A short Lesson.[3] Now unto the King eternal, immortal, invisible, the only God, be honour and glory, for ever and ever. Amen. (1 Tim. i. 17.)

Thanks be to God.

Answer. O Jesu Christ, Son of the living God; have mercy upon us.

Verse. Thou who sittest at the right hand of the Father;

Answer. Have mercy upon us.

Glory be to the Father, &c.

O Jesu Christ, &c.

Verse. O Lord, arise, help us;

Answer. And deliver us for Thy Name's sake.

iii. Kyrie eleison.

iii. Christe eleison.

---

[1] Psalms xxii.-xxvi. were used only on Sundays, and they were omitted between Christmas Day and the Second Sunday after Epiphany, and between Easter and the first Sunday after Trinity. Between Septuagesima and Easter, Psalm xciii. was used instead of Psalm cxviii.

[2] This Antiphon was used on the Sundays when all the Psalms were said. On festivals and week days other Antiphons were sung.

[3] This short lesson, or *Capitulum*, was used on all Sundays and festivals. On week days generally it was, "Love the truth and peace, saith the Lord Almighty," &c., Zech. viii. 19; but between Easter and Pentecost, and on certain vigils, it was, "O Lord, be gracious unto us; we have waited for Thee," &c., Isaiah xxxiii. 2.

iii. Kyrie eleison.

Our Father, &c.

O, let my soul live, and it shall praise Thee;
And Thy judgments shall help me.

I have gone astray like a sheep that was lost;
O, seek Thy servant, for I do not forget Thy commandments.

THE CREED.

I believe in God the Father Almighty, &c.

Let my mouth be filled with Thy praise;
That I may sing of Thy glory and honour all the day long.

O Lord, turn Thy face from my sins, &c.   (Ps. li. 9-12.)

*   *   *   *   *   *

Deliver me, O Lord, from the evil man;
And save me from the wicked man.

*   *   *   *   *   *   *Latin*

So will I alway sing praise unto Thy Name;
That I may daily perform my vows.

Hear us, O God of our salvation;
Thou that art the hope of all the ends of the earth, and
of them that remain in the broad sea.

O God, make speed, &c.

Holy God, holy mighty, holy and immortal. O Lamb of
God, that takest away the sins of the world;
Have mercy upon us.

Bless the Lord, O my soul;
And all that is within me, bless His holy Name, &c. (Ps.
ciii. 1-5.) [1]

---

[1] The antiquity of these *Preces* is shown by their being found in an Anglo-
Saxon Service Book, which is interlined with a very ancient Anglo-Saxon
version, belonging to the ninth century, but supposed to be a copy from
services at least two centuries earlier. They are headed, "Incipiunt capitulæ ad primam."—Rituale Eccles. Dunelm.

The Priest then said the Confession: [1]

I confess to God, to blessed Mary, to all saints, and to you, I have sinned exceedingly, in thought, word, and deed, by my fault. I pray holy Mary and all the saints of God and you to pray for me.

The Choir made answer :

[1] This confession illustrates the development in unscriptural ways of thought which advanced during the middle ages. In the Anglo-Saxon Service Book, referred to in the last note, this *Confiteor* is as follows :—

"Confiteor Domino et tibi frater quia ego peccavi nimis in cogitatione et in locutione et in operatione et in multis criminibus, in quibus omnibus malis excogitare potui, propterea precor te frater ora pro me peccatore."

The earliest form of this confession, in which mention of the saints is found, occurs in the ancient Benedictine Breviary of the Monastery of Monte Casino.and is as follows :—" I confess to God and to all His saints, and to thee, O father, that I have sinned," &c.—Martene, De Antiq. Monach. Ritibus, lib. i., c. iii. The origin of this confession to the saints can be traced to some very beautiful forms of confession in a very ancient Missal :—" I confess my sins to Thee, O eternal High Priest .... I confess to Thee, because I am not only the debtor to Thee of the ten thousand talents of my sins, but I owe Thee also the account of my whole life. . . . And now, O Lord, I come before Thy face in confession, and, *in sight of angels and all the saints*, I confess to Thee my sins," &c. After which is added another form in which these words are used :—" I, a miserable sinner . . . confess to the Lord, and to all His saints."—Martene, De Antiq. Eccles. Ritibus, lib. i., cap. iv., art. xii. ordo 4. In the Roman Breviary confession is made "to blessed Michael the Archangel, to blessed John Baptist, the holy Apostles Peter and Paul, and to all saints," &c. This form was ordained for general use both in the Mass and in other offices, A.D. 1314, by the Third Council of Ravenna, canon 15, for the stated purpose of paying reverence to the saints, as follows :—" Rubric 15. *De Veneratione sanctorum in confessione habenda.* Quoniam devotio et pulcritudo demonstratur in uniformitate ecclesiæ quæ sub specie unius columbæ describitur, et in confessionibus quæ fiunt publice in introitu Missæ et alias varii perfunctorie et diversimode confitentur ; statuimus et de cætero observari præcipimus per totam provinciam Ravennatem confessiones hujusmodi fieri sub hac formâ : Confiteor Deo omnipotenti, beatæ Mariæ virgini, beato Michæli archangelo, beato Joanni Baptistæ, sanctis Apostolis Petro et Paulo, et omnibus sanctis."—Labbe's " Councils," tom xi., p. 1614.

Almighty God, have mercy upon you, and pardon all your sins; deliver you from all evil; preserve and confirm you in good; and bring you unto life everlasting. Amen.

The same confession was then made by the Choir, to whom the Minister made answer as above, adding :

Absolution and remission of all your sins, space for true repentance, amendment of life, grace and comfort of the Holy Ghost, may the Almighty and merciful Lord grant you. Amen.

Wilt Thou not turn again, and quicken us;
    That Thy people may rejoice in Thee?
O Lord, shew Thy mercy upon us;
    And grant us Thy salvation.
Vouchsafe, O Lord, to keep us,
    This day without sin.
Have mercy upon us, O Lord,
    Have mercy upon us.
O Lord, let Thy mercy be shewed upon us,
    As we do put our trust in Thee.[1]
Turn us again, O Lord God of hosts,
    Shew the light of Thy countenance, and we shall be whole.
O Lord, hear my prayer,
    And let my cry come unto Thee.
The Lord be with you.
    And with thy spirit.

[1] On week days the following were inserted here :—

Hear my voice, O Lord, when I cry unto Thee,
    Have mercy upon me and hear me.

Psalm li. Have mercy upon me, O Lord, &c.
Then the Priest, standing up, shall say,

O Lord, arise, help us;
    And deliver us for Thy Name's sake.
Turn us again, &c., as above.

Let us pray.

The Collect. O Lord, Holy Father, Almighty, everlasting God, who hast safely brought us to the beginning of this day, &c.   (Third Collect for Grace.)

The Lord be with you, &c.[1]

Precious in the sight of the Lord,
    Is the death of His saints.

May holy Mary, mother of our Lord Jesus Christ, and all the holy just ones and elect of God, intercede and pray for us sinners to the Lord our God, that we may be helped and saved by Him, who liveth and reigneth, &c.

iii. O God, make speed to save us.

iii. O God, make haste to help us.

Glory be to the Father, &c.

Kyrie eleison, &c.

Our Father, &c.

Let Thy loving mercy come also unto me, O Lord ;
    Even Thy salvation, according unto Thy word.

Shew Thy servants Thy work,
    And their children Thy glory.

And the glorious majesty of the Lord our God be upon us ;
    Prosper Thou the work of our hands upon us ; O prosper Thou our handy work.

Let us pray.

The Collect. O Lord God, vouchsafe, we beseech Thee, to direct, sanctify, and govern both our hearts and bodies, &c. (Second Collect at the end of the Communion Service.)

---

[1] A list of persons to be prayed for was read during Prime, apparently here ; and on Sundays, when Psalm cxxiii. had been said in Lauds, Psalm cxxi., " I will lift up mine eyes unto the hills," &c., was said immediately afterwards, and different *preces,* instead of the above, together with this additional collect, " Assist us mercifully, O Lord, in these our supplications and prayers, and dispose the way of Thy servants," &c.—First Collect at the end of the Communion Service.   On festivals a different collect was said in place of the above.

The Lord be with you, &c.
Let us bless the Lord.
Thanks be to God.

The Services for the Third, Sixth, and Ninth Hours were shorter, and as they have not been formed into a distinct service for public use, it seems unnecessary to give an example of them here.

The Services for Vespers and Compline from which our Evening Service has been formed, were as follows:—

The Evening Service.

The service began with preparatory prayers the same as in Mattins; see above, page 124.

Then followed these PSALMS, *every one with its* Antiphon.[1]

Psalm cx. The Lord said unto my lord, &c.

Psalm cxi. I will give thanks unto the Lord, &c.

Psalm cxii. Blessed is the man that feareth the Lord, &c.

Psalm cxiii. Praise the Lord, ye servants, &c.

Psalm cxiv. When Israel came out of Egypt, &c.

A short Lesson.[2] The Lord direct your hearts into the love

---

[1] Different Psalms, with appropriate Antiphons, were appointed for every day in the week, but always five in number. These were always used, except that on Easter Day it appears that Psalms cxiii. and cxiv. were omitted.

On Monday, Psalms cxv., cxvi., cxvii., cxx., cxxi.

On Tuesday, Psalms cxxii.-cxxvi.

On Wednesday, Psalms cxxvii.-cxxxi.

On Thursday, Psalms cxxxii., cxxxiii., cxxxv.-cxxxvii.

On Friday, Psalms cxxxviii.-cxlii.

On Saturday, Psalms cxliv.-cxlvii. (Psalm cxlvii. was divided into two Psalms at verse 12.)

[2] This was generally the same for every day except Saturday, when the short lesson, or *Capitulum*, was taken from 2 Cor. i. 3, 4, " Blessed be God

of God, and into the 'patient waiting for Christ. (2 Thess. iii. 5.)

Thanks be to God.

HYMN.[1] Blest Creator of the Light (Hymns A. and M., 38).
Verse. O Lord, let my prayer be set forth;
Answer. In Thy sight as the incense.

Antiphon.[2] These things have I spoken unto you; that when the time shall come, ye may remember that I told you of them. Alleluia.

MAGNIFICAT. S. Luke i. 46.
My soul doth magnify the Lord, &c.

THE COLLECT FOR THE DAY.

(*On week days the* Preces *from Lauds were used here, with* Psalm li., *after which the Priest stood at the choir step, and said the Suffrages :* O Lord, arise, help us: And deliver us for Thy Name's sake, &c.)

Then followed the Memorial of S. Mary ; *with the* Vespers of our Lady.

Then followed the Memorial of the Holy Ghost.

Then followed the Memorial of All Saints.[3]

Then followed the Memorial of Peace, *as follows :*

even the Father of our Lord Jesus Christ," &c. But a proper *Capitulum* was appointed for Saints' days and festivals, and for the Sundays between Septuagesima and Trinity. The festivals began with the Vespers of the day before.

[1] This was the usual Vesper hymn, except on Saturdays, when the hymn (A. and M., 14), " O Trinity most Blessed Light," was sung. But a different hymn was appointed for every day during the weeks between Advent and Lent, and proper hymns for all festivals.

[2] This Antiphon, like that to *Benedictus* in Lauds, carried on the teaching of the Sunday or festival during the week. The above is the Antiphon for the Sunday after Ascension Day. See above, p. 130.

[3] For these Memorials see above, p. 132, in Mattin Lauds.

Antiphon. Give peace in our time, O Lord, because there is none other that fighteth for us, but only Thou, O Lord.

Verse. Peace be within Thy walls, O Lord :

Answer. And plenteousness within Thy palaces.

The Collect. O God, from whom all holy desires, all good counsels, &c. (Second Collect at Evening Prayer.)

The Lord be with you, &c.

Let us bless the Lord.

Thanks be to God.

The Service for **Compline** here began.[1]

Our Father, &c. Hail Mary, &c.

Turn us, O God, our Saviour.

And let Thine anger cease from us.

O God, make speed, &c.

Glory be to the Father, &c.

Alleluia.

Antiphon. Have mercy upon me, O Lord, and hearken unto my prayer.

Psalm iv. Hear me when I call, &c.

Psalm xxxi. In Thee, O Lord, have I put my trust, &c.

Psalm xci. Whoso dwelleth under the defence of the Most High, &c.

Psalm cxxxiv. Behold now praise the Lord, &c.

A short Lesson. Thou, O Lord, art in the midst of us, and we are called by Thy Name; leave us not, O Lord our God. (Jerem. xiv. 9.)

HYMN. Before the ending of the day (Hymns A. and M., 15).

---

[1] This service was the same daily throughout the year, with the exception that on twenty-two days a proper Antiphon was appointed, and occasionally a different hymn and an additional collect. In the Roman Breviary this service is much altered and shortened.

Verse. Keep us, O Lord:
Answer. As the apple of Thine eye;' hide us under the shadow of Thy wings.

Antiphon. Come, O Lord, and visit us in peace, that we may rejoice before Thee with a perfect heart.

NUNC DIMITTIS. S. Luke ii. 29.
Lord, now lettest Thou Thy servant depart in peace, &c.

iii. Kyrie eleison.
iii. Christe eleison.
iii. Kyrie eleison.
Our Father, &c.
I will lay me down in peace:
    And take my rest.

THE CREED.
I believe in God the Father, &c.

Let us bless the Father and the Son with the Holy Ghost.
    Let us praise and magnify Him for ever.
Blessed art Thou, O Lord, in the firmament of heaven.
    And to be praised and glorified and magnified for ever.
May the Almighty and merciful Lord bless and keep us.
    Amen.
Then the Minister and Choir made confession, as before in Prime, and the Absolution was said.
Wilt Thou not turn again, and quicken us:
    That Thy people may rejoice in Thee.
O Lord, shew Thy mercy upon us:
    And grant us Thy salvation.[1]

*   *   *   *   *   *

[1] These *preces* were the same as those which followed the Confession in Prime, p. 137, with the exception that "this night" was said instead of "this day;" and Psalm li. was added at certain times of the year, as in Prime.

The Collect. Lighten our darkness, we beseech Thee, O Lord, &c. (Third Collect for Aid against all Perils.)

Then followed Prayers for the Peace of the Church. Psalm cxxiii. Unto Thee lift I up mine eyes, &c, Kyrie eleison.
Christe eleison.
Kyrie eleison.
Our Father, &c.
O Lord, arise, help us;
And deliver us for Thy Name's sake.
Turn us again, O Lord God of Hosts:
Shew the light of Thy countenance, and we shall be whole.
O Lord, hear our prayer, &c.
Let us pray.
The Collect. O Lord, we beseech Thee, mercifully receive the prayers of Thy Church, that being freed from all adversities and errors, it may serve Thee in all godly quietness: and grant us Thy peace all the days of our life, through Christ our Lord. Amen.

The above sketch gives an idea of the ancient services for Sundays. But no idea can be formed from it of the extreme intricacy of the services which were directed to be used for any particular day. In the Breviary the regular order of the services was appointed in that portion which contained the " Psalter." But the chief part of every service was contained in what was called the " Temporale," which consisted of the antiphons, hymns, verses, lessons, responses, and collects *proper* for every day in the year. But on Saints' days an additional complication arose. The fixed parts of the services were to be sought for in the " Commune Sanctorum " on all days dedicated to Apostles, Evangelists, Martyrs, Confessors or Virgins. Then the parts *proper* to the particular saint were to be taken from the " Proprium Sanctorum," which contained the antiphons, hymns, verses, lessons, &c., *proper* for every saint's day throughout the year. If it is remembered that nearly every day in the year was dedicated to some saint, and that a varying amount of respect was shown to these saints, it will be seen at once that as the Sundays and other movable feasts fell on this or that saint's day, the confusion between the various services belonging to the same day must have been very great.[1] Difficulties occur even in the present day, in knowing how to make a choice between the lessons or the gospels, when Sundays and other festivals happen to coin-

[1] The patience of few readers will last out sufficiently to read through the following description of festivals. It is a curious illustration of mediæval ceremonial. The complication of festivals under the Sarum Use was so great, that there were no less than twenty-five degrees of importance assigned to them. Festivals belonged to one or other of two classes, and were called either double or single. There were four kinds of DOUBLE FESTIVALS :—1, *Principal*, such as Christmas, Easter, &c. ; 2, *Greater*, such as the Purification, Trinity Sunday, &c.; 3, *Less*, such as S. Stephen, S. John, Holy Innocents, &c.; 4, *Least*, such as S. Andrew, S. George, S. Augustine, &c.

SINGLE FESTIVALS were far more complicated. They were of three kinds, according as the " Invitatory " was *triple, double,* or *single.*

A. Single Festivals with *triple* Invitatory consisted of Saints' Days, such as S. John ante Portam Latinam, &c.: and Octaves, which were of two kinds, either with continual rule of the choir, or with rule of the choir on the eighth day only.

B. Single Festivals with *double* Invitatory consisted of days with rule of choir, and days without rule of choir. Days with rule of choir included, 1, Saints' Days; 2, days within Octaves; 3, Commemorations : 4, certain Sundays which belonged to four classes. Days without rule of choir included Saints' days of two kinds, and Octaves of three kinds.

C. Single Festivals with *single* Invitatory consisted of Saints' days of two kinds, and certain week days which belonged to four classes.—Index to " Sarum Breviary," Cambridge edition.

cide; but in the times before the Reformation the difficulties must have been very much greater. For the assistance of the reader, whose duty it was to find out how the
service for any particular day was to be arranged, directions
were minutely given in thirty-five tables, commonly named
Pica Sarum, or " the rules called the Pie." These tables
were placed in the Breviary before certain Sundays, in the
" Temporale," and took the place of our modern almanacks.[1] In some cases they referred to the services of a
single week; for instance, there was a different table, or
Pica, for every week in Advent. Other tables referred
to the whole time during which a series of lessons from
some one book of Holy Scripture was read, and were
named after that book; for instance, *Historia Job* was the
heading of the *Pica* for the time during which Job was
read. These " rules of the Pie " were arranged according to the seven Sunday letters. From the beginning
of August until the following Second Sunday after
Epiphany, the arrangement was comparatively simple.
To find out the service for any day, one needed to know
the Sunday letter; and directions would be found under
that letter for each week included in the particular table,
showing what relative importance should be assigned to
the Saints' days, the Sunday, and the weekly commemorations which happened to coincide during that week.
But at other times of the year the tables were more complicated, and showed wonderful ingenuity. The *Pica*
preceding the Sunday after the Octave of the Epiphany
(Second Sunday after the Epiphany), was headed by a

---

[1] See introduction to Procter and Wordsworth's " Sarum Breviary." The
rules are such that a life-long study and use of the Breviary seem to be
needed to enable anyone to interpret them with certainty.

table showing the connection between the Golden Number
and the Sunday Letter, by which all calculations were
determined.   In all the following tables of *Pica* rules,
until the beginning of August, every Sunday Letter was
necessarily represented under five divisions.   And in
looking out the services, it was necessary to find the particular division which was adapted to the year in accordance with the table of connection between the Golden
Number and the Sunday Letter.   In other words, every
reader was compelled to form his own almanack in accordance with tables such as those at the beginning of the
Book of Common Prayer; but without the assistance of
the dates and explanations there given; and under the
complicated concurrences of innumerable festivals.   From
which it came to pass, as may easily be imagined, "that
to turn the book only was so hard and intricate a matter,
that many times there was more business to find out
what should be read, than to read it when it was found
out." [1]

[1] Preface to Book of Common Prayer.

CHAPTER V.

"Faxit Deus ut juxta votum et intentionem meam, sic exeant (hi libelli) ut et tibi sint grati . . . atque a barbaricâ contra vetusta sacra et antiquas Ecclesiæ ceremonias gigantomachiâ salubriter deterreant et avertant."— *Johan. Cochlæus*, A.D. 1534.

THE English Book of Common Prayer has been brought by degrees into its present form, and the consideration of its contents is complicated by the changes introduced at different times. In order to form a just opinion of the character of the English services, it will be necessary to prepare the way : *First*, by studying the history of the various revisions, the circumstances of the times, and the objects which the revisers had in view ; and, *Secondly*, by referring to the forms of worship which were in use in other countries, and can be proved to have been within reach of our reformers. It will then be possible to examine our English services as they are, without stopping to inquire into the steps by which their present form was reached.

At the time of the Reformation a fresh sense of Christian duty respecting the worship of God had arisen in the minds of Englishmen, and a very slight acquaintance with the character of the mediæval services which were in use in England at the beginning of the sixteenth century will be sufficient to explain what was then regarded

as necessary, as described in the Preface to the Book of
Common Prayer, " Concerning the Service of the Church."
The work which men felt that they were called on to
undertake included four things: (1) to turn the Latin
forms of devotion into the English tongue, (2) to restore
the ancient practice of reading Holy Scripture in large
and continuous portions, (3) to remove what was super-
stitious and objectionable, (4) to simplify the services in
such a way that they might be made practically useful for
ordinary people.

The task was extremely complicated. Mistakes had
been accumulating for a thousand years, until men had
grown so accustomed to them that they were ignorant
of the fact that their ways of thought and worship were
no longer in accordance with the original faith and practice of the Church of Christ. Developments had been
introduced so gradually that they were unnoticed at the
time, and these were intertwined so closely amidst the
framework of the services that it was a very difficult
matter to remove them without destroying the framework itself. Moreover, the very abundance of the materials, rich in beauties, and drawn from the devotional
spirit of the saints of earlier and purer days, was itself a
serious difficulty.

The result of the labours of the English reformers is
before us in " The Book of Common Prayer and Administration of the Sacraments." The Bible and Prayer Book
together now supply the place of the Missal and Breviary;
and the Prayer Book by itself is a sufficient handbook for
the congregation in all public services.

The work of revising the English services was gradually effected by means of various measures, spread over

many years; and though no attempt was made to put forth an English Prayer Book in the reign of Henry VIII., many steps were taken which prepared the way for it to be accomplished afterwards. The first and most important reform was in respect of the public use of the Holy Scriptures in English. In response to a petition from Convocation, the king assented to the circulation of an English version, which was a revision of that made by Tyndal and Coverdale, and an injunction was issued, A.D. 1538, requiring a copy of what was called "The Great Bible," printed by Grafton and Whitchurche, to be set up in some convenient place in every church, where the parishioners might most commodiously resort and read it. The sensation which was created is well known. Eager crowds availed themselves of a privilege never granted before, and a knowledge of Holy Scripture spread amongst all classes.[1]

In the work of translating the Bible into English our reformers were following in the steps of Erasmus, who had fought the battle of vernacular versions twenty years before, and had succeeded in convincing the world that the Vulgate was not infallible. His edition of the New Testament was published in 1516, under the name "Novum Instrumentum," and included the Greek text (then first published), a new Latin version, and annotations. A preface was prefixed entitled "Paraclesis," in which he urged that Christians should learn from the teaching of Christ Himself, rather than from the subtleties of the schoolmen, and that even the commentaries of the best of the Fathers were to be used with judgment, being the

---

[1] See Collier, Eccles. Hist., vol. v., p. 52, 83; Hook, "Lives of Archbishops," vol. vii., p. 141.

work of " men ignorant of some things and mistaken in others." To this end he boldly declared his opinion that it ought to be possible for all to read the Holy Scriptures in their vulgar tongue. As might be expected, his work was received with no little hostility by the party opposed to reform, who regarded the Vulgate as the sacred text, and viewed suggestions of possible improvements as undermining the authority of Holy Scripture. But the book met with the warm approval of the learned both in England and on the Continent, and reached a fourth edition by 1527.[1]

The zeal with which Cranmer threw himself into the study of Holy Scripture may be proved by his library; for in addition to the Fathers and Schoolmen, the student may find, amongst the books bearing the autograph

---

[1] Novum Instrumentum, Basle, 1516; "The Oxford Reformers," by Fred. Seebohm, pp. 312-336, 395-402. Erasmus was himself following in the steps of the editors of the Complutensian Polyglott, but he outstripped them. For though the Polyglott was printed in 1514-1517, its publication was delayed until 1522. (See Scrivener, " Introduction to New Testament Criticism," third edition, pp. 423-433.) The first four volumes of this noble work contain the Old Testament in Hebrew, Greek, Chaldee, and Latin; the fifth volume contains the New Testament in Greek and Latin, with a Greek vocabulary; the last volume is a Hebrew and Chaldee vocabulary or lexicon. Vernacular versions of portions of the Scriptures in most of the European languages had been in use long before. In the British Museum are copies of German editions of the Old Testament assigned to 1466 and 1475, and of four dated editions between the latter year and 1507; there are also copies of four Italian editions between 1471 and 1484, and of a French edition of (apparently) 1515. But Erasmus evidently gave a fresh impetus to the study of the Scriptures. The French Bible was re-published at Lyons, 1521, a copy of which belonged to King Henry VIII. (Brit. Mus. 466. d. 6); Luther's German version of the whole Bible appeared 1527; and an Italian version, 1538. England was the last of these countries to obtain a printed edition of the Bible in the vernacular.

" Thomas Cantuarien.," the celebrated Complutensian Polyglott, edited under the auspices of Cardinal Ximenes, 1514 ;[1] the Vulgate with the Commentary of Nicholas de Lyra; the Hebrew Bible of 1525 ; and the Paraphrases and Annotations of Erasmus upon the New Testament, with many other commentaries. And the archbishop was no mere collector of books. His volumes of MS. collections of extracts, which are still in existence, containing quotations from Holy Scripture and the Fathers upon every subject of interest, afford clear signs of his diligence as a student.[2] And portions of an earlier Hebrew Bible have been preserved, containing the Books of Joshua, Psalms, Proverbs, Job, Daniel, Ezra, Nehemiah, and 1 and 2 Chronicles, interleaved with a MS. Latin translation in the archbishop's handwriting ;[3] and this is not merely an independent ver-

[1] For the use made of this Polyglott in the revised edition of Coverdale's Bible of 1539, see his Letters to Cromwell, dated from Paris, 1538.— " Remains," Parker Soc., pp. 492-4.

[2] Brit. Mus., Royal MSS., 7 B., xi., xii. ; Lambeth MSS., 1107. " There was no book either of the ancient or modern writers, especially upon the point of the Eucharist, which he had not noted with his own hand in the most remarkable places. . . . So that his library was the storehouse of ecclesiastical writers of all ages, and which was open for the use of learned men. Here old Latimer spent many an hour."—Strype's " Cranmer," vol. i., p. 630. See " Catalogue of Archbishop Cranmer's Library."

[3] Printed at Soncino, 1488. (Brit. Mus., Press mark C. 23. c. 10.) Attention has been before called (p. 91) to the words " give thanks " and " thanksgiving," as having been more uniformly adopted in Cranmer's Bible in place of *confiteor*, and this accords with the invariable use of the word *celebro* in this MS. version as the translation of the verb *Hodah*, apparently in every case, except Ps. xxxii. 6, where *confiteor* is used. The following passage is another illustration of the independence of this version. It Psalm lxxxviii. 10, the Vulgate, following the Septuagint, gives the curious translation—" Aut medici suscitabunt et confitebuntur tibi ? " which is followed by Coverdale and Matthew, " Can the physicians raise them up again

sion, but contains suggestions for many of the improvements adopted in the Bible of 1539, commonly known as Cranmer's Bible, which was reprinted in 1540 with a preface by the archbishop.

Another important step was taken through the publication of books of devotional instruction. The use of what were called Primers, containing the Creed, the Lord's Prayer, and the Ten Commandments, in the vulgar tongue, had been customary from early times, and other offices of devotion had been added by degrees, so that there was nothing new in principle in putting forth such books for general use. But in the publication of "The Institution of a Christian Man,"[1] commonly called "The Bishop's Book," A.D. 1537, a fresh step was taken, inasmuch as it not only contained the Creed, the Lord's Prayer, and the Ten Commandments, but explained their contents, and defined the meaning of the sacraments and

that they may praise Thee?" But in Cranmer's version the words are translated tentatively thus, " Num manes surgent(?) [sic] celebrabunt te ? " and in 1539 the English was given according to the sense now generally accepted, " Shall the dead rise up again and praise Thee ? " It is interesting to find *manes* suggested in Gesenius as the meaning of the word *rephaim* which is here used.

[1] For a full account of the contents of this book, see Collier, Eccles. Hist., vol. iv., p. 400. He says :—The clergy " were to govern themselves in the instruction of their flocks by this rule. It was an authoritative explanation of the doctrines of faith and manners, and a sort of standard for the desk and pulpit. It is ranged under these divisions : the Creed, the Seven Sacraments, the Ten Commandments, the Lord's Prayer, the Ave-Maria, Justification, and Purgatory." Amongst other things worthy of notice, it may be mentioned that " hell " in the Creed is taken to be the place of the damned ; the Church of Rome is described to be no more than a part of the Catholic Church ; though seven Sacraments are described, the Sacraments of Baptism, of Penance, and of the Altar are declared to be of greater dignity than the rest ; it is taught that images may be retained in churches for memory and instruction, but men must not bow down to them nor give them

other religious acts.   This was afterwards revised and
republished, A.D. 1542, under the name of " A Necessary
Doctrine and Erudition for any Christian Man," and was
commonly called " The King's Book." [1]

A yet nearer approach to a revision of the Service
Books was made in the same year, when, after a motion to
that effect in Convocation, it was made known that "it was
the king's pleasure that all mass books, antiphoners, and
portuasses (breviaries) should be examined and reformed
from all mention of the Bishop of Rome's name ; from all
apocryphas, feigned legends, collects, versicles, and
responses ; and that the names and memories of all saints
which are neither mentioned in the Scriptures, nor by
authentical doctors, should be deleted in the same books
and calendars." [2]   Two years later Cranmer was directed
by the king to prepare and set forth a Litany in English ;
and amongst other things the king, in his letter to the
archbishop, takes notice " that the prayers being formerly
in an unknown tongue made the people negligent in

any worship; the invocation of saints is restricted to intercession. and men
are instructed that to pray to them for good things is to injure the majesty
of God ; and the Ave-Maria is declared to be no prayer, properly speaking,
but of the nature of a hymn.

In the Library at Lambeth there is a MS. collection of extracts, mainly
in Archbishop Cranmer's handwriting, in which these subjects are discussed
as follows :   " De numero, usu, et efficacia sacramentorum magna est con-
troversia in ecclesia.   Scholastici contendunt septem esse, et per hæc con-
ferri gratiam ex opere operato.   Alii affirmant tria tantum esse necessaria,
quæ oporteat etiam cum fide accipi.   Anabaptistæ negant," &c., fol. 84.
In the following pages the seven sacraments are described, but their necessity is stated to depend upon their signifying the remission of sins; and the
three, " 1. Baptismus ; 2. Cœna Domini ; 3. Absolutio," are singled out for
this reason.   (Lambeth MS. 1107.)

[1] Collier, Eccles. Hist., vol. v., pp. 98-105.
[2] *Ibid.*, vol. v., p. 89 ; Hook, " Lives of Archbishops," vol. vii., p. 194.

coming to church." This Litany was published in 1544, and, being that which is still in use, it continues to bear striking testimony to the devotional spirit of Cranmer, as well as to his power as a master of the English language. It is a translation of the old Sarum Litany with many alterations and additions, which the reader will find described in a letter from the archbishop to the king, dated Oct. 7th, 1544, and with the more remarkable improvement, which Cranmer passes over without notice, caused by compressing the almost innumerable invocations of the saints into three sentences, whereby the Litany was restored to its original purpose, as a supplication addressed to God.[1]

By these and such like measures the way was prepared for taking in hand the general revision of the ancient services, and shortly after the accession of Edward VI., a Committee of Divines, including most of those who had been appointed A.D. 1540 to consider various questions connected with the Sacraments, together with several new members, "were commanded to draw up an order for administering the Holy Eucharist in English under both kinds."

The result of their deliberations was put forth in March, 1548; by means of which the first great alteration of the Service of the Mass was introduced into England.[2] The service continued, as usual, in Latin to the

---

[1] Collier, Eccles. Hist., vol. v., p. 136; Hook, "Lives of Archbishops," vol. vii., pp. 204-206. For the full text of this Litany, see below, Chapter IX., Litanies and Invocations of Saints.

[2] The commissioners began by considering various questions respecting the receiving of the Sacrament of the Altar, to which every member gave his answer in writing. See Collier, Eccles. Hist., vol. v., p. 247. The committee consisted of eighteen bishops and six divines, viz., Archbishops

end of the Canon; but after this an Office in English for the Communion of the people was inserted as follows :—

THE ORDER OF THE COMMUNION, OF 1548.

First the Parson, Vicar, or Curate, the next Sunday, or holy day, or at the least, one day before he shall minister the Communion, shall give warning to his Parishioners, or those which be present, that they prepare themselves thereto, saying to them openly and plainly as hereafter followeth, or such like:

Dear friends, and you especially, upon whose souls I have cure and charge, upon ——day next I do intend by God's grace to offer to all such as shall be thereto Godly disposed, the most comfortable Sacrament of the body and blood of Christ, to be taken by them in the remembrance of his most fruitful and glorious Passion : by the which Passion we have obtained remission of our sins . . . and to forgive other as you would that God should forgive you. And if there be any of you whose conscience is troubled and grieved in any thing, lacking comfort or counsel let him come to me, or to some other discreet and learned Priest taught in the law of God, and confess and open his sin and grief secretly, that he may

Cranmer of Canterbury and Holgate of York ; Bishops Bonner of London, Tunstal of Durham, Heath of Worcester, Reps of Norwich, Parfew of S. Asaph, Salcot (*alias* Capon) of Salisbury, Sampson of Coventry and Lichfield, Aldrich of Carlisle, Bush of Bristol, Ferrars of S. David's, Gooderich of Ely, Holbech of Lincoln, Day of Chichester, Skip of Hereford, Thirlby of Westminster, and Ridley of Rochester ; Doctors Cox, May, Taylor, Heynes, Robertson, and Redmayne.

The use of the new service was pressed upon the clergy by a letter from the Privy Council drawn up by Archbishop Cranmer, addressed to the bishops.—Calendar of State Papers, Edw. VI., March 15, 1548. The letter is given in full by Collier, vol. v., p. 256. Coverdale, writing to Calvin from Frankfort, March 26, 1548, rejoices over this "little book in English" as the "first-fruits of godliness."—" Remains," Parker Soc., p. 525.

receive such ghostly counsel, advice and comfort that his conscience may be relieved, and that of us, as a minister of God and of the Church, he may receive comfort and absolution, to the satisfaction of his mind, and avoiding of all scruple and doubtfulness : requiring such as shall be satisfied with a general confession, not to be offended with them that doth use, to their further satisfying, the auricular and secret Confession to the Priest; nor those also which think needful or convenient for the quieting of their own consciences particularly to open their sins to the Priest, to be offended with them which are satisfied with their humble confession to God, and the general confession to the Church; but in all these things to follow and keep the rule of charity, &c.

The time of the communion shall be immediately after that the Priest himself hath received the sacrament, without the varying of any other rite or ceremony in the Mass . . . and (he) shall thus exhort them as followeth.

Dearly beloved in the Lord, ye coming to this holy communion, must consider what S. Paul writeth to the Corinthians, how he exhorteth all persons, &c. [With a few verbal alterations the same Exhortation as is still used.]

Then the Priest shall say to them which be ready to take the Sacrament.

If any man here be an open blasphemer, an advouterer, in malice, &c. [The same warning as now forms part of our First Exhortation.]

Here the Priest shall pause a while, to see if any man will withdraw himself . . . and after a little pause the Priest shall say.

You that do truly and earnestly repent you of your sins . . . make your humble confession to Almighty God, and to his holy Church here gathered together, in his name, meekly kneeling upon your knees.

Then shall a general Confession be made . . .

Almighty God, Father of our Lord Jesus Christ, &c.

Then shall the Priest stand up, and turning him to the people, say thus.

Our blessed Lord who hath left power to his church to absolve penitent sinners from their sins, and to restore to the grace of the heavenly Father such as truly believe in Christ, have mercy upon you, pardon and deliver you from all sins, confirm and strength you in all goodness, and bring you to everlasting life.

Hear what comfortable words, &c.

Come unto me all that travail, &c.

Then shall the Priest kneel down and say, in the name of all them that shall receive the Communion, this prayer following.

We do not presume to come to this thy table . . . and to drink his blood, in these holy Mysteries, that we may continually dwell in him, and he in us, that our sinful bodies may be made clean by his body, and our souls washed through his most precious blood. Amen.

Then shall the Priest rise, the people still reverently kneeling, and the Priest shall deliver the Communion, first to the Ministers, . . . and when he doth deliver the sacrament of the body of Christ he shall say to every one these words following.

The body of our Lord Jesus Christ, which was given for thee, preserve thy body unto everlasting life.

And the Priest delivering the Sacrament of the blood, and giving everyone to drink once and no more, shall say.

The blood of our Lord Jesus Christ, which was shed for thee, preserve thy soul unto everlasting life.

Then shall the Priest turning him to the people, let the people depart with this blessing.

The peace of God which passeth all understanding, keep your hearts and minds, in the knowledge and love of God, and of His Son Jesus Christ our Lord. *Amen.*

Note that the Bread that shall be consecrated shall be such as heretofore hath been accustomed. . . .

Note that if it doth so chance that the wine hallowed and con-secrate doth not suffice or be enough for them that do take the Communion, the Priest, after the first Cup or Chalice be emptied, may go again to the altar, and reverently and.devoutly prepare and consecrate another, and so the third or more, like-wise beginning at these words, Simili modo postquam cœnatum est, *and ending at these words,* Qui pro vobis . . . peccatorum, *and without any levation or lifting.*[1]

In the following September the Committee of Bishops and Divines were again summoned, and were directed to draw up an English Prayer Book to provide an uniform service for the whole kingdom in place of the various Uses of Sarum, York, Bangor, and Lincoln. Their labours resulted in the publication of the First Prayer Book of King Edward VI., which was ordered to come into use at Pentecost (*i.e.* on Whitsunday), 1549.[2]

PRAYER BOOK OF 1549.

The Order for Morning and Evening Prayer was almost the same as in our present Prayer Book, with the exception that the services began with the Lord's Prayer, and ended at the third Collect, and no alternative Psalms in place of Bene-dictus, Magnificat, and Nunc dimittis were provided.

[1] Taken from Parker Society's volume, "Liturgies of Edward VI," according to the copy in the University Library, Cambridge. It is entitled "The Order of the Communion." Printed in London, March 8th, 1548.

[2] The committee was much smaller than before. Only seven bishops took part in it, viz., Canterbury, Ely, Lincoln, Chichester, Hereford, Westmin-ster, and Rochester; but all the divines who were in the previous commis-sion assisted. Of the other bishops, London, Durham, Worcester, Norwich, S. Asaph, and Bristol, had declared their opinion against the use of English for the whole service. But amongst the committee were two bishops, viz., Chichester and Hereford, who had taken the same view.—Collier, vol. v., p. 252.

The Communion Service was headed, THE SUPPER OF THE
LORD, AND THE HOLY COMMUNION, COMMONLY CALLED THE
MASS.   The opening Rubrics were substantially the same as
now, with the exception of the last, which directed—*The Priest
that shall execute the holy ministery, shall put upon hym the
vesture appointed for that ministration, that is to saye : a white
Albe plain, with a vestment or Cope.   And where there be many
Priests or Deacons, there so many shall be ready to help the
Priest, in the ministration, as shall bee requisite : And shall have
upon them likewise the vestures appointed for their ministery,
that is to say, Albes with tunacles.*
   The Communion Service was begun by the Priest saying
"afore the middes of the Altar" the Lord's Prayer, with the
Collect for Purity.   Then followed the *Introit*, or Psalm ap-
pointed for the purpose, for every Sunday and holyday.   Then,
   iii. Lorde have mercie upon us.
   iii. Christ have mercie upon us.
   iii. Lord have mercie upon us.
   Glory be to God on high, &c.   (Omitting the repetition,
"Thou that takest away the sin of the world, have mercy
upon us.")
   The Lord be with you.
   And with thy spirit.
   Let us pray.
   Then followed the Collect for the Day, one of the two
Collects for the King, the Epistle and Gospel, the Creed, the
Sermon or Homily, the Exhortation, "Dearly beloved in the
Lord," and the Offertory.   After the oblation of Bread and
Wine, with "a little pure and clean water," had been made,
the Priest said,
   The Lord be with you, &c.
   Lift up your hearts, &c.
   After the Sanctus, which still contained the words, "Ho-
sanna in the highest," &c., the Priest or Deacon said,

Let us pray for the whole state of Christe's Churche.

The Prayer which followed took the place of the ancient Canon, and included our present Prayer for the Church Militant, our Prayer of Consecration, and our Post-Communion Prayer, with the following additions : The Prayer for the Church contained a thanksgiving in commemoration of the Blessed Virgin Mary, the patriarchs, prophets, apostles, and martyrs, and a prayer for the departed as follows : " We commend unto Thy mercy, O Lord, all other Thy servaunts, which are departed hence from us, with the signe of fayth, and nowe do reste in the slepe of peace ; Graunte unto them, we beseche Thee, Thy mercy and everlastinge peace, and that at the daye of the general resurrection we and all they which be of the mystical body of Thy Sonne maye altogether be set on His right hand, and hear that His most joyful voice, Come unto me," &c.   The Prayer of Consecration contained these words : " With Thy Holy Spirite and Worde vouchsafe to ble ✠ sse and sancti ✠ fie these Thy gifts, and creatures of breade and wyne, that they may be unto us the bodie and bloode of Thy most derely beloved Sonne Jesus Christ, who

in the same nyghte that He was betrayed
Here the Priest must take the bread into his handes. tooke breade, and when He had blessed, and geven thankes, He brake it, and gave it to His disciples sayinge, Take eate ; this is my bodye whiche is given for you, do this in remembrance of me.

" Lykewise after supper He tooke the cuppe, and when He had geven thanks, He gave it to them,
Here the Priest shall take the cup into his handes. saying, Drinke ye all of this, for this is my bloude of the New Testament," &c.

" Wherefore, O Lorde and heavenly Father, according to the institution of thy derely beloved Sonne, our Savioure Jesu Christe, we thy humble servauntes doe celebrate and make here before thy Divine Majestie, with these thy holy giftes, the memoriall which thy Sonne hath willed us to make ; having in remembraunce his blessed passion, mightie resurreccion, and glorious ascencion ; renderynge unto thee moste heartye thankes for the innumerable benefites procured unto us by the same : entyrely desiring thy Fatherly goodnes mercyfully to accept thys our sacrifice of prayse and thankesgevinge," &c.

After this the Lord's Prayer followed immediately with a preface, " As our Saviour Christe hath commanded and taughte us, we are bold to saye, Our Father," &c.

" The peace of the Lorde be alway with you.

" And wyth thy spirite.

" Christe our Pascal Lambe is offered up for us once for all, when He bare our sinnes on His body upon the crosse. for He is the very Lambe of God that taketh away the sinnes of the worlde ; wherefore let us kepe a joyfull and holy feast with the Lorde."

Then came the Invitation, " You that do truly and earnestly repent," &c.; the Confession; the Absolution, the same as now; the Comfortable Words ; and the Prayer of Humble Access, as in " The Order of Communion." Then the Communion, with the same words of administration as in " The Order of Communion," except that the words " body and soul" were used in both forms. The " Agnus Dei" in English was appointed to be sung " in the Communion time." Sentences of Scripture followed, of which one was to be said or songe every day after the Holy Communion. Then the Post-Communion Thanksgiving, the same as now ; and the Blessing in the full form as now.

Rubrics followed, directing that " forasmuch as the pastors and curates within this realm shall continually find at their cost and charges in their cures, sufficient bread and wine for the Holy Communion, it is therefore ordered that . . . the parishioners . . . shall offer every Sunday at the time of the Offertory the just value and price of the holy loaf," &c.

M

The Litany followed the Communion Office. This was the Litany translated by Cranmer A.D. 1544, with the omission of the three verses of invocations of saints and angels, and was the same as now, except that it contained a clause which was omitted in 1559, " From the tyranny of the Bishop of Rome and all his detestable enormities ; Good Lord deliver us," and the concluding Benediction was absent.[1]

The First English Prayer Book came into use at Whitsuntide, 1549. It was generally accepted throughout the kingdom, though some bishops and priests were slow to give up the old forms. For instance, in the Calendar of State Papers, Edward VI., under date Aug. 2, 1549, a letter is mentioned which was sent by the king to the Bishop of London (Bonner), stating that, through his evil example, the people absent themselves from Prayer and Holy Communion, and he is peremptorily commanded to reform his neglect. Heads are prescribed for his first sermon at S. Paul's, particularly against the " sin of rebellion." These instructions refer to the neglect of Bishop Bonner in introducing the new services at S. Paul's, and to the insurrections which had arisen in Devonshire, Norfolk, and Yorkshire, amongst the peasantry, supported by various country gentlemen, in opposition to the religious changes which had been introduced, and as a protest against the alienation of various abbey lands which had been used in former times as common pastures.[2] These disturbances were not quelled without much bloodshed and difficulty.

[1] This Communion Service in full is given by Collier, Eccles. Hist., vol. ix., p. 247. It will be found, with the spelling modernized, in Parker Society's volume, " Liturgies of Edward VI."

[2] The document is given in full by Collier, Eccles. Hist., vol. v., p. 346.

About the same date another letter is stated to have been sent by the king to Princess Mary, in which he marvels at her refusing to conform to the Common Prayers, and grants a dispensation for her having private service in her chamber. But with these exceptions the new Prayer Book met with general approval.

In the course, however, of the next few months objections to the English services began to arise from the opposite quarter. A spirit of fanaticism had been encouraged by an act passed in November, 1549, calling in all the old Service Books, commanding the churchwardens and others to deliver them over to the bishop under penalties of fine and imprisonment, and directing that "if the bishops failed to execute the act, and did not burn, deface, and destroy all the said books within forty days after they received them, they were to forfeit forty pounds, half of which sum was for the king, and the other moiety for the informer," which resulted in the utter destruction of almost the whole series of English Uses. This spirit of fanaticism was further inflamed in two ways; first, in respect of what were termed the ecclesiastical "habits," by the refusal of Hooper to wear the episcopal vestments after being nominated to the bishopric of Gloucester in the summer of 1550; and, secondly, in respect of the arrangements of the churches by a letter from the king dated November 24, 1550, requiring all altars to be taken down. So that whilst the new Book of Common Prayer was publicly commended to the people as ordaining " that nothing be read but the very pure Word of God, or what is evidently grounded upon the same," a spirit of opposition to its instructions was being generally fostered.

Before this time, moreover, many signs had been given of the difficulty of satisfying the more ardent reformers. For instance, Calvin, in a letter to the Protector Somerset, dated Oct. 22 (apparently in the year 1549), made objection to the First Prayer Book, upon the ground that no additions to the express declarations of Scripture respecting the rule of worship are allowable. And in particular he strongly denounced the praying for the dead in the Communion Service, though he admitted that it was an ancient custom in the Church, and that the words used do "not imply any approbation of the Popish Purgatory."[1] It is evident that Cranmer felt it to be necessary to take steps to endeavour to pacify such objectors, however unreasonable they might be, in order to save the English Church from utter disruption. Consequently, towards the end of 1550, the archbishop wrote to Martin Bucer, who had been appointed Divinity Professor at Cambridge, desiring his opinion of the Book of Common Prayer; and in order that Bucer might study it the more easily, the book was translated into Latin for his use. His opinion was published in a letter to Archbishop Cranmer, which is commonly spoken of as the *Censura* of Martin Bucer. He began by stating that in the description of the Communion and daily prayers he saw nothing enjoined in the book but what was agreeable to the word of God, either in word, as in the Psalms and Lessons, or in the sense, as in the Collects. But he desired alterations in respect of the following matters: That there should be stricter discipline to exclude scandalous livers from the sacrament; that the old habits (*i.e.* vestments) should be laid aside; that the

[1] Collier, Eccles. Hist., vol. v., p. 364.

first half of the Communion Service should not be said at the altar when there was no sacrament; that the frequency of communion should be increased; that distinct reading of the prayers should be practised; that the sacrament should be delivered into the hands of the people; that prayers for the dead should be given up; and that the prayer that the elements might be to us the body and blood of Christ might be varied so as to bring it nearer to a scriptural form.[1]

The result was that a second revision of the English Prayer Book was taken in hand. It is evident that the objections of the foreign Protestants, especially Calvin, Bucer, and Martyr, had great weight in urging the king and Privy Council to appoint a commission for this purpose. It is singular that little is known for certain about the members of it. But all that seems to have been recorded is that "these revisers were Cranmer, Ridley, and certain other doctors, whereof Dr. Cox was one." [2]

It has been commonly asserted that the changes which were now made were due to the demands of the foreign divines, in accordance with the remark of Bishop Burnet that "almost in every particular the most material things

[1] Censura super libro sacrorum seu ordinationis Ecclesiæ, printed in " Martini Buceri Scripta Anglicana," Basil, 1577. (British Museum.) An analysis of the *Censura* was made by Rev. A. Roberts, 1853. See also Strype, " Memorials of Cranmer," vol. i., p. 300; Burnet, " Hist. of Reform.," part ii., book i., p. 319.

[2] Strype, " Memorials," book ii., chap. xv., p. 20. Both Strype and Burnet pass over their account of the work very briefly, apparently taking for granted that the advice which the foreign divines were pressing upon the English bishops sufficiently explains the alterations which were made, and not appreciating the complete change which was produced in the order of the service.

which Bucer excepted to were corrected afterwards." [1] But a reference to Bucer's *Censura*, quoted above, will show that the changes recommended by him did not touch upon the arrangement of the prayers. Even though Bishop Burnet's remark be true, it will not explain the changes now made, by which the whole order of the Communion Service was completely altered; whilst on the other hand there is evidence which points in the opposite direction, leading to the conclusion that the alterations were the independent work of the commissioners themselves, and were not the result of consultation with these foreign divines. For Peter Martyr mentions in a letter to Bucer, that "the archbishop had told him that the bishops had met about this business, and concluded on a great many alterations; but what these corrections were Cranmer did not acquaint him, neither durst he take the freedom to enquire." [2]

The part which Cranmer took in this second revision may be gathered from Strype's account of the archbishop. He says,—

"As his authority was now very great, so there was undoubtedly a great deference paid to it, as also to his wisdom and learning, by the rest of the divines appointed to that work; so that nothing was by them inserted into the Liturgy but by his good allowance and approbation; so neither would they reject or oppose what he thought fit should be put in or altered." [3]

But the difficulties which he had to encounter must have been very great in consequence of the readiness of

---

[1] Burnet, "Hist. of Reformation," part ii., book i., p. 319.
[2] Collier, Eccles. Hist., vol. v., p. 434.
[3] Strype, "Memorials of Archbishop Cranmer," vol. i., p. 381.

the Privy Council to listen to objections. This has been brought to light by a letter from Cranmer to the Privy Council, which is described in the Calendar of State Papers, and which has been lately published in full.[1] It appears from this that the printing of the New Prayer Book was stopped, Sept. 26, 1552, by a letter from the Privy Council to Grafton the printer, in consequence of objections raised by Knox to kneeling at the time of Communion. The character of these objections will explain the dangers through which the English Church was guided at this period under the good providence of God. They were as follows : (1) Because there is no commandment or example of Jesus Christ nor of His Apostles about kneeling, but it is the imagination of man proceeding from false opinions ; (2) It is idolatrous ; (3) The weak brethren are offended thereby ; (4) It is not suitable for the joyful approach of men as reconciled sons to the Table of the Lord. The objections were sent to Cranmer, and in reply he wrote to the Council, under date Oct. 7th, 1552:—

" Some be offended with kneeling at the time of receiving the Sacrament, and would that I, calling to me the Bishop of London and some other learned men as Mr. Peter Martyr or such like, should with them . . . weigh the said prescription of kneeling . . . I trust that we with just balance weighed this at the making of the Book, and not only we but a great many bishops and òther of the best learned within this realm, and appointed for that purpose."

---

[1] Calendar of State Papers, Edward VI., 1552, October 7th, vol. xv., 15. The letter was published in full by Rev. T. W. Perry, " Declaration on Kneeling," p. 77. See also P. Lorrimer, " John Knox and the Church of England."

He then goes on to point out the serious importance of altering what had been approved by Parliament with the Royal assent (January, 1551-2), and adds,—

"I trust ye will not be moved by these glorious and unquiet spirits, which can like nothing but that is after their own fancy, and cease not to make trouble and disquietness when things be most quiet and in good order. If such men should be heard, although the Book were made every year anew, yet should it not lack faults in their opinion."

However, the result was that on October 27th the Council accepted the addition of what is called "the Black Rubric" at the end of the Communion Service. Its abrupt and confused style bears testimony to its hasty composition, and marks of indignation and annoyance are plainly to be seen in it. There is no doubt that it must be regarded as a compromise, and it is probable that it was suggested and drawn up by Cranmer to avoid the risk of further alterations.[1]

"The Black Rubric," which was thus hastily inserted by the authority of the Privy Council alone, was as follows :—

[1] This is rendered the more probable by the fact that his chaplain, the Rev. Thos. Becon, is found to have expressed himself in very similar language a few years afterwards, evidently regretting the removal of this note from the Prayer Book of 1559. In "A new Catechism set forth dialogue wise in familiar talk between the Father and the Son," which was printed apparently in 1560, he says, "I would wish with all my heart that either this kneeling of the Sacrament were taken away, or else that the people were taught that that outward reverence were not given to the Sacrament and outward sign, but to Christ which is represented by that sacrament and sign."—Becon's works, publ. by Parker Society, vol. ii., p. 298. P. Lorrimer, "Knox and the Church of England," chap. iii. In the first edition of the Prayer Book of 1552, this rubric is printed upon a separate leaf and pasted in ; and several copies are without it.

" Although no order can be so perfectly devised, but it may be of some, either for their ignorance and infirmity, or else of malice and obstinacy misconstrued, depraved and interpreted in a wrong part; and yet because brotherly charity willeth that, so much as conveniently may be, offences should be taken away ; therefore we willing to do the same ;—Whereas it is ordained in the Book of Common Prayer, in the Administration of the Lord's Supper, that the communicants kneeling should receive the holy Communion; which thing being well meant, for a signification of the humble and grateful acknowledging of the benefits of Christ given unto the worthy receiver, and to avoid the profanation and disorder which about the holy Communion might else ensue. Lest yet the same kneeling might be thought or taken otherwise, we do declare that it is not meant thereby, that any adoration is done, or ought to be done, either unto the Sacramental Bread or Wine there bodily received, or unto any real and essential presence there being of Christ's natural flesh and blood," &c.

The result of this second revision of the services appeared in the Second Prayer Book of 1552. The alterations in the words of the prayers were few, and comparatively unimportant. But the changes in the order and arrangement of them, and the omissions in deference to the objections of the Protestant party, were very considerable.

PRAYER BOOK OF 1552.

The chief alterations in the daily prayers were as follow : The Sentences, Exhortation, Confession, and Absolution, were prefixed to Mattins. Psalm c. was inserted for alternative use in place of Benedictus ; the Creed was placed before instead of after the lesser Litany; and Psalms xcviii. and lxvii. were inserted in the Evening Prayer.

In the Communion Service the following changes were made. The rubric respecting the vestments of the Priest and his assistants was omitted; and, instead of it, the following rubric was placed at the beginning of the daily Prayers : "And here it is to be noted, that the Minister at the time of the Communion, and at all other times in his ministration, shall use neither alb, vestment, nor cope; but being Archbishop, or Bishop, he shall have and wear a rochet; and being a Priest or Deacon, he shall have and wear a surplice only." The words "at the north side of the Table" were introduced in place of the words "afore the middes of the Altar." The Introits were omitted. The Ten Commandments and the responses to them took the place of the nine repetitions of the Kyries alone. The "Gloria in Excelsis" was removed to the end of the service. The Prayer for the Church received the addition of the words "accept our alms" before the words "receive these our prayers," and was placed immediately after the Offertory. This partially supplied a great deficiency in the First Book, which contained no prayer, *super oblata*, in connection with the oblations. At the same time the Commemoration of the Saints, and the intercessions for the faithful departed were omitted, and the words "Militant here on earth" were inserted.

The Exhortation, "Dearly beloved in the Lord," &c., which in the First Prayer Book was appointed to follow immediately after the Sermon, but only "if the people be not exhorted (therein) to the worthy receyving of the Holy Sacrament of the body and bloude of our Saviour Christ," was now removed to its present position, and the first form of instruction, "Dearly beloved, on —day next, I purpose," &c., which had come after, was now placed before it, and a second instruction, composed by Peter Martyr, was added to meet the difficulty, which had already been felt, of the negligence of the people to come to the Holy Communion.

The Invitation, Confession, Absolution, and Comfortable Words were brought here from their former position after the Prayer of Consecration.

The " Sanctus " was altered by the omission of the words " Osanna in the higheste. Blessed is he that cometh in the name of the Lorde ; " and by the use of the words " Glory be to Thee O Lord most high," in place of " Glory to Thee O Lorde in the higheste."

The Prayer of Humble Access was removed from its position immediately preceding the Communion, and placed after the " Sanctus " ; the words " in these Holy Mysteries " were omitted, and the last clauses arranged as they are now.

The Prayer of Consecration was now reduced in proportions and character, and brought into a short form consisting only of the Commemoration of the Lord's Passion and Institution of the Holy Sacrament. This was effected by taking away the first part of the Prayer of 1549, and using it as was mentioned before in its present position as a Prayer for the Church Militant ; and by removing the latter part of it into the position of a Post-Communion Prayer. The rubrics prescribing the Manual Acts were also omitted.

The words of administration were now altered : the former words being replaced with the words " Take and eat this in remembrance," &c.

The Lord's Prayer was omitted from the end of the Prayer of Consecration, and was ordered to be said after the Communion ; and the introduction to it was removed.

A Post-Communion Prayer was now provided for alternative use with the Thanksgiving, as above mentioned, by cutting off what had been the last portion of the Prayer of Consecration, and placing it here.

The singing of " Agnus Dei " during the Communion was

discontinued; and "Gloria in Excelsis" was brought to its present position, with the addition of a second repetition of the words "Thou that takest away," &c., apparently in place of "Agnus Dei."

By these changes the service was so completely altered that it is hardly possible to compare together the two Prayer Books of 1549 and 1552. The service of 1549 was the old Roman Liturgy revised; but the resemblance between the present order of Holy Communion, which in the main is that of 1552, and the ancient Sarum order is now confined to comparatively narrow limits. Consequently the objections which have been raised against the Second Prayer Book of 1552 have been very numerous.[1] They are founded for the most part upon the supposition that the Roman Liturgy was the only orthodox guide which our reformers could use, and consequently that its principal features ought to have been maintained at all costs. To those who take this view the changes in the Second Prayer Book of 1552 are unintelligible; it appears to them that the various parts of the service have been wilfully and unreasonably mixed up together, and that the whole has been thrown into confusion.

But there is a difficulty in accepting such a view of the service of 1552. When the known learning, ability, and experience of Archbishop Cranmer are taken into consideration, and it is remembered that he framed our English Litany with its wonderfully perfect rhythm, and translated the Collects with such devotional skill and power that the faithful are never wearied of using them,

---

[1] References to the most important of these objections will be found in the notes to the Service of Holy Communion in Chapter VII.

the question may well be raised whether the apparent confusion into which the Communion Service was thrown by the revision of 1552 may not be explained on other grounds than wilful or ignorant perversity.

It has been the custom to regard the Communion Service of the Second Prayer Book of 1552 as if it were nothing more than a further revision of the ancient service, carried out in continuation of the work begun in the First Prayer Book of 1549, and in accordance as before mentioned with the suggestions of the foreign Protestants. But it appears very doubtful whether this is a correct view of the circumstances of the time. Dean Hook in his life of Cranmer raises the question, but dismisses it for lack of evidence without discussion, saying, " Whether the alterations introduced into the Second Prayer Book were all of them improvements is a subject upon which opinion is divided, and as we know not the precise line taken by Cranmer it does not fall within my province to discuss it." [1]

The difficulties which beset the rulers of the Church of England at this time must have been very great. It does not appear that they desired any alteration of the First Prayer Book of 1549. For in the Act of Uniformity which ordained the use of the Second Prayer Book (5 and 6 Edward VI., Cap. I., January, 1551-2), the First Book was described as " a very godly order agreeable to the word of God and the primitive Church, very comfortable to all good people desiring to live in Christian conversation, and most profitable to the estate of this realm." And it has been pointed out before that the " censures " of Bucer, who may be regarded as the leader

[1] " Lives of the Archbishops," vol. vii., p. 285.

of the more moderate section of the party that was pressing for a revision, referred only to a few of the points involved in the changes above described. But there was another and more extreme section of men, of whom Calvin and Knox were the spokesmen, and these showed that they would be satisfied with nothing short of an utter sweeping away of the ancient forms of religion. The episode connected with the direction upon kneeling is a sufficient proof both of the unreasonableness and of the political power of this party.

The problem which Archbishop Cranmer and his fellow-commissioners were set to solve was how to satisfy this fierce desire for change, and yet to retain an order of service " agreeable to the word of God and the primitive Church." And the question still remains to be considered, whether some other ancient form of service, distinct from the Roman Liturgy, was not taken as a guide, which influenced this revision in a Catholic direction.

There is no doubt that the work of revision in the First Prayer Book of 1549 was affected by the increasing knowledge of Greek authors in this country during the early part of the sixteenth century, and especially by the recent publication of the Liturgy of S. Chrysostom. This is proved by the addition of "The Prayer of S. Chrysostom " at the end of the Litany, and by the change in the form of the words of institution, from " The day before He suffered," &c., to " In the same night that He was betrayed," &c.[1]   But with respect to the second revision

---

[1] The first of these extracts from the Liturgy of S. Chrysostom seems without doubt to have been due to Cranmer's own study of it (see above, page 42); the latter may have been accepted at second hand from Herman's " Consultation." See next chapter, page 192.

of 1552 it seems probable that we must look in another direction to discover the guide which was followed. For it has been often observed that the arrangement of the prayers of our English Communion Service agrees in a remarkable manner with that of the ancient Gallican Liturgy, and a glance at the Comparative Table of Liturgies will show how far this agreement extends.[1] For instance, the non-juror Collier, speaking of the difference between the Roman and the Gallican services, says, " From hence likewise we may discover that the English prelates at the Reformation rather followed the latter; and where there happened to be a difference were more governed by the British or Gallican than by the Roman form." [2] But there has been a difficulty in accepting this idea, because the ancient Gallican Liturgy was so completely replaced by the Roman in the ninth century, that no copies of the former were known to exist, until the discovery of three MSS., which had belonged to the Monastery of Fleury, near Orleans, and which were published by Cardinal Thomasius in 1680.

It is, however, quite possible that our reformers became acquainted with the Gallican order of service through the Spanish form of it described in the writings of Isidore, Bishop of Seville, *circa* A.D. 603, and lately published to the world by Cardinal Ximenes under the name of the Mozarabic Missal.[3] The arguments in

[1] See " Comparative Table of Liturgies," fronting the title-page.

[2] Collier, Eccles. Hist., vol. i., p. 117. In this statement Collier follows Bishop Stillingfleet ; see " Antiquities of British Churches," p. 356.

[3] An account of Isidore's Treatise upon this Liturgy, and how it became known to our reformers will be found in the next chapter, p. 196. The use of this ancient Liturgy had lingered on amongst certain congregations of Christians who were scattered amongst the Moorish conquerors of Spain. The

support of this suggestion may be briefly stated. The connection between this country and Spain was very close about that period, in consequence of the marriage of King Henry VIII. with Queen Katharine, his brother's widow. And since she was daughter of Isabella of Castile, to whom Ximenes, who was then Archbishop of Toledo, acted as confessor, it may be regarded as certain that the knowledge of this newly discovered Missal would be brought to England by the chaplains in attendance upon the queen.[1] Moreover, Wolsey succeeded to part of the revenues of the archbishopric of Toledo after the death of Ximenes, and he could hardly fail to be acquainted with the peculiar rites which were there celebrated.[2] And as the principles of the Reformation spread, the interest which would be felt in a service differing altogether from the Roman Mass would naturally be considerable, and this might be expected to influence

name Mozarabes was given to these Christians by the Moors, and from this their service books have been called the " Mozarabic Missal and Breviary." When the Moors had been finally conquered by King Ferdinand, towards the end of the fifteenth century, Cardinal Ximenes became Archbishop of Toledo, and finding that the Mozarabic rites were still in use there, but in danger of being soon forgotten and lost, he endowed a chapel at Toledo for the support of some of the priests accustomed to the services, and charged them with the duty of maintaining the use of them; and there they have continued to be used to the present day. At the same time the Service Books were carefully edited under the directions of Ximenes, and the Missal was published A.D. 1500.

[1] It is well known that Spaniards settled in London in large numbers in the reign of Henry VIII.; see ballad, " An Evil May Day," published in Collection of Old Ballads, by T. Evans, 5 vols., 1810. I am indebted to the authoress of " The Armourer's Prentices," Miss C. M. Yonge, for this information.

[2] A yearly pension of seven thousand five hundred ducats from the revenues of the bishoprics of Toledo and Valencia had been granted to Wolsey by the Emperor Charles V. and Pope Leo X.—Lingard, " History of England,"

in a special degree those who were engaged in the revision of the old services. At the same time, the extreme party would be likely to regard with suspicion any references to the rites which were in use in the country where the worst powers of the Inquisition were then in special activity. Consequently it is not to be expected that our bishops and divines, who were engaged in the difficult task of satisfying the extreme Protestants whilst they preserved the services of the Church from destruction, would give any prominence to the fact that they had taken this form of service as their guide.

But whether this be the case or not, the facts remain the same, viz., that under the providence of God changes which cannot be exactly explained have brought the English Service into close agreement with the arrangement of the ancient Gallican Liturgy; and that whilst it is true that the ancient order of the Roman Liturgy has been abandoned to a very great extent, it is a mistake to conclude that the order of Holy Communion is therefore at variance with primitive usage.

The Second Prayer Book remained in force only a few months. It began to be used in November, 1552, and the king died in July, 1553. Shortly after the accession of Queen Mary an Act was passed to repeal the various Acts which had established the use of the English

vol. iv., p. 192. Shakespeare alludes to Wolsey's desire to obtain the archbishopric of Toledo after the death of Ximenes in 1517 :—

> " 'Tis the cardinal;
> And merely to revenge him on the emperor,
> For not bestowing on him, at his asking,
> The archbishopric of Toledo, this is purposed."
> *King Henry VIII.*, act ii., scene 1.

N

Services, and the clergy were forbidden to use the English Prayer Book after December 20th.

With the accession of Elizabeth in 1558 a return was made to the principles of the Reformation. A committee was appointed to revise the services a third time, and by an Act of Uniformity the Third English Prayer Book was ordered to come into use June 24th, 1559.

THE PRAYER BOOK OF 1559.

The changes now made were few in number.

The Ornaments Rubric was altered; instead of the " surplice only " of the Second Book, the minister was directed to " use such ornaments as were in use by authority of Parliament in the second year of the reign of King Edward VI."

The Prayers " For the Queen's Majesty," and " For the Clergy and People," which now form part of the Morning and Evening Prayer, and the concluding Benediction, were added to the Litany ; and the petition for deliverance " from the tyranny of the Bishop of Rome " was removed from it.

In the Communion Service, in the words of administration the two forms of the previous books were combined together ; and " The Black Rubric " upon kneeling was omitted.

The changes introduced in the next revision of the Prayer Book at the Hampton Court Conference were of small importance.

THE PRAYER BOOK OF 1604.

In the Title to the Absolution the words " or remission of sins " were added.

The Prayer " For the Royal Family," and various Thanksgivings for Special Occasions, were added at the end of the Litany.

After the restoration of Charles II. the Savoy Conference was held, which resulted in the last revision of 1662. The following changes were then made, bringing the services into their present order.

THE PRAYER BOOK OF 1662.

The Sentences, Exhortation, Confession, and Absolution were printed before Evening Prayer, as well as Morning Prayer.

The word " Minister " in the Title to the Absolution, and in other places, was changed into " Priest ; " the Rubric, " In quires and places where they sing," &c., was inserted after the Third Collect ; and the five following Prayers were brought there from the Litany. The following additions were also made : the two Prayers for use in the Ember Weeks, the Prayer for the Parliament, the Prayer for all conditions of men, the General Thanksgiving, and the Thanksgiving for restoring Peace at home.

In the Communion Service, important additions were made to the Prayer for the Church Militant by the introduction of the rubric directing the Bread and Wine to be then placed upon the holy Table, and by the insertion of the words " and oblations " at the beginning, and of the last paragraph at the end, " We also bless Thy holy Name for all Thy servants departed," &c. Alterations were made in the arrangements of the Exhortations. The rubric directing the Priest duly to order the Bread and Wine was prefixed to the Prayer of Consecration ; the rubrics respecting the manual acts, which had been left undescribed since 1552, were inserted ; and the rubrics which direct the Priest how he shall consecrate more Bread and Wine, and how he shall reverently cover what remaineth of the consecrated Elements, were added. The Lord's Prayer was now printed at length ; and the ascription added, " For Thine is the Kingdom," &c.

" The Black Rubric" upon kneeling, omitted in.1559, was replaced with certain alterations, which removed the signs of irritation at the.misconstruction placed upon the practice, as explained above; and avoided the apparent denial of the reality of the spiritual presence of Christ in the Holy Sacrament, by the substitution of the word " corporal " in place of the words "real and essential."[1]

[1] Other changes took place in the Occasional Offices both in 1604 and in 1662, but these do not strictly belong to the subject of this Book.

CHAPTER VI.

" Mihi placet ut sive in Romana, sive in Gallicanarum, seu in qualibet
ecclesia aliquid invenisti quod plus omnipotenti Deo possit placere, sollicite
eligas; et in Anglorum ecclesia . . . infundas."—*Gregory the Great*.
(Sixth century.)

MANY circumstances prepared the way for the
Reformation besides those which were apparent
in its progress. Similarly, there were many men who
greatly influenced the religious character of the move-
ment, though they took no prominent part in it, or
passed away before it was carried out. Foremost
amongst those who revolted against the absence of spiritual reality prevailing at the close of the fifteenth century
was Dean Colet. His sermons at S. Paul's stirred the
religious feelings of the citizens and others in an unwonted
manner, and awakened a desire for the spiritual realities
belonging to the rites of Christianity which had been
long forgotten. Men had been content with the outward
shell, and Colet led them to seek the substance within.
Consequently, in searching for the patterns which guided
our reformers in their revision of the services, it is
necessary to consider first the spiritual influences which
led Colet and others to desire something better than the
mediæval formularies.

First and foremost amongst the causes which raised the spiritual tone of the nation was the revival of the study of Holy Scripture.   When Colet, in 1496, began a course of lectures at Oxford upon S. Paul's Epistles, he was introducing to the learned what was practically a new study.   Hitherto theological students had studied not the Bible, but the scholastic interpretations of the Bible.[1]   In the course of a few years the study of Holy Scripture rapidly spread, and by drawing from the fountain source, men began to obtain clearer ideas of spiritual truths, and higher aspirations after spiritual nourishment than they had before.   Consequently, the first place amongst the works which guided our reformers must be given undoubtedly to Holy Scripture itself.

Next to Holy Scripture attention is due to a remarkable series of writings which have come down to us under the name of S. Dionysius the Areopagite.   The importance of these works can hardly be overstated.   For though they are little studied in the present day, their influence upon the course of thought in the past was very great.   This was the source from which the principles of Scholasticism took their rise.   Here may be found the elaborate ideas about the harmony of the spheres and the order of the celestial beings on which poets have fed their imaginations, and from which the lines of the great Puritan, Milton, have derived their peculiar grandeur. Little can be stated about their date or author.   Until the beginning of the sixteenth century they were universally accepted as the work of that Dionysius the Areopagite who was one of S. Paul's converts at Athens ; but under a more critical examination their claim to this extreme

---

[1] "The Oxford Reformers," by F. Seebohm, pp. 1-35.

antiquity was found to be false, and they are now assigned by modern authorities to about the end of the fifth century.[1] But their main interest is independent of their origin, being due to our knowledge of the high value attached to them by such men as Dean Colet, who wrote a summary of their teaching expanded according to his own idea of spiritual truth,[2] and as Archbishop Cranmer, who relied upon them as teaching the true doctrine about the heavenly realities of the Sacraments.[3]

Dionysius does not mention the words used in the service which he expressly names " Communion," but he gives a very full description of the order of its several parts, followed by an account of their spiritual meaning, and he assigns special importance to the act of communicating.[4] The passage is full of interest because of the

[1] The variety of Latin versions of these works which appeared between the ninth and the sixteenth century attests their wide influence; and the fact that the Greek Text was published as early as 1516 proves the importance that was assigned to them. For a full account, see Smith's ·· Dict. of Christ. Biog."; " Contemp. Review," No. XVII., May, 1867 ; " The Oxford Reformers," by F. Seebohm.

[2] " Dean Colet on the Hierarchies of Dionysius," by J. H. Lupton.

[3] Cranmer refers to the Ecclesiastical Hierarchy of Dionysius, cap. iii., in the following passage, saying, " Although the bread and wine be figures, signs and tokens of Christ's flesh and blood (as St. Dionyse calleth them both before the consecration and after), yet the Greek annotations upon the same Dionyse do say that the very things themselves be above in heaven."— " Defence of the True and Catholick Doctrine," in " Remains of Thomas Cranmer," by H. Jenkins, vol. ii., p. 402, vol. iii., p. 237. Cranmer quotes these writings frequently in his MS. Collections. The passage upon the Holy Communion will be found, vol. i., fol. 213, 214 ; see also fol. 20, 148 (Brit. Mus. Royal MSS., 7 B. xi., xii.). The archbishop's copy of the Latin version of the works of Dionysius is in the Cathedral Library at Wells; published at Paris by Henry Stephens, 1515.

[4] In the *Scholia* occurring in this edition a table is given of the rites thus described, together with those still observed, showing that only thirteen out

early date to which this description of the Holy Communion belongs, but it becomes of peculiar value when
it is regarded as one of the patterns which in all probability helped to guide our reformers in restoring to
the Eucharist its ancient character. The facts already
mentioned might be regarded as leading to this conclusion, but all doubt respecting it is removed by the words
of Martin Bucer. When the " Simplex ac pia Deliberatio " of Archbishop Herman appeared, a furious attack
was made against the principles on which the book was
founded, and especially because it allowed a celebration
of the Eucharist only when there was a congregation, and
exhorted the worshippers to receive. Martin Bucer set
himself to defend the book, and in the course of his
arguments he referred his opponents to the description
given by Dionysius of the service of Holy Communion,
and pointed out that it differed wholly from the Roman
Service, but agreed with the form which was suggested
by Herman, and which will be presently shown to have
been followed in many respects by our English reformers.[1]

The description given by Dionysius is as follows :—

" *The Mystery of the Assembly or Communion.*[2] — The
Hierarch (*i.e.* the Bishop) having finished a holy prayer at

of twenty rites mentioned were then in use. Attention is thus called to the
omission of psalms, the dismissal of catechumens, the kiss of peace, the
recitation of names, and the exhortation to the people to communicate.—
Dionys., Eccles. Hierarch., cap. iii., p. 64.

[1] " Martini Buceri defensio . . . deliberationis Hermanni," p. 338,
Basle, 1618. (British Museum.) The MS. is in Corpus Christi College
Library, Cambridge.

[2] The above version is a translation from the Greek. The Latin version
in Cranmer's copy is as follows :—" *Mysterium synaxeos sive communionis.*
Itaque pontifex quidem ubi orationem sanctam supra divinum altare peregit,

the divine altar, censes it first, and then makes a circuit of
the whole sanctuary; and returning again to the divine altar,
begins the sacred melody of the Psalms, and the whole body
of ecclesiastics join with him in the singing. Next follows the
reading of the sacred Scriptures by the ministers. Afterwards
the Catechumens go out of the sanctuary, and also the Energumens and Penitents; and those only who are worthy of a sight
of the divine (mysteries) and of Communion remain. And
some of the ministers stand beside the closed gates of the
temple, and others do something else belonging to their order.
But certain who are chosen from the order of the deacons,

ex ipso incensum adolere inchoans, omnem phani ambitum circuit. Demum ad sanctum altare iterum rediens, psalmorum incipit melos; concinen-
tibus secum sacra carmina omnibus ecclesiastici ordinis gradibus; deinde
ministrorum officio sanctarum scripturarum lectio suo ordine recitatur.
Post hac, extra delubrum catechumini fiunt, et cum ipsis energumini, et ii
quoque qui in pœnitentia sunt; manent autem intus soli qui divina spectare
merentur atque percipere. Porro ministrorum alii quidem pro clausis
templi foribus astant; alii proprii aliquid muneris agunt. Qui vero ipsius
ordinis præcipui sunt, una cum sacerdotibus sanctum panem et benedictionis calicem sacrosanctis altaribus imponunt, cum ante præcesserit ab
omni clero universalis laus atque confessio. Ad hæc venerandus antistes
orationem sanctissimam peragens, pacem sanctam omnibus nunciat; et cum
se mutuo omnes salutaverint mystica sanctorum recitatio fit   Ubi vero
manus tum antistes tum sacerdotes aqua laverunt, pontifex ad medium
divini assistit altaris; circumstant autem soli cum sacerdotibus electi
quique ex ministrorum numero. At vero pontifex cum divina munera
laude prosecutus fuerit, sacrosancta et augustissima mysteria conficit, et quæ
(ante) laudaverat venerandis operta atque abdita signis in conspectum agit;
divinaque munera reverenter ostendens, ad sacram illorum communionem
et ipse convertitur, et reliquos ut communicent hortatur.   Sumpta demum
atque omnibus tradita communione divina gratias referens finem mysteriis
imponit.   Ac multi quidem sola in signa divina prospiciunt; ipse autem
semper divino spiritu ad excelsa signorum initia fælicibus et intelligibilibus
intuenda luminibus, pontificia dignitate ac merito mundiciaque singulari
divini capaciorisque sensus attolitur."—Dionysius, Eccles. Hierarch., cap.
iii., pars ii., p. 63; quoted in Cranmer's MS. Collections, vol. i., fol. 213,
214.

with the priests, place upon the divine altar the sacred bread and the cup of blessing, after that the Catholic hymn of praise has been first confessed by the whole body of the Church. After this the divine Hierarch concludes the sacred prayer, and declares the holy peace to all; and after all have kissed each other, the mystical reading of the sacred tablets is observed. And the Hierarch and the priests having washed their hands in water, the Hierarch stands in the midst of the divine altar, and those alone who are chosen from the deacons stand round with the Priests. And the Hierarch, when he has sung of the sacred work of God,[1] consecrates the divine (mysteries), and brings under view the things sung of by means of the sacredly offered symbols. And having displayed the gifts belonging to the Work of God, he approaches to the sacred communion of them himself, and encourages the rest to do the same. And after he has received and distributed the divine communion, he concludes with sacred thanksgiving. And herein, whilst the multitude have only gained a glance at the divine symbols, he is himself continually led up by the Divine Spirit to the holy originals of the mysteries, by blessed contemplation of the mind, in a hierarchic manner, in the purity of a divine habit of being."

The points in this quotation which deserve special notice from English churchmen are the following :—

1. The dismissal of all unworthy to communicate after the instruction is finished.   2. The act of united worship preceding the Offertory, which from ancient times was interpreted as meaning the Creed.   In the Greek text this " Catholic Hymn of Praise " is afterwards described as " named by some the symbol of worship, by others in my opinion in a more divine manner, the Hierarchic

---

[1] This appears to refer to the work of Redemption. It is so explained by Dean Colet, " On the Hierarchies," p. 93 ; and by M. Bucer, *ut supra.*

Eucharist (or thanksgiving), as comprising the divine
gifts which come from God to us."[1] It seems, therefore, to support the view that a Eucharistic meaning
should be attached to every part of the service ; as
is presently expressed in our Prayer for the Church,
in which we mention that God has taught us " to make
prayers and supplications and to give thanks for all
men." 3. The Kiss of Peace and reading of the diptychs, which agree with the Gallican practice, though
in the reverse order. 4. The simplicity of the description
of the Canon of Consecration, which accords in a remarkable manner with our English service. After the Hierarch has taken his stand at the middle of the altar, he
sings of the sacred work of God." This appears to correspond with the Preface and Sanctus. He then " consecrates the divine mysteries." This is afterwards
explained as including " an act of humble confession of
unworthiness, and a prayer that he may be made worthy
for his office, and as much as possible like Christ, to the
end that he may duly consecrate and distribute the sacrament, and that those who draw near to communicate
may receive worthily."[2] This seems to correspond very
closely with our Prayer of Humble Access preceding the
Commemoration of Redemption and the Consecration.

[1] Eccles. Hierarch., cap. iii., pars iii., Latin Version, p. 66 ; see
above, note 3, p. 183.
[2] " Quocirca reverenter simul et ex pontificali officio post sacras divinorum
operum laudes, quod hostiam salutarem (quæ supra ipsum est) litet, se
excusat, ad ipsum primo decenter exclamans, tu dixisti, Hoc facite in meam
commemorationem. Deinde tanto ministerio ad imitationem Dei instituto
dignus fieri postulat, et similis ipso Christo pro viribus evadere, ut et sacra-
menta sancte conficiat et caste distribuat, et qui ad communionem accessuri
sunt digne participent: sicque venerandissima mysteria consummat."—
Eccles. Hierarch., cap. iii., pars iii., p. 67.

5. The Communion of the People, which follows immediately without mention of the Lord's Prayer. 6. The concluding Thanksgiving, which is mentioned as the fitting end of the service.

Besides these ancient writings there were other more modern works which helped to guide the course taken in the formation of our English Prayer Book. It is evident that the desire for reform was not confined to English churchmen in the middle of the sixteenth century, for both in France and Germany previous attempts had been made by those in authority to amend the existing services. The result of these attempts had been recently made public, and there is no doubt that they largely influenced our reformers in carrying out their work.

Urged by the growing desire for reform, Herman, Archbishop of Cologne and Prince Elector, held what was called " a simple and religious consultation," for determining " by what means a Christian reformation, and founded in God's Word, of Doctrine, Administration of the divine Sacraments, of Ceremonies, and the whole cure of souls and other ecclesiastical ministeries may be begun." The result was published in Latin, A.D. 1535, in the form of suggestions rather than of the offices themselves, and without any appearance of ecclesiastical authority.[1] It was afterwards published in English,

---

[1] Dean Hook mentions that the copy of this original edition, entitled " Hermanni . . . simplex ac pia deliberatio," &c., Bonnæ, 1535, which belonged to Archbishop Cranmer and bears his autograph, is in the Library of Chichester Cathedral.—Hook, " Lives of Archbishops," vol. vii., p. 289.

In the following year a Provincial Council was held at Cologne, "auctoritate Hermanni Archiepiscopi (qui postea in hæresim lapsus est) pro refor-

A.D. 1547, and a revised edition was printed the following year, only a few months before our First English Prayer Book was brought out.[1] It has been commonly ascribed to the labours of Melancthon and Bucer, upon the authority of Strype, who says of it, " It is an excellent book, and was compiled, if I mistake not, by the pains and learning of Melancthon and Bucer, and reviewed, examined, and allowed by the Elector himself."[2] There can be no doubt that this book exerted a great influence in the progress of the Reformation. It is marked throughout by a tone of deep piety, reverence, and knowledge of Holy Scripture. Strype adds the following testimony to its value :—

" Oct. 30th, 1547, came forth translated into English the Book of the Reformation of the Church of Colen ; whereof

matione clericorum et cærimoniarum ecclesiæ celebratum."—Labbe, Concilia, A.D. 1536, tom. xiv., p. 484. Labbe makes no mention of any formal acceptance of this work, but he records many canons which urge attention to the spiritual side of religion. *Pars* vii. is devoted to the instruction of the people, and urges that men should often receive the Communion after preparing for it, and, if necessary, after private confession (Can. 18-21); that the sacrifice of the Mass is a *representative* sacrifice (Can. 27); that prayers for the dead are of primitive origin, but that men must live in a manner agreeable to such prayers in order to be benefited by them (Can. 28). Cranmer frequently refers to these canons in his MS. Collections under the title " Capitulum Coloniense," vol. i., fol. 112, 253, vol. ii., fol. 177; but no reference has been found to the book above mentioned. The Canons were published at Cologne, 1538 (British Museum), with a tract on Christian Doctrine by Archbishop Herman, named " Enchiridion ; " but Cranmer's copy has not yet been found.

[1] " A simple and religious Consultation of us Herman, &c.," London, 1547; revised edition, 1548. (British Museum.)

[2] This is confirmed by the work, before mentioned, " Martini Buceri defensio," Basle, 1618. The opening chapter is addressed in the name of Herman to Christian readers, and Martin Bucer is specially mentioned as having been singled out for attack for the part which he had taken.

Herman, the good Archbishop and Elector, was the great instrument. This book showed itself in this kingdom at this juncture undoubtedly by the means of Archbishop Cranmer, and probably of the Protector, as a silent invitation to the people of the land to a reformation, and as a motive to incline them to be willing to forsake the old superstition when they should see the beauty of a reformed Church so lively laid before them in this book. And perhaps it was intended to serve as some pattern to the heads and governors of this Church, whereby to direct their pains they were now ere long to take about the emendation of religious worship." [1]

The suggestions "how the Lord's Supper must be celebrated" were in striking contrast with the ceremonial ordained in the Sarum Rubrics, but some of them would have led to the overthrow of beliefs and practices which had been held dear from the earliest times. Happily our reformers were guided to reject what was novel in this "Consultation," whilst they made use of what was in harmony with the teaching of the ancient Liturgies. It should be noticed especially that the example of true and pure-hearted devotion, which was here given, evidently helped to give a tone of scriptural calmness and earnestness to our English service. The following extracts will give an idea both of what was accepted and of what was rejected by our reformers :—

The Simple and Religious Consultation of us Herman,
by the Grace of God Archbishop of Cologne,
and Prince Elector.

*When the people be come together, forasmuch as before all things
we should acknowledge and confess our sins . . . the Minister*

[1] Strype, Eccles. Memor., vol. ii., part i., p. 41.

when he shall come to the Altar shall make a confession in the name of the whole congregation, after this sort :

Almighty Everlasting God, the Father of our Lord Jesus Christ, the Maker of all things, the Judge of all men, we acknowledge and we lament that we were conceived and born in sins . . . have mercy upon us, most merciful Father, through Thy only Son our Lord Jesus Christ, &c.

One of the following five Gospels should then be said :

S. John iii. God so loved . . . everlasting Life.

Or 1 Tim. i. This is a sure saying . . . save sinners.

Or S. John iii. The Father loveth the Son . . . everlasting Life.

Or Acts x. All the Prophets bear witness . . . through Him.

Or 1 S. John ii. My little children, if any have sinned . . . for our sins.

The Pastor shall say further.

Because our Blessed Lord hath left this power to His Congregation that it may absolve them from sins and restore them into favour of the Heavenly Father which being repentant for their sins do truly believe in Christ the Lord, I the Minister of Christ and the Congregation declare and pronounce remission of sins, the favour of God and life everlasting through our Lord Jesus Christ, to all them which be sorry for their sins, which have true faith in Christ the Lord, and desire to approve themselves unto Him.

The Clerks shall then sing something in Latin out of Holy Scripture, for an Entrance *or* Beginning. *After which* Kyrie Eleison *and* Gloria in excelsis, *and let the people sing both in Dutch (i.e. German).*[1]

A COLLECT (which should agree with the words "The Lord be with you," and the response of the people, "and

[1] This is of great interest, for it set the example of using the vulgar tongue in Church services, though the confusion of the two languages here suggested would have been intolerable.

with thy spirit," as signifying that they also pray together with the Minister, for so Chrysostom interpreteth this saying).

THE EPISTLE ; *to be followed by the* Graile *or some* Sequence.

THE GOSPEL ; *after which an* Interpretation and Ordinary Sermon.

After the Sermon, a Prayer for all states of men and necessities of the Congregation, *after this sort.*

1, We must desire remission of sins and the Holy Ghost to be given unto us ; 2, for the Church and Ministers ; 3, for the King, Archbishop, Prince, and Magistrates ; 4, for those which yet pertain not to God's Kingdom ; 5, for the tempted and afflicted ; 6, for the Congregation.

THE CREED, *to be sung by the whole Congregation, during which the faithful are to offer their oblations, every man according to the blessing which he hath received of God.*[1]

The Priest. The Lord be with you.

The People. And with thy spirit.

The Priest. Lift up your hearts.

The People. We have unto the Lord.

The Priest. Let us give thanks, &c.

THE PREFACE ; THE SANCTUS.

Then the Priest shall sing the words of the Lord's Supper in Dutch (i.e. German).

Our Lord the night in which He was delivered, &c.

These words must be sung with great reverence, and plainly. And the people shall say to these words "Amen," *which all the old Church observed, and the Greeks do yet observe the same.*

The Priest shall add, Let us pray.

Our Father, which art in heaven, &c.

The People. Amen.

---

[1] This should be compared with the Account of the Holy Communion by Pseudo-Dionysius, see above, p. 186.

The Priest. The Lord's peace be ever with you.

The People. And with thy spirit.

After this they which be admitted to the Communion . . . shall come to the Lord's Board religiously. First men and then women, and the whole Sacrament shall be given to them all, that they may be partakers of the Body and Blood of the Lord, receiving not only Bread, but also the Cup, even as He instituted it.

At the exhibition of the Body let the Pastor say : Take and eat to thy health the Body of the Lord which was delivered for thy sins.

At the exhibition of the Cup : Take and drink to thy health the Blood of the Lord which was shed for thy sins.

After the Communion let Agnus Dei *be sung; and hymns, if the Communion shall give so much time and leisure.*

When the Communion is ended let the Priest sing, turning to the people :

The Lord be with you, &c.

Let us pray.

Almighty, Everlasting God, we give thanks to Thy exceeding goodness, because Thou hast fed us with the Body of Thy Only Begotten Son, and given us His Blood to drink. We humbly beseech Thee work in us with Thy Spirit, that as we have received this divine Sacrament with our mouths, so we may also receive and ever hold fast with true faith Thy grace, remission of sins, and communion with Christ Thy Son. All which things Thou hast exhibited unto us in these Sacraments, through our Lord Jesus Christ, &c.

Last, let the Pastor bless the people with these words :

The Lord bless thee and keep thee, &c.

Or,

The Blessing of God the Father, the Son, and the Holy Ghost, be with us and remain with us for ever.[1]

[1] That our reformers took counsel with Archbishop Herman is well

O

The references made in the above suggestions to Chrysostom, and to the practice of the congregation joining in *Amen,* which "the Greeks do yet observe," are of great interest and value, because they prove distinctly that at the time of the Reformation men were not only acquainted with the early Greek Fathers, but were also studying the Greek Liturgies. This is confirmed by the discovery of the Latin version of the Liturgy of S. Chrysostom made by Erasmus for Bishop Fisher, which has been given in a previous chapter. The knowledge of this Liturgy is hereby brought home to our own divines in England at this period. So that we are prepared not merely to acknowledge the possibility of a resemblance between our English Service and the Greek Liturgies, but to look for such a likeness.[1]

It is doubtful whether the Clementine Liturgy, which

known. Cardwell says that King Edward VI. " appointed the Archbishop of Canterbury and others to draw an order of divine worship, having respect to the pure religion of Christ, taught in Holy Scripture, and to the practice of the primitive Church." . . . " Cranmer corresponded with Herman, and interested the King's Council in his behalf; and it cannot be doubted that his book was much employed by the commission assembled at Windsor in the compilation of their new form of Common Prayer."—Cardwell, " Two Liturgies of Edward VI.," Preface, xvi. The above extracts are taken from the edition published in London, 1548, fol. cci.-ccxii.

[1] Amongst the particulars for which our English Service is indebted to the Eastern Liturgies may be mentioned : the commencement with a form resembling a Litany ; the prayer for the Queen; the quotation, " God so loved the world," &c. ; the humble form of the prayer, " We do not presume," &c. ; the brief consecration prayer; the Invocation of the Holy Spirit in the Prayer Book of 1549 (now omitted); the form of the words of institution, " In the same night," &c.; the addition to the Lord's prayer of the ascription, " For Thine is the kingdom," &c. These particulars were for the most part strange to the Western Church of the sixteenth century. Many of them may have been adopted through the suggestions of Herman, but some seem to have been taken direct from the Liturgy of S. Chrysostom.

is found in the Apostolical Constitutions, may be added amongst the examples of Communion Services within reach of our reformers. If it could be proved to have been known to them it might be supposed that their authority for the omission of the Lord's Prayer after the Prayer of Consecration had been discovered. But without further knowledge than is at present possessed it cannot be asserted that the Constitutions were known to Archbishop Cranmer.[1]

The use which was made of the suggestions of Archbishop Herman and of the Liturgy of S. Chrysostom in drawing up the Order of Communion in 1548, and the First Prayer Book of 1549, will be recognized at once. But it has been pointed out in the previous chapter that

[1] This work was first made known to the world by its discoverer, Carolus Capellius, a Venetian noble, by means of extracts, which he named Epitome Apostolicarum Constitutionum, published at Ingolstad, 1546. (Durham University Library.) The book contains a letter dated 1545, from Joh. Cochlæus to Capellius, urging him to publish the full text whilst the Council of Trent was sitting, and a dedication from Capellius to Pope Paul III., dated 1544, discussing the causes of the sad state of the Church, and expressing the hope that the antidote would be found in the Apostolical Constitutions. The epitome itself consists of twelve pages, and is confined to extracts about the dignity of the ecclesiastical orders, taken, with the exception of the first two pages, from Apost. Constit., lib. iii., cap. 10, 11, lib. ii.,cap. 27-34. It was reprinted in Crabbe's Concilia, 1551, pp. 27-30. The earliest known version of the full text of the Constitutions, translated into Latin by Car. Bovius, was published at Venice, 1563, and dedicated to certain bishops then at the Council of Trent. The Greek Text, edited by Franciscus Turrianus, issued from the same press in the same year. Neither editor mentions the other; but Turrianus states that he made use of three MSS., one from Calabria, one from Sicily, and the third from Crete. (Both of these books are in the British Museum.) The Apostolical Constitutions soon became known, and were quoted by M. Harding in his controversy with Jewel, which was published 1565.—Jewel's works (Parker Soc.), pp. 110, 111, 267.

the difference between these services and the Communion Service of the Second Prayer Book of 1552 is
so great that it is necessary to look for some other guide
which may have led our reformers in this revision of their
work.

It is well known that about this period, by the help
of the printing press, many ancient works became
known to the world at large for the first time.
Amongst others, a short treatise in two books upon
" The Offices of the Church " was published simultaneously in two editions at Leipsic and Antwerp
in 1534, which had been written by Isidore, Bishop of
Hispalis (Seville), A.D. 603-636.[1]   It is dedicated to
Dr. Robert Ridley (uncle of Nicholas Ridley, who afterwards became Bishop of Rochester), and mention is
made in the dedication that the editor, Johannes Cochlæus, had previously sent him a letter " by the hands of
the king's ambassador, Sir Thomas Cranmer, that learned
man and renowned theologian."[2]   The dedication ends
with the prayer that " God may bring my purpose to

---

[1] Isidori Hispalensis, de Officiis Ecclesiasticis.   Lipsiæ, 1534, 4to.;
Antwerp, 1534, 8vo. (British Museum.)

[2] Cranmer was appointed as orator at the Imperial Court by commission
dated January, 1530-1.   Whilst " in this ambassage with the Emperor, the
Archbishop of Canterbury, William Warram, being departed this transitory
life, the said Dr. Cranmer was nominated and elected Archbishop of Canterbury in his room."—Ralf Morice, " Anecdotes of Archbishop Cranmer,"p.244,
edited by Nicholls, Camden Society.   He was consecrated March, 1533.
So that by the time this book was published he was archbishop.   It is
interesting to find that his learning was recognized by the literary men of
the day, and the mention of his name in the dedication may be accepted
as a sure proof that the book was brought under his notice ; whilst the
expressions there used would lead him to accept it as a help against the
violent views of the extreme party.   But no copy has been found bearing
his autograph.

pass, that it may fruitfully admonish our bishops and presbyters of their duty, and recall the leaders of the new sects from their impious attempts, and deter them from their wild contest, like the battle of the giants, against the ancient rites and ceremonies of the Church." That this work became well known in the course of the next twenty years is evident from the frequent references to it which are found in the writings of the reformers.[1]

Isidore lived in Spain at about the time when Gregory the Great was Pope of Rome, and as Gregory revised the Roman Liturgy, which for all future generations bore his name, so Isidore of Seville revised the Spanish form of the Gallican Liturgy, which in consequence was ever afterwards spoken of as "secundum regulam Beati Isidori." This Liturgy he describes in the above mentioned treatise, "Upon the Offices of the Church." He states that it consists of seven prayers; and instead of describing the perfection of the one prayer of the Roman Canon, he supposes that there is a necessity for the number of the prayers being seven, " either as represent-

---

[1] For instance, Bullinger, who was minister of the church at Zurich, quotes (Decades, vol. i., p. 692, Parker Society), De Eccles. Officiis, lib. i., cap. x., to the effect that prayers and lessons should be said in the language of the people, so that all might join in them. Pilkington, Bishop of Durham, shows (Works, page 497, Parker Society) that he was aware of the Liturgy herein described by Isidore, for he asks, " What order or Mass was it?—was it Chrysostom's, Basil's, Justin's, Tertullian's, Austin's, Dionysius', Isidorus', Gregory's, Rabanus', the Romans', or whose else?" and (page 503) he quotes from the beginning of the very chapter which contains the account of the Liturgy, de Eccles. Offic., lib. i., cap. xv. [In this volume a different reference is given, viz., lib. i., cap. v., de origine officiorum, evidently in error.] Becon, Whitgift, and Jewel also quote from the works of Isidore.

ing the perfect universality of the Church, or because of the sevenfold gifts of the Holy Spirit." He then gives the following brief description of the seven prayers, to which careful attention is invited. He says, " The first is a prayer or address of admonition towards the people that they may be aroused to pray God earnestly.[1] The second is a prayer of invocation upon God, that He may mercifully receive the prayers of the faithful, and their oblations. But the third is poured forth for those who offer, or for the faithful departed, that by the same sacrifice they may obtain pardon.[2] The fourth is introduced afterwards for the Kiss of peace, that all being reconciled in charity one with another may unite together as worthy of the Sacrament of the Body and Blood of Christ, because the indivisible Body of Christ allows not of the dissension of anyone.[3] The fifth comes as an Introduction (or Preface) in the sanctification of the oblation, in which also the creatures of earth and the whole company of heavenly powers are called out to the praise of God, and Hosanna in the Highest is sung, because by the birth of the Saviour, of the family of David, salvation has come to the world even to the highest.[4] Moreover, the sixth then follows as the confirmation of the sacrament, that

[1] The first prayer may be compared with the English Exhortation, " Dearly beloved in the Lord; " and the words *Fratres charissimi* are found in it in almost every service.

[2] The second and third prayers take the place of our prayer for the Church Militant. Special notice should be paid to the fact that the prayer for the Church was thus separated from the Consecration Prayer.

[3] The fourth prayer may be compared in respect of its position and intention with our Invitation, Confession, Absolution, and Comfortable Words. See this further explained in Chapter VII., page 225.

[4] The fifth prayer corresponds with our Preface, Sanctus, and Prayer of Consecration.

the oblation which is offered to God, being sanctified by the Holy Spirit, may be confirmed (as the oblation) of the Body and Blood.[1] The last of all is the prayer which our Lord taught His disciples to pray, saying, Our Father, &c."[2]

It has been explained in the previous chapter that the ancient Liturgy here described had been recently published to the world by Cardinal Ximenes under the name of the Mozarabic Missal; and that the close connection between this country and Spain at the beginning of the sixteenth century makes it improbable that it could have been unknown to Archbishop Cranmer.[3] A

[1] The sixth prayer may be compared, in respect of the contents of many examples of it, with our Prayer of Humble Access.

[2] *De missa et orationibus.* "Ordo autem Missæ vel orationum quibus oblata Deo sacrificia consecrantur, primum a sancto Petro est institutus, cujus celebrationem uno eodemque modo universus peragit orbis. PRIMA earundem oratio admonitionis est erga populum, ut excitentur ad exorandum Deum. SECUNDA invocationis ad Deum est, ut clementer suscipiat preces fidelium oblationemque eorum. TERTIA autem effunditur pro offerentibus sive pro defunctis fidelibus, ut per idem sacrificium veniam consequantur. QUARTA post hæc infertur pro osculo pacis, ut charitate omnes reconciliati invicem, digni sacramento corporis et sanguinis Christi consocientur, quia non recipit dissensionem cujusquam Christi indivisibile corpus. QUINTA infertur illatio in sanctificatione oblationis, in qua etiam ad Dei laudem terrestrium creatura, virtutum cœlestium universitas provocatur, et Osanna in excelsis cantatur, quòd salvatore de genere Dauid nascente, salus mundo usque ad excelsa pervenerit. Porro SEXTA exhinc succedit confirmatio sacramenti ut oblatio quæ Deo offertur, sanctificata per Spiritum sanctum corporis et sanguinis confirmetur. Harum ULTIMA est oratio quam Dominus noster orare discipulos suos instituit, dicens, Pater noster, &c." Isidore Hispalensis, de Eccles. Officiis, lib. i., cap. xv. See Comparative Table of Liturgies facing the title-page.

[3] This Missal is now easily accessible, having been published in Migne's Patrologia, vol. lxxxv. It is described thus : "Missale Mixtum secundum regulam beati Isidori, dictum Mozarabes." In the course of the nine centuries which had elapsed between the age of Isidore and the time when

specimen of its services is here given, which will furnish
an idea of the scriptural tone of its prayers, and make it
possible to compare their arrangement with the order of
this Missal was brought out of its obscurity by Cardinal Ximenes, some
additions and changes had been introduced which need to be considered and
cleared away before the original service can be studied in its purity. But
these changes are few and unimportant in comparison with those which had
been introduced into other Missals of the West, and in a general way they
can be detected with certainty. The ritual directions, including almost all
of the more modern additions, are found chiefly in the service for the First
Sunday in Advent (folio 1-7), and in the service headed "Omnium
Offerentium," with its preliminary matter (folio 217-234); and the student
should be on his guard against accepting these rubrics and devotions without due consideration. The words "si placuerit" in certain rubrics point
to alterations which were not universally followed; as, for instance, "Hic
ponat incensum in thuribulo et incenset sacrificium si placuerit; postea
inclinet se sacerdos in medium altaris junctis manibus" (folio 3). Similarly,
the rubrics relating to the offering of the oblations point clearly to a variation of custom between the ancient and the more modern Mozarabic Ritual.
The ancient custom was for clergy and people to offer their gifts whilst the
Sacrificium or Offertory was sung (*vide* note to folio 119). That this custom
fell into disuse is clear from the rubric, "Sacerdos vertat se ad populum; et
faciat offertorium si voluerit" (folio 3). The devotions preparatory to the
Mass (folio 217-220) are clearly additions to the ancient services, adopted
from mediæval missals; and under the service named "Omnium Offerentium," other comparatively modern directions are given according as the
Mass was private or public (*vide* note to folio 223). Attention will presently
be called to a more important alteration in the form of the Prayer of Consecration, but in general the Missal is singularly free from such additions
and changes, and in every service the seven prayers described by Isidore
stand out clearly, and form the "Missa Fidelium" as in ancient times.

[Since the above was in type the author has had the opportunity of
examining two out of the three Missals of the tenth century which have
been recently acquired by the British Museum (Addit. MSS. 30844, 30846).
The MSS. are incomplete; but one service contains the "Sanctus" at length
(MS. 30844, fol. 48), and is probably as full a guide to the services as was
then given. They prove that the old services had undergone very considerable revision when they were edited by Cardinal Ximenes. No trace of the
service "Omnium Offerentium" is found, though the services "Feria vi
Paschæ" and "Octava Paschæ," between which it now occurs, are given

our English Communion Service. It is not to be expected that any special resemblance will be detected between the words of these prayers and our own, because almost every prayer in every service throughout the year is different. But attention should be paid to the resemblance in the general arrangement and character of the prayers in the two services, especially in the following particulars : *Preces,* or a Litany of a peculiar character preceding the Epistle, which may have encouraged the use of the commandments in the English Service; the form of exhortation contained in the first prayer; the prayers for the Church coming next, instead of in the Prayer of Consecration ; the giving of the Kiss, and the prayer for true peace with God, corresponding with the position of the Confession, Absolution, and Comfortable Words ; the short form of Consecration Prayer; the prominence given to the act of communion of the people, mention of which was omitted in all other existing service books; the omission of *Agnus Dei ;* the form of post-Communion Thanksgiving, followed by words of exultation, which may have given support to the plan of placing " Gloria in excelsis " here. On the other hand, when we consider the differences between the service described by Isidore and our own, we find that they are mainly confined to the omission of the sixth prayer and of the Lord's Prayer after the Consecration.[1]

very nearly the same as now (MS. 30846, fol. 36-57 ; Migne, fol. 211-214, 234-237). The Lections were different, and Sermons followed the Gospel. But the prayers were the same as now, though frequently arranged under different days ; and " Post Sanctus" ended with the words " Christus Dominus," or " Christus," instead of "Ipse Dominus ac Redemptor eternus " (MS. 30844, fol. 48 ; 30846, fol. 44).]

[1] It has been thought by some that the Consultation of Herman may

THE GALLICAN LITURGY, ACCORDING TO THE MOZARABIC RITE.[1]

The ante-Communion Service consisted of an Introit, named "The Office at the Mass," consisting of a verse of Holy Scripture with the "Gloria." This was followed on Sundays and

have been a sufficient guide to our reformers in the changes of the Second Prayer Book. But against this view it must be considered, that in this case we might expect that the Confession, Absolution, and Comfortable Words would have been found in the position of the Ten Commandments; that the Consecration Prayer would have consisted of the words of institution alone, concluding with the Lord's Prayer; that the singing of the *Agnus Dei* during the Communion would have been continued; and that the Blessing would have followed the post-Communion Thanksgiving. If the object of Archbishop Cranmer had been merely to satisfy the extreme Protestant party, nothing would have been so likely to effect this as to have followed the Consultation of Herman; by which means a service would have been produced similar to that which is described as now prevailing in the Lutheran churches of Saxony and Prussia.

[1] Reference is made to the Mozarabic Missal as being an example of the ancient Gallican Liturgy which was actually in use at the time of the Reformation. In France the use of the ancient form of service had been superseded by the introduction of the Roman Canon since the beginning of the ninth century. Four specimens of Gallican Missals are in existence, printed in Muratori's Liturgia Romana vetus, viz., Missale Gothicum, Missale Francorum, Missale Gallicanum vetus, and Sacramentarium Gallicanum, or Codex Bobiensis. But of these the first alone contains the ancient Gallican Service in its integrity; the others consist of services adapted for use with the Roman Canon, in which the Gallican and the Roman Liturgies are mingled together. In the Missale Gothicum the seven prayers described by Isidore are found in the same positions as in the Mozarabic Missal, and correspond with them, though under different names, being headed thus:—*Præfatio; Collectio sequitur; Collectio post nomina; Collectio ad Pacem; Contestatio,* or *Immolatio Missæ,* and *Post Sanctus; Post mysterium,* or *Post secreta;* and *Ante orationem Dominicam.* After which are added, *Post Orationem Dominicam; Benedictio Populi; Post Communionem,* or *Post Eucharistiam;* and *Consummatio Missæ.*

Festivals by "Gloria in excelsis Deo."[1] Then came the Collect ; then a reading from the Prophets ; then the "Hymn of the three Children," *Benedicite omnia opera,* followed by Psalm cvi., *Confitemini Domino ;*[2] then an Anthem named "Psallendo ;"[3] and in Lent and on certain other days *Preces,* or a Litany, followed, and a Prayer *post precem.*[4] Silence was then proclaimed, and the Epistle was read, "Thanks be to God" having been first sung. Then the words "Glory be to Thee, O Lord," followed by the Gospel. The versicle and response, "The Lord be with you always. And with thy spirit," were repeated at the end of both Epistle and Gospel. After this was sung an Anthem, named "Lauda," consisting of Alleluia, with a verse, generally from the Psalms.[5]

In the Gallican Church the Sermon or Homily came next,

[1] Folio 1, 220, 221. This may have been an addition to the original service, for there is no sign of the use of "Gloria in excelsis" in Gallican Missals in this position. In the Gallican Sacramentary, or "Liturgia Bobiensis," it occurs after the Roman Canon, as though it was sung after the Communion at the time when the use of the "Missa Romensis" was first introduced into the Gallican Church.—Muratori, vol. ii., pp. 776, 780. But see Addit. MS. 30844, fol. 39, where a similar form of words, if not the same, is appointed.

[2] Folio 93. Fourth Council of Toledo (A.D. 633), Canon 14, directed that the Hymn of the three Children should never be omitted.—Labbe's Concilia, vol. v., p. 1704. Psalm cvi. seems to have been added to this at some later period.

[3] This seems to be referred to by Isidore under the name of *Responsoria,* which, he says, "came long ago from Italy ; being so called because, after it had been sung by one, the choir repeated it in response."—Isidore, de Eccles. Offic., lib. i., cap. viii.

[4] Folio 94. Compare the use of a Litany between the Epistle and Gospel in the Stowe Missal.

[5] Isidore, de Eccl. Offic., lib. i., cap. xiii., describes "Laudes" as consisting of the repetition of Alleluia, the Hour Service of this name being then known by the name of Mattins ; cf. "Ratio institutionis cursuum eccles.," at end of Gallican Sacram.—Muratori, vol. ii., p. 966.

followed by the dismissal of the Catechumens, but no mention of either appears in the modern Mozarabic Rite.[1]

The Offertory or *Sacrificium* was then sung, whilst the people and clergy offered their oblations. Incense was then used, after which the washing of hands followed.[2] Then came the seven main prayers of the Liturgy, the first of which was introduced by the words " Incipit Missa."

The following are the Seven Prayers which form the Service for the Sunday after the Ascension.[3]

First Prayer, named Missa.

Dearly beloved Brethren, now that the mystery of the Resurrection is completed, let us all exult in body and heart. Let us not now weep with the guardians of the tomb, keeping watch over the sacred Body; but mingle our rejoicings with the Angels who tell of the risen Saviour. For He dispenses now with any care being spent upon His corpse, since He returns to the Father, and would have an end put to the watches of death that is death no more. Let us be indeed assured of the consummation of our hope, for He led captivity captive as He returned on High, and He will give the promised gifts to men. *Amen.*

[1] See the description of the Gallican Service in the Exposition given by Germanus.—Martene, lib. i., cap. iv., art. 12, ordo 1. Such sermons are also provided in the tenth century Missals before mentioned.

[2] Folio 3, 224. These were very ancient customs, but probably the present rubrics and devotions are additions of more modern times. No mention of them has been found in the above-named MSS.

[3] Folio 254-256. *Missa.* Mysterio Resurrectionis impleto : et corporibus, Fratres Carissimi, cuncti exultemus et cordibus. Nec jam cum sepulchri custodibus sacri corporis defleamus excubias : sed cum Angelis qui redivivum nunciant Salvatorem nostra gaudia misceamus. Etenim deinceps curam sibi funeris excusat impendi : qui rediens ad Patrem vacuatæ mortis excubias vult privari. Simus sane de spei nostre consummatione securi : nam qui in altum remeans captivitatem duxit: dabit dona hominibus que promisit. *Resp.* Amen.

Through Thy mercy, O our God, who art blessed, and livest and rulest over all for ever. *Amen.*

Let us pray.

Answer. Hagios, Hagios, Hagios. O Lord God, King Eternal, to Thee be praise and thanks.

The Holy Catholic Church let us remember in our prayers: that the Lord may graciously vouchsafe to increase it in faith and hope and charity. All the fallen, the prisoners, the sick, and the travellers let us remember, that the Lord may graciously vouchsafe to redeem, to heal, and to comfort them.

Answer. Grant it, Eternal Almighty God.

Second Prayer, For the Holy Church, *named* Alia Oratio.

O Christ our God, who hast withdrawn Thy bodily presence from Thy disciples by ascending into Heaven, grant us in spirit to love Thee, whom now in the flesh we cannot see, and yet faithfully expect for judgment. Create a new heart and a right spirit within us, that we who have now celebrated the festival of Thine Ascension may obtain the promised aid of Thy Holy Spirit. *Amen.*

Fixed ending. Per misericordiam tuam Deus noster qui es benedictus et vivis et omnia regis in secula seculorum. *Resp.* Amen.

[The resemblance to Eastern forms here and elsewhere should be noticed ; above, pp. 46, 47.]

Oremus. *Resp.* Agyos, Agyos, Agyos. Domine Deus Rex eterne tibi laudes et gratias.

Ecclesiam sanctam catholicam in orationibus in mente habeamus : ut eam Dominus fide et spe et charitate propicius ampliare dignetur : omnes lapsos captivos infirmos atque peregrinos in mente habeamus : ut eos Dominus propicius redimere : sanare et confortare dignetur. *Resp.* Presta eterne omnipotens Deus. (Folio 3.)

Alia oratio. Christe Deus qui ascendendo in celos presentiam corporalem tuis subtraxisti discipulis : permitte nos ut te spiritu diligamus quem in carne nunc videre nequimus : et tamen ad judicium fideliter expectamus. Crea in nobis cor novum et spiritum rectum. Ut qui jam Ascensionis tue celebravimus festum : promissum a te mereamur suscipere Spiritum Sanctum. *Resp.* Amen.

Through Thy mercy, O our God, in whose sight the names of the saints, apostles and martyrs, confessors and virgins are recited.

Recital of the Names of the Departed.

Third Prayer, named Post Nomina.

Thy creatures are glad that Thou, the Son of God, hast ascended into Heaven to the Father. Therefore we humbly pray, with contrite hearts, that Thou wilt both fulfil in us the promise of Thy Spirit, and also grant unto those who are departed the gift of everlasting rest. *Amen.*

For Thou art the life of the living, the health of the sick, and the rest of all the faithful departed, for ever and ever. *Amen.*

Fixed ending. Per misericordiam tuam Deus noster in cujus conspectu Sanctorum Apostolorum et Martyrum Confessorum atque Virginum nomina recitantur. *Resp.* Amen.

[Offerunt Deo Domino oblationem Sacerdotes nostri : Papa Romensis : et reliqui pro se et pro omni clero ac plebibus ecclesie sibimet consignatis : vel pro universa fraternitate : item offerunt universi Presbiteri Diachoni : Clerici ac populi circumastantes : in honorem sanctorum pro se et suis. *Resp.* Offerunt pro se et pro universa fraternitate.

Facientes commemorationem beatissimorum Apostolorum et Martyrum: gloriose Sancte Marie Virginis, Zacharie, Joannis, Infantum, Petri, Pauli, Johannis, Jacobi, Andree, Philippi, Thome, Bartholomei, Matthei, Jacobi, Symonis et Jude, Matthie, Marci et Luce. *Resp.* Et omnium martyrum.

Item pro spiritibus pausantium, Hilarii, Athanasii, Martini, &c. *Resp.* Et omnium pausantium. (Folio 4.) These Commemorations are not found in the ancient Missals before mentioned.]

Post nomina. Ascendisse te in celos ad Patrem Dei Filium creatura tua letatur. Et ideo suppliciter cordis contritione exposcimus ; ut et in nobis pollicitationem tui spiritus impleas, et defunctis donum eterne quietis impertias. *Resp.* Amen.

Fixed ending. Quia tu es vita vivorum : sanitas infirmorum : ac requies omnium fidelium defunctorum in eterna secula seculorum. *Resp.* Amen. (Folio 4.)

Fourth Prayer, named Ad Pacem.

O God, who hast gone up on high, leading captivity captive, give gifts unto men of eternal peace : that though Thou hast withdrawn Thyself in a bodily sense from human view by ascending into heaven, Thou mayest graciously be pleased to be present in our hearts. *Amen.*

For Thou art our true Peace, and Love that cannot be dis‑ solved, who livest and reignest with the Holy Spirit, One God, for ever and ever. *Amen.*

The grace of God the Father Almighty, the peace and love of our Lord Jesus Christ, and the fellowship of the Holy Spirit be ever with us all.

Answer. And with men of good will.

As ye stand, give the peace.

The Kiss of Peace.

After this the Priest bows and says : I will go unto the altar of God.

Answer. Even unto the God of my joy and gladness.

Ad Pacem. Deus qui ascendisti in altum : captivam ducens captivatem : da dona hominibus pacis eterne. Ut qui te humanis obtutibus ad celos ascendens corporaliter subtraxisti : in nostris cordibus digneris propiciatus infundi. *Resp.* Amen.

Fixed ending. Quia tu es vera pax nostra, et charitas indirupta vivis tecum (*sic*) et regnas cum Spiritu Sancto unus Deus in secula seculorum. *Resp.* Amen.

Gratia Dei Patris omnipotentis : pax ac dilectio Domini nostri Jesu Christi : et communicatio Spiritus Sancti : sit semper cum omnibus nobis. *Resp.* Et cum hominibus bone voluntatis. [This should be compared with the corresponding words in Eastern Liturgies ; see above, pp. 32, 38 (note), 54.]

Quomodo astatis pacem facite. *Resp.* Pacem meam do vobis, &c. (Folio 4.)

[" They give then the peace of Christ to one another, that they may pre‑ serve in themselves the effect of love by kissing one another ; so that if any one is bearing the dark shade of illwill, he may quickly seek for grace, or beg pardon of the Lord, lest by a pretended gift of peace he joins company

Priest. Your ears unto the Lord.

Answer. We give them to the Lord.

Priest. Lift up your hearts.

Answer. Let us lift them up unto the Lord.

Priest. To our God and Lord Jesus Christ, the Son of God, who is in Heaven, let us render worthy praise and thanks.

Answer. It is meet and right.

Fifth Prayer, named Illatio.

It is meet and right that we should at all times give thanks unto Thee, O Lord, holy Father, everlasting Almighty God, through Jesus Christ Thy Son our Lord; who therefore withdrew from us the presence of His human Body, that we might learn to love Him spiritually; and who gave commandment to His disciples to remain in private until they should be strengthened with the presence of the Holy Spirit coming down upon them; to whom with the Father and the Son, one God, ever reigning, all the attendant angels with one voice proclaim, saying,

Answer. Holy, holy, holy, &c.

with the traitor."—Ancient Commentary by S. Germain, *circa* A.D. 555.— Martene, lib. i., cap. iv., art. 12, ordo 1. With this should be compared our Confession, Absolution, and Comfortable Words. See below, Chap. VII., p. 225.]

Postea inclinet se Sacerdos junctis manibus et dicat. Introibo ad altare Dei mei. *Resp.* Ad Deum qui letificat juventutem meam.

Presbiter ponat manus super calicem et dicat. Aures ad Dominum. *Resp.* Habemus ad Dominum.

Sursum corda. *Resp.* Levemus ad Dominum.

Deo ac Domino nostro Jesu Christo Filio Dei : qui est in celis dignas laudes dignasque gratias referamus. *Resp.* Dignum et justum. (Folio 4.)

[The use of the word *levemus* here in place of the usual *habemus* is worthy of notice, as it may possibly have supplied the expression, " We *lift* them up." In the translation of Herman's Consultation, printed at London 1547 and 1548, the words are, "Lift up your hearts. We have unto the Lord."]

Illatio. Dignum et justum est: nos tibi semper gratias agere Domine

Post Sanctus. Truly holy and truly blessed is our Lord
Jesus Christ, Thy Son, who was borne upon the arms of
angels, and ascended into Heaven, and now sitteth at the right
hand of God the Father. He, our Lord and Redeemer (in the
night in· which He was betrayed, took bread, and when He
had given thanks, &c.).

Sancte Pater eterne omnipotens Deus per Jesum Christum Filium tuum
Dominum nostrum. Qui nobis ideo presentiam subtraxit nativitatis corpore :
ut eum spiritaliter disceremus amare. Quique discipulis intra suarum
mentium (*forte,* suorum mœnium) claustra tamdiu presidere precepit :
quousque supervenientis firmarentur presentia Spiritus Sancti. Cui cum
Patre et Filio uni Deo jugiter in sempiternum regnanti omnes Angeli
famulantes una voce proclamant ita dicentes. *Resp.* Sanctus, sanctus,
sanctus, Dominus Deus Sabbaoth : pleni sunt celi et terra gloria majestatis tue : osanna filio David : osanna in excelsis. Benedictus qui venit in
nomine Domini : osanna in excelsis.

Post Sanctus. Vere sanctus et vere benedictus Dominus noster Jesus
Christus Filius tuus. Qui angelorum evectus ulnis ascendit in celos, et
nunc sedet ad dexteram Dei Patris. Ipse Dominus ac redemptor æternus.

(Adesto, adesto Jesu bone Pontifex in medio nostri : sicut fuisti in
medio discipulorum tuorum : sanctifica hanc oblationem : ut sanctificata
sumamus per manus sancti angeli tui sancte Domine ac Redemptor eterne.
Dominus noster Jesus Christus in qua nocte tradebatur accepit panem : et
gratias agens benedixit ac fregit : deditque discipulis suis dicens. Accipite
et manducate. Hoc est corpus meum, quod pro vobis tradetur. *Hic elevetur
corpus.* Quotiescumque manducaveritis : hoc facite in meam commemorationem. Similiter et calicem postquam cenavit dicens. Hic est calix novi
testamenti in meo sanguine qui pro vobis et pro multis effundetur in remissionem peccatorum. *Hic elevetur calix coopertus cum filiola.* Quotiescumque biberitis hoc facite in meam commemorationem. *Resp.* Amen.
Quotiescumque manducaveritis panem hunc. et calicem istum biberitis :
mortem Domini annunciabitis donec veniet. In claritatem de cœlis. *Resp.*
Amen. Folio 5.)

[The words of Consecration have been altered, but at what period is
uncertain. Other Gallican Missals end the fifth prayer with the words
" Qui pridie quam pateretur, &c. ; " and the following prayer is here named
" Post pridie," though the word *pridie* is replaced by the words " in qua
nocte tradebatur." As the form now differs from the Roman form, the
alteration must have been an ancient one; and it is possible that we have

P

Sixth Prayer, named Post Pridie.

O Christ, desiring to behold Thy Presence, who didst seek the things above, without deserting the things of man; we pray and beseech Thee, that having carried into Heaven the pledge of the Flesh which Thou hast taken, Thou wilt grant us the comfort of Thy Holy Spirit; and by His presence now both sanctify these gifts which we offer unto Thee, and enlighten our inward hearts. *Amen.*

Thou fulfilling it, holy Lord, because Thou createst all these things for us, Thine unworthy servants, to be very good; Thou sanctifiest, blessest, and grantest them to us, that they may be blessed by Thee our God, for ever and ever. *Amen.*

The Lord be ever with you.

Answer. And with thy spirit.

The faith which we believe in our heart, let us now say with our mouth.

here the ancient Spanish form, agreeing with the Eastern form of Consecration. It should be noticed that our English form follows the same pattern, instead of the usual Western one. The addition beginning "Adesto, adesto Jesu bone Pontifex" is a curious feature of this Liturgy; it is evidently an interpolation, since it does not fit in with the words with which the *Post Sanctus* prayer invariably ends. No trace of it appears in the ancient Missals before mentioned.]

Post Pridie. Contueri tuam Christe cupientes præsentiam: qui humana non deserens: appetisti superna: petimus et rogamus: ut qui pignus assumpte carnis intulisti in celos: consolationem nobis Sancti Spiritus largiaris. Cujus nunc presentia et apposita hæc tibi oblata sanctifices: et nostrorum cordium arcana perlustres. *Resp.* Amen.

Fixed ending. Te prestante sancte Domine: quia tu hec omnia nobis indignis servis tuis: valde bona creas: sanctificas vivificas benedicis ac prestas nobis: ut sit (*forte* sint) benedicta a te Deo nostro in secula seculorum. *Resp.* Amen.

Dominus sit semper vobiscum. *Resp.* Et cum spiritu tuo.

Fidem quam corde credimus ore autem dicamus. Credimus in unum Deum, &c. (Folio 5-6.)

Post hec frangat Presbyter. Eucharistiam in medium: et ponat mediam

We believe in one God, the Father Almighty, &c.

The Priest then broke the Eucharist into nine parts, which were arranged in the form of a cross.

Prayer before the Lord's Prayer, which is the Seventh Prayer.

Let us pray.

O God, Son of God, who in ascending to the Father didst promise that Thou wouldest come again to us; come to us and make Thine abode with us; showing Thyself to us, whom Thou hast taught to pray acceptably in this manner from earth;

Our Father which art in Heaven, &c.

Delivered from evil, confirmed ever in good, may we be permitted to serve Thee, our God and Lord. Put an end to our sins; give joy to those in trouble; grant redemption to captives, health to the sick, and rest to the departed. Bestow peace and security all our days; break down the boldness of our foes; and answer, O God, the prayers of all faithful Christians, Thy servants, this day and ever, through our Lord

partem in patena: et de alia parte faciat quinque particulas et ponat in patena: et accipiat aliam partem et faciat quatuor particulas et ponat in patena similiter per ordinem factas per perscriptas rotas.

[The particles were named after the events in the Life of our Lord: Corporatio (*i.e.* Incarnatio); Nativitas; Circumcisio; Apparitio (*i.e.* Epiphania); Passio; Mors; Resurrectio; Gloria; Regnum.]

Ad orationem Dominicam. Oremus. Deus Dei Filius qui cum ad Patrem ascenderes venturum te iterum ad nos voce promisisti, veni ad nos et apud nos facito mansionem; manifestans te ipsum nobis, quibus precepisti sic exorare e terris.

Pater noster qui es in celis. *Resp.* Amen. Sanctificetur nomen tuum. *Resp.* Amen. Adveniat regnum tuum. *Resp.* Amen. Fiat voluntas tua: sicut in celo et in terra. *Resp.* Amen. Panem nostrum quotidianum da nobis hodie. *Resp.* Quia tu Deus es. Et dimitte nobis debita nostra: sicut et nos dimittimus debitoribus nostris. *Resp.* Amen. Et ne nos inducas in temptationem. *Resp.* Sed libera nos a malo.

Liberati a malo: confirmati semper in bono: tibi servire mereamur Deo ac Domino nostro. Pone Domine finem peccatis nostris, &c.

Jesus Christ, Thy Son, who liveth and reigneth with Thee and in the unity of the Holy Spirit, God for ever and ever. *Amen.*

The Priest then takes the particle called Regnum *from the Paten, and places it over the Chalice, saying thrice,*

The Lion of the tribe of Judah, the root of David, is Victor. Alleluia.

Answer. Who sittest above the Cherubim; the root of David. Alleluia.

Holy things to the holy; and may the conjunction of the Body of our Lord Jesus Christ be for pardon to us who receive and drink; and to the faithful departed may it be for rest.

The Priest places the particle into the Chalice, saying,

Bow down for the blessing.

The Lord be ever with you.

Answer. And with thy spirit.

The Blessing.

May Christ the Lord be your Helper, who ascended into Heaven, and now sitteth at the right hand of the Father. *Amen.* (Other blessings follow.)

Sic faciat Presb. Accipiat modo particulam que dicitur regnum *de Patena : et ponat super calicem : in tempore resurrectionis videlicet dicat tribus vicibus.* Vicit leo de tribu Juda radix David alleluja. *Resp.* Qui sedes super Cherubin radix David alleluja.

Et postea dicat istam orationem inter se submissa voce. Sancta sanctis et conjunctio corporis Domini nostri Jesu Christi : sit sumentibus et potantibus nobis ad veniam : et defunctis fidelibus prestetur ad requiem.

Et mittat particulam in calicem et cooperiat calicem : et dicat alta voce sic : si non fuerit ibi Diachonus. Humiliate vos benedictioni. Dominus sit semper vobiscum. *Resp.* Et cum spiritu tuo. (Folio 6.)

[The words " Sancta sanctis " agree with the Eastern Liturgies; cf. Apost. Constit., S. Cyril, S. Chrysostom, pp. 36, 61. The word *Conjunctio* seems to be used instead of the usual *commixtio*, in accordance with Fourth Council of Toledo, A.D. 633, Canon 18: "Post orationem Dominicam et con-

The Summons to draw near.

Rejoice, ye people, and be glad; an Angel sat upon the Lord's stone; he himself has preached the good news to you; Christ is risen from the dead, &c.

The Communion.

Anthem after Communion.

Refreshed with the Body and Blood of Christ, we praise Thee, O Lord. Alleluia, Alleluia, Alleluia.

Post-Communion Thanksgiving.

Having rendered to Thee, O Lord, our bounden duty and service in this holy solemnity, we give Thee thanks and praise,

junctionem panis et calicis benedictio in populum sequatur, et tunc demum corporis et sanguinis Domini sacramentum sumatur."—Labbe, Concilia, vol. v., p. 1704. For the mediæval use, see above, page 101.]

Benedictio. Christus Dominus sit auxiliator vestri; qui adsumptus in celos; sedet nunc ad dexteram Patris. *Resp.* Amen.

Corpus quoque vestrum nullis torpentibus patiatur passionibus mancipari: qui illud glorificatum in celos adsumpsit. *Resp.* Amen.

Ut qui ascendentis vidimus gloriam : judicantis non puniamur sententia. *Resp.* Amen.

Ipso prestante qui cum Deo Patre vivit et regnat in unitate Spiritus Sancti in secula seculorum. *Resp.* Amen.

Dominus sit semper vobiscum. *Resp.* Et cum, &c.

Ad accedentes. Gaudete populi et letamini: Angelus sedit super lapidem Domini: ipse vobis evangelizavit. Christus surrexit a mortuis Salvator mundi; et explevit omnia suavitate: gaudete populi et letamini, &c.

[At other times of the year the anthem " O taste and see, &c." was used, whilst the people came up to communicate. The directions which are given in Folios 7, 233, point to the prevalence of private masses instead of the ancient communions for which the services were originally provided.]

Communio. Refecti Christi corpore et sanguine : te laudamus Domine alleluja : &c.

[In the Prayer Book of 1549 similar anthems were provided, named *Communio.*]

through the help of Thy gift of mercy; beseeching Thee, O God, to cleanse us from our sins, and to grant us to exult in Thy praises for ever. *Amen.*

Through Thy mercies, who, &c.

Priest. Let us exult and be glad this day; the King of Glory everlasting is risen, our Resurrection; let all flesh bless the Lord.

Answer. It is time to exult and be glad; the Lamb our Passover is slain, who hath purged away our miseries; to Him let us give thanks.[1]

Oratio. Expletis Domine in hac sacra solennitate nostre servitutis obsequiis gratias tibi laudesque referimus dono tuo miserationis adjuti. Precantes te Deus: ut a peccatis nos abluas et in tuis semper laudibus exultare concedas. *Resp.* Amen.

Exultemus et letemur hodie: resurrexit Rex eterne glorie: nostra resurrectio: benedicat omnis caro Domino. *Resp.* Exultandi et letandi tempus est: pascha nostrum immolatus agnus est: qui nostras miserias expurgavit: illi demus gratias.

[On other days different endings to the service were provided. The following seems to have been a usual form: "Dominus sit semper vobiscum. *Resp.* Et cum. Solennia completa sunt in nomine Domini nostri Jesu Christi. Votum nostrum sit acceptum cum pace. *Resp.* Deo gratias."]

[1] The Mozarabic Missal was first printed A.D. 1500. There is a copy of the original edition in the Library of Emmanuel College, Cambridge. It was presented by Simeon Ashe, a Puritan minister, in 1651, who thereby testified to his appreciation of the pure and scriptural character of this Liturgy. There is also another copy in the British Museum.

The description of the seven prayers of the Liturgy given by Isidore, de Officiis Ecclesiæ, lib. i., cap. xv., is contained in the collection by Hittorpius, de Officiis Divinis. An explanation of their spiritual meaning may be found in the commentary assigned to S. Germain, A.D. 555.—Martene, lib. i., cap. iv., art. xii., ordo i.

CHAPTER VII.

THE ENGLISH ORDER OF HOLY COMMUNION.

"The sacrement of the auter

*　　*　　*　　*　　*

whilk ilk man and woman, that of eld is,
aught for to resceyve anes in the yhere,
that is at sai at Paskes, als hali kirke uses,
when thai er clensed of syn through penaunce
of payne of doying out of hali kirke."

Archbp. Thoresby's Catechism, A.D. 1357.

IN the last chapter attention has been called to the various forms of service which were within reach of our reformers to help them in the work of revising the Communion Service. The result proves that they probably made use of them all to some extent, and that they followed the advice given to Augustine by Pope Gregory nine hundred years before, in choosing out of the services of various countries such parts as seemed best suited for the purpose of forming a Liturgy for the English Church. For whilst the English Service is distinct from all other Liturgies, its various parts correspond more or less closely with ancient examples, if they have not been taken directly from the services of former times.

It is probable that few who have made the ancient Liturgies their study will assert that the English Service of Holy Communion is in every respect perfect, though they may admire and value it very highly. For it is commonly found that improvements in various directions are regarded as desirable when the matter is considered from a theoretical point of view. But our reformers had the practical difficulty before them of reconciling antagonistic parties; and they acted accordingly. Similarly, in the present day, in dealing with the form of service which has been accepted by the Church of England, it is necessary to remember that theoretical improvements are matters on which opinion is divided, and are of little practical importance. Attention will be therefore directed to the different parts of the service with the view of pointing out the extent of their agreement with the general practice of the Church, without entering into debatable matters or considering whether these forms, which have been ordained by the authority of the Church of England, are the best which could be devised or not.

The Order of Holy Communion begins with the Lord's Prayer and Collect for Purity which formed part of the private preparations of the priest and attendant ministers under the Sarum rite. And the traditional custom of allowing the priest alone to say the Lord's Prayer here, contrary to the general rule, is a sign that this preparation is still regarded as belonging specially to himself.

The responses to the commandments recall by their name, *Kyries*, a very ancient practice, which had been but slightly represented in the mediæval missals. From very early times in the Eastern Church a litany has always formed part of the opening portion of the service. Similarly, the rubric at the beginning of the

Gregorian Canon is a proof that the same custom once prevailed in the Roman Church.[1] In the Church of Milan a litany is still used here during Lent ; and in the Mozarabic Missal a kind of litany is still provided for similar use under the name of *Preces,* varying for different days.[2] But in the mediæval missals the only trace of such litanies which remained was the repetition of *Kyrie eleison.*[3] Upon this, with the help of the suggestions gathered from other churches, our reformers founded the penitential form of preparation, peculiar to the Anglican Liturgy, in which the priest rehearses the Ten Commandments, and the people kneeling are directed to " ask God mercy for their transgression thereof for the time past, and grace to keep the same for the time to

[1] Pages 30, 45, 69.

[2] See Chapter IX., LITANIES AND INVOCATIONS OF SAINTS.

[3] In the Sarum Use a custom prevailed of using what were called *farced* (*i.e.* stuffed) Kyries on festivals. In the magnificent Sarum " Graduale," published at Paris, 1532 (British Museum), eight forms of such farced Kyries are given with the musical notation. The first is specially worthy of notice, because it introduces Greek words in addition to the common word *eleison,* which seem like relics of the Eastern origin of the Liturgical Litany.

" Deus creator omnium tu *theos ymon* nostri pie eleyson.

Tibi laudes conjubilantes regum rex *christe* (cf. 1 Sam. xii. 3, 5, Vulgate) oramus te eleyson.

Laus, virtus, pax et imperium cui est semper sine fine eleyson.

Christe rex unice patris almi nate coeterne eleyson.

Qui perditum hominem salvasti de morte reddens vitæ eleyson.

Ne pereant pascuæ oves tuæ Jesu pastor bone eleyson.

Consolator Spiritus supplices *ymas* te exoramus eleyson.

Virtus nostra domine atque salus nostra in æternum eleyson.

Summe deus et unæ vitæ dona nobis tribue misertus nostri quæ tu digneris eleyson."

In three of the forms the lines begin in a more formal manner ; the first three with the word *Kyrie,* the next three with the word *Christe ;* the last three with the word *Kyrie ;* and every line ends with *eleyson.*

come, saying, Lord, have mercy upon us, and incline our hearts to keep this law." [1]

The use of a Collect for the Queen in this place is peculiar to the English Service. The idea is probably taken from the Eastern Liturgies, where similar petitions form part of the litanies above mentioned.

The Collect for the Day,[2] the Epistle and Gospel,[3]

[1] The Commandments and Responses were inserted in the Second Prayer Book of 1552, in place of the threefold repetition—" iii. Lord have mercy," &c. It is possible that the idea was taken from Coverdale's " Ghostly Psalms and Spiritual Songs," which are assigned to some date previous to 1539. For, amongst other similar translations, the Ten Commandments are given in metre, with the word " Kirieleyson " following each verse.— " Remains," Parker Soc., pp. 543-549, 562. Or the practice may have been derived from the Liturgy of the Strasbourg refugees at Glastonbury (published in Latin by Valerandus Pollanus, 1551), in which the Commandments were so used in rhyme at the beginning of the service. The spiritual meaning assigned to the Ten Commandments by our Blessed Lord had been already set forth in the Catechism contained in the Prayer Book of 1549 ; and this was in accordance with the general teaching of the Primers, and especially of one published in 1535, in which every person was directed to examine his practice by the Ten Commandments with the view to true confession. Similar teaching had been enforced by the " Institution of a Christian Man," and the " Erudition."—Collier, Eccles. Hist., vol. iv., pp. 315, 406 ; v., p. 98.

[2] The English Church cannot sufficiently express the debt of gratitude which is due to Archbishop Cranmer for his translation of the Collects. All that can be said in explanation is that he was guided by the Holy Spirit of God to choose such words that the ear never wearies of hearing them. Out of our fifty-four Sunday Collects, thirty-seven are direct translations, four are free translations, and three are adaptations of the ancient Collects. The new Sunday Collects, are : 1 Advent, 2 Advent, 3 Advent, Sunday after Christmas, 6 Epiphany, Quinquagesima, 1 Lent, 1 Easter, 2 Easter, and the Sunday after Ascension, which is formed upon an Antiphon for Ascension Day. The new Collects for Festivals and Fasts are Circumcision, Ash Wednesday, Good Friday, SS. Andrew, Thomas, Matthias, Mark, Philip and James, Barnabas, John Baptist, Peter, James, Matthew, Luke, Simon and Jude, and All Saints.

[3] The Epistles and Gospels are the same as were appointed in the Sarum

and the Nicene Creed follow the ancient order of the
Sarum Service.

The rubric directing that the Sermon or Homily shall
come next has restored the primitive custom of preaching,
which was maintained for many centuries, but which had
been very generally neglected in the times preceding
the Reformation.[1]

Missal, with such slight variations as are hardly worth mentioning. The
Epistles for 4 Epiphany, 6 Epiphany, and Easter Day, are new; and for
the following Festivals : S. John, Circumcision, Epiphany, SS. Philip and
James, Barnabas, John Baptist, James, Matthew, Michael, Luke, and
Simon and Jude, and on some other days a few verses have been added
or removed. The Gospels are the same as formerly, except for Sunday
after Christmas, 6 Epiphany, and Easter.

[1] The Sermon has always formed one of the special observances of the
Lord's Day. Justin Martyr refers to it, A.D. 137: " On the day called
Sunday all gather together and the memoirs of the apostles or the writings
of the prophets are read as long as time permits ; after which he who takes
the lead verbally instructs and exhorts."—" Apology," I., 67. It appears
from this that from the earliest times the accustomed place of the Sermon
was immediately after the Gospel. Similarly, in Apostol. Constit., lib.
viii., 5, the Bishop is directed to greet the church, after the readings from
the Prophets, Epistles and Gospels, saying, " The grace of our Lord," &c.,
and after this to address the people with words of exhortation. Cæsarius
of Arles, A.D. 502-542, in order to prevent the congregation leaving before
the Sermon, is said to have very often caused the doors to be shut after the
Gospel. And he persisted in preaching incessantly every Lord's Day and
Festival, and frequently also in Mattins and Evensong. And when unable
to preach himself, he took care that his presbyters and deacons should take
his place and preach homilies written by himself or one of the fathers.—
" Life of Cæsarius," lib. i., c. 14, 29, quoted by Martene, de Antiq. Eccles. ritibus, lib. i., cap. iv., art. 5 ; lib. iv., cap. ix. In the Council in Trullo, at Constantinople, A.D. 691, the following directions are given about preaching on the
Lord's Day, according to the words of Scripture as laid down by the ancient
fathers ; Canon 19 : "Ὅτι δεῖ τοὺς τῶν ἐκκλησιῶν προεστῶτας ἐν πάσῃ μὲν
ἡμέρᾳ, ἐξαιρέτως δὲ ταῖς κυριακαῖς πάντα τὸν κλῆρον καὶ τὸν λαὸν ἐκδιδάσκειν
τοὺς τῆς εὐσεβείας λόγους, ἐκ τῆς θείας γραφῆς ἀναλεγομένους τὰ τῆς ἀληθείας
νοήματά τε καὶ κρίματα, καὶ μὴ παραβαίνοντας τοὺς ἤδη τιθέντας ὅρους, ἢ

With the return of the priest to the Lord's Table, the more solemn part of the service, or the Liturgy proper, may be considered to begin. The Offertory, or anthem to be sung or said whilst the offerings are made, is found in all liturgies; and is followed by various forms of prayer for the acceptance of the gifts. In the English Service the form which follows includes the Prayer for the whole state of Christ's Church. It had been the custom of the Western Church, in accordance with the Roman Liturgy, to defer the Prayer for living and departed until the Canon, or great Prayer of Consecration, in which the petitions for the living come at the beginning before the act of Consecration, and the petitions for the departed after it. And in the Eastern Liturgies, with the excep-

τὴν ἐκ τῶν θεοφόρων πατέρων παραδόσιν.—Beverege, "Canons," tom. i., p. 177.

The ancient exposition of the Mass, named "Gemma Animæ," describes the Sermon as following the Gospel, in which "the Bishop instructs the people in repentance, faith, and confession of sin. After this the people say *Kyrie eleison*, and the clergy sing *Credo in unum Deum.*"—Gemma Animæ, lib. i., cap. xxv. From this we learn that the position of the Sermon was not altered by the introduction of the Creed. But in the English Church in mediæval times the Sermon seems to have been sometimes placed after the Offertory, before the *Secreta*. A Bidding Prayer in English preceded it, examples of which are found dating back before the Conquest, differing but little from the Bidding Prayer still in use in cathedrals and at the universities.—"Lay Folks Mass Book," Simmons, pp. 212, 316-319. In the *excerpts* of Egbert, Archbishop of York, A.D. 732-766, this order is given, "ut omnibus festis et diebus Dominicis unusquisque sacerdos Evangelium Christi prædicet populo."—"Pontifical of Egbert." But in the times immediately preceding the Reformation, the Sermons seem to have been very infrequent. Possibly the Homilies on the Gospel for the day, which were provided as the Lessons of the Third Nocturn at Mattins according to Sarum Use, see pp. 123, 128 (note 3), may have had something to do with the neglect of preaching, because in these homilies the learned were already provided with discourses full of thought and spiritual teaching.

tion of the Liturgy of S. Mark, the whole of these petitions are deferred until after the Consecration. But, on the other hand, in the Mozarabic Missal, the prayers for the living and departed come before *Sursum Corda*. Consequently our reformers, in deciding upon the present order of the service, have followed the example set in the ancient Gallican Liturgy of the French and Spanish Churches; and in doing so they returned to the practice of the Celtic or ancient British Church as well.[1]

The addition of the words " Militant here in earth," points out one of the chief alterations introduced by our reformers into our English Services. By this means attention was called to the fact that the whole system of prayers for the departed, as understood and practised by the Mediæval Church, was deliberately abandoned. There is no doubt that such prayers were given up with regret by those who took the lead in the reformation of the Church of England. Men of the most extreme opinions, such as Calvin, as well as the more moderate, such as Bucer, distinctly admitted that the references to the departed which were retained in the Prayer Book of 1549 were in accordance with primitive custom.[2] It is interesting also to be able to trace in various parts of our English Services words and phrases which still remain to prove that the practice is in no sense condemned by the Church of England, and which furnish to those who desire it the opportunity of remembering

[1] See F. E. Warren's " Liturgy and Ritual of the Celtic Church." The Stowe Missal shows that even after the Roman Canon had been introduced, these prayers still retained their place in the early part of the Liturgy. See Table of Anglican Communion Services, at end of this chapter.

[2] See above, page 164.

before God those who have gone to their rest.[1] But the popular objections to the continuance of public prayers for the departed were too strong to be neglected. The corruptions belonging to this practice, as it had been carried out in the mediæval services, were so great, that the necessity of sweeping away the whole system was accepted by our reformers. And in the Prayer Book of 1552 the passages referring to the departed, which had been retained in the Prayer Book of 1549, were omitted, and the words, "Militant here in earth," were inserted. It is probable that in thus abolishing the mediæval system of prayer for the departed, we lost something which was dear to the early Church. But a careful distinction is necessary between that "something" which was primitive, and the system with which our reformers had been familiar. There is no doubt but

---

[1] The whole subject is carefully discussed in the "Church Quarterly," April, 1880, pp. 1-25, wherein the changes in the different revisions of the Book of Common Prayer touching upon the prayers for the departed are examined. Special attention is paid to the omission of any mention of such prayers in the Thirty-nine Articles. The author argues that the omission was designedly made in order to leave the matter open to individual judgment, and that this is proved by the fact that the words "de precatione pro defunctis," which are found in the Latin MS. of Article XXII., disappeared before the Articles were promulgated. Another point which meets with very careful consideration is the addition of the last clause to the Prayer for the Church Militant. Its importance appears when it is taken in conjunction with the uncertainty of the title to this prayer. This was repeatedly altered during the last revision of 1662 ; the suggestion of Bishop Cosin being alternately received and rejected : " Let us pray for the good estate of the Catholick Church of Christ." The words in the Post-Communion Collect " that . . . we and all Thy whole Church may obtain remission," are regarded as furnishing another proof that the whole subject is left open to the judgment of individuals, whether they will mean more or less in the words they use ; for there can be no question that, as Bishop Cosin says,. " The whole Church consists of more than those that are upon the earth."

that a certain kind of prayers for the departed had been used from the first by Christians, who had derived the practice from ancient Jewish custom. But between the prayer of S. Paul for his (apparently) departed friend Onesiphorus, "The Lord grant unto him, that he may find mercy of the Lord in that day," and the mediæval masses and prayers for the deliverance of souls out of Purgatory, there was a difference so great as to make it difficult to compare them together.[1]

The departure of non-communicants at this point in the service is a distinctive feature of the English Church. No order respecting this withdrawal is now given in the Prayer Book, but it seems to have been founded upon a rubric in the Service of 1549, immediately after the Offertory,—" All other (that mind not to receive the said Holy Communion) shall depart out of the quire, except the ministers and clerks." There is no doubt that this order may be traced to the directions for the dismissal of catechumens and penitents in the ancient Church, and the importance that was attached to it by spiritually-minded men, in the times preceding the Reformation, may be illustrated by the comment of Dean Colet upon the description of the service given by Dionysius the (so-called) Areopagite. After mentioning that the catechumens, energumens, and penitents, when the performance of the sacred rites was at hand, were driven out of the temple, he adds :—

"Therefore all the profane, imperfect, shortcoming, back-sliding, are kept away from the mysteries. . . . For the sacred

---

[1] 2 Tim. i. 18. See Additional Note B, "ON PRAYERS FOR THE DE-PARTED," at the end of this chapter. It should be noticed that the Commemoration of the Departed was restored to this Prayer in 1662.

things of God require no common light of faith. . . . Thus, then, there are left in the temple only the pure, the enlightened, and the perfect, wholly without spot, viz., the most holy bishop, the priests, deacons, ministers, and holy people." [1]

In the Exhortations a practice has been adopted which seems to have been customary in ancient times, in England, on the rare occasions when the Communion was administered. For an ancient form of Exhortation in English has been discovered, containing many points of resemblance with our present Exhortation.[2] It has been also shown in the previous chapter that in the ancient Gallican Liturgy an admonition to the people, containing the familiar mode of address, " Dearly beloved Brethren," was the first of the seven regular forms of prayer. So that our reformers had several examples to guide them in this respect.[3]

---

[1] Dean Colet, " On the Hierarchies of Dionysius," by J. H. Lupton, page 88. See the Catalogue of Cranmer's Library.

[2] Blunt, " Annotated Prayer Book."

[3] Objections are urged against the use of this exhortation upon two grounds; first, because "it is peculiarly out of place, the subject matter being proper for the Sermon ; " and, secondly, because "it speaks of the Holy Sacrament as if it were then present, whereas the consecration is yet to follow."—J. D. Chambers, " Divine Worship in England in Thirteenth Century," page 350. But a reference to the Mozarabic Liturgy above referred to will show that the position of our Exhortation is not so indefensible as has been thus represented. And it will be found that in various prayers preceding Consecration reference is frequently made to the pleading of Christ, as if the Holy Sacrament were already present, *e.g.,* " Famuli tui indigni et exigui sacerdotes tremendæ majestati tuæ spirituales victimas immolantes, offerimus tibi Deus hostiam immaculatam . . . hanc tibi summe Pater offerimus pro sancta Ecclesia tua," &c.—*Post nomina,* in Nativitate Domini Nostri. And in the *Missa,* or first prayer of the same service, these words occur, " Panis vivus credentibus datus est; hunc sumamus. Fons perennis fidelibus ortus est; animas impleamus." (Folio 39, 38.)

The Invitation, Confession, Absolution, and Comfortable Words, which come next, are in some respects peculiar to our English Service. Forms of Confession are universally met with in mediæval missals, but they are differently expressed; and whilst our own form is evidently based upon the Confession in Herman's Consultation,[1] its contents are a distinct feature of our own service. The Absolution is almost entirely taken from the Sarum form.[2] The Comfortable Words are from Herman, but in a different position. It seems not improbable that our reformers may have regarded these forms as in some degree taking the place of the ancient Kiss of Peace. A reference to the Sarum Absolution will show that it was followed by the kiss, which was peculiar to the Sarum Use; and a reference to the Mozarabic Service will show that the kiss and its accompanying Collect held the very same position that is now filled by our Confession, Absolution, and Comfortable Words.[3] The sense of peace with God through perfect peace with a man's self, as well as with his fellow man, was the true meaning of the ancient symbol of a kiss.[4] The kissing of a

[1] See above, page 191.　　　[2] See above, page 92.
[3] See above, page 207.
[4] The following explanation of the kiss is given for the instruction of the laity, *circa* A.D. 1150 :—

" There when tho prest tho pax wil kis,
knele thou & praye then this ;
God's lamb, that best may,
do tho synne of this world away
of us haue merci & pite,
and graunt us pese & charite.
For in charyte are thre kyns loues　　(*kinds of love.*)
That to parfite pese nedlyng behoues.　(*peace. necessarily. are fitting.*)
Tho first loue is certenly

Q

metal pax[1] must have been felt to be but the shadow or
skeleton of the old reality; and the humble confession,
the authoritative message of pardon, and the comforting
assurances of the Saviour's work of salvation, were provided to bring home to men's souls the substance itself,
even the peace of God.[2]

Then follows the part of the service of which there are
the earliest and most widely-spread evidences, viz.,
Sursum Corda, "Lift up your hearts," &c., and the
Preface which introduces the Angels' Hymn of Praise,
"Holy, Holy, Holy." This portion of the service is the

> to loue the Lord souerenly.
> Tho secunde is a prive loue
> by twix my soule & my body.
> Tho thrid loue is with outen
> to loue ilk neghtbur me abouten."
> "Lay Folks Mass Book," page 48.

[1] See note 1, page 102.

[2] The position of the Confession and Absolution has been described as
"a most unhappy misplacement."—"Divine Worship in England in
Thirteenth Century," page 352. But the prayers ad Pacem, which hold a
similar position in the Mozarabic Liturgy, show a singular resemblance in
spirit and idea to our English forms. For instance, "O Christ the Son of
God, who by Thy Cross didst make peace in heaven and earth, we pray
Thee make us rich in that peace . . . that Thou mayest always come to us,
and with the Father abide in us, and so make us Thine own that Thou
mayest grant the grace of Thy Holy Spirit to dwell within us."—*Ad Pacem,*
Oratio for the Sunday before Ash Wednesday. "O Saviour of the world
. . . cleanse our heart from every charge, and all blindness of ignorance :
so that preparing in our hearts a cleansed abode for Thee, Thou mayest
grant us . . . to retain in truth the love of our neighbour, by which we may
reach to Thee and know indeed Thy love."—*Oratio,* First Sunday in Lent.
"O God . . . hear our prayers, and disperse the storms of those passions by
which we are tossed, and infuse the Peace of Thine own calm ; so that by
Thy merciful pity we may obtain that which we have lost by our excessive
sins."—*Oratio,* Wednesday after Third Sunday in Lent. (Folio 87,
96, 122.)

same in effect in every known Liturgy, though the Prefaces themselves are provided in endless variety, both in the ancient Roman Sacramentaries and in the Gallican and Mozarabic Missals.[1]

The "Prayer of Humble Access," with respect to its position, is a peculiar feature of our English Service.[2]

[1] The words of the "Sanctus" were changed in 1552 by the omission of the words "Hosannah in the Highest, Blessed is He that cometh in the name of the Lord;" and by altering the last clause, "Glory to Thee, O Lord, in the highest," to "Glory be to Thee, O Lord, most High." The omission commends itself to our minds, in consideration of the fact that the words of the "Sanctus" are addressed to the Blessed Trinity, whilst the words omitted seem to be restricted to the praise of the Incarnate Son of God. The alteration of the last words may be explained in the same way. It is worthy of notice that at certain seasons the Mozarabic form ends, "Agyos, Agyos, Agyos, Kyrie o Theos" (fol. 229); for the words may have suggested the expression "Lord most High," which is not otherwise met with.

[2] Its position between the Preface and that to which the Preface leads—the Prayer of Consecration—appears to break the continuity of the act, and consequently the Prayer of Humble Access has been vehemently objected to. But perhaps to members of the Eastern Churches, who are accustomed to have the Prayer of Consecration immediately after the Preface, the early part of the Roman Canon seems as great an intrusion and interruption to the sense. No similar prayer is found in any existing Liturgy in this position; but probably this humble expression of unworthiness and anxiety for worthy reception comes as a relief to the minds of a large proportion of devout worshippers. The thoughts to which the Preface leads are too high to be maintained. From joining with the angels we are driven to prostrate ourselves beneath a sense of sin. It seems therefore most natural to regard this prayer as a sort of parenthesis, to be said as it were "aside," as the expression of individual unworthiness to join in the supreme act belonging to the office of priesthood. And since all Christians are in a certain sense "priests unto God," and are about to claim their share in the priestly act by the "Amen" at the conclusion, the priest is directed to say these words, not for himself alone, but "in the name of all them that shall receive the Communion." It was probably felt by our reformers that this prayer took the place of the act of humiliation preceding the *Orate* in the Sarum Service, beginning, "In the spirit of humility," &c., page 97.

But similar prayers for a worthy approach to God's Holy Table may be found in various Liturgies of East and West, both before and after the Prayer of Consecration. The prayer in the Clementine Liturgy immediately preceding the words "Holy things to the Holy," is an example; and the words in corresponding prayers in the Liturgy of S. Chrysostom, beginning "To Thee we commit our whole life," and, "Attend, O Lord Jesus Christ," are still better examples.[1] Whilst the similar prayer in the Liturgy of S. Basil seems even more closely allied to it : "Cleanse Thou us from all pollution of flesh and spirit, &c. . . . that in receiving our portion of Thy sacred mysteries, we may be united with the Holy Body and Blood of Thy Christ; and by receiving them worthily may have Christ dwelling in our hearts, and be made the temple of Thy Holy Spirit."[2] Attention has been already called to the use of a confession here in ancient times, as mentioned by Dionysius the (so-called) Areopagite.[3] It is interesting to find a paraphrase of the passage by Dean Colet, which seems to prove that the spiritually minded, in the times preceding the Reformation, felt the need of some such expression of unworthiness in connection with the Prayer of Consecration. He says :—

"When the Bishop with his priests has made mention of what Jesus the Son of God did for us, he then proceeds to complete what remains, with meet symbols appointed by God.

---

[1] Pages 36, 59, 61,

[2] Dr. C. A. Swainson, "The Greek Liturgies," p. 85. The prayers named *Post Pridie* in the Mozarabic, and *Post mysterium* or *Post secreta* in the Gallican Missals, are in many cases very similar.

[3] See above page 187, and the Catalogue of Cranmer's Library.

He makes heartfelt excuse for himself, and declares himself unworthy to approach so great a mystery; he prays that he may worthily consecrate, may rightly distribute to the Church standing by, and that the Church may duly participate." [1]

The great Prayer of Consecration, which in the Roman Liturgy was called " The Canon," had been endeared to Christians of the West by the usage of at least a thousand years. It must have needed no slight effort and courage on the part of our reformers to give it up. But, as has been already shown, the character of this ancient form of prayer had been much altered by the insertion of rubrics and many new ceremonies, and when it is compared with the Consecration Prayers of other Liturgies, it is seen to be by no means free from blemishes. [2] Composed by an unknown scholastic, the Canon originally had no peculiar sanction of authority in its favour. [3] And our reformers, having removed the intercessions for the Church to the beginning of the service, did not hesitate to remodel the actual Prayer of Consecration after the patterns of other Liturgies. The result is, that we possess a Consecration Prayer which in its general character resembles the ever-varying forms of the Gallican and Spanish Services, whilst in its fulness of statement with respect to the work of Redemption and the institution of the memorial

[1] Dean Colet, " On the Hierarchies of Dionysius," by J. H. Lupton, page 93.
[2] Page 98. See also Additional Note A, " ON THE CANON," at the end of Chap. III.
[3] S. Greg. the Great, Epist., lib. vii., ii., 64: " It seemed to me extremely inconvenient that we should say over the oblation a prayer which some scholastic had composed, and that we should not say over His Body and Blood that very traditional form which our Redeemer composed."

of the Sacrifice of the Cross, it follows the pattern of the Consecration Prayers of the Eastern Liturgies.[1]

The rubrics appointing the manual acts to be performed in the course of the Prayer of Consecration were

---

[1] The English Prayer of Consecration has been sometimes spoken of in a contemptuous manner, upon the supposition that the form in the Roman Canon is the only one that can be accepted as Catholic. For instance, it has been recently described as containing " a recital of some truisms ending, ' Hear us, O merciful Father,' which is not found in any previous formulary of any Christian Church in the world."—" Divine Worship in England in Thirteenth Century," p. 373. Those who are acquainted with the ancient Gallican Liturgy are aware that the Prayer of Consecration varied with every service, and commonly contained some such " recital of truisms." The character of these prayers may be learned from the following specimens from the Mozarabic Missal: " Truly holy . . . Jesus Christ Thy Son : who in place of the rejected idea of any impure libation, instituted the simple rite of the New Covenant; and taught His disciples through these most sacred solemnities to make the pure vow of innocence, and offer to God alone the sacrifice of praise."—*Post Sanctus*, 6th S. after the Octave of Epiphany.   " Truly holy and true Jesus, Son of God ; who ascended the Cross that, through His death, Death might lose all its force; who descended into hell that . . . He might burst the bars of its gates by His own powerful hand, &c."—*Post Sanctus*, Saturday before Easter.   " Truly holy and blessed art Thou, O God, Father Almighty ; who didst cause our Lord Jesus Christ, Thy Son . . . to undergo death, that He might loose the chains of our sins, and triumphing over hell, might return free to Thy throne."—*Post Sanctus*, Monday after Easter. (Folio 79, 192, 200.)

Similarly the words, " In the same night that He was betrayed," have been objected to as " a novel recital for the first time introduced into the Canon, instead of ' Who the day before, &c.,' the original form."—J. D. Chambers, " Divine Worship in England in Thirteenth Century," p. 373. It is curious to find that the Mozarabes, or Spanish Christians under dominion of the Moors, introduced the same change into the Mozarabic Liturgy. At what time the change was made is not known.   It seems to be evident that the words originally used were, " Who the day before," &c., since the following prayer is named *Post Pridie*. But when the Mozarabic Missal was printed in 1500, the words were found to be, " In the same night that He was betrayed." It is singular also that the author above quoted should not be aware that the Churches of the East have universally used the same formula :

re-added at the last revision of the Prayer Book in 1662. This is a singularly clear proof that the absence of rubrical directions is no sure sign of the absence of ceremonial. For it is difficult to believe that the consecration was performed for more than a hundred years without any breaking of the Bread. In the First Prayer Book of 1549 the following rubrics were inserted in the Prayer of Consecration : " Here the Priest must take the Bread into his hands ;" " Here the Priest shall take the Cup into his hands." But no directions were given for the breaking of the Bread. It may be supposed that this would be naturally observed by those who had been accustomed to the elaborate ritual of former times, the many crosses over the elements, and the fraction and commingling which were practised under the Sarum rite. But these rubrics were omitted in 1552, and the clergy were left to follow such ceremonial as their own unaided judgment prescribed. Probably the matter is of less importance than it appears at first sight to be. For, whilst the earliest name of the service—the Breaking of Bread—proves that the fraction as a ceremonial act, and not observed for the mere purpose of distribution, was handed down from the beginning, history proves that such ceremonial acts of consecration have varied very much in different churches and at different times.[1]

" In the same night that He was betrayed," &c.—Apost. Constit., lib. viii., cap. xii. ; Dr. C. A. Swainson, " The Greek Liturgies," Liturgy of S. Mark, p. 50, S. Basil, p. 81, S. Chrysostom, p. 91, S. James, p. 272. See Comparative Table of Liturgies, facing the title-page.

[1] Objections have been raised to the order in which the manual acts are here prescribed, on the ground that " it is certain that according to the account of the original institution, as interpreted by the universal practice of the whole Western and Eastern Churches, this is not the proper time for

The omission of the Lord's Prayer after the Prayer of Consecration is unlike all other changes in our service, for no reason for it has been discovered, and it is opposed to the universal practice of all branches of the Church of

this fraction, which is a principal and integral part of the whole rite, and if wrongly performed may vitiate the whole."—" Divine Worship in England in Thirteenth Century," p. 374. It is not known when the practice of the solemn fraction *after* Consecration, which is here referred to, first arose. It is not found in the most ancient forms either of East or West. For instance, there is no mention of this rite in the so-called Liturgy of Clement, Apostolical Constitutions, lib. viii., cap. xii. ; nor in the Catechetical Lectures of Cyril, in which a corresponding Liturgy is expounded. Neither is it found in the Sacramentary of Gregory. But Martene mentions it amongst the additions which were made at different times to the Canon.— Martene, de Antiq. Eccles. Rit., lib. i., cap. iv., art. 9. It does not seem to have been introduced at the beginning of the ninth century, since nothing is said about it in the exposition of the Roman Mass, supposed to belong to *circa* A.D. 800.—*Ibid.*, art. 11. Directions are given about dividing the bread, after the giving of peace, in the first *Ordo Romanus* (Muratori, vol. ii., p. 984), but no devotions accompany it, and it seems to be connected with the practical purpose of distribution. In this as in every other ritual act much diversity of practice is found to have existed in different times and countries. In the Ambrosian Liturgy of Milan, which probably preserves in many respects the customs of the days of S. Ambrose himself, *circa* A.D. 374, the fraction is made immediately after the Prayer of Consecration, with the words " Corpus tuum frangitur Christe." And the same practice is found to have been followed in the ancient Celtic Church.—Stowe Missal, in F. E. Warren's " Liturgy and Ritual of Celtic Church." But in later times it became a serious offence if the priest, in forgetfulness, broke the bread before the Lord's Prayer.—Martene, de Antiq. Monach. Rit., lib. ii., cap. vii., 23, extract from MS. of the monastery of Corbey. In mediæval times, as shown in the Sarum Missal, the fraction was performed after the Lord's Prayer and before the Peace (page 101) ; and the same is continued in the modern Roman use.

The rite was practised in very early times in the Gallican Church, for it is mentioned as an important part of the ritual in the exposition of the ancient Gallican Liturgy, supposed to have been composed by Germanus, Bishop of Paris, *circa* A.D. 555 ; and a prayer is found in Missale Gothicum, headed *Coll. ad Panis Fractionem.*—Martene, de Antiq. Eccles. Rit., lib. i.,

Christ. Yet since our reformers, who had been accustomed to its use here all their lives, were led by the providence of God to remove it to its position after the Communion, there was doubtless some good and sufficient reason, unknown in these days, for its removal.[1] There are, moreover, certain notices in ancient works which prove that it was not always used in this position. No mention of it occurs in the description of " The Communion," by Dionysius the (so-called) Areopagite.[2] The Clementine Liturgy affords another example of its omission ; but that it was unusual to omit it, even so early as the fourth century, is proved by Cyril's lecture upon the Liturgy in use at Jerusalem, A.D. 347.[3] S. Augustine also shows that in his days, *circa* A.D. 400, there were some who did not use it in this position, by remarking that " nearly every church concludes the whole act of praying with the Lord's Prayer." [4] And a passage in a letter of Pope Gregory the Great throws much doubt upon the Roman practice, *circa* A.D. 590, for he upholds his introduction of the Lord's Prayer " immediately after the

cap. iv., art. xii., ordo 1 ; Muratori, vol. ii., p. 594. In the Liturgy of S. Chrysostom the fraction is now observed with much ceremony, and is followed by another rite, of adding warm water to the cup (page 61).

[1] In Cranmer's MS. Collections, vol. ii., p. 175, a quotation from Gregory is given, referring to the use of the Lord's Prayer in the Consecration, which shows that it was designedly omitted. See above, page 77.

[2] Page 186.   [3] Page 36, note 1.

[4] S. Augustine, Epist. 59, ad Paulinum. Discussing the meaning of the words used with respect to prayer in 1 Tim. ii. 1, he says : " Eligo in his verbis hoc intelligere . . . ut *precationes* accipiamus dictas, quas facimus in celebratione Sacramentorum, antequam illud quod est in Domini mensâ incipiat benedici ; *orationes* cum benedicitur et sanctificatur et ad distribuendum comminuitur, quam totam petitionem fere omnis ecclesia Dominicâ oratione concludit."

Canon," by the singularly weak argument that it was the custom of the Apostles to consecrate by the use of this prayer alone; and this is understood by some to imply that he was the first to introduce it into the service, and by others that he only altered its position.[1]

The use of the Lord's Prayer here was regarded with such reverence that it was introduced in all Liturgies by a special form, which called attention to its supreme solemnity. In the Roman Liturgy this form was invariable: "Admonished by saving precepts and following the pattern of the divine institution, we are bold to say, Our Father, &c." In the Eastern Liturgies a similar form is used, varying in length, but always containing such words as these: "Make us worthy, O Master, with boldness and without condemnation to venture to call upon Thee, the Heavenly God, the Father, and to say, Our Father, &c."[2] But in the Gallican Missals this preface varied daily; the following is for the Festival of the Epiphany, "Not presuming upon our own merits, but obeying the command of our Lord Jesus Christ, Thy

---

[1] Gregory the Great, Epist., lib. vii., ii., 64, to John, Bishop of Syracuse, in answer to various questions about certain changes in the Roman Liturgy and variations between different Liturgies, amongst which was the question, Why the Lord's Prayer was said "immediately after the Canon," *mox post canonem :* " Orationem vero Dominicam idcirco mox post precem dicimus quia mos Apostolorum fuit, ut ad ipsam solummodo orationem hostiam consecrarent.　Et valde mihi inconveniens visum est ut precem quam scholasticus composuerat supra oblationem diceremus, et ipsam traditionem quam redemptor noster composuit supra ejus corpus et sanguinem non diceremus.　Sed et Dominica oratio apud Græcos ab omni populo dicitur, apud nos vero a solo sacerdote."

It should be noticed that the author of " Gemma Animæ," quoted above, p. 77, note 1, assumes that Gregory did not merely change the position of the ·Lord's Prayer, but introduced its use here.

[2] Page 60.

Son, whom Thou hast sent. We are unworthy indeed of the name of sons; yet we are bidden to say, Our Father, &c." [1] Special prominence also was given in most Churches to the part taken by the people. In the Eastern Church, and in the Gallican, the whole congregation joined in saying it. And in the Spanish Church a peculiar custom was adopted under the Mozarabic rite, for the people responded to every petition " Amen," except after the petition for daily bread, when the response was made, " For Thou art God." But in the Roman Liturgy the people responded only at the last petition, " But deliver us from evil." [2]

But notwithstanding this marked use of the Lord's Prayer in other Liturgies, our reformers were led to omit it from the conclusion of the Prayer of Consecration, and to place it after the Communion; probably with the intention of its being used for the purpose of summing up the private devotions of the worshippers, and in this sense carrying out the idea referred to by S. Augustine, of concluding the whole act of praying.[3]

[1] Missale Gothicum. *Missa in diem Sanctum Epiphaniæ :* " Non nostro præsumentes, Domine, merito, sed Domini nostri Jesu Christi filii tui, quem ut nos a tenebris et umbra mortis liberaret misisti, obedientes imperio. Indigni quidem sumus nomine filiorum ; sed jubemur dicere, Pater noster." —Muratori, vol. ii., p. 544.

[2] For the Eastern method, see p. 60, and also the quotation, note 1, p. 234, where both the Greek and the Roman custom are mentioned by Gregory. The ancient Gallican method is proved by a story told by Gregory, Bishop of Tours, A.D. 573-594, of a dumb woman who recovered her speech : " It came to pass that whilst the Lord's Prayer was being said, with open mouth she began to repeat with the rest the holy prayer."—Gregor., de Mirac. S. Martini, lib. ii., 30, quoted in Mabillon, de Liturgia Gallicana, cap. v. For the Mozarabic method, see note above, p. 211.

[3] Note 4, p. 233.

It has been shown before that an exaggerated importance is sometimes attached in the present day to various
parts of the act of Eucharistic celebration. And this
may be especially noticed in the discussions which have
been raised at different times upon the absence of any
direct invocation of the Holy Spirit in the English Service.
So essential has this form of petition appeared to some
that the remark of Bishop Seabury, the first American
bishop, has been quoted without any expression of dis-
approval : "To confess the truth, I hardly consider the
form to be used (viz. the English Prayer of Consecration) as strictly amounting to a consecration." And that
this view is maintained in the present day may be proved
by the words of his successor, the present Bishop of Con-
necticut, who says that in giving the primitive form of
consecration, "Scotland gave us a greater boon than
when she gave us the Episcopate."[1]   Yet when the subject is investigated by a comparison of different Liturgies,
the English Church is found to stand by no means alone
in this particular. It is well known that there is no
direct invocation in the Roman Canon; and when it is
remembered that the changes which took place in mediæval times were in the shape of additions, not of omissions, the importance of this example is seen to be very
great ; for it carries us back to the practice of the latter
part of the sixth century for certain, and in all reasonable
probability to that of the first days of the Roman Church.
We find similar testimony in the practice of the Gallican
Church preceding the ninth century. In the " Missale
Gothicum," which represents the form of Gallican Service

[1] "The Annotated Scottish Communion Service," by Dr. John Dowden,
pp. 115, 117 ; but see also p. 207.

previous to the introduction of the Roman Canon, a prayer
named *Post mysterium* follows the words of institution.
Herein the universal occurrence of the invocation would
naturally be looked for, if the practice was regarded as
being of supreme importance. Yet what do we find?
A direct invocation is rarely met with; and, as a general
rule, no mention of the Holy Spirit occurs even indirectly.[1]
But it may be said that the practice of the Spanish Church
of the seventh century testifies clearly to the importance
of the invocation, since Isidore describes the sixth prayer
of the Liturgy as " The Confirmation of the Sacrament;
in order that the oblation which is offered to God should
be sanctified by the Holy Spirit and confirmed (as the
oblation) of the Body and Blood of Christ."[2] Yet when
we turn to the Mozarabic Missal we find that its testimony
is not so clear as might be expected. The prayer *Post
Pridie* is most frequently a prayer that the Lord will
sanctify or bless the offering; direct invocation of the
Holy Spirit is only occasionally met with, and very often
no mention at all of the Holy Spirit's work is made.[3] We
are thus led to conclude that, whilst we may regret the
omission of the Invocation of 1549, we may suppose that
in all Liturgies much which is not actually expressed may
be understood to be implied.

We come now to the main point which has made the

---

[1] Miss. Goth., in Muratori, Liturg. Rom. vetus, vol. ii. The invocation
occurs pp. 534, 548, 565, 651; it is wanting, pp. 518, 522, 526, 647, 649,
652, 656. This prayer is sometimes named *Post Secreta*.

[2] Isidore, de Officiis Eccles., lib. i., cap. 15. See above, page 199, note 2.

[3] Mozarabic Missal. The ordinary prayer for the Lord's blessing occurs
folios 5, 9, 12, 16, &c.; direct invocation, or prayer that the Holy Spirit
may be sent, folios 69, 79, 97, 112, 114, 120, &c.; no reference to the Holy
Spirit's work, folios 50, 57, 63, 88, 92, 103, 108, &c.

English Service distinct from all the services which have
been handed down from mediæval times, viz., the importance attached to the act of communicating. A reference to the specimens of early services, both of the
Eastern and Western Churches, which have been given
in former chapters, will show that in introducing the
Communion of the people, our reformers were returning
to what was originally the universal practice of the Church.[1]
But so little attention was paid to this in the Mediæval
Church, that no rubrical directions for the general Communion of the people are given in the Sarum Missals.
The only reference which remained at the time of the
Reformation is found at the end of the Missal in a service for those undertaking a journey, in which it is
directed that certain prayers should be added after the
usual service, and that the persons should then communicate and depart.[2]

It is quite possible to trace out how this neglect of
Communion arose. It has been already shown that in
the early Liturgies directions were given for the Communion of the people. Thus, in the Clementine Liturgy
the words of administration are mentioned, and Psalm
xxxiv. is appointed to be sung whilst all are receiving ; and in the Lecture of Cyril upon the Liturgy,
minute instructions are added to teach the people how
they should reverently receive both the Bread and the
Cup.[3] In the early Roman Liturgy the rubric arranges

---

[1] Pp. 24, 27, 37, 62, 79, 186, 213.

[2] *Missa pro iter agentibus.* After the mass the priest is directed to add
certain prayers, after which this rubric follows : " Deinde°communicentur,
et ita recedant in nomine Domini."

[3] Page 37.

for the Communion of the people in order, and the practice is confirmed by much later testimony in the rubrical directions of various editions of the Ordo Romanus.[1] Similarly, in the ancient Gallican Church mention is made of the people coming up to the altar to communicate.[2] In accordance with this universal practice of regular communion in the ancient Church, the prayers which were appointed to be used after the Consecration commonly referred to the reception of the Holy Communion by the worshippers. In the ancient Sacramentaries there are many such post-Communion prayers.[3] And the same or similar prayers were handed on in the missals of the Western Church throughout the Middle Ages.[4] Such prayers also occur continually in the Gal-

[1] Page 79, note 1.

[2] Mabillon refers to a story related by Gregory of Tours, of a paralytic girl suddenly healed, who "by the mercy of the Lord went up to the altar to communicate by her own unaided steps." The Second Council of Tours, A.D. 567, Canon 4, directs that "the sanctuary should be open for prayer and for communicating both to lay men and women according to custom." But the custom was different in Spain; the Fourth Council of Toledo, A.D. 633, Canon 18, directs "that the priests and levites (deacons) should communicate before the altar, the other orders in the choir, and the people outside the choir."—Mabillon, de Liturgia Gallic., cap v. ; Labbe, Concilia, tom. vii., p. 1711.

[3] In the Sacramentary of Leo: "Ab omni nos Domine, quæsumus vetustate purgatos Sacramenti veneranda perceptio in novam conferat creaturam; Per, &c." "Supplices te rogamus Domine Deus noster, ut qui percepimus cœlestis mensæ substantiam, ad vitam pertingamas æternam; Per, &c." And the same and similar prayers are continued in the Sacramentaries of Gelasius and Gregory.—Muratori, vol. i., pp. 297, 357, &c.

[4] Thus in the Sarum Missal, "Grant, we beseech Thee, O Lord, that by this Sacrament, which we have received, our devout affections may thither ascend, where our Lord is with Thee ; Through, &c."—*Post communio,* Vigil of Ascension. See also 6 Sunday after Trinity, 10 Sunday after Trinity, 12 Sunday after Trinity, &c.

lican Missals, and psalms were sung whilst the people communicated.[1] But the people were not always earnest in their desire for communion. Even as early as the sixth century, Cæsarius, Bishop of Arles, A.D. 502-542, complains in one of his Homilies : " When the greatest part of the people, yea, what is worse, almost all go out of church after the Lessons have been read, to whom is the priest to say, *Sursum Corda?* Can they respond, when in body as well as in heart they are departing hither and thither through the streets ?"[2]

In the course of the Middle Ages the custom of communicating the people with the Bread which had been first dipped into the Chalice came into use. It began no doubt from reasons of convenience or necessity in the communion of the sick, and was sometimes condemned, and at other times decreed. But in the twelfth century it became general, and was upheld as avoiding the danger of spilling the consecrated wine, and of irreverence in reception.[3] But many years before this the ancient

[1] Missale Gothicum : " Accepto cœlesti corporis sacramento, et salutis æternæ calice recreati, Deo Patri Omnipotenti gratias agamus, laudesque dicamus : Per, &c."—Muratori, vol. ii., page 649. Mabillon, de Liturgia Gallicana, cap. v., quotes " Psallendo omnes communicare," from the Rule of Aurelian, Bishop of Arles.

[2] Cæsarius Arelatensis, Hom. xii. ; Menard, notes to Sacram. S. Gregorii, under the words " Sursum Corda."

[3] In the very ancient service edited by Matthias Flaccus Illyricus instructions are given for Communion, as follow : " *Deinde presbyteris et diaconis corpus in manus accipientibus et communicantibus, dicitur singulis.* Pax tecum. *Respons.* Et cum spiritu tuo. *Alia.* Verbum caro factum est et habitavit in nobis. *Calicem vero cum sacrosancta commixtione dando unicuique dicat,* Hæc sacrosancta commixtio Corporis et Sanguinis D. N. J. C. prosit tibi ad vitam æternam. *Populo quidem communicando dicat :* Corpus et Sanguis D. N. J. C. prosit tibi in remissionem omnium peccatorum, et ad vitam æternam. Amen." In the MS. Pontifical of Prudentius, Bishop of

practice of regular communion had fallen into disuse, notwithstanding various attempts to introduce a better state of things. The people would not communicate, and the priest was left to receive alone. Councils had decreed that all laymen should receive three times a year

Troye, A.D. 860, after instructions for the communion of the priest: " *Quando datur hostia sacra populo Christiano* : Corpus Domini nostri J. C. maneat ad salutem et conservet animam tuam in vitam æternam. Amen. *Ad sanguinem Domini* : Sanguis Domini nostri Jesu Christi sanctificet corpus et animam tuam in vitam æternam. *Ad utrumque :* Perceptio corporis et sanguinis Domini nostri J. C. prosit animæ tuæ in vitam æternam. Amen. *Item alia :* Corpus Domini nostri J. C. quo pasti sumus, et sanguis ejus quo potati sumus, adhæreat in visceribus nostris, et non nobis veniat ad judicium, neque ad condemnationem, sed proficiat nobis ad salutem, et ad remedium vitæ æternæ. Amen."

These extracts show that up to the middle of the ninth century the Communion of the people continued to be the regular practice, and that the Sacrament was administered in one of two ways, either in both kinds separately, or both together.

In a MS. Pontifical of Salzburg, about A.D. 1100, after the communion of the priest, this rubric occurs : " *Deinde cum cœperit communicare clerum sive populum dicat singulis :* Perceptio Corporis Domini nostri sit tibi vita, et salus, et redemtio omnium tuorum peccatorum." No other directions are given. From which it appears that Communion in the one kind only was becoming the custom at the end of the eleventh century.

In a MS. Missal according to the use of the Church of Evreux, about A.D. 1400, full directions are given for the communion of the priest: " *Hic se communicet dicendo :* Corpus Domini nostri Jesu Christi custodiat corpus meum et animam meam in vitam æternam. Amen. *Ad sanguinem:* Corpus et Sanguis Domini nostri Jesu Christi non sint mihi ad judicium, sed ad remedium animæ meæ in vitam æternam. Amen." But there are no instructions for the communion of the people; but instead : " *Postea signet populum de Calice dicendo :* Benedicat vos divina Majestas et una Deitas, Pater et Filius et Spiritus Sanctus. Amen." From which it appears that by the end of the fourteenth century the Benediction with the sign of the Cross by means of the empty chalice had taken the place, in an ordinary way, of the Communion of the people.—Martene, de Eccles. Ritibus, lib. i., cap. iv., art. xii., ordo 4, 6, 13, 28.

Similarly, in the Sarum Missal elaborate rubrics direct the priest in his

R

at least, but the decrees were neglected, and once a year was then accepted as the rule. Thus private Masses became general, and the ancient prayers which continued in use became " a mass of absurdities, whilst they prayed and gave thanks to God for the whole congregation as communicants, when there was not so much as one communicant, properly speaking, among them." [1]

The rubrics and words of administration in our English Service brought in the attempt to restore the ancient custom, not only of the Communion of the people, but also of receiving in both kinds. [2]   The steady growth which is now going on in the number of intelligent communicants in the Church of England is a sign that the attempt made by our reformers is being at length carried out successfully, through the revival of the ancient principles of Church teaching, and it may be accepted as a true cause of thankfulness on the part of the faithful.

own communion, and in the manner of making the ablutions; but no instruction is given for the Communion of the people.

See authorities mentioned in Martene, de Eccles. Rit..lib. i., cap. iv., art. x. Examples of the mediæval words of administration to the sick are found in fragments of Celtic Missals, edited by Rev. F. E. Warren in "Liturgy and Ritual of Celtic Church" :—" Corpus cum sanguine Domini nostri Jesu Christi sanitas sit tibi in vitam perpetuam et salutem." (Book of Deer.) In a more ancient fragment called the Book of Dimna the words are " Corpus et sanguis Domini nostri Jesu Christi filii Dei vivi conservat animam tuam in vitam perpetuam."

[1] Bingham, Antiq., book xv., chap. ix., 5, 6.

[2] The form of words for the administration consists of two parts. The first part is in accordance with the words used in the ancient Gallican Church. They are found in the Mozarabic Missal : " Corpus et sanguis Domini nostri J. C. custodiat corpus et animam meam in vitam æternam," fol. 7. The same words were used also, as stated in note on page 241, in the Church of Evreux in Normandy. The second part was added to the first in the revision of the Prayer Book, A.D. 1559, having been the form alone appointed in the second Prayer Book of 1552.

The rubric which prescribes how the priest shall consecrate more bread and wine was added in 1662. Similar directions with respect to the cup had been given in "The Order of Communion," 1548, but these were omitted in the First Prayer Book, 1549. In the mediæval missals no such directions are found, because in the general absence of communicants they could not be wanted. But it is interesting to discover that the instructions now given are in accordance with the ancient rules which were laid down for the guidance of the priest in cases of accident.[1]

The use of the Lord's Prayer as the commencement of the post-Communion prayers and thanksgivings is a peculiar feature of our service. But, as Wheatley says, "It cannot be anywhere used more properly ; for having now received Christ in our hearts, it is fit that the first words we speak should be His." Knowing that " to as many as receive Christ, He gives power to become the sons of God," we may well call upon God, saying, " Our Father."

---

[1] See above, page 15ᶿ. These instructions have been sometimes objected to without much reason. For amongst the *Cautelæ* to be observed respecting the Consecration of the Eucharist according to the Sarum Use, we find the following :—" Si sacerdos in actu consecrationis deficiat, verbis aliquibus jam in parte prolatis, sed in toto non completis, secundum Innocentium, alius sacerdos debet incipere ab illo loco, Qui pridie."

" Si tamen sacerdos deficiat, consecrato corpore sed non sanguine ; alius sacerdos compleat consecrationem sanguinis, incipiens ab illo loco, Simili modo."

Similarly, If after the consecration of the Blood he should find that there was no wine, but only water in the chalice, or if poison should be found therein, he is to prepare the chalice over again and resume the Consecration at the words, " Simili modo."—Sarum Missal.

The English rubric is thus shown to be founded upon the rule ascribed to Pope Innocent, A.D. 402-417.

Two forms of post-Communion prayer follow. The first revives the ancient sacrificial view of the Eucharist. Its words are founded upon expressions which, in the course of the Middle Ages, had lost their original signification.[1] But now in its English form, " Sacrifice of Praise and Thanksgiving," the ancient expression *sacrificium laudis* has regained its ancient meaning. And the sacrifice which we offer is described as being that which the early Church delighted to offer, a sacrifice of many kinds.[2] It is, first and chiefly, our Eucharist: our Thanksgiving for the Redemption of mankind through the Sacrifice of the death of Christ. It is also our sin-offering, the pleading of the merits of that death, in

---

[1] See the prayer which follows the " Orate," in the Sarum Missal, p. 97 ; and Note A., On the Canon, following Chapter III.

[2] Hence we find that words in the plural number are continually used in phrases which cannot be restricted to references to the Elements of Bread and Wine. For instance :—

In the Sacramentary of Leo : " Lord, we beseech Thee mercifully sanctify these gifts (*dona*), and receiving the offering of our spiritual sacrifice (*hostiæ spiritalis*) make us ourselves an offering for ever unto Thee (*nos met ipsos tibi perfice munus æternum*)." " It is very meet . . . wherefore rejoicing before Thine Altar, O Lord of Hosts, we offer sacrifices of praise unto Thee (*hostias tibi laudis*)."

" Receive, O Lord, we beseech Thee, the sacrifices of our humble service (*hostias nostræ devotionis*)."

In the Sacramentary of Gelasius : " We bring Thee, Lord, sacrifices (*hostias deferimus pro*) for the manifestation of the Birth of Thy Son."

In the Missale Gothicum : " We beseech Thee, O Lord, mercifully look upon the sacrifices before Thee (*sacrificiis præsentibus*), in which not gold, incense, and myrrh are brought, but that which is declared by such gifts is offered, slain, and taken."—*Post mysterium, i.e.,* prayer after consecration.

" Come into our souls, Almighty Everlasting God, and enter the temples which that Corner-Stone hath founded ; and through Him may we be able to offer unto Thee the sacrifices prepared for Thy Majesty (*majestati hostias præparatas*)."—Muratori, vol. i., pp. 318, 352, 502 ; vol. ii., pp. 544, 648.

order that "through faith in His Blood we may obtain
all the benefits of His Passion." And with these Sacrifices of Thanksgiving and Pleading, " we offer ourselves,
our souls and bodies, to be a lively sacrifice unto God."
The alternative form of post-Communion Thanksgiving follows the old Sarum rite, which differed here
from the Roman Liturgy in providing a form of thanksgiving for the blessings of Communion, in accordance
with the more ancient Eastern pattern. It should be
noticed that these two prayers together take the place of
the old post-Communion Collect and the Thanksgiving,
to which the English Church had been accustomed under
the Sarum Use.

The position of "Gloria in Excelsis" is another peculiar feature of our English Service. It is evident that
our reformers felt that thanksgiving naturally ends in
praise, and that, therefore, it was more fitting for this
ancient hymn to come at the end than in its old position
at the beginning of the service. It has been already
shown that the Western Church had lost to a great extent the idea of thanksgiving in connection with this
service, and therefore it is not to be wondered at that no
such act of praise is to be found in mediæval missals.[1]
But it is quite in accordance with the devotions with
which the Eastern Liturgies end, and with descriptions
of the ancient Gallican Liturgy also.[2] A comparison of

[1] Pp. 91 note 2, 109, 110.

[2] The use of *Gloria in Excelsis* here, instead of at the beginning of the
service, has been objected to upon various grounds. " It is here very inop-
portune ; acts of worship and petitions for mercy ought to precede rather
than follow after partaking of a Divine privilege ; " " at variance with all
ancient authority and principle ; " " its continual iteration every day without
variation only adds to the already too chilling monotony and unsuggestive

our present form of " Gloria in Excelsis" with the ancient
copies of it leads to the conclusion that "Agnus Dei,"
which used to be sung before or during the Communion,
has been incorporated with it.

bareness of the Anglican Offices."—" Divine Worship in England in
Thirteenth Century," page 413. Yet with the exception of the Roman
Liturgy something corresponding to this hymn is found in most Liturgies.
In the East this may be traced from the beginning, for in " The Doctrine of
the Twelve Apostles," the Thanksgiving after Communion ends with these
words, " Let grace come and this world pass away. Hosanna to the Son of
David," page 24. In the Liturgy of S. Chrysostom the post-Communion acts
of worship include various prayers and praises ; see above, page 62.

Similarly, in the Gallican Church the ancient Liturgy ended with a hymn
of praise to the Trinity. It was called *Trecanum.* No example has been
found of it, but it is mentioned at the end of the ancient exposition of the
Gallican Service attributed to Germanus, Bishop of Paris, *circa* A.D. 555,
as follows : " Then the Trecanum, which will be sung, is a sign of the
Catholic Faith about the belief in the Trinity."—Martene, lib. i., cap. iv.,
art xii., ordo 1. It is interesting to find that when the Roman Canon was introduced into the Gallican Liturgy, *Gloria in Excelsis* was also brought into
use ; but it occurs at the end of the Canon, headed " Gloria ad Missam
decantanda," and it is followed by various prayers which carry on its petitions.—Sacrament. Gallicanum, Muratori, vol. ii., p. 780. Whether it
may be concluded from this that it was so used at the end of the service is
uncertain, but other post-Communion Prayers in Gallican Missals show that
such a mingling of praise and prayer seemed to the ancient Gallican Church
to be an appropriate ending of the service, as the following instance proves :
" Filled with heavenly Food, ... Dearly beloved Brethren, let us give
praise and thanks unceasingly to the Lord our God ; beseeching that we
who have spiritually received the Body of our Lord Jesus Christ, being
freed from carnal vices, may be made spiritual, through our Lord."—*Post
Communionem, in die Nativitatis Domini,* Missale Gothicum, Muratori, vol. ii.,
page 523. And in the Mozarabic Missal such mingling of exultation and
petition is appointed for the conclusion of the service at various seasons ; as
for instance, " Having fulfilled our bounden duty and service in this sacred
solemnity, we give Thee, O Lord, thanks and praise, through the aid of
Thy merciful gift ; beseeching Thee, O God, that Thou wilt wash us from
our sins and make us to exult always in Thy praises. Amen. Through
Thy mercy, O our God, who art blessed and livest and reignest for ever and

" O Lamb of God, that takest away the sins of the world, have mercy upon us.

" O Lamb of God, that takest away the sins of the world, have mercy upon us.

" O Lamb of God, that takest away the sins of the world, grant us Thy peace."

In the First Prayer Book of 1549, when these words were appointed to be sung during the Communion, " Gloria in Excelsis" was recited without the repetition, " Thou that takest away, &c." But in the Second Prayer Book of 1552, " Agnus Dei" was omitted, and " Gloria in Excelsis" was brought here from the beginning of the service with the repetitions to which we are accustomed.[1]

The service ends with a benediction in place of the ancient form of bare dismissal. Such an ending is found in the Clementine Liturgy, which probably carries us back to the beginning of the fourth century.[2] Benedictions seem to have been once used in the Roman Liturgy, instead of the mere giving of peace, before the Communion.[3] And these benedictions were a marked feature of

ever. Amen. The Lord be with you, &c. Let us exult and rejoice to-day, &c. It is time to exult and rejoice, &c."—*In die Resurr. Domini,* folio 198. See also the instance of a similar form in the service given in the last chapter, page 214.

[1] The above suggestion is rejected as improbable by Professor Dowden, who says, " Clumsy as no doubt the revision sometimes was, this mode of treatment seems incredible."—" Scottish Communion Office," p. 230. But when it is remembered that our reformers were accustomed to the insertions in honour of the Virgin Mary, which are described page 94, the improbability is much lessened, especially if the natural fitness and the rhythmical beauty of the threefold repetition are considered.

[2] Page 38.

[3] Pages 77, 78.

the ancient Gallican and Anglo-Saxon as well as of the Mozarabic Services.[1]   The fixed ending of the Roman benedictions had been, " The blessing of God the Father, and of the Son, and of the Holy Ghost, and the peace of the Lord be always with you."   Upon this it is evident our own very beautiful blessing has been founded, amplified by the reminder of S. Paul, " that it passes all understanding." [2]

[1] Pages 86 (note 2), 87, 212.
[2] Phil. iv. 7.

A COMPARATIVE TABLE OF A

The Order of Communion, 1548, in Latin.	*The First Prayer Book, 1!*
Come, Holy Ghost. Collect for Purity. Ps. xliii. Our Father. Ave Maria.	Lord's Prayer. Collect for Purity.
Introit. Confession. Absolution. Kiss. Incense. iii. Kyrie. iii. Christe. iii. Kyrie eleison. Gloria in Excelsis. Collect. Epistle. Gospel. Nicene Creed. [Sermon.]	Introit. iii. Lord. iii. Christ. iii. Lord, ! Glory be to God on High, &c. Collect. Collect for King. Epistle. Nicene Creed. Sermon. Exhorta:
The Offertory. *Suscipe Sancta Trinitas.* *Orate* and Answer. *Secretum*, varying daily.	The Offertory.
The Lord be with you. And with thy spirit.	The Lord be with you. And with thy spirit.
Sursum Corda. Preface (nine proper), ending with Sanctus.	Sursum Corda. Preface (five proper), ending with Sa:
Roman CANON, with Sarum Rubrics. Prayer for Peace of Church. Sacrifice of Praise for Redemption. Commemoration of departed Saints. Oblation of whole Family of God. Words of Institution: " Day before He suffered." Offering in Remembrance of Passion. Prayer that it be accepted as Abel's. Prayer that these be carried to Altar on High. Prayer for Faithful departed and fellowship with them. Ascription to Trinity. Lord's Prayer, with unvarying Preface.	Let us pray for the whole state of Chri: (Present prayer for Church Militant.) Commemoration of Saints and prayer fo Prayer of Consecration. Prayer for Ho Words of Institution : "In the same ! (Priest taking the bread into his hands, Memorial of Passion. " Mercifully accept this our Sacrifice." Prayer for Ministry of Angels. Lord's Prayer, with short Preface.
The Peace of the Lord. Communion of the Priest. English Exhortation. Invitation. Confession. Absolution. Comfortable Words. Prayer of Humble Access. Communion. (?) Agnus Dei.	The Peace of the Lord. Christ our Pa: Invitation. Confession. Absolution. Prayer of Humble Access. Communion. Agnus Dei.
(?) Thanksgiving. (?) Post-Communion Collects. The Peace of God, &c.	Sentences of Holy Scripture, one daily. The Lord be with you. Thanksgiving. The Peace of God . . . . and the Bless

The Second Prayer Book, 1552.	
Lord's Prayer. Collect for Purity.	**Preparation of the Priest.**
Ten Commandments and Responses. Collect. Collect for King. Epistle. Gospel. Nicene Creed. Sermon or Homily.	**Instruction and Preparation of the People.**
The Offertory. Prayer for Church Militant. [1662, " and oblations." " We also bless Thy."] Exhortation.	**The Offertory.**
Invitation. Confession. Absolution. Comfortable Words.	**Preparation of the Faithful.**
Sursum Corda. Preface (five proper), ending with Sanctus.	**Praise and Thanks.**
Prayer of Humble Access. Prayer of Consecration, containing Commemoration of Sacrifice of Death of Christ ; and Words of Institution : " In the same night that He was betrayed." (No Manual Acts mentioned.) [Added again 1662.]	**The Consecration, including the Great Thanksgiving for Redemption.**
	The Communion.
Communion.	
Lord's Prayer. Post-Communion Prayer, or Thanksgiving. Glory be to God on High. The Peace of God . . . . and the Blessing.	**Thanksgiving, Praise, and Blessing.**

Additional Note, B ; On PRAYERS FOR THE DEPARTED.
(To page 223.)

THE object of this note is to consider the subject of Public Prayers for the Departed, pointing out their original limitation, and tracing the result of disregarding it in later times. It is not intended to discuss the subject of Private Prayers for the Departed. Since the days of S. Augustine there have always been some who have thought it necessary to pray for those dear to them, as he prayed for his mother, on the ground that even the most holy are imperfect.—Confessions, lib. ix., cap. 13. Whilst others have thought it unnecessary, either because they have confidence that the Almighty " doth so put away the sins of them that truly repent that He remembereth them no more" (Sacram. Gelas., *Reconcil. pœnitentis ad mortem*, Muratori, vol. i., p. 552, and English Office for the Visitation of the Sick), or because they feel that it is too late to pray for them when amendment of life is impossible, and they must be left simply to the mercy of God. And since the Church of England has left the whole subject of such private prayers undefined, with the exception of condemning " the Romish doctrine concerning Purgatory," there is no necessity to express any opinion here. But the case is different with respect to Public Prayers for the Departed, because the Church of England has been compelled to take the extreme measure of omitting what had previously been the universal custom of the Church of Christ, and to remove from the service all direct prayers for the dead. It is therefore necessary to consider, as exactly as possible, what the custom of the Church has been from the earliest times.

The character of early Liturgical Prayers for the Departed has been already shown by extracts from the Liturgy contained in the Apostolical Constitutions ; see above, p. 34. Such prayers were offered in the Eucharist in respect of the great and good of former ages, such as the patriarchs, prophets, apostles, and the blessed Virgin Mary, and in respect of martyrs and confessors of more recent times. When the names of the departed were mentioned, those only were commemorated whose memory was recalled with reverence and awe. There is no doubt that such prayers were regarded as an honour paid to the memory of the departed more than as intercessions on their behalf. Thereby the belief in the Communion of Saints was vividly set forth, and the departed were regarded as joining in the great act of the

Church's worship. But the need of praying for the pardon of their sins was disregarded. For instance, Cyprian, Bishop of Carthage, A.D. 250, forbids men to honour the memory of a certain Victor, because he had committed the ecclesiastical offence of nominating a presbyter as guardian under his will. He had acted contrary to the express decision of the bishops, therefore no offering should be made in his name, neither should the sacrifice be celebrated in commemoration of his falling asleep. " Episcopi censuerunt ne quis frater excedens ad tutelam vel curam Clerum nominaret; ac si quis hoc fecisset non offeretur pro eo, nec sacrificium pro dormitione ejus celebraretur. [For this use of *pro*, see page 109.] Neque enim apud altare Dei meretur nominari in sacerdotum prece, qui ab altari sacerdotes voluit avocare."—Cyprian, ad Presbyt. et Diac. Furnis., Epist. I., *aliter* lxv. See note, Oxford edition, 1682.

The above example proves that a Christian might lose the privilege of being publicly commemorated after death in consequence of a breach of ecclesiastical rule. It is therefore evident that such prayers did not involve the idea of any necessity of praying for the pardon of the departed; for if it had been otherwise it would have been felt that such an offence rendered intercession to be the more necessary. This is further confirmed by obser-. ving that the intercession offered in these early liturgical prayers was of a very general character. This appears in the Liturgy above referred to, and also in the later prayers of other Liturgies. Nothing is said to lead to the idea that those who are prayed for are in need of any propitiatory offering. They are described as " orthodox " and " righteous," and the petition is confined to the simple entreaty that God will remember them and give them rest.

But by the middle of the fourth century, as we learn from the Catechetical Lectures of Cyril (see above, p. 34), a distinction was made in these prayers between saints and martyrs who were commemorated only, and others for whom intercessions were offered ; and then the prayer was introduced that God would regard the intercessions of the former on behalf of the worshippers, and give rest to the latter. Thus we find that in the Liturgy of S. Chrysostom the prayer for the departed has taken this shape : " We offer to Thee this reasonable service for those who have fallen asleep in faith, our forefathers . . . the most blessed ever-virgin Mary . . . the holy and renowned Apostles, and all Thy saints; at whose intercessions look down upon us, O God. And remember all who sleep in hope of the Resurrection of life eternal (*here he commemorates whom he will*) and give them rest, where the light of Thy countenance shines upon them." See above, p. 58. This is almost exactly reproduced in the Liturgy of S. James, to which Cyril probably referred.—Swainson's " Greek Liturgies," pp. 293, 301.

The advance from these views respecting prayers for the departed to the mediæval ideas respecting the need of making propitiatory offerings on their behalf may now be traced. The distinction thus made between saints and others was clearly unscriptural. For Holy Scripture regards all Christians as " called to be saints" (1 Cor. i. 2 ; Ephes. i. 1, &c.), and describes all consistent members of Christ by the same term (Acts ix. 32, 41,&c.). A departure from scriptural modes of thought having been once made, the way was opened for wider developments which can have been little expected in those early days. By degrees the object of the prayers, which had been confined to pious wishes for the rest and enjoyment of the *blessed* dead, was enlarged, and the remembrance of the departed before God was understood to imply intercessions for the pardon of their sins. There is abundant evidence to prove that in the age of Gregory the Great, A.D. 590-604, the practice of offering the Eucharistic Sacrifice in a propitiatory sense on behalf of the dead, who were not supposed to be at rest, was a new addition in the Roman Church ; and that such intercessions were being gradually introduced amongst the private devotions of the people instead of, or in addition to, the ancient commemoration of the departed. For in urging this practice upon his people Gregory found it necessary to confirm the usefulness of such prayers by the help of a number of curious stories, from which he draws the conclusion that "if the Eucharistic offering can help those who are not aware that it is being offered, it will assist the dead, if their sins are not insoluble."—Greg. Magn., Dial., lib. iv., cap. 55, 56. But the conclusion which may be drawn from these stories in the present day is somewhat different. For if they are genuine, they show the difficulty which was felt at the end of the sixth century in spreading a practice to which the Church was not accustomed ; and if they have been interpolated by a later generation, they show how slight was the foundation of the practice in which men wished to be able to trust. Archbishop Cranmer calls attention to these opinions of Gregory, in his MS. Collections, vol. ii., p. 175.

There is a doubt whether the "Memento," or prayer for the departed, formed a part of "The Canon" before the days of Gregory; see above, page 75. But whether it was used or not, it is clear that he could not appeal to it in support of the views he was encouraging. According to the actual words of "The Canon," the practice of the mediæval, as of the modern Roman Church, has been to pray only for those who already "sleep in the sleep of peace." The arguments of Gregory were used to support the practice of praying for those who were not in peace.

At about the same period Isidore of Seville, A.D. 603-636, mentions the custom of offering for the dead as an ancient tradition which, as was usual with respect to anything of unknown antiquity, he refers to the Apostles.

He takes the view that unless the Catholic Church believed that sins could be remitted to the dead it would not pray for them; and he shows that such ideas had been prevalent from the end of the fourth century at least, by quoting S. Augustine's teaching about such offerings, as being " for the very good, thanksgivings ; for those not very bad, propitiations ; and for the very bad, a consolation rather for the survivors than a benefit to the dead."— Isidore, de Eccles. officiis, lib. i., cap. xviii. ; Augustine, Enchiridion, cap. cx.; de Civit. Dei, lib. xxi., 24. An example of the earliest form of such prayers " for those not very bad " is found in *Missale Gothicum*, a Gallican Missal belonging to about the beginning of the eighth century, as follows, "For these and all who rest in Christ, grant, Lord, a place of refreshment, light, and peace; and if some, by reason of their sins, are detained in the shades and punishments of Hades, grant the kind things of Thy mercy, and direct them to cross over into rest, and permit them to share in the first resurrection with Thy saints and elect, that they may be Thy portion in the land of the living ; through Christ, our Lord."—Muratori, vol. ii., p. 646.

The development of this practice of pleading for the departed extended during the Middle Ages, until it was universally believed that such prayers were necessary in order to gain for Christians pardon and peace. What was regarded in the times of Cyprian as an honour which should be forfeited for the least offence, was turned into an ordinance which was necessary for salvation, as appears from the following prayers from the Sarum Services :—

" O Lord Jesu Christ, the King of glory, deliver the souls of all faithful departed from the hand of Hades, and from the deep lake; save them from the mouth of the lion ; let not Hell suck them in, nor let them fall into dark places of the shades," &c.

" O God, whose nature and property is always to have mercy and to spare, be gracious unto the soul of Thy servant, and pardon all his sins, that being freed from the bonds of death he may pass over unto life ; through," &c.

" Grant, O Lord, we beseech Thee, that the soul of Thy servant, the anniversary of whose death we are keeping, being cleansed by these sacrifices, may receive both pardon and everlasting rest ; through," &c.

" O God, the Creator and Redeemer of all the faithful, grant unto the souls of all faithful departed remission of all their sins ; that by our dutiful supplications they may obtain the pardon they have longed for ; who with the Father," &c.—Collects from *Missa pro defunctis et in anniversariis*, Sarum Breviary, Psalterium, pp. 527-532.

The practice of mediæval prayers for the dead may be further illustrated by an admonition which appeared in a primer printed A.D. 1535, in which the author complains of " several books that mislead the people in their application to the Saints, make them believe their addresses before some images would be more particularly significant, that they would deliver a certain number of souls out of purgatory," &c. And he illustrates his assertion by mention of the legend of " The Mass of the Five Wounds," as follows : " Boniface, byshop of Rome, lay sycke and lyke to dye, to whome our Lord sent the arc-angel Raphael with the office of the Masse of the Five Wounds, sayeing, Ryse and write this office and saye it five tymes, and thou shalt be restored to thy health immediately. And what preste soever shall say this office . . . . and that it be sayd for the soule of the deade, anone as it shall be sayd and ended fyve times, his soul shall be ryd from paynes."— Collier, Eccles. Hist., vol. iv., p. 314 ; Burton, Three Primers of the reign of Henry VIII., p. 5 ; Sarum Missal, *Missa de quinque vulneribus*, amongst the " Missæ votivæ " at the end.

Justification through a living and working faith in Christ was thus ob- scured, and in place of it men were taught to trust to the prayers which should be offered for them after death. With these instances before us, there can be little wonder that our reformers felt it necessary to sweep away the whole system of such prayers for the departed, in order to lead men to know that this life is the time to gain pardon and salvation through Christ, and that the paying for such prayers to be said after their death could not take the place of personal repentance and faith. There is no doubt that Archbishop Cranmer was much influenced in this decision by his study of the works of Dionysius the (so-called) Areopagite. For in his Book of Extracts from Holy Scripture and the Fathers, he enters very carefully into the subjects of purgatory and of prayers for the dead, and quotes largely from Dionysius.—MS. Collections, vol. ii., pp. 265, 335-348. The question is raised by Dionysius, " What is the use of asking God's mercy for the dead ? " And in his answer he declares positively that Scripture teaches that the prayers of the righteous, whether for the living or the departed, can profit those only who are worthy. He asks, " How did the prayer of Samuel profit Saul, or the intercession of the prophets the people of Israel ? " And he compares the man who seeks the prayers of the saints, without striving after a holy life, to the man who would gaze upon the sunlight after having put out his own eyes.—Dionys., Eccles. Hierarch., cap. vii., pars iii., p. 96. This is expanded with great force by Dean Colet in his summary.—Colet, " On the Hierarchies of Dionysius," by J. H. Lupton, pp. 145-147. The system of prayers for the dead to which the Church was accustomed in the beginning of the sixteenth century included prayers for the unworthy. In the First Prayer Book of 1549 the attempt was made to retain what was primitive and to reject what was ob- jectionable, but it failed to satisfy those who had been accustomed to the system all their lives, and it was deliberately abandoned in 1552.

CHAPTER VIII.

THE COMMON PRAYERS.

" Si quis diligenter animadverterit et vetus Patrum consilium institutum-
que consideraverit, plane intelliget hoc Breviarium non tam esse novum
inventum, quam Breviarii antiqui adhibito quodam temperamento restitu-
tionem."—*Cardinal Quignonius*, A.D. 1537.

A T the time when "The Consultation" of Archbishop
Herman was brought out in Germany, A.D. 1535, a
similar attempt to revise the Breviary was being prepared in France, which proved to be equally useful to
our reformers in their still more complicated work of
revising the Common Prayers, or "Divine Service" of
the Church.[1]

The specimen of the Hour Services which was given
in a previous chapter from the Sarum Breviary will have
explained the urgent need for revision which existed at
the beginning of the sixteenth century; and when Archbishop Cranmer and the Commissioners appointed for
the purpose gave their attention to these services, with
the view of publishing an English form of daily prayers,

---

[1] " The Common Prayers in the Church, commonly called Divine Service."
—Preface concerning the service of the Church in the Book of Common
Prayer.

they found ready to hand a revised Breviary which had been prepared at the express desire of Pope Clement VII. by Cardinal Quignon, General of the Franciscan Order and Legate to Spain. This was published at Rome, Lyons, and other places, by authority, and with the sanction of Pope Clement's successor, Paul III., and the King of France, A.D. 1535, 1536. From the words of the preface to this reformed Breviary it is clear that the objections to the old services which were felt by churchmen in Italy and France were very similar to those which were held by our English reformers. And in the preface "Concerning the Service of the Church," in our Book of Common Prayer, frequent use has been made of the expressions previously used by Cardinal Quignon.[1] There is no doubt that he did a valuable work in his attempt at revising the services. For he freed the Breviary from its very difficult rules, removed the vast mass of vain repetitions, shortened the services, lengthened the readings from Holy Scripture, and expunged from the lessons the foolish legends about the saints who were commemorated. But he did not venture to alter the ancient arrangement of the services according to the eight Offices finally fixed by the Rule of S. Benedict, *circa* A.D. 530.

A specimen of the course of daily services thus prepared is here given, from which the reader can judge for himself the value of this work by comparing them with those of the Sarum Breviary previously given.[2]

[1] These two prefaces are compared together in Palmer's Origines Liturgicæ, vol. i., p. 230.
[2] See above, Chapter IV.

𝕸attins.

Our Father. Ave Maria.

Confession.

I confess to God Almighty, blessed Mary ever a virgin, blessed Michael the Archangel, blessed John Baptist, the holy Apostles Peter and Paul, to all saints, and to you, Father, that I have sinned exceedingly in thought, word, and deed, by my fault, by my fault, by my very great fault. Therefore I pray blessed Mary, &c., to pray the Lord our God for me.

Absolution.

Almighty God have mercy upon you, and, forgiving you all your sins, bring you to life everlasting.

Response. Amen.

Verse. Pardon, absolution, and remission of our sins may the Almighty and merciful Lord grant us.

Response. Amen.[2]

---

[1] Breviarium Romanæ Curiæ, 1537, small 8vo., second edition. In the Preface addressed to Pope Paul III., Cardinal Quignon states that the work lately issued had been carried out at the express desire of Pope Clement. He mentions that it was so well approved by many that they thought that no alterations were needed, but that at the request of others he had added some things and altered others, thoroughly revising the whole. The Preface is followed by a faculty from Pope Paul III. authorizing its sale, and giving a dispensation to all clerics to use it in place of the old Breviary. A copy of this edition is in Corpus Christi College Library, Cambridge. It is evident that many other editions were printed. I have found the following :— 1543, 4to. Lugduni, and 1549, 16mo. Parisiis, Durham University Library ; 1546, fol. Lugduni, Bodleian ; 1547, 4to. Venetiis ; 1551, 8vo. Lugduni, and 1557, 16mo. Antwerp, British Museum.

[2] The preparatory part of the service was thus shortened by omission of the Creed, and its spiritual character improved by the Confession, &c., brought here from *Prime.* This example was not followed in England until the Second Prayer Book of 1552.

Verse. O Lord, open Thou my lips.
Response. And my mouth shall show forth Thy praise.
Verse. O God, make speed to save us.
Response. O Lord, make haste to help us.
Glory be to the Father, &c. Alleluia.

VENITE ; *with* INVITATORY, *said only at beginning and end.*

HYMN.

ANTIPHON. Three PSALMS. ANTIPHON *repeated.*[1]

Our Father, &c.

1st LESSON, *from the OLD TESTAMENT ; preceded by*
" Command, Lord, a blessing ; "[2] *and the Benediction,* " God
the Father Almighty, be merciful and gracious unto us.
R. Amen ; " *and followed by,* " Do Thou, O Lord, have mercy
upon us. *R.* Thanks be to God."

2nd LESSON, *from the NEW TESTAMENT ; preceded by*
the Benediction, " The only begotten Son of God, vouchsafe to
bless and help us;" *and ending as the first.*

3rd LESSON, *from a HOMILY upon a Text ; preceded by*
the Benediction, " May the grace of the Holy Spirit illuminate
our senses and our hearts ; " *and ending as the first.*

TE DEUM ; *or, in Advent and Lent,* PSALM LI.

---

[1] The Psalms were arranged for a weekly course, three for every office,
except Lauds. The Antiphons were said in part before, and wholly after
the Psalms, except on double Feasts, when they were said both before and
after.

[2] " Jube Domine benedicere ; " we may learn from the Primers that this
was understood as a prayer to God, not as a request to the priest. For
instance, in Bishop Hilsey's Primer, 1539, it is translated, " Lord, we
beseech thee of thy blessing," to which is added, " *The answer,* With a blessing perpetual Bless thou us Father eternal."—Burton's Three Primers,
p. 336 ; but see also above, p. 80.

Lauds.[1]

Verse. O God, make speed to save us, &c.
Glory be to the Father, &c. Hallelujah.
Antiphon.   Two PSALMS ; BENEDICITE OMNIA
OPERA, *on Sundays, and some other Old Testament Canticle
on Week Days.*   BENEDICTUS.   Antiphon *repeated.*[2]
Verse. O Lord, hear my prayer.
Response. And let my crying come unto Thee.

Let us pray.

COLLECT FOR THE DAY.

Commemoration *of the BLESSED VIRGIN, consisting of
Antiphon, Verse and Response, and Collect.*
Commemoration *of the SAINTS, consisting of Antiphon,
Verse and Response, and Collect.*
Verse. Let us bless the Lord.
Response. Thanks be to God.
Verse. May the souls of the faithful, through the mercy of
God, rest in peace.
Response. Amen.

Prime.

Our Father.   Ave Maria.
Verse. O God, make speed to save us, &c.
Glory be to the Father, &c.   Hallelujah.

---

[1] A rubric states that *Lauds* is not to be considered a distinct office, but
a part of Mattins. Therefore there is no preparatory part before it, and
no hymn.

[2] It should be noticed that the services were greatly simplified in respect
of the Antiphons.   Here the two Canticles as well as the two Psalms were
included under one Antiphon.

HYMN.

ANTIPHON. Three PSALMS. ATHANASIAN CREED *on Sundays; * APOSTLES CREED *on Week Days.* ANTIPHON *repeated.*

Verse. O Lord, hear my prayer.

Response. And let my crying come unto Thee.

Let us pray.

THIRD COLLECT FOR GRACE.

Verse. Let us bless the Lord, &c.; *same ending as to Lauds.*

And after Prime shall be said:

The COMMEMORATION *of the Saint whose Festival is observed.*

Or else immediately,

Verse. Precious in the sight of the Lord

Response. Is the death of His Saints.

May S. Mary and all the Saints intercede for us to the Lord, that we may obtain help and salvation from Him who liveth, &c.

Verse. May the Lord Almighty dispose our days and our doings in His peace.

Response. Amen.

The Evening Services were drawn up after the same plan.

Vespers.

Our Father. Ave Maria.

Verse. O God, make speed to save us, &c.

Glory be to the Father, &c. Hallelujah.

HYMN.

ANTIPHON. Three PSALMS. MAGNIFICAT. ANTIPHON *repeated.*

Verse. O Lord, hear my prayer, &c.

Let us pray.

COLLECT FOR THE DAY.

Commemorations *as in Lauds.*

Compline.

Our Father. Ave Maria.

Verse. Turn us, O God, our Saviour.

Response. And let Thine anger cease from us.

Verse. O God, make speed to save us, &c.

Glory be to the Father, &c.   Hallelujah.

HYMN.

Antiphon.   Three PSALMS.   NUNC DIMITTIS.   Antiphon *repeated.*

Verse. O Lord, hear my prayer, &c.

Let us pray.

Visit, we pray Thee, O Lord, this habitation, and drive far from it all snares of the enemy; may Thy holy angels dwell herein, and keep us in peace; and may Thy blessing be upon us for ever, through, &c.

Verse. Let us bless the Lord, &c., *as in Lauds.*

After which shall be said,

The Commemoration *of the Blessed Virgin.*

It will be seen at once that whilst the evils of repetitions in the old services were removed, a new evil was introduced by the formality of the plan of the new services. The new Breviary consisted of a repetition of services one after another, which were drawn up on the same plan, and were almost alike. And there is little cause for wonder that after about thirty years' trial it was replaced by a new version under a bull of Pope Pius V.,

A.D. 1568, which brought back again the old services, with all their old blemishes, but also with their ever-varying beauties, through the combination of fixed with movable portions, in verses, responses, psalms, anthems, and preces.

At the same time it is clear that many very useful suggestions were thus made, which assisted our reformers in their revision. Cardinal Quignon's Breviary led the way towards the formation of one service in place of several, and by its rejection of a multitude of details, which, though beautiful and devotional in themselves, were practically unsuited for congregational use, it pointed out the parts which were most worthy to survive.[1] Our reformers were thus encouraged boldly to abandon what experience had proved to be impracticable. The ancient course of frequent services, beautiful in theory, aimed too high. Necessity had already reduced them in practice to two, or at the most three meetings for worship. The English Church has gone one step further, and in abandoning the shadow of many services has secured the substance of daily Morning and Evening Prayer expressed in the words of the ancient Hour Offices; and this she alone has secured of all the Churches of the West.[2]

[1] Cardinal Quignon himself calls attention to the beauty of the various devotions which he had omitted, and to the necessity of omitting them. As early as 1544 Archbishop Cranmer, in a letter to King Henry VIII. respecting the Litany which he had translated, singles out for special mention the main portions of the daily services, showing that their importance was already recognized. He recommends that the Litany "be sung distinctly and devoutly, as be in the matins and evensong, *Venite*, the hymns, *Te Deum*, *Benedictus*, *Magnificat*, *Nunc dimittis*, and all the psalms and versicles."—Hook, Lives of Archbishops, vol. vii., p. 204.

[2] Freeman, Principles of Divine Worship, vol. i., pp. 278-281.

But whilst our reformers took their ideas from Cardinal Quignon, they took their matter from the old services to which they had been accustomed at home. It is evident that a great resemblance ran through the " Hour Offices " of the different Churches of the West. With the exception of those which used the Mozarabic and the Ambrosian Rites, all followed one plan and order. Yet there were local peculiarities belonging to the services not only of the monastic bodies, but also of different countries and dioceses. And it is interesting to be able to trace some of the old English peculiarities which still stand out prominently in our Mattins and Evensong. Our services are still distinctly English, even as they were in the times before the Reformation. For instance, the Sarum Lessons were peculiar to the English Use, and our English Lectionary still stands alone and preeminent. The rubric directing the priest to stand up to say the *Preces* is taken from the old Sarum rubric in Lauds, but it does not appear in the Roman Breviary.[1] The third collect at Evening Prayer, " Lighten our darkness, &c.," is found in the Sacramentary of Gelasius, but it was a distinctive feature of the English " Compline;" for in the Roman Breviary another collect was provided, which was continued in Quignon's Breviary, and is still used.[2] The importance given to the Festival of the Trinity through the numbering of the Sundays for the rest of the year as Sundays after Trinity, is

---

[1] See above, p. 131.

[2] The Collect in the Roman Compline is as follows: " Visita quæsumus Domine habitationem istam, et omnes insidias inimici repelle ; Angeli tui sancti habitent in ea, qui nos in pace custodiant, et benedictio tua sit super nos semper. Per Dominum." See above, p. 260.

another English custom shared from ancient times with
the Gallican Church, but not adopted by the Roman.
The observance of Trinity Sunday began in France about
the eighth century, being mentioned in a letter to the
Emperor Charlemagne. Its observance is also provided
for in an ancient MS. of the monastery of S. Denys, and in
another belonging to Tours, *circa* A.D. 900. It seems also
to be referred to in the Pontifical of Egbert, Archbishop
of York, A.D. 732-766.[1] The Festival was not generally
admitted into the Roman Service Books until the fifteenth century, when it was ordered to be observed by
Pope John XXII., and the Sundays in the Roman Ser-

[1] Martene, de Antiq. Eccles. ritibus, lib. iv., cap. xxviii., 22, mentions
that in the Pontifical of Egbert, the Episcopal Benediction for First Sunday
after Pentecost accords with the Festival of the Holy Trinity. It is as
follows :—

"Omnipotens Trinitas, unus et verus Deus, Pater et Filius et Spiritus
Sanctus, det vobis desiderare fideliter, agnoscere veraciter, diligere sinceriter.
Amen.

"Æqualitatem atque incommutabilitatem suæ essentiæ ita vestris mentibus
infigat, ut ab eo numquam vos quibuscunque fantasiis oberrare permittat.
Amen.

"Sicque vos in sua fide et caritate perseverare concedat ut per ea postmodum ad sui manifestationem visionemque interminabilem introducat.

"Quod ipse, &c."—Pontif. of Egbert, publ. by Surtees Society, p. 71.
But the Sundays are named after Pentecost.

In the Leofric Missal of the Church of Exeter of the ninth century, the
Service for *Domin. octavis pentecostes* is taken from the Gelasian Sacramentary,
and the Collect for Second Sunday after Pentecost is that for First Sunday
in the Gregorian Sacramentary ; and the other Sundays follow in the same
way. But there is no reference to the Festival of the Holy Trinity on the
Sunday after Pentecost. The Service for the Holy Trinity containing our
present collect is, however, placed first amongst the *Missæ votivæ* which
follow the services for saints' days. The same service is added in an eleventh
century hand to the Codex Othob. of the Gregorian Sacramentary.—Leofric
Missal, edited by Rev. F. E. Warren ; Muratori, Liturg. Rom. vetus, vol. ii.,
p. 582.

vice Books are still counted from Pentecost.[1] But in the Sarum Missal and Breviary the Sundays were numbered, the same as in our English Prayer Book, as Sundays after Trinity.

Yet at the same time, whilst the signs of the peculiarity of the ancient English use are still maintained, our services are in general accord with the most ancient western forms of daily service. The Psalms and Canticles are the same as of old. The greater number of our Collects, which in almost all cases are translations of the old Sarum Collects, are to be found in the ancient Sacramentaries.[2] The *Preces* are the same as were used in the original Benedictine Services appointed by the Rule of S. Benedict, A.D. 530.[3] It is true that many parts of

[1] In the Roman Missal, as it was revised at the Council of Trent, the Service for the Festival of the Trinity appears after the services for Whitsun Week, in conjunction with the service provided for the First Sunday after Pentecost. But in earlier missals the " Missa in honore Trinitatis " is found added after all the other " Missæ " of the year ; showing its late introduction. See, for instance, Roman Missal printed at Lyons, A.D. 1500. (British Museum.)

[2] See above, page 66, and note 1, page 132.

[3] The first two verses are now omitted, and the concluding verses respecting the faithful departed. The Benedictine *Preces* were as follow, according to an ancient Breviary of the monastery of Monte Casino, preserved in the Library of the Oratory at Paris :—

> Ego dixi Domine misereri mei
>> Sana animam meam
> Convertere Domine aliquantulum
>> Et deprecare
> Fiat Domine misericordia tua super nos
>> Sicut speravimus
> Sacerdotes tui induant justitiam
>> Et sancti tui exultent
> Domine salvos fac reges
>> Exaudi nos

the ancient offices—hymns, verses, responses, anthems, and *preces*—were necessarily omitted, because, though beautiful in themselves, they interfered with the simplicity of arrangement, without which the services could not become fit for congregational use. But with the exception of these omissions, and the additions of the preparatory part at the beginning and the prayers after the third collect, our Mattins and Evensong consist of the very same devotions which Christians have used from the sixth century, stripped of repetitions, shortened, and made suitable for general use.

The main point to be noticed is the orderly arrangement of our English Services. Each service now follows a systematic and well-defined plan, according to which the different acts of worship come in their assigned places.

These different acts of worship are thus described in the Exhortation. We meet together—1, to render thanks; 2, to set forth God's praise ; 3, to hear His Word ; 4, to ask those things which are requisite for soul and body. Thanksgiving belongs specially to the Service of the Eucharist, and, therefore, does not hold any distinct place in our Morning and Evening Prayer. But the other three divisions of worship are arranged in a regular order. After the introductory preparation for the service which is to follow, Praise forms the first great division of

Salvum fac populum tuum Domine et
  Benedic hæreditati tuæ
Reges eos et
  Oremus pro fidelibus defunctis
      *   *   *   *   *

—Martene, de Antiq. Monach. rit., lib. i., cap. iii., 15. Cf. Sarum *preces*, page 131.

our daily worship; next comes the hearing of God's Word, with Canticles intermingled with the Lessons; and, lastly, the Prayers. Under the old system, in which one service was repeated after another, these three divisions of worship were confused together. In the English Services they are arranged in regular order.

It has been explained before that the three Offices of Mattins, Lauds, and Prime formed together one service in the mediæval Church. Our Morning Service has been compiled out of the same three Offices. This has been effected by the omission of repetitions and devotions unsuited for congregational use, and by the rearrangement of the Psalms and Lessons.

The preparatory sentences, exhortation, confession, and absolution were prefixed in the Second Prayer Book of 1552. Our reformers, following the example set by Cardinal Quignon, decided that confession and absolution should come at the beginning, instead of at the end, of the service, as in the old arrangement. And the forms which were then drawn up are generally acknowledged to be singularly weighty and full of matter, and to show a deep knowledge of Holy Scripture.

In the Lord's Prayer, which in the first Prayer Book had been the only preparation for the following acts of worship, we may now detect the influence of the recent knowledge of the Eastern Services, through the addition of the ascription, " For Thine is the kingdom," &c., for this had been unknown in the Western Offices, though always used in the Greek.[1]

[1] Added in 1662. See above, page 60. The Lord's Prayer seems to have been first printed at full length in the Scottish Prayer Book of 1637. Mention of the Ascription is made in Archbishop Herman's " Simplex ac pia de-

Then the Service of Praise begins, as of old, with the Versicles :—

" O Lord, open Thou our lips, &c.

O God, make speed, &c.

Glory be to the Father," &c.

" Praise ye the Lord," is in place of the Hebrew exclamation, " Hallelujah ;" and the fitting response, " The Lord's Name be praised," is new.[1]

Then the great act of Praise follows, consisting of the fixed Invitatory Psalm *Venite*, and the daily portion of the Psalms, as in the ancient Mattins. The chief alteration is in the arrangement of the Psalter for a monthly, instead of a weekly, course. A comparison of the present with the ancient order will show how much the service has gained in simplicity, in the omission of Antiphons, and in the regular use of the "Gloria" after every Psalm. Attention should be paid also to two particulars mentioned in the preface to our Book of Common Prayer :— " Note that the Psalter followeth the division of the Hebrews, and the translation of the great English Bible, set forth and used in the time of Henry VIII. and Edward VI." The numbering of the Psalms in the Vulgate follows that in the Septuagint version, and differs from the numbering in the Hebrew text.[2] Consequently

liberatio," 1535, in the exposition of the prayer, but only the first few words of the prayer itself are printed. Bishop Cosin also, 1627, adds "the Doxology" to his description of the Lord's Prayer, but the prayer itself occurs without it in the accompanying offices.—" Private Devotions," pp. 26, 60 (Oxford, 1867).

[1] Added in 1604.

[2] In the Septuagint, Psalms ix. and x. form one Psalm, and all the following Psalms are numbered x., xi., xii., &c., instead of xi., xii., xiii., as far as Psalm cxlvii., which being counted as two Psalms brings the total to be the same as in the Hebrew.

the numbers of our English Psalms, both in the Prayer Book and Bible version, vary in the same way from the numbers referred to both in Greek and Latin Service Books. The mention of "the great English Bible" leads us to understand that the rhythmical beauty of our Psalter is due to the unrivalled power which Cranmer possessed of rendering the devotional expressions of other languages into the English tongue.

The second division of our daily acts of worship then follows, viz., the devotional hearing of the Word of God. This arrangement follows the order of the ancient Mattins, but here especially we notice the practical character of the work of our reformers. The old lessons had varied in number, being twelve on Sundays and certain festivals, six on others, and three on others and on ordinary week days. They were excessively short, and appointed in such a way that no regular course of Bible reading was followed. The present order of the Lessons is one of the distinguishing excellences of the English Prayer Book.

The Calendar is now arranged, not merely to give the course of the Festivals throughout the year, as in former times, but to give also the fixed order of daily lessons from Holy Scripture. The many lessons of the old services have been reduced to two, both being taken wholly from Holy Scripture; and in place of the often repeated and complicated arrangement of Responds and Verses, the Canticles are appointed to be sung after each Lesson, according to a fixed order, viz., *Te Deum* from Mattins after the First Lesson, and *Benedictus* from Lauds after the Second Lesson. To these *Benedicite* [1]

---

[1] In other churches *Benedicite* has been held in higher esteem than amongst ourselves. It was appointed to be sung before the Gospel in the

from Lauds was added in the Prayer Book of 1549, for
use during Lent, in place of *Te Deum.* This restriction

Gallican Church, and S. Germain, *circa* A.D. 555, explained that it was so
used to represent the Old Testament saints waiting for the coming of the
Lord. For like as the Angel came to the Three in the furnace, and " made
as it had been a moist whistling wind," so the Son of God came to those who
were looking for Him, breaking the powers of hell and bringing the joy of
the Resurrection which the Gospel teaches.—Martene, de Eccles. ritibus,
lib. i., cap. iv., art. xii., ordo 1. *Benedicite* was ordered to be similarly used in
the Spanish Liturgy (Fourth Council of Toledo, Canon 14), and is found in the
Mozarabic Missal in the Service for the First Sunday in Lent. Many versions of this hymn occur, all of which differ considerably from our English
arrangement. In the Mozarabic Missal, the hymn begins at verse 29 of the
English Version of the Apocryphal addition to the Book of Daniel, " Blessed
art Thou, O Lord God of our fathers ; and to be praised and exalted above
all for ever ; " and the later verses are placed together, so that the response
occurs only a few times ; and all the verses which refer to inanimate nature
are omitted. Similarly, in the Mozarabic Breviary, *Benedicite*, which forms
part of *Lauds*, is called *Benedictus* from the first word of the verse with
which it begins. After the *Antiphon* it is arranged as follows :—

" Blessed art Thou, O Lord God of our Fathers," &c. (ver. 29-32, English
Version of Apocryphal addition to the Book of Daniel).

" O all ye works of the Lord, ye heavens : angels, and all who are above
the heavens, bless ye the Lord.

" O all ye powers, sun and moon, rain and dew : every wind, fire and heat,
nights and days, light and darkness.

" O ye winter and summer, frosts and snow : lightning and clouds.

" O ye earth, mountains, and hills : and all things that grow upon the earth.

" O ye seas, and floods and fountains: whales and all that move in the waters.

" O ye fowls of the air, beasts and cattle : sons of men, Israel, priests,
servants of the Lord, spirits and souls of the righteous, holy and humble
men of heart.

" O Ananias, Azarias and Misael, bless ye the Lord : and exalt Him
above all for ever. Amen."

Antiphon repeated. " Bless ye the Lord all ye His saints," &c.

" Glory be to the Father," &c.

Antiphon repeated again.—Breviarium Gothicum. (Folio 6.)

In the Rule of S. Benedict *Benedicite* was regarded as holding a very
important position in the morning service of *Lauds*, and was called *Benedictio.*—Martene, de Antiq. Monach. ritibus, lib. i., cap. iii.

was afterwards removed, and *Benedicite* as well as *Jubilate*,[1] which was introduced also from Lauds, became available for alternative use.

Amongst the numerous omissions which were made in this part of the Morning Service we may notice that many repetitions of the Lord's Prayer were struck out, together with varying Verses and Benedictions, and the fixed Psalms of Lauds and Prime, accompanied with a complicated system of Anthems. In removing these our reformers closely followed the guidance of Cardinal Quignon.[2]

---

[1] *Jubilate* was one of the fixed Psalms for *Lauds* on Sundays ; see above, page 129. Its alternative use instead of *Benedictus* was a permission added in the Second Prayer Book of 1552. Many persons have a strong objection to using it in place of the New Testament canticle, considering that as a memorial of the incarnation *Benedictus* ought never to be omitted. On the other hand, Hooker, book v., chap. xl., mentions that amongst the Puritans in Queen Elizabeth's time great objections were raised to the use of all the New Testament canticles. How little reason they had for their objections Hooker, as usual, ably shows, whilst he reminds them that by the appointment of alternative Psalms, "the choice was left free for the minister to use indifferently the one or the other ; " which seems a sufficient answer to both parties. It may be added that in the original institution of *Lauds* no particular importance was assigned to *Benedictus*. The Rule of S. Benedict merely appointed that two Canticles should be sung, one from the Old Testament, and one from the New Testament ; and the Canticle which was held in the highest estimation was *Benedicite*.—Martene, de Antiq. Monach. ritibus, lib. i., cap. iii. In the Eastern Church, *Benedictus* does not appear to be used in the regular Hour Services ; neither is it appointed for daily use in the Spanish Breviary according to the Mozarabic Rite.

[2] Respecting the omission of many details in the old services, Cardinal Quignon gives this explanation: " Versiculos responsoria et capitula omittere idcirco visum est, non quod hæc supervacanea, aut inutilia viderentur, augent enim pietatem et sunt scripturæ sacræ particulæ ; sed quoniam cum introductæ sint ad cantus potissimum modulandos, et legentes sæpe morentur cum molestia quæritandi, locum relinqui voluimus continenti lectioni scripturæ sacræ, quæ magis facit ad pietatem atque doctrinam . . . Nec

But two omissions were made, which were of a different character, and can only be regarded with regret, viz., the Invitatory to *Venite*, which struck the keynote of the Festival, and the Antiphon to *Benedictus*, which pressed home the teaching of the Gospel of the day, and maintained the memory of it during the succeeding week. It is evident that the present position of *Benedictus*, immediately after a *varying* lesson from the New Testament, makes it impossible that an antiphon from the *fixed* Gospel of the Sunday or Festival should be used with it. But the case in respect of *Venite* is different; and the absence of any distinctive mark of the Festival from the beginning of the service must always be felt to be a matter for regret.[1]

In the Sarum Use both the Athanasian Creed and the Apostles' Creed formed part of the unchanging service of Prime. Our present practice is a good illustration of the character of our reformers' work in removing unreasonable repetitions.[2] The position of the Creed here

enim ad precandum cuncta utilia et salubria congeri debent, ne clerici graventur iniquiore pondere. Atque utinam tam robusti essemus ut totum etiam vetus testamentum in anno perlegere non gravaremur, libenter enim omnes illius libros legendos proponeremus; sed (ut dictum est) habenda fuit ratio ne precandi labor in tanta clericorum infirmitate modum excederet."
—Preface to Reformed Breviary, second edition, 1537.

[1] See note 1, page 125, and note 4, page 130. A future revision of the Prayer Book seems at present to be a matter beyond the bounds of probability. But it may be worthy of consideration whether it is impossible for a verse to be introduced before *Venite* upon the Great Festivals, as our hymns are introduced, with the sanction of the Ordinary and by general consent, for the purpose of marking the special lesson of the day, as the Service of Praise is begun.

[2] From ancient times, according to the Rule of S. Benedict, the Creed came after the Lord's Prayer and before the other prayers at Prime. But it appears that according to some Rules two lessons from the Old Testa-

agrees with all the most ancient examples. It has always been appointed to come after the acts of Praise and of hearing God's Word, and at the commencement of the final prayers. It may be regarded as taking an intermediate place between revelation from God and prayer to God. It expresses in the briefest form the summary of all the teaching of God's Word, and it describes the grounds on which all prayer is founded. We believe in God as the Creed declares, because He has so revealed Himself in Holy Scripture. We pray to God in perfect confidence that He will hear and answer, because we have so learned to believe in Him.

The last division of our daily worship then begins with the invitation "Let us pray." The "Preces" which follow are mainly taken from the ancient "Preces" of weekday Lauds, with a few omissions. They have been selected, no doubt, in such a way as to express all the main wants of God's people. It is interesting to find that the same versicles had been selected probably as early as the seventh century for use in the Anglo-Saxon Church in Northumbria, and were headed in such a way as to point out the intention with which they were appointed to be used, viz., for the clergy, for our king, for our bishop, for all Christian people, for the peace and soundness of the Church.[1] Our English "Preces" are now

ment and New Testament were read after the Psalms and *Quicunque vult*, then the Lord's Prayer and Apostles' Creed, after which the *preces* and other prayers followed, but in all cases the position of the Creed was very similar to that which it still holds, except that it followed instead of preceding the Lord's Prayer.—Martene, de Antiq. Monach. ritibus, lib. i. cap. iv.

[1] They occur under the head *Vespertinæ laudis*, after a preparatory prayer, "Actus nostros hodiernos, quæsumus, in beneplacito unigeniti filii

arranged so as to point out six subjects of prayer, as follows :—
1. For carrying Christ's work into effect through His Church :—

" O Lord, shew Thy mercy upon us ;
And grant us Thy salvation "—

tui dirigas et gubernes, omnipotens Deus, quousque referamus tibi gratias incolumes vespertinis horis dicentes :

> Deus in adjutorium, &c.
> Gloria Patri, &c.
> Pater noster, &c.
> Adjutorium nostrum, &c.
> Ego dixi, &c.
> Ostende nobis, &c.

Then follow various preces under separate headings :—
Pro omni gradu ecclesiastico. "Sacerdotes tui Deus induantur justitiam et sancti tui lætentur."
Pro rege nostro. "Domine salvum fac regem et exaudi nos in die qua invocaverimus te."
Pro episcopo nostro. "Salvum fac servum tuum, Deus meus, sperantem in te."
Pro omni populo Christiano. "Salvum fac populum tuum Domine et benedic hereditati tuæ, et rege eos et extolle illos usque in æternum."
Pro pace et sanitate ecclesiæ. "Fiat pax in virtute tua et habundantia in turribus tuis."
And many others, including *Pro omnibus adversantibus et calumpniantibus nobis.* "Domine Jesu Christe, ne statuas illis hoc in peccatum, nesciunt enim quid faciunt."—Anglo-Saxon Rituale Eccles. Dunelm., pp. 175, 176.
The first of our "Preces" is from the "Preces" of Prime and Compline which came after *Confiteor*, according to Sarum Use.
"Ostende nobis Domine misericordiam tuam. Et salutare tuum da nobis."
The next four are from Lauds, with the exception that the versicle for Peace is differently expressed.
The last is from the "Preces" of Prime which came after the Creed, being formed out of parts of two versicles.

T

which is presently expressed more at length in the Collect for the Day.

2. For the Queen :—

" O Lord, save the Queen ;
And mercifully hear us when we call upon Thee "—

which is continued in the prayers for the Queen's Majesty, and for the Royal Family.

3. For the clergy, and, through their ministrations, for the happiness of the elect :—

" Endue Thy ministers with righteousness,
And make Thy chosen people joyful "—

which is continued in the prayer for the clergy and people.

4. For the people at large :—

" O Lord, save Thy people ;
And bless Thine inheritance "—

which is extended in the prayer for all conditions of men.

5. For peace :—

" Give peace in our time, O Lord ;
Because there is none other that fighteth for us, but only Thou, O Lord "—

which is continued more at length in the Second Collect for Peace.

6. For the Holy Spirit :—

" O God, make clean our hearts within us ;
And take not Thy Holy Spirit from us "—

which is continued in the Third Collect for Grace.

The Collects which follow are taken from the ancient services. The Collect for the Day came immediately after the "Preces" in Lauds, and the Second Collect followed in the Memorial of Peace.[1] The Third Collect for Grace came after the "Preces" in Prime, on Sundays and all days except Double Feasts.[2] The prayers which follow were printed at the end of the Litany until the last review in 1662. The Prayer for the Queen's Majesty was first placed there in 1559; but it is found in "A Book of Prayers," which was printed in 1547, and in the Primer of 1553. The majesty of the language and the direct urgency of the petitions in this

[1] The ancient Collect for Peace has been handed down from the times to which the Sacramentary of Gelasius belonged; it is as follows :—
"Deus auctor pacis et amator, quem nosse vivere, cui servire regnare est, protege ab omnibus impugnationibus supplices tuos; ut qui in defensione tua confidimus, nullius hostilitatis arma timeamus; Per Dominum."—Sarum Breviary, Temporale, p. xi. This Collect formed the post-Communion Collect in a Service *Pro Pace* in the Gelasian Sacramentary.—Muratori, vol. i., p. 727.

[2] The Collect for Grace first appears in the Sacramentary of Gregory edited by Menard, where it is in this form : "Deus qui nos ad principium hujus diei pervenire fecisti, da nobis hunc diem sine peccato transire, ut in nullo a tuis semitis declinemus; sed ad tuam justitiam faciendam nostra semper procedant eloquia per," &c. (Menard, p. 212), which is evidently founded upon a prayer in the earlier form of this Sacramentary, containing a thanksgiving for having been brought safely through the night, and a petition that the day may be passed without sin.—Muratori, vol. ii., p. 234. It is found in a slightly different form in the Anglo-Saxon Ritual of Durham, following the *preces ad primam*, and it is the same in the Roman Breviary. But in the Sarum Breviary from which our English Collect is taken it is as follows : "Domine sancte Pater omnipotens æterne Deus qui nos ad principium hujus diei pervenire fecisti; tua nos hodie salva virtute, et concede ut in hac die ad nullam declinemus peccatum, nec ullum incurramus periculum; sed semper ad tuam justitiam faciendam omnis nostra actio tuo moderamine dirigatur: per, &c."—Sarum Breviary, Psalterium, page 54.

prayer become the more apparent when it is compared
with the form, which seems to have held the place of it
in the ancient services, in the Mass for the King.[1] The
Prayer for the Royal Family was added in 1604. In the
Eastern Liturgies we find prayers for the Queen, and for
"all in the palace and in the camp;"[2] but there seems
to be no example of such a prayer in the Western Services. The Prayer for the Clergy and People was added
to the Litany in 1559; it came from the end of the Sarum
Litany, and may be traced back to very early times.[3]
The Prayer of S. Chrysostom was placed at the end of
the Litany of 1544. The history of this prayer has been
mentioned in a previous chapter, and also the means by
which Archbishop Cranmer probably became acquainted
with it.[4] The Grace was added in 1559. Its use seems
to have been a novelty in the Western Church, as no trace
of it appears in the Breviary or Missal. It occurs in all
Eastern Liturgies as the commencing Benediction of the
Anaphora, or more solemn portion of the Liturgy; and it
has been fitly added to the previous prayer in place of

---

[1] "Quæsumus omnipotens Deus ut famulus tuus Rex noster *N.* qui tua
miseratione suscepit regni gubernacula, virtutum etiam omnium percipiat
incrementa; quibus decenter ornatus, et vitiorum voraginem devitare et
hostes superare, et ad te qui via, veritas et vita es, gratiosus valeat pervenire;
per Dominum."—*Oratio in Missa pro rege,* Sarum Missal. This Collect is
from the Gregorian Sacramentary.—Muratori, vol. ii., p. 188.

[2] Dr. C. A. Swainson, "Greek Liturgies," Liturgy of S. James, p. 285.

[3] "Omnipotens sempiterne Deus, qui facis mirabilia solus, prætende
super famulos tuos Pontifices et super cunctas congregationes illis commissas
spiritum gratiæ salutaris: et ut in veritate tibi complaceant perpetuum eis
rorem tuæ benedictionis infunde."—*Sarum Breviary, Psalterium, p. 254.*
It is found also in the Gelasian Sacramentary as the Collect for *Missa in
Monasterio.*—Muratori, vol. i., p. 719.

[4] Pages 41, 174.

the corresponding ascription with which Eastern prayers conclude.[1]

The omissions from the ancient Offices in the last part of the Daily Service are more numerous than in the previous acts of worship. They will be fully appreciated by all who have attempted to master the complicated rules of the old services. From the various memorials at the end of Lauds the Second Collect for Peace alone has survived. A complicated system of services in connection with the veneration paid to the Blessed Virgin Mary was thus abolished. Whole services in her honour were conducted daily and weekly, in addition to others on certain festivals. They were called " Servitium Beatæ Mariæ," or " Hours of our Lady." They were much shorter and simpler than the ancient Hour Services, and seem to have been very popular.[2] The whole of the psalms of Lauds and Prime have also been omitted, together with a vast mass of versicles and responses, which recurred again and again in these offices,

---

[1] Pages 32, 47, 54.

[2] The MS. Books of Hours which may frequently be met with in private collections and museums commonly contain these services. Such expressions as the following are frequent : " Sancta Maria . . . . tuum nobis impende solatium ; ut cœlestis regni per te mereamur habere præmium." " Deus . . . . tribue, quæsumus, ut ipsam pro nobis intercedere sentiamus per quam meruimus auctorem vitæ suscipere; Dominum nostrum," &c.

The Eastern Church was, and is still, equally involved in the adoration of the Blessed Virgin. An Antiphon in her honour, called *Theotokion*, occurs in every service. This is one : " Refuge, terrible in strength and that cannot be put to confusion, Mother of God, pass not by our supplications; confirm the state of the orthodox ; preserve those whom thou hast chosen to rule, and give them from heaven victory; because thou who only art to be praised didst bring forth God."—Office of Lauds, Neale's *Eastern Church*.

and which appear as if they must have been both confusing and wearisome.

c / 1 : ə ∩

The Evening Service was formed in a similar way out of the ancient offices of Vespers and Compline. The same care has been taken as in the Morning Service to form a well-arranged course, including the three acts of devotion—praise, hearing, and prayer. The chief alterations have been made in the arrangement of the psalms in connection with the monthly course, instead of the appointment of fixed psalms for the different days of the week, and in the introduction of lessons corresponding with those in the morning, instead of the very short lesson, or *Capitulum*, of the ancient services. Again, as in the morning, we have lost the varying anthem which was appointed to be sung before *Magnificat*, and which struck the keynote of the Festival, or maintained the Sunday teaching during the week.[1] But the other omissions were similar to those in the morning, and tended only to make the service practically useful.

A reference to the old services will best explain the formation of our English Evensong. *Magnificat* is taken from Vespers; *Nunc dimittis* from Compline. Psalms xcviii. and lxvii. were added in 1552 for alternative use. The Creed came from Compline; it was there followed by *Preces*, which have served as the pattern for our own. The Collect for the Day occurred in Vespers, and also the Second Collect for Peace.[2] The Third Col-

---

[1] Page 140.

[2] Various memorials were used in Vespers, as in Lauds. The Collect from the Memorial for Peace was as follows :—

" Deus a quo sancta desideria, recta consilia, et justa sunt opera, da servis

lect for Aid against all Perils was one of the distinguishing features of the Office of Compline according to Sarum Use.[1]

. The concluding prayers were added to the Evening Service, 1662. Regrets have been often expressed that the same forms were used for this purpose as in the Morning Service; and it seems strange that the commissioners, having the vast wealth of ancient collects from which to make a selection, should have decided upon this repetition.

tuis illam quam mundus dare non potest pacem, ut et corda nostra mandatis tuis dedita et, hostium sublata formidine, tempora sint tua protectione tranquilla. Per Dominum."—Sarum Breviary, Temporale, page xi. This Collect is found in the Sacramentary of Gelasius, in *Missa pro Pace.*—Muratori, vol. i., p. 727.

[1] " Illumina quæsumus Domine Deus tenebras nostras : et totius noctis insidias tu a nobis repelle propicius. Per."—Sarum Breviary, Temporale, page xiv. This Collect also is found in the Sacramentary of Gelasius amongst *Orationes ad Vesperum.*—Muratori, vol. i., p. 745. See above, page 262.

CHAPTER IX.

" Notandum est autem Litanias non tantum dici illam recitationem no-minum, qua Sancti in adjutorium vocantur infirmitatis humanæ; sed etiam cuncta quæ supplicationibus fiunt rogationes appellari. Litania autem sanctorum nominum posteà creditur in usum adsumpta quam Hieronymus martyrologium conscripsit."—*Walafridus Strabo.* (Ninth century.)

FOR the original pattern of forms of prayer correspond-ing with our Litany we must look to the Eastern Church; and it is interesting to find that the earliest examples of such forms accord most nearly with our own. The most ancient specimen occurs as the introductory part of the so-called Liturgy of S. Clement.[1] The first part of the service is divided into portions, each one in the form of a Litany, for catechumens, energumens, the newly baptised, the penitents, and the faithful. The plan of the service is set forth as follows :—

"*All standing up, let the Deacon say,* Pray, ye Catechumens.

And let all the faithful heartily pray for them, saying, Lord, have mercy.

And let the Deacon minister for them, saying, For the Cate-chumens let us all beseech God, that He may graciously hear their prayers and supplications . . . . that He may reveal to

[1] See above, page 30. The whole service is found in the Apostolical Constitutions, book viii., cap. 6-15 ; Patres Apostolici, edited by Cotelerius. The Litanies are quoted in full by Bingham, Antiq., book xiv., cap. v., sect. 3-10.

them the Gospel of His Christ; that He may enlighten them and make them wise; . . . . *And to each of these things which the Deacon proclaims, as we said before, let the people say,* Lord, have mercy."

In the portion which relates to the faithful, the following prayers are found :—

" For the peace and tranquillity of the world, and of the holy Churches let us beseech; that the God of the Universe may give us His everlasting and irremovable peace, so as to keep us persevering in the fulness of piety and virtue.

For the holy Catholic and Apostolic Church from one end of the earth to the other, let us beseech; that the Lord may preserve it unshaken and untossed until the end of this world, founded upon the rock . . . .

For the whole Episcopate throughout the world, even those who rightly divide the word of Thy truth, let us beseech; and for our Bishop *'*. . . . that the merciful Lord will grant, &c.

And for our presbyters let us beseech, &c.

For all who serve as deacons, and ministers, let us beseech, &c.

For readers, singers, virgins, widows, and orphans.

For those in matrimony and child bearing . . . .

For those who bear fruits in the holy Church by their gifts, and alms to the poor . . . .

For those afflicted with weak health.

For those who travel by sea and land.

For those in mines, exile, prison, and bonds for the Name of the Lord.

For our enemies and those who hate us.

For those who persecute us for the Name of the Lord; that the Lord may soften their heart and disperse their wrath against us.

For those who have wandered and strayed from the way; that the Lord may convert them.

Let us remember the young children of the Church, that God will perfect them in His fear, and bring them to their full age.

For one another let us beseech.

For every Christian soul . . . .

Save and lift us up, O God, in Thy mercy."

In the Eastern Church at the present day the services of Holy Communion still begin in this way with the Litany, which is called "The great Collect," and other Litanies occur in different parts of the service, which closely correspond with the very ancient example here given, and the people respond as here directed, *Kyrie eleison,* "Lord, have mercy," after every verse.[1]

In the Western Church there is little doubt but that a similar Litany was originally used in the opening part of the Liturgy. The rubric at the beginning of the earliest copy of the Sacramentary of Gregory, refers to the occasional use of the Litany in this place; and in the Liturgy of the Church of Milan, as also in the Gallican Liturgy according to the Mozarabic Rite, Litanies are so used to this day on the Sundays in Lent, after the pattern of the form above given.[2]   But the occasional

---

[1] 'Η Μεγάλη Συναπτή.—Dr. C. A. Swainson, "The Greek Liturgies," *passim.*

[2] See note 1, page 69.   Confirmation of this practice is found in a book of offices compiled by Alcuin, in which a Litany occurs under Feria V., named "The Deprecation of Pope Gelasius," as follows:—

"Dicamus omnes Domine exaudi et miserere.

Patrem Unigeniti, et Dei Filium genitoris ingeniti, et sanctum Deum Spiritum, fidelibus animis invocamus.

Pro immaculata Dei vivi ecclesia, sacerdotibus ac ministris, divinam bonitatis opulentiam deprecamur.

use of the Litany referred to in the Sacramentary of
Gregory evidently fell into disuse in the Western Church
in very early times, so that few traces of it can be discovered. Yet an interesting relic of it remained in the
repetition here of the words *Kyrie eleison,* which is still

Pro sanctis Dei magni sacerdotibus et ministris . . . ."
with many more petitions, but no invocations of saints as in other Litanies
which he gives.—Alcuin, Officia per ferias, p. 560; Migne, Patrol., tom. ci.

In the Church of Milan Litanies which have been handed down probably
from the days of Ambrose, *circa* A.D. 380, are used as follows. On the First,
Third, and Fifth Sundays in Lent, the deacon, or priest himself if there be no
deacon, is directed to say these *Preces,* the choir or minister answering to
every verse, *Domine miserere,* " Lord, have mercy," thus, " In supplication
for the gift of divine peace and pardon, with our whole heart and mind we
pray Thee. *R.* Lord, have mercy. For Thy Holy Church which is spread
here and over the whole world we pray Thee. *R.* Lord, &c." In the following verses prayers are made for mercy in respect of the pope, bishop,
and clergy; the emperor, the king, and all his army, the peace of churches,
the calling of the nations, and the quietness of the people; for the state, its
manner of life, and all its inhabitants; for mildness of climate, the crops,
and the fruitfulness of the lands; for virgins, widows, and orphans, captives,
and penitents; for those journeying by sea and land, and those detained in
prison, chains, the mines, or exile; for those suffering under all kinds of infirmities and evil spirits; and for those who yield abundant fruits of charity
in Christ's Holy Church. (Compare with this the petitions in the Clementine Liturgy, above, page 281.)

On the Second and Fourth Sundays in Lent a different Litany is used,
and the response is in the Greek form, *Kyrie eleison.* " O Lord God Almighty of our fathers. *R.* Kyrie. Behold from heaven, O God (de cœlo
Deus), and from Thy holy seat. *R.* Kyrie." And it ends with the words
which follow our English Litany, " O Lord, arise, help us, and deliver us
for Thy Name's sake."

Other instances of ancient Liturgical Litanies, free from invocations of
saints, occur in a MS. of the monastery of Fulda (Bingham, Antiq., book
xv., ch. i., 2), and in the Stowe Missal of the Celtic Church, entitled *Depre-
catio S. Martini* (Warren, " Liturgy and Ritual of the Celtic Church ").
And in the Mozarabic Missal such Litanies are provided under the name of
preces for the first five Sundays in Lent. That on the First Sunday is a
supplication for pardon, and the response is *Placare et miserere,* " Be

maintained in the Roman Service,[1] and which has been replaced in our English Communion Service with the petitions for pardon and grace in connection with the Ten Commandments.[2]

Litanies for separate use, apart from the Service of Holy Communion, were introduced into the Western Church by Mamertus, Bishop of Vienne in France, A.D. 450. They formed part of penitential services appointed for use on the three days preceding Ascension Day,

gracious and hear." On the Second Sunday there is a more humble confession and entreaty for pardon, with the response, *Quia peccavimus tibi*, " For we have sinned against Thee." On the Third Sunday the supplication is more general, for protection, peace, and plenty, and with the response, *Jam miserere, peccavimus tibi*, " Now have mercy, we have sinned against Thee." On the Fourth and Fifth Sundays the Litany is of an unusual character. The versicles describe our Lord's sufferings, and are as if spoken by Himself; and the responses follow, *Miserere Pater juste et omnibus indulgentiam dona*," Have mercy, righteous Father, and give pardon to all ; " and *Tu Pater sancte miserere et libera me*, " Do Thou, holy Father, have mercy and deliver me." The verses are such as these, " Sent by the Father I came to seek for the lost and to redeem with blood those who had been taken by the enemy ; the unhappy people rejected me. *R.* Have mercy, &c. With bad thieves suspended on the Cross; with bitter food fed ; and with the sharp cup handed over to punishment. *R.* Have mercy," &c.—Mozar. Missal, folios 94, 105, 117, &c.

[1] Cardinal Bona says that *Kyrie eleison* seems to be the natural cry of the hearts of men, and is therefore universally used.—Rerum Liturg., lib. ii., cap. iv., sect. 1. He gives five specimens of *farced* Kyries, and states that the additions were made without authority.—*Ibid.*, sect. 2. He explains that formerly on occasions when " Gloria in excelsis," was not used, immediately after *Kyrie eleison* followed *Preces* for all conditions of men, similar to the petitions called *Irenicæ* or *Diaconicæ* by the Greeks; and that this custom prevailed in the Latin Church until the ninth century, and is still observed in the Church of Milan. He adds specimens of such *Preces*, transcribed by Wicelius from the ancient MS. in the monastery of Fulda, and also of the Milan Litany for First Sunday in Lent, as above in the last note.—*Ibid.*, sect. 3.

[2] See above, note 1, page 218.

which were named in consequence Rogation Days.[1] Unfortunately, in the course of the next four hundred years,
the introduction of the practice of the Invocation of
Saints altered the ancient Litanies so completely that
their original form has been almost entirely lost. But
amidst the general wreck one specimen seems to have
escaped to represent the original form of the Rogation
Service. It belonged to a monastery in Bavaria.[2] After
describing the origin of these fasts, the MS. contains
directions that the people shall abstain from rich clothes,
wine, and feasting; that they shall not ride on horse-
back, but walk barefoot, and all together chant *Kyrie
eleison* with contrition of heart, beseeching God's mercy
for their sins, and with respect to the preservation of

---

[1] See a letter from a contemporary of Mamertus quoted by Bingham,
Antiq., book xiii., chap. i., sect. 10.

[2] *Ex pervetusto Codice Pontificali seu ordine Romano Wertinensis cænobii
in diœcesi Monasteriensi.* " De Litania Minori. Tres autem dies qui cele-
brantur ante ascensionem Domini juxta morem Gallicanæ Ecclesiæ constituit
S. Mamertus Viennensis Episcopus, ob incursionem scilicet malarum bes-
tiarum, quæ tunc temporis gravissime afficiebant populum Domini, quæ
consuetudo apud nos usque hodie pro diversis calamitatibus devotissime re-
colitur. Nullus autem his diebus vestimenta pretiosa induatur, quia in sacco
et cinere lugere debemus. Prohibeantur ebrietates et comessationes quæ
fiunt in vulgari plebe. Nemo ibi equitare præsumat, sed discalciatis pedibus
omnes incedant. Nequaquam mulierculæ choros ducant, sed omnes in com-
muni *Kyrie eleison* decantent, cum contritione cordis Dei misericordiam
exorent pro peccatis, pro pace, pro peste, pro conservatione frugum, et pro
ceteris necessitatibus."

Sequitur antiphona: Exurge Domine. *Psalm:* Deus auribus nostris.
Gloria. *Qua finita ponendi sunt cineres super capita, sicut antiphona testatur.*
Immutemur . . . . *Sequitur versus Letaniæ hujusmodi.*

Dicamus omnes, Domine miserere.

Versus. Ex toto corde et ex tota mente, oramus te.

Pro sancta ecclesia catholica quæ est in toto orbe diffusa supplicamus te,
Domine," &c.—Martene, de Antiq. Eccles. ritibus, lib. iv., chap. xxvii.

peace, the averting of pestilence, the protection of their crops, and other necessities. Then follows Psalm xliv., "O God we have heard with our ears," &c., with the *Antiphon,* "O Lord, arise, help us, and deliver us for Thy Name's sake," and the *Gloria,* as in our English Litany. Then this Litany :—

> "Let us all say, Lord, have mercy.
> With our whole heart and mind we pray Thee.
> For the Holy Catholic Church which is scattered throughout the whole world, Lord (have mercy).
> For our pastor and all his clergy, we implore Thee.
> For our King *N.* and all his army, we beg Thee.
> For our Bishop *N.* and the flock committed to him, we beseech Thee.
> For remission of sins or amendment of our lives, we beseech Thee.
> Hear us, O God, in all our prayer, O Thou who art kind.
> Then a great number of *Antiphons,* without any accompanying Psalms."

One ancient Service Book still remains in use which is free from any trace of the Invocation of Saints. The Mozarabic Breviary seems to have handed down the original forms of service which were used in Spain before the practice of the Invocation of Saints was introduced. And numerous short Litanies occur in it, which are appointed to be used on the annual fasting days, under the name of *Preces.* The following examples will give an idea of their character :—

> "Let us all say, Have mercy, O Lord, and hear us.
> *People.* For Thou art kind.
> From our whole heart and mind beseeching, hear us, O Lord.

People. For Thou art kind.

Thou who dwellest in heaven and hast respect unto the lowly, give pardon to the penitent. *People.* For, &c.

This city and all who dwell herein protect, O Christ, by the right hand of Thy might. *People.* For, &c.

Remission of sins and amendment of life, grant, O Lord. *People.* For, &c."

" Our iniquities are many.

People. Have mercy upon us, O Lord.

Our love grows cold. *People.* Have mercy, &c.

Against Thee only have we sinned. *People.* Have mercy, &c.

O Christ, Redeemer of the world. *People.* Have mercy, &c."

" Have mercy and spare Thy people, O most merciful Lord. *People.* For we have sinned against Thee.

For our wickedness we are the more severely punished, and for our crimes we are the more blinded, yet we weep not for the evils we have done. *People.* For we have sinned against Thee.

Remove famine, and give the gracious shower, and afford a large abundance of crops, as well as the longed-for pardon of our sins.

Take away pestilence, O Redeemer most High; let us not be overwhelmed with sudden death; whilst we kneel let not punishment fall: give pardon to sinners.

Fill our breasts with worthy tears; let the spirit of charity flow down upon us, whereby we may be delivered from the falls of sin."[1]

[1] " Dicamus omnes. Miserere Domine et exaudi nos. *P.* Quia pius es. *V.* Ex toto corde et ex tota mente orantes ad te exaudi Domine. *P.* Quia. *V.* Qui habitas in cœlis et humilia respicis, pœnitentibus dona indulgentiam. *P.* Quia. *V.* Civitatem hanc et omnes habitantes in ea protege Christe dextera virtutis. *P.* Quia. *V.* Remissionem peccatorum et emendationem morum concede Domine. *P.* Quia pius es."—Ad tertiam, in i. die Jejuniorum ante Festum S. Cypriani.

Very little is known about the form of the Litanies which were in use in the early Roman Church. When Gregory the Great revised the Roman Sacramentary, *circa* A.D. 590, the practice of using Litanies was encouraged in various services.   It is probable that at first they consisted largely of the repetition of *Kyrie eleison.* Gregory describes this practice in one of his epistles, saying, " We have not been accustomed, neither do we now say *Kyrie eleison* as the Greeks do.   For amongst the Greeks all say it together, but with us it is said by the clergy, and then answer is made by the people, and *Ohriste eleison* is said by us the same number of times, which is not said at all by the Greeks."[1]   It has been

" Dicamus omnes, Miserere Domine   *P.* Miserere.   *V.* Iniquitates multæ sunt.   *P.* Miserere.   *V.* Charitas refrigescit.   *P.* Miserere.   *V.* Tibi soli peccavimus.   *P.* Miserere.   *V.* Christe Redemptor mundi.   *P.* Miserere."—Ad nonam, in ii. die Jejuniorum ante Festum S. Cypriani.

" Miserere et parce, clementissime Domine, populo tuo.   *P.* Quia peccavimus tibi.   *V.* Pro nostris malis flagellamur acrius, et pro delictis obcæcamur durius ; nec deflemus mala quæ commisimus.   *P.* Quia.   *V.* Remove famem, et da imbrem gratiæ, fructuumque largam præbe abundantiam, atque optatam peccatorum veniam.   *P.* Quia.   *P.* Amove pestem, Redemptor Altissime, ne obruamur repentina morte ; dum prosternimur non detur pœna ;   veniam da peccantibus.   *P.* Quia.   *V.* Lachrymis nostra dignis reple pectora ; affluat in nos charitatis spiritus ; qua eruamur vitiorum lapsibus.   *P.* Quia peccavimus tibi."—Ad tertiam, in ii. die Jejuniorum ante Festum S. Martini.—Breviarium Gothicum, folios 434, 439, 444 ; Migne's Patrol., tom. lxxxvi.

[1] Gregory, Epist., lib. vii., ii., 64, to John, Bishop of Smyrna. It appears from this that the threefold repetition :—

Lord, have mercy,
Christ, have mercy,
Lord, have mercy,

was not the original practice.   This is confirmed by ancient examples of Litanies in which *Kyrie eleison* is followed by *Christe eleison*, each being said once, or three times.   To this was frequently added *Christe audi nos*, but this

already mentioned that, by the introduction of the Invocation of Saints in the Western Church, the form of the original Litanies was superseded so completely that few examples remain to show what the older ones were like. But it is interesting to find that the commencement of our Litany appears in a very ancient Roman Pontifical, which contains this description of the form which was appointed to be used at the Benediction of a Church :—

> *" Then the Clergy begin the Litany.*
> Lord, have mercy.
> Christ, have mercy.
> O Christ, hear us.
> O God, the Father of Heaven, have mercy upon us, &c.
> *And let the Bishop prostrate himself upon what is strewn in the middle of the Church, until the Choir say, O Lamb of God."* [1]

The brief description thus given excites regret that so little is told. But it proves the antiquity of the phrase " O God the Father of Heaven," which has been handed down to us through the Sarum Litany.

From the Roman Church the use of the same kind of

was not always repeated the same number of times. Litanies were begun in this way down to the time of the Reformation. But at the end of the Litany the threefold repetition to which we are accustomed was generally adopted. See Martene, lib. iv., cap. xxiv., &c. ; Sarum Breviary, Psalterium, pp. 250-253 ; notes in Menard's Sacram. S. Gregorii, Feria ii. of week before Ascension, where a Litany of *circa* A.D. 840 is given.

[1] *" Inde incipit Clerus Letaniam :*
> Kyrie, eleison.
> Christe, eleison.
> Christe, audi nos.
> Pater de cœlis, Deus.   Miserere nobis, &c.
> *Et prosternat se Pontifex super stramenta in medio Ecclesiæ, usque dum dicat schola :*
> Agnus Dei."—Muratori, vol. ii., p. 472.

Litanies was introduced into the Anglo-Saxon Church. Canon 16 of the Council of Clovesho, A.D. 747, prescribes that " Litanies should be reverently performed after the Roman manner on S. Mark's Day (vii Kalend. May), which was accordingly named ' Lætania Major,' and that also, according to the custom of their forefathers, the three days before the Ascension of the Lord should be observed with fasting, not with the admixture of vanities, as was the manner of many through negligence or ignorance, *i.e.*, with sports and horse-racing and banquets, but with fear and trembling, with the Cross, the sign of Christ's passion and our redemption, and with the relics of the saints borne before, and all the people kneeling and humbly beseeching the pardon of God for their sins."[1]

The exact date of the introduction of Invocations of Saints is not known.   But certainly by the eighth century a Litany was understood in the Western Church to mean the invocation of the prayers of a vast number of saints.   In the Pontifical of Egbert, which is assigned to the ninth century, an interesting example of such a Litany occurs in the Service for the Dedication of a Church.   It begins with *Kyrie eleison, Christe eleison, Christe audi nos*, followed immediately, without any further invocation of God, by ninety-six invocations of saints.   The approximate date is fixed by the name of the most recent of these saints, S. Guthlac, a monk of Croyland, who flourished at the end of the seventh and beginning of the eighth century.[2]

---

[1] Haddan and Stubbs' Councils, vol. iii., p. 368.

[2] Pontifical of Egbert, A.D. 732-766, page 27.   The petitions which follow the invocations show the original form of much of our English Litany, and reference will presently be made to them again.

At this time Litanies were variously described in the Western Church, according to the method employed in the arrangement of the invocations. In a ninth century version of the Sacramentary of Gregory,[1] mention is made of several of these kinds of Litanies. On the Saturday before Easter, when baptisms were solemnly performed, the rubrics direct "that the choir shall go down to the font to perform the Litany, waiting ready for the Bishop to come. And those who are bidden perform a sevenfold Litany" (*Litania septena*). After the children are baptized, " the choir who are appointed perform a fivefold Litany (*Litania quina*) at the font." The confirmation of the newly baptized followed, " after which those who are bidden begin in the Church a threefold Litany (*Litania terna*), and when they have said, ' O Lamb of God,' the church is lighted up, &c. After which the Bishop says *Gloria in excelsis.*" These Litanies are explained in a Roman Missal of *circa* A.D. 1490,[2] as follows :—

" Whilst the lessons are being read seven subdeacons are prepared, one of whom should carry the Cross to the font,

---

[1] Sacram. S. Gregorii, edited by Menard.

[2] " Sabbato sancto dum lectiones leguntur vii subdiaconi præparantur quorum unus portet crucem ad fontem, et faciunt ibi letaniam septenam, quinam, et ternam hoc modo ; viz. prior subdiaconus incipit *Kyrie eleison*, secundus et ipse idem dicit, *Kyrie eleison*, et tertius postea, *Kyrie eleison*, deinde quilibet usque ad septimum singulatim dicit *Kyrie eleison.* Prior vero postquam omnes dixerint singulatim *Kyrie eleison*, dicit *Christe eleison* et omnes septem dicunt singulatim *Christe eleison.* Postea prior dicit *Christe audi nos*, et quilibet singulatim dicit *Christe audi nos ;* et prosequitur totam letaniam usque ad finem. Et dicuntur de quolibet choro septem sancti, septem de Apostolis, septem de Martyribus, septem de Confessoribus, et septem de Virginibus. Et postmodum fit letania quina per quinque sub-

and they perform there a sevenfold, fivefold, and threefold
Litany in this way. The first subdeacon begins *Kyrie eleison,*
then the second *Kyrie eleison,* and the third, and so on; then
the first says *Christe eleison,* and one after the other the rest
say the same; then the first says *Christe audi nos,* and the
others the same. The whole Litany is then carried on to the
end, but only seven Saints are mentioned, seven Apostles,
seven Martyrs, seven Confessors, and seven Virgins. The fivefold Litany is said by five subdeacons, after the same manner,
except that five Saints, &c., only are mentioned; and the
threefold Litany the same."[1]

diaconos, per omnia ut supra, excepto quod de quolibet choro dicuntur
quinque sancti; et deinde letania terna per tres subdiaconos, per omnia
ut supra, excepto quod de quolibet choro dicuntur tres sancti."—Martene,
lib. i., cap. i., art. xviii., ordo 19, ex vet. Missali Romano ad usum fratrum
minorum accommodato circiter A.D. 1490.

[1] The same kind of service was appointed for this day in the Statutes of
the Cathedral of S. Andrew at Wells. "*Processio quomodo fit ad fontem in
Vigilia Paschæ.* Finita septiformi Letania quæ a septem pueris in superpelliciis dicatur in medio chori, et quinque partita Letania a quinque Diaconis
de secunda forma similiter in medio chori inchoata in superpelliciis ad pro-
lationem ' Sancta Maria ora pro nobis ' eat processio ad fontes."—Reynolds'
Wells Cathedral, p. 31.

In some churches a method was adopted which was not quite so elaborate
as that before described. Martene gives a further explanation of these
Litanies from a MS. of the Church of Soissons, according to which every
saint was invoked seven times in the first, five times in the second, and
three times in the third Litany; but only fourteen saints were invoked
in each Litany. This would amount to 210 invocations, instead of
the 332 invocations of the former method. Such accounts reveal very
plainly the need of reformation in the sixteenth century.—Martene, lib. iv.,
cap. xxiv.

But these repetitions were not universally practised. In the Mozarabic
Missal what appears to be the original form of Litany for this occasion is
found in the service for the day. The rubrics are in considerable confusion,
proving that the service has been altered in later times. In the earlier part
of the service a Litany of the usual mediæval type occurs, with ninety-one
invocations for the prayers of saints. Then follow various prayers, the

It was mentioned before that the Anglo-Saxon Church observed the Festival of S. Mark with a special Litany after the Roman rite, as well as the Rogation-tide which their forefathers had learned to observe, probably from the Gallican Church. It is recorded that the Litany for S. Mark's Day was instituted by Gregory the Great, after the example of Mamertus, on the occasion of a pestilence, and that it was of a peculiar character. It was called *Litania Septiformis*, a Litany in seven divisions, and it was carried out in the following manner : Seven processions were arranged to start from different churches at the same time, formed of different classes of persons, ecclesiastics in one, men in another, monks in a third, maidens, matrons, widows, and poor people in the rest. And a similar procession was continued down to the end of the seventeenth century at Tours on S. Mark's Day, when from different approaches seven bodies of eccle-

benediction of the water, and the baptism of the infants. Then a second Litany is given as follows :—

" Be merciful, Spare us, O Lord.
From all evil, Deliver us, O Lord.
From the snares of the Devil, Deliver.

   *   *   *   *   *   *   *   *

We sinners, Beseech Thee to hear us.
That Thou wilt grant us peace, We beseech Thee.
That Thou wilt govern and defend Thy Church, We beseech Thee.
That Thou wilt vouchsafe to bless and consecrate this font, We beseech Thee.
O Son of God," &c.

The petition for the benediction of the font seems to mark this Litany as a more ancient form, to which the other Litany with its accompanying prayers was prefixed by the Mozarabes in mediæval times. Martene gives this service, but mentions only the first verse of this Litany, omitting the reference to the consecration of the font which makes it different from all other Litanies for this day.—Martene *ut supra ;* Mozarabic Missal, folio 189.

siastics were accustomed to assemble at the Church of
S. Martin and sing Litanies.[1]

One other use of the word Litany remains to be
noticed. The use of Litanies in procession gave rise to
the custom of calling any processional service a Litany; and
Antiphons were provided in great numbers by Gregory
the Great, which might be sung in procession. The use
of such Antiphons in connection with Litanies has been
before referred to, and in course of time the Antiphon
itself, when so used, was called a Litany.[2] The ancient
English historian, the Venerable Bede, describes how
Augustine and his companions approached the city of
Canterbury singing in this way : " It is said that as
they drew near to the city, bearing according to their
custom the holy Cross and image of the great King our
Lord Jesus Christ, they sang with one voice this Litany :
We implore Thee, O Lord, in Thy great mercy to turn
away Thy wrath and anger from this city, and from Thy
holy dwelling, for we have sinned. Alleluia." [3]

Illustrations of all these kinds of Litanies may be
found in the Sarum Processional, or Litany Book. The
Litanies provided for use on Wednesdays and Fridays in
Lent consisted entirely of invocations, with different
lists of saints for each day, and the priest was directed
to begin the *Officium Missæ* immediately after, without
any verse or collect.[4] The Litanies described as sevenfold and fivefold, which were appointed to be said on the
Saturday before Easter, also consisted wholly of invocations, but with this difference, that they were addressed

---

[1] Martene, lib. iv., cap. xxvii., sect. 1.   [2] Page 286.
[3] Bede, Hist. Eccles., lib. i., 25.
[4] Processionale ad usum Sarum, fol. xli.

entirely to the saints, and an explanation was given why no invocations were addressed to God on that day.[1] For the processions on the Rogation Days various Antiphons were provided, with a verse and *Gloria Patri.*[2] On S. Mark's Day three forms were provided, the first metrical, and the last ending with the Preces which are now placed at the end of our English Litany.[3] And besides these, there was the common form of Litany, which will be presently described at length.

But in course of time, notwithstanding the prevalence of the practice of invoking the saints who were best known in this or that country, the character of the petitions which came after the invocations gradually assumed more of the form with which we are familiar. Mingled with the dependence upon the prayers of the departed, a spirit of true devotion to God and of trust in the help of

---

[1] Fol. xciv.

[2] Fol. cxvi. " 1. *Antiphon.* Exurge Domine adjuva nos et libera nos propter nomen tuum. Alleluia.

Presbyter. Deus auribus nostris audivimus, patres nostri annunciaverunt nobis.

Gloria Patri, &c.

Antiphon. Exurge, &c.

2. *Antiphon.* Surgite sancti dei de mansionibus vestris, loca sanctificate, plebem benedicite, et nos humiles peccatores in pace custodite. Alleluia.

Presb. Deus misereatur nostri et benedicat nobis, illuminet vultum suum super nos et misereatur nostri.

Gloria Patri, &c.

Antiphon. Surgite, &c."

Various other *Antiphons* follow.

[3] Fol. cxxxi. The first Litany begins, " Kyrie eleison qui precioso sanguine mundum eripuisti de maledicti fauce draconis. *Chorus.* Kyrie.

Sancta Maria quæsumus almum poscere regem jure memento salvet ut omnes nos jubilantes. *Chorus.* Kyrie.

Sancte Michael quæsumus almum, &c."

the Saviour was at work, guiding the mediæval church to lay the foundations on which the various divisions of our English Litany are built, as the following ancient specimen of a French Litany will show. It is from the library of the Abbey of Corbey, and belongs to the ninth century.[1]

" iii. Kyrie eleison.
iii. Christe eleison.
iii. O Christ, hear us.
O Christ, have mercy upon us.
O holy God of saints, have mercy upon us,
O holy Virgin of virgins, intercede for us.
O holy Mother of God, intercede for us.
O holy Mary, pray for us.
O holy Peter, pray for us.
(Then follow separate petitions to fifty-two Saints, Apostles, Martyrs, Bishops, Abbots, Virgins, Matrons.)
O all Saints, pray for us.
Be gracious unto us, Spare us, O Lord.
Be gracious unto us, Deliver us, O Lord.
From all evil, Deliver us, O Lord.
From all temptations of the devil, Deliver, &c.
From all evil thoughts . . . .
From all wickedness.
From all filthiness.
By Thy Cross, Deliver us, O Lord.
We sinners, Beseech Thee to hear us.
That Thou wilt grant us peace, Lord Jesus, we beseech Thee.
That Thou wilt grant peace and quietness to Thy Church.
That Thou wilt remove Thy wrath from Christian people.
That Thou wilt defend us from all dangers of our enemies.

[1] Given in Menard's notes to the Sacramentary of Gregory, under Monday in Rogation week.

That Thou wilt pardon our offences.

That Thou wilt give us remission of our sins.

That Thou wilt mercifully pour into our hearts the grace of Thy Holy Spirit.

That Thou wilt grant us the intercession of Thy saints.

That Thou wilt give us a right faith.

That Thou wilt give us a firm hope in Thy goodness to us.

That Thou wilt give us eternal life.

That Thou wilt give us everlasting light.

Son of God, we beseech Thee to hear us.

Lamb of God, which takest away the sins of the world, Have mercy upon us.

iii. O Christ, hear us.

iii. Kyrie eleison.

iii. Christe eleison.

iii. Kyrie eleison.

Our Father which art in Heaven, &c.

A Collect after the Litany. O God of Hosts, &c."

The history of our English Litany now claims consideration. In 1543 a special Procession and Litany had been ordered under the fear of famine. King Henry VIII., not satisfied with the way in which the order was carried out, instructed Archbishop Cranmer to translate a Litany which should be published with authority for general use. In 1544 this was done; and the Litany was sent to the king with an interesting letter from the archbishop describing how he had " felt constrained to use more than the liberty of a translator," in adding some verses and omitting others.[1] This Litany, with the exception of a few words, is the same as that which we have now. A comparison between it and the ancient Sarum Litany will

[1] Hook, Lives of the Archbishops, vol. vii., pp. 203-205.

enable the reader to see exactly what was done, and the accompanying notes will suggest the probable sources from which the additions were derived. The following particulars should be specially noticed. First, that the orderly arrangement of our English Litany is a distinguishing feature, which gives it a peculiar value. It is true that in the Sarum Litany the general divisions are the same as in our own; the invocations, deprecations, pleadings, intercessions, and concluding supplications come in the same order. But there is an absence of any regular arrangement of the petitions, especially of the intercessions, which are mixed up with the personal petitions in the main part of the Litany, and then recur again after the Lord's Prayer. Secondly, that the reduction of the invocations of the saints and angels to three petitions was a bold step, which brought into prominence the fact that the Litany was in the main a prayer to God the Son. Thirdly, that the spiritual tone of the petitions was raised in a remarkable degree by the repeated prayer that the Word of God, now at length accessible to clergy and people, might be taken by both as the guide of life under the leading of the Holy Spirit; and that the Lord's people might regard the heart as the seat of that love and fear of God on which acceptable service depends.

The formation of this Litany was the first step in the revision of the ancient services after the publication of the English Bible; and whether we regard the devotional tone of the petitions or the masterly English in which they are expressed, our deep thanks are due to Almighty God for this work of Archbishop Cranmer.[1]

[1] The text of the English Litany is taken from the Parker Society's volume, entitled " Private Prayers—Queen Elizabeth," where it is printed

LITANY OF 1544.	SARUM LITANY.
	Kyri eleyson. Christe eleyson.
	Christe audi nos.
O God the Father of Heaven: have mercy upon us, miserable sinners. *R.* O God, &c.	Pater de cœlis Deus : Miserere nobis. *R.* Pater, &c.
O God the Son, Redeemer of the World; have mercy upon us, &c. *R.* O God, &c.	Fili Redemptor mundi Deus: Miserere nobis. *R.* Fili, &c.
O God the Holy Ghost, proceeding from the Father and the Son: have mercy upon us, &c. *R.* O God, &c.	Spiritus sancte Deus: Miserere nobis. *R.* Spiritus, &c.

in the appendix. It is stated to be copied from the edition in the University Library, Cambridge, entitled " An Exhortation unto Prayer, thought mete by the Kinges maiestie, and his clergy, to be read to the people in every church after Processyons. Also a Letanie with Suffrages to be said or song in the tyme of the said processyons." Imprinted at London, 1544. The spelling is given as modernized in the above volume.

The Latin text is taken from Breviarium ad usum Sarum, Psalterium, pp. 250-260.

In the following notes it is shown that much assistance was derived from two Litanies published in the same year : one in a primer commonly called Marshall's Primer, 1535, and the other in " Simplex ac Pia Deliberatio " of Archbishop Herman before described. The former is given in full by Collier, Eccles. Hist., vol. iv., p. 316. It is also printed with the spelling modernized in Burton's " Three Primers put forth in the reign of Henry VIII.," p. 124. It is curious to find so many points of agreement between this Litany and that of Herman. The author of the primer was evidently an ardent reformer, and since a former edition of his primer is mentioned as possessing no Litany, and this edition is dated June 16th, 1535, it is possible that he may have had some knowledge of the " Deliberatio."

LITANY OF 1544.

O Holy, blessed, and glorious Trinity, one God: have mercy, &c. *R.* O Holy, blessed, &c.

Saint Mary, Mother of God, our Saviour Jesu Christ, pray for us. *R.* Saint Mary, &c.

All Holy Angels and Archangels, and all holy orders of blessed spirits, pray for us. *R.* All holy, &c.

All holy Patriarchs and Prophets, Apostles, Martyrs, Confessors, and Virgins, and all the blessed company of heaven, pray for us. *R.* All Holy Patriarchs, &c.[1]

Remember not, Lord, our offences, &c.[2] *R.* Spare us, good Lord.

SARUM LITANY.

Sancta Trinitas unus Deus: Miserere nobis. *R.* Sancta, &c.

Sancta Maria: Ora pro nobis. *R.* Sancta, &c.

. . . . .

Sancte Michael ora pro nobis. *R.* Sancte Michael, &c.

[Twenty-eight invocations were appointed for regular use; then forty more for each day of the week; a different list for every day.]

Propitius esto: parce nobis Domine. *R.* Propitius, &c.

[1] This was the first attempt at reducing the invocations of saints in an English Litany. Even Marshall's Primer, 1535, contained the usual long list of saints. The same is found in Bishop Hilsey's Primer of 1539. And a new edition of the Processionale ad usum Sarum, with all the old invocations, was published in this very year 1544. But Archbishop Herman in his "Deliberatio," 1535, had boldly omitted them altogether from his Litany.

[2] This was the Antiphon to the Seven Penitential Psalms, which commonly preceded the Litany: "Ne reminiscaris Domine delicta nostra vel parentum nostrorum neque vindictam sumas de peccatis nostris. Parce Domine parce populo tuo quem redemisti pretioso sanguine tuo ne in æternum irascaris nobis; et ne des hæreditatem tuam in perditionem : ne in æternum obliviscaris nobis."—Sarum Breviary, Psalterium, p. 249.

The shortening of the responses from this point to the verse beginning "We sinners do beseech Thee," &c., should be noticed.

LITANY OF 1544.	SARUM LITANY.

From all evil and mischief; from sin, from the crafts and assaults of the devil; from Thy wrath,[1] and from everlasting damnation.
R. Good Lord, deliver us.

Ab omni malo : libera nos Domine. *R.* Ab omni, &c.
Ab insidiis Diaboli : libera, &c. *R.* Ab insidiis, &c.
A damnatione perpetua : libera, &c. *R.* A damnatione, &c.
Ab imminentibus peccatorum nostrorum periculis : libera, &c. *R.* Ab imminentibus, &c.

From blindness of heart; from pride, vain-glory and hypocrisy; from envy, hatred and malice, and all uncharitableness. *R.* Good, &c.

Ab infestationibus dæmonum : libera, &c.
A spiritu fornicationis : libera, &c.
Ab appetitu inanis gloriæ : libera, &c.

From fornication and all deadly sin; and from all the deceits of the world, the flesh and the devil. Good Lord, &c.

Ab omni immunditia mentis et corporis : libera, &c.
Ab ira, et odio, et omni mala voluntate : libera, &c.
Ab immundis cogitationibus : libera, &c.
A cæcitate cordis : libera, &c.

From lightning and tempest; from plague, pestilence, and famine;[2] from battle and

A fulgure et tempestate : libera, &c.

---

[1] "Ab irâ tuâ" is found in the Roman Litany. The petition may have been taken from Quignon's Breviary, second edit., 1537, p. 506.

[2] This verse seems to be founded upon the words of the Litany in the Primer printed in 1535, "From sodeyn and unprovided dethe, delyver us

LITANY OF 1544.	SARUM LITANY.
murder, and from sudden death. *R.* Good Lord, &c.	A subitanea et improvisa morte: libera, &c.

From all sedition and privy conspiracy; from the tyranny of the Bishop of Rome, and all his detestable enormities; from all false doctrine and heresy; from hardness of heart, and contempt of Thy word and commandment.[1] *R.* Good Lord, &c.

| By the mystery of Thy holy incarnation; by Thy holy nativity and circumcision; by Thy baptism, fasting, and temptation.[2] *R.* Good, &c. | Per mysterium sanctæ Incarnationis tuæ: libera, &c. Per Nativitatem tuam: libera. Per sanctam Circumcisionem tuam: libera. |

Lorde. From pestilence and famine. . . From all mortal warre. . . From lyghtnynge and tempestious wethers."—Collier, Eccles. Hist., vol. iv., p. 316. The words ἀπὸ λοιμοῦ, λιμοῦ, occur in the Liturgy of S. Mark.— Swainson, Greek Liturgies, p. 18. But there is no evidence to show that this was known in the West at this time, since the earliest known edition is by Ambrose Drouard, Paris, 1583. In Herman's Litany in the "Deliberatio" of 1535, these words occur, "a peste et fame, a bello et cæde."

[1] Very similar words are found in the Liturgy of S. James, διασκέδασον τὰ σκάνδαλα· κατάργησον τοὺς πολέμους· παῦσον τὰ σχίσματα τῶν ἐκκλησιῶν· τὰς τῶν αἱρέσεων ἐπαναστάσεις ἐν τάχει κατάλυσον·—Swainson, p. 286. But the earliest known edition is by Morel, Paris, 1560. In the Primer of 1535 these words occur, "From seditions and schismies;" and in Herman's Deliberatio, "a seditione et simultate," and "ut sectæ et omnia scandala tollere digneris." But the last clause appears to be Archbishop Cranmer's own.

[2] "By thy baptisme, fastings and temptations," Primer, 1535. "Per tentationes tuas," Herman.

LITANY OF 1544.	SARUM LITANY.
	Per Baptismum tuum: libera. Per Jejunium tuum: libera.
By Thine agony and bloody sweat;[1] by Thy cross and passion ; by Thy precious death and burial;[2] by Thy glorious resurrection and ascension; by the coming of the Holy Ghost.[3]	Per Passionem et Crucem tuam: libera. Per pretiosam Mortem tuam: libera. Per gloriosam Resurrectionem tuam: libera. Per admirabilem Ascensionem tuam: libera. Per gratiam Sancti Spiritus Paraclyti: libera.
In all time of our tribulation; in all time of our wealth;[4] in the hour of death; in the day of judgment.	In hora mortis: Succurre nobis Domine. In die judicii: libera nos Domine.
We sinners do beseech Thee to hear us, O Lord God; and that it may please Thee to rule and govern Thy holy	Peccatores: te rogamus audi nos. *R.* Peccatores, &c. Ut pacem nobis dones. *R.* Te rogamus, &c.

[1] "By thy painful agony in sweating blood and water," Primer, 1535. " Per sudorem tuum sanguineum," Herman.

[2] " By thy death and buryuge," Primer, 1535. In the Roman Litany also the burial is mentioned, " Per mortem et sepulturam tuam," Quignon's Breviary, p. 506.

[3] " By the comynge of the Holy Ghoste," Primer, 1535. " Per adventum Spiritus Sancti," Quignon's Breviary.

[4] "In tyme of our tribulations . . . In the tyme of our felicitie," Primer, 1535. " In omni tempore tribulationis nostræ, in omni tempore felicitatis nostræ," Herman.

church universal in the right way. *R.* We beseech Thee to hear us, good Lord.

That it may please Thee to keep HENRY the VIIIth Thy servant, and our king and governor.[1]

That it may please Thee to rule his heart in Thy faith, fear and love, and that he may ever have affiance in Thee, and ever seek Thy honour and glory.[2]

That it may please Thee to be his defender and keeper, giving him the victory over all his enemies.

That it may please Thee to keep our noble Queen

Ut misericordia et pietas tua nos custodiat. *R.* Te ro-gamus, &c.

Ut ecclesiam tuam regere et defensare digneris.

. Ut domnum Apostolicum, et omnes gradus ecclesiæ in sancta religione conservare digneris.

Ut Episcopos et Abbates nostros in sancta religione conservare digneris.

Ut regi nostro et Princi-pibus nostris pacem et veram concordiam atque victoriam donare digneris.

---

[1] "That thou vouchsafe to preserve our moste gracious Soveraign Lorde and Kynge Henry the eyghte, his most gracious quene Anne, all their posterite, ayders, helpers, and true subjects."—Primer, 1535.

[2] These petitions seem to be Archbishop Cranmer's own.

LITANY OF 1544.   SARUM LITANY.

CATHERINE in Thy fear
and love; giving her increase
of all godliness, honour, and
children.

That it may please Thee to
keep and defend our noble
Prince EDWARD, and all the
king's majesty's children.

That. it may please Thee
to illuminate all Bishops,
Pastors, and Ministers of the
church, with true knowledge
and understanding of Thy
word; and that both by their
preaching and ` living they
may set it forth and shew it
accordingly.[1]

That it may please Thee to
endue the lords of the council,
and all the nobility with

---

[1] "That thou vouchsafe that our byshops, pastors, and ministers of thy
Churche may in holy lyfe, and in thy sound and holy worde, fede thy
people."—Primer, 1535. Prayers for the various orders of the Clergy,
"who rightly divide the word of Thy truth," τῶν ὀρθοτομούντων τὸν λόγον
τῆς σῆς ἀληθείας, are frequently met with in the Eastern Liturgies. See
above, pages 34, 58; Swainson, page 132. The petition for "true knowledge
and understanding of Thy word" was appropriately put forth here by
Archbishop Cranmer, who had devoted years of labour to promote the
spread of Biblical study. The Bible was first published with his name on the
title-page in 1540, and a revised edition appeared in 1541. This was the
Bible usually read in the English Church until 1568, and from it the Prayer
Book Psalms are taken.—Hook, Lives of the Archbishops, vol. vii., pp. 136-
147. See above, pp. 150-152.

X

LITANY OF 1544.

grace, wisdom and under-
standing.[1]
That it may please Thee to
bless and keep the magistrates,
giving them grace to execute
justice, and to maintain truth.[2]
That it may please Thee to
bless and keep all Thy people.
That it may please Thee to
give to all nations unity,
peace and concord.[3]
That it may please Thee to
give us an heart to love and
dread Thee, and diligently
to live after Thy commandments.[4]

SARUM LITANY.

Ut congregationes omnium
sanctorum in tuo sancto ser-
vitio conservare digneris.

Ut cunctum populum Chris-
tianum pretioso Sanguine tuo
redemptum conservare dig-
neris.

[1] Prayers for "all in the palace and the camp," παντὸς τοῦ παλατίου καὶ στρατοπέδου, are common in Eastern Liturgies. See above, page 34; Swainson, page 133. "That our ministers and governours may vertuously rule thy people," Primer, 1535.

[2] No prayer corresponding to this has been met with. It has been recorded that in the Church of Soissons on certain days devotions named *Laudes* were anciently used between the Collect and Epistle, in which the words occur, "Omnibus judicibus et cuncto exercitui Francorum vita et victoria."—Martene, lib. i., cap. iv., art. iii., 13, quoted in Palmer's Origines, vol. i., p. 325. But the words do not seem to be quite analogous.

[3] This seems to be taken from the ancient form used in the Anglo-Saxon Church: "Ut cuncto populo Christiano pacem et unanimitatem largire digneris," Pontif. of Egbert, page 30. "That thou vouchsafe to give universal peace amonges all kings and other rulers," Primer, 1535.

[4] The true insight into the foundation of spiritual life expressed in the first half of this verse should be noticed; the words are peculiar to our Litany. The latter half may be founded upon the words "ut congregationem istam in sancta religione conservare digneris," Pontif. of Egbert, page 30;

LITANY OF 1544.	SARUM LITANY.
That it may please Thee to give to all Thy people increase of grace to hear meekly Thy word, and to receive it with pure affection, and to bring forth the fruits of the Spirit.[1]	Ut omnibus benefactoribus nostris sempiterna bona retribuas. Ut animas nostras et parentum nostrorum ab æterna damnatione eripias.
That it may please Thee to bring into the way of truth all such as have erred and are deceived.[2]	Ut fructus terræ dare et conservare digneris.
That it may please Thee to strengthen such as do stand; and to comfort and help the weak hearted; and to raise up them that fall; and finally to beat down Satan under our feet.[3]	Ut oculos misericordiæ tuæ super nos reducere digneris. Ut obsequium servitutis nostræ rationabile facias.

or possibly it may be an interpretation of the Sarum words " obsequium . . . rationabile."

[1] " That thou vouchsafe Lord to gyve the herers of thy worde lyvely grace to understand it, and to worke thereafter, by the vertue of the Holy Ghost," Primer, 1535. But the verse seems to be founded upon the words in Herman's Litany, " ut incrementum verbi et fructum Spiritus cunctis audientibus donare digneris."

[2] " That all wĥich doe erre and be deceived may be reduced into the way of verite," Primer, 1535. " Ut errantes et seductos reducere in viam veritatis digneris," Herman.

[3] This verse seems to be founded upon expressions in Herman's Litany, " ut Satanam sub pedibus nostris conterere digneris," " ut lapsos erigere et stantes confortari digneris," " ut pusillanimes et tentatos consolari et adjuvare digneris." But similar petitions occur in the Primer, 1535, " That we may the devyl with all his pomps frusbe and trede under foote," " That they which are weyke in vertue, and soon overcome in temptation, thou of thy mercye wilt helpe and strengthen them."

LITANY OF 1544.	SARUM LITANY.
That it may please Thee to succour, help and comfort all that be in danger, necessity and tribulation.[1]	Ut mentes nostras ad cœlestia desideria erigas.
That it may please Thee to preserve all that travel by land or by water, all women labouring of child, all sick persons and young children, and to shew Thy pity upon all prisoners and captives.[2]	Ut miserias pauperum et captivorum intueri et relevare digneris.
That it may please Thee to defend and provide for the fatherless children and widows, and all that be desolate and oppressed.[3]	
That it may please Thee to have mercy upon all men.[4]	Ut omnibus fidelibus defunctis requiem æternam dones.
That it may please Thee to	

[1] These words seem to be taken from the Liturgy of S. Chrysostom, ἀπὸ πάσης θλίψεως, ὀργῆς καὶ ἀνάγκης; see above, note to p. 45. Similar words are also found in Herman's Litany, "ut afflictos et periclitantes respicere et salvare digneris;" and in the Primer, 1535, "That thy people in affliction or in peryl and daunger by fyre water or lande thou wilte vouchsafe to defende and preserve."

[2] Such words are common in the Greek Liturgies, see Liturgy of S. Chrysostom, *ut supra.* The improvement upon the few words of the Sarum Litany should be noticed. Similar expressions are found in Herman's Litany, and in the Primer, 1535.

[3] These words seem founded upon Herman's Litany, " ut pupillos et viduas protegere et providere digneris," but similar petitions occur in the Primer, 1535.

[4] " That unto all people, Lorde, thou wilte shewe thy inestimable mercy," Primer, 1535. " Ut cunctis hominibus misereri digneris," Herman.

LITANY OF 1544.

SARUM LITANY.

forgive our enemies, persecutors and slanderers, and to
turn their hearts.[1]
That it may please Thee to
give to our use the kindly
fruits of the earth, so as in
due time we may enjoy them;
and to preserve them.[2]
That it may please Thee to   Ut nos exaudire digneris.
give us true repentance; to
forgive us all our sins, negli-
gences and ignorances; and
to endue us with the grace of
Thy Holy Spirit to amend
our lives according to Thy
holy word.[3]
Son of God, we beseech   Fili Dei : te rogamus audi
Thee to hear us. *R.* Son of   nos. *R.* Fili Dei, &c.
God, &c.
O Lamb of God: that takest   Agnus Dei qui tollis pec-

---

[1] " That thou wilte forgyve all warryars, persecutors, and oppressours of thy people, and to convert them to grace," Primer, 1535. " Ut hostibus persecutoribus et calumniatoribus nostris ignoscere et eos convertere dig- neris," Herman. But the same prayer had been in use in the Anglo-Saxon Church of the seventh century—" Pro omnibus adversantibus et calumpnian- tibus nobis," see above, page 273—and still more anciently in the Liturgy of the Apostolical Constitutions, see page 35.

[2] This petition is founded upon the words in the Sarum Litany ; see a few verses above.

[3] The summing up of our spiritual needs in this verse is a peculiar beauty of the English Litany. The petition for true repentance occurs in the Roman Litany, and may have been taken from Quignon's Breviary, " ut nobis indulgeas . . . ut ad veram pœnitentiam nos perducere digneris," p. 506.

LITANY OF 1544.

away the sins of the world. R. Grant us Thy peace.

O Lamb of God: that takest away the sins of the world. R. Have mercy upon us.

O Christ, hear us. R. O Christ, &c.[1]

Lord, have mercy upon us.

Christ, have mercy upon us.

Lord, have mercy upon us.

Our Father, which art in heaven; *with the residue of the Pater noster.*

And suffer us not to be led into temptation. R. But deliver us from evil. Amen.

The *Versicle.* Lord, deal not with us after our sins.

The *Answer.* Neither reward us after our iniquities.[2]

SARUM LITANY.

cata mundi: exaudi nos Domine. R. Agnus, &c.

Agnus Dei qui tollis peccata mundi: parce nobis Domine. R. Agnus, &c.

Agnus Dei qui tollis peccata mundi: miserere nobis. R. Agnus, &c.

Kyri eleyson.

Christe eleyson.

Kyri eleyson.

Pater noster, &c.

Ostende nobis Domine misericordiam, &c.

Et veniat super nos misericordia, &c.

Peccavimus cum patribus, &c.

Domine non secundum peccata nostra facias nobis. Neque secundum iniquitates nostras retribuas nobis.

The word "ignorances" seems to be taken from the expression repeatedly used in the Liturgy of S. Chrysostom, τῶν ἡμετέρων ἁμαρτημάτων καὶ τῶν τοῦ λαοῦ ἀγνοημάτων; see above, pp. 50, 52.

[1] These words are in the Roman Litany, though not in the Sarum. See Quignon's Breviary, p. 507.

[2] It will be noticed that this *Versicle* is the only one retained out of several

LITANY OF 1544.	SARUM LITANY.
Let us pray.	Oremus pro omni gradu Ecclesiæ, &c.
O God, merciful Father, &c.[1]	Pro fratribus, &c.
R. O Lord, arise, help us, and deliver us, for Thy honour.	Pro cuncto populo, &c. Domine fiat pax in virtute, &c.
O God, we have heard, &c.	Animæ famulorum, &c.
R. O Lord, arise, help us, and deliver us, for Thy name's sake.	Domine exaudi orationem, &c. Dominus vobiscum, &c,
Glory to the Father, the Son, and to the Holy Ghost, as it hath been from the beginning, is, and shall be ever, world without end. Amen.[2]	

in the Sarum Litany. This selection had already been made in Herman's Litany.

[1] This prayer is in place of the Intercessions which were introduced again here in the Sarum Litany. It was the Collect belonging to Sarum *Missa de tribulatione cordis.* Our translation has evidently been made from a slightly altered version of it, which is found here in Herman's Litany.

[2] This is an interesting illustration of the ancient Antiphons. The form is taken from a service to be used on the Monday in Rogation week, consisting of various Antiphons and verses, thus: " *Ordo processionis in secunda feria in rogationibus. Hæc sequens Antiphona cantatur a choro in stallis:* Exurge Domine adjuva nos et libera nos propter nomen tuum. Alleluia. *Presbyter.* Deus auribus nostris audivimus, patres nostri annunciaverunt nobis. *Non dicatur nisi primus versus, sed statim sequatur.* Gloria Patri. *Deinde repetatur,* Exurge." Then other Antiphons follow in a similar manner.—Processionale ad usum Sarum, fol. cxvi. The great antiquity of this form of service has been mentioned above, p. 286.

LITANY OF 1544.

SARUM LITANY.

From our enemies defend us, O Christ.

R. Graciously look upon our afflictions.

Pitifully behold the dolour of our heart.

R. Mercifully forgive the sins of Thy people.

Favourably, with mercy, hear our prayers.

R. O Son of David, have mercy upon us.

Both now and ever vouch-safe to hear us, Christ.

R. Graciously hear us, O Christ: graciously hear us, O Lord Christ.[1]

The *Versicle.* O Lord, let Thy mercy be shewed upon us.

---

[1] These versicles are appointed for use in time of war, in the third Litany for S. Mark's day, according to Sarum Use, as follows :—

"Ab inimicis nostris defende nos Christe. *R. Idem.*
Afflictionem nostram benignus vide. *R. Idem.*
Dolorem cordis nostri respice clemens. *R. Idem.*
Peccata populi tui pius indulge. *R. Idem.*
Orationes nostras pius exaudi. *R. Idem.*
Fili dei vivi miserere nobis. *R. Idem.*
Hic et in perpetuum nos custodire digneris Christe. *R. Idem.*
Exaudi nos Christe, exaudi exaudi nos Christe."—Processionale ad usum Sarum, fol. cxxxiv. They are found also in the Litany of the Anglo-Saxon Church of the eighth century.—Pontif. of Egbert, p. 32. The use of the words, "O Son of David," apparently for the sake of rhythm, should be noticed.

The *Answer.* As we do put our trust in Thee.[1]

Let us pray.

We humbly beseech Thee, O Father, mercifully to look upon our infirmities, and for the glory of Thy name's sake, turn from us all those evils, that we most righteously have deserved. Grant this, O Lord God, for our mediator and advocate, Jesus Christ's sake. Amen.[2]

O God, whose nature and property, &c.

Almighty and everliving God, which only workest great marvels, send down upon our bishops, &c.

We beseech Thee, O Lord,

Oremus.

Deus cui proprium est misereri semper et parcere, &c.

(Various other Collects.)

---

[1] This versicle was in frequent use, being appointed as the *Verse* between Mattins and Lauds, and occurring again amongst the *Preces* in Lauds, Prime, and Compline. The words *Priest* and *Answer*, now found here, are thus accounted for ; being in place of the words above, which were used at first because the *versicle* was brought here from other services, but in later times became unintelligible.

[2] This Collect is formed out of an ancient collect, " Infirmitatem nostram quæsumus Domine propitius respice, et mala omnia quæ juste meremur, omnium Sanctorum tuorum intercessione averte. Per."—Sarum Processional, fol. ccvi., quoted in Palmer's Origines, vol. i., p. 330. It should be noticed that the words " for the glory of Thy Name's sake " now take the place of the mention of the intercession of the saints.

to shew upon us Thine ex-
ceeding great mercy, &c.

Grant, we beseech Thee, O
Almighty God, that we in our
trouble put our whole confidence upon Thy mercy, that
we may against all adversity
be defended under Thy protection.   Grant this, O Lord
God, for our mediator and
advocate, Jesus Christ's sake.
Amen.

A prayer of Chrysostome.

Almighty God, which hast
given us grace, &c.[1]

---

[1] This prayer ended the Litany until 1559. See Liturgy of S. Chrysostom, above, p. 47.   It appears to have been translated direct from the
Greek by Archbishop Cranmer.   He had a Latin version of it by Erasmus ;
but in his MS. collections he uses a Latin version of his own.   See above,
page 42, note 1, and " Catalogue of Cranmer's Library."

CHAPTER X.

THE CREEDS ; THEIR ORIGIN, AND USE IN ACTS
OF WORSHIP.

" Priusquam incipiam de ipsis sermonum virtutibus disputare, illud non
importune commonendum puto, quod in diversis Ecclesiis aliqua in his verbis
inveniuntur adjecta. In Ecclesia tamen urbis Romæ hoc non deprehenditur
factum . : . in ceteris autem locis, quantum intelligi datur, propter non-
nullos hæreticos addita quædam videntur."—*Rufinus, expositio in Symbolum.*
(Fourth century.)

THE Christian faith was set forth in its briefest form
by our Lord Himself, who laid this charge upon
His Apostles, " Go ye, and make disciples of all nations,
baptizing them in the name of the Father, and of the Son,
and of the Holy Ghost." [1] Wherefore Tertullian, writing
circa A.D. 200, correctly states that Christians receive the
Creed, or *Regula Fidei*, " as instituted by Christ." [2]

It is not known whether any longer form was drawn up
at once, and used by the Apostles ; but many passages in
the New Testament seem to lead to this conclusion.
Thus S. Paul exhorts the Thessalonians, " Hold fast the
traditions which ye were taught." [3] Writing to Timothy
he speaks more plainly, " Hold the pattern of sound
words ; " and again, " The things which thou hast heard
from me among many witnesses, the same commit thou

[1] S. Matt. xxviii. 19.
[2] Tertullian, de Prescript., cap. xiv.
[3] τὰς παραδόσεις ἃς ἐδιδάχθητε εἴτε διὰ λόγου εἴτε δι' ἐπιστολῆς ἡμῶν.—
2 Thess. ii. 15.

to faithful men."[1]   And to Titus he describes the man
fit to be a bishop, as " holding to the faithful word which
is according to the teaching."[2]   All these expressions
seem to point to some fixed form of Christian doctrine,
and history confirms this view.   For as soon as the full
form of the Apostles Creed is found in Christian writings,
viz., about the end of the fourth century, it is found connected with the tradition that it had been so fixed by the
Apostles, as the rule of what their preaching should be.[3]

But whether the Apostles drew up an enlarged form of
belief or not, this at least is certain, that through the
formula of Christian baptism, established by our Lord,
the doctrine of the Trinity became the foundation of
Christian worship ; and the knowledge of the Creed
which contained and expressed this faith became the
symbol or watchword by which a Christian was recognized.   At what date the baptismal formula was first enlarged into the Creed, as we have it, cannot be known ;
because as long as persecution lasted the form in which
the Christian faith was repeated was necessarily con-

[1] ὑποτύπωσιν ἔχε ὑγιαινόντων λόγων, ὧν παρ' ἐμοῦ ἤκουσας.—2 Tim. i. 13.
ἃ ἤκουσας παρ' ἐμοῦ διὰ πολλῶν μαρτύρων, ταῦτα παράθου πιστοῖς ἀνθρώποις.
—2 Tim. ii. 2.

[2] ἀντεχόμενον τοῦ κατὰ τὴν διδαχὴν πιστοῦ λόγου.—Titus i. 9.   But see
p. 22, where " The Teaching of the Apostles" bears a wider meaning.

[3] Rufinus, Expositio in Symbol. Apost., at end of Cyprian's Works,
Oxon, 1682.   This is repeated in a sermon attributed to S. Augustine, but
included amongst his doubtful works, and probably belonging to a later
writer: " Sancti Apostoli certam regulam Fidei tradiderunt, quam secundum
numerum Apostolicum duodecim sententiis comprehensam, Symbolum voca-
verunt; per quam credentes Catholicam tenerent unitatem et per quam
hæreticam convincerent pravitatem."—Sermo de Temp., 181, tom. x., p.
687.   And this statement was afterwards exaggerated by assigning the
various articles of the Creed to the various Apostles.—Sacrament. Gallic.,
sub finem, Muratori, vol. ii., p. 967.

cealed from the heathen, otherwise Christians would not have known whom they might trust. Moreover, for a long time after persecution ceased, it was considered wrong to make public the form of Christian words, lest the heathen should profane the name of God.[1] But whilst the faith was one and the same amongst all Churches of the East and West, it is evident that the symbol of the faith, or Creed, which was used in the solemn profession of Christianity at baptism, was not drawn up universally in the same form of words. But from the earliest times two distinct types of Creed can be traced, corresponding with the two Creeds with which we are familiar under the names of the Apostles Creed and the Nicene Creed.[2]

---

[1] For instance, Cyril of Jerusalem, in his catechetical lectures delivered A.D. 347, exhorts those preparing for baptism: "Take thou and hold the faith which is by the Church delivered unto thee. For since all cannot read the Scripture, that the soul may not perish for lack of instruction, in these few articles we comprehend the whole doctrine of the faith. This I wish you to remember in the exact words, and to rehearse it with all diligence amongst yourselves; not writing it on paper, but by memory graving it on your heart, as on a monument." He then goes on to warn them against letting other persons hear them repeating it, and against admitting any different form of words, quoting, "Though we or an angel from heaven preach any other gospel, let him be accursed;" and he assures them that like as the seed contains the tree, so this faith in a few words enfolds the whole knowledge of godliness contained in the Old and New Testaments.— Cyril, Catech. Lecture V., 12; Mozarabic Missal, folio 151; Rufinus, Expos. in Symb., *ad init.*

[2] Rufinus, *ut supra ;* Suicer, "Thesaurus," under the word Σύμβολον. The history of the formation of these Creeds is very complicated, as is shown by the many volumes which have appeared on the subject. The author desires to mention that, whilst he alone is responsible for the following statements, he is indebted to the Rev. Preb. E. C. S. Gibson, Principal of Wells Theological College, for much valuable criticism, as well as help, in pursuing the course which has been taken.

SECTION I.—*The Apostles Creed.*

The first specimen of the Creed is found in the earliest of the Latin Fathers, Tertullian, a presbyter of the African Church, *circa* A.D. 200. He mentions the Creed in various passages, under the term *Regula fidei*, as "having been instituted by Christ and received amongst Christians without questioning, except that raised by heretics." And though he does not record the full words of the Creed in any one of these passages, doubtless for the reason stated before, yet it is possible to construct the substance of it from them as follows. The Christian's faith is to believe

"in one God only, Almighty, maker of the world. And in His Son Jesus Christ, [who was sent down by the Spirit and power of God the Father], born of the Virgin Mary, [suffered], was crucified under Pontius Pilate, [dead and buried according to the Scriptures]; the third day He was raised again from the dead, and received in heaven; He sitteth now at the right hand of the Father; He will come to judge the quick and the dead, through the resurrection even of the flesh. [Who sent . . . the Holy Spirit, the Comforter, and Sanctifier,] [to bring the saints into the enjoyment of life everlasting . . . . with the restitution of the flesh]." [1]

---

[1] Tertullian de Virgin. veland., cap. i.; the words in [ ] are added from adv. Prax., cap. ii., and de Prescript., cap. xiii.: "Regula quidem fidei una omnino est, sola immobilis, et irreformabilis, credendi scilicet in unicum Deum omnipotentem mundi creatorem. Et Filium ejus Jesum Christum [delatum ex Spiritu Patris Dei et virtute] natum ex virgine Maria, [passum], crucifixum sub Pontio Pilato, [mortuum et sepultum secundum Scripturas], tertia die resuscitatum a mortuis, receptum in cœlis,

Similar outlines of a Creed can be gathered from the writings of Cyprian, Bishop of Carthage, A.D. 248-258. He refers to the questions used in baptism in connection with what he speaks of as the baptismal *Symbolum*, and states that besides the profession of faith in God the Father, Christ the Son, and the Holy Ghost, this also was demanded, " Dost thou believe in the remission of sins and the life everlasting through the Holy Church ?"[1] It is clear from these words that the questions asked in baptism were distinct from the Creed itself as early as the third century. And a comparison of these questions with the interrogatories in baptism in later times will show that there is no reason to suppose that Cyprian was thus stating the whole or the actual words of the Creed of the African Church in his day.[2] On the contrary, they furnish good evidence of the existence of the Creed in full; the remainder of which may be gathered from another passage, where he refers to the events in the life of Christ as forming part of the necessary belief in God,

sedentem nunc ad dexteram Patris, venturum judicare vivos et mortuos per carnis etiam resurrectionem. [Qui miserit. . . Spiritum Sanctum, Paracletum, sanctificatorem,] [ad sumendos sanctos in vitæ æternæ fructum . . . cum carnis restitutione.] "

[1] Cyprian, Epist. lxix., *al* lxxv. to Magnus : " Sciat, . . . non esse unam nobis et schismaticis symboli legem, neque eandem interrogationem. Nam cum dicunt ; Credis remissionem peccatorum et vitam æternam per sanctam ecclesiam ; mentiuntur in interrogatione, quando non habeant ecclesiam." See also Epist. lxx., *al.* lxix. to Numidian Bishops.

[2] See below, p. 342. Dr. J. R. Lumby, in his " History of the Creeds," pp. 17, 115, assumes on the contrary that the interrogatories and the Creed were the same ; but he does not mention the grounds upon which this supposition is founded. The same is repeated in his article on the Creeds in " Prayer Book with Commentary," published by S. P. C. K. Unnecessary doubt seems to be thus thrown upon the existence of the Creed in the third century.

and uses expressions corresponding with many words of the Creed, though no decided reference is made to it.[1]

Evidence is thus given by the writings of Tertullian and Cyprian in proof of the existence of the Creed in the Church of North Africa from the end of the second century in substantially the same form as it has been handed down to the present day. Every article of the Creed is found to be represented in the extracts above given, and the only expressions omitted are "descended into hell," and " the Communion of Saints."

But whilst the Creed was thus known and referred to in the third century, it was still considered wrong to commit the complete form of words to writing. Consequently we must pass over another century and a half before we find a copy of the full rule of faith of the Western Church in Latin. This is given for the first time in the writings of Rufinus, presbyter of the Church of Aquileia in the north of Italy, *circa* A.D. 397. He has left behind a careful exposition of every article of the Creed. In the preface he states that there was an old tradition, that when the Apostles were departing to preach the Gospel in every land, they first laid down in common the rule which should be followed in their preaching, in order that there might be no diversity amongst their converts, and that this Creed was the result. He compares it to the watchword amongst soldiers, and declares that for this reason the Apostles taught that it should

---

[1] Cyprian de Idol. vanit., *ad finem:* "Ipse prædixerat . . . oportere illum pati . . . et cum passus esset ad superos regredi . . . Fidem itaque rerum cursus implevit. Nam et crucifixus . . . et die tertio rursus a mortuis sponte surrexit . . . Tunc in cœlum . . . sublatus est, . . . venturus e cœlo ad pœnam diaboli et ad censuram generis humani."

not be written down on paper or parchment, but retained in the heart, that there might be no risk of anyone learning it otherwise than by Apostolic tradition. In the course of his treatise he adds some wise remarks about the substantial agreement between different churches, though verbal differences might be found existing in their forms of Creed. For instance, under the first article, "I believe in God the Father Almighty," he refers to the fact that in various churches other words were added to the form which he was expounding, such as the words "invisible and impassible" in the Creed of Aquileia, which were wanting in the Creed which was used at Rome; and he explains that in his opinion the reason was this : "In other churches it seemed necessary to add such words on account of novelties introduced by various heretics, in order that it should be impossible for such new meanings to be put upon the ancient words of the Creed ; whereas in the Roman Church no heresy had arisen, and the old custom was retained of repeating the Creed exactly word for word as from the beginning, without any addition being permitted." He calls attention also to the words "descended into hell," which occur for the first time in the Creed as he gives it, stating that they were not found in the Roman Creed, nor amongst the Churches of the East, though, in his opinion, the truth which they expressed was included in the word "buried," which those other Creeds contained.[1] And very similar

[1] The Creed as expounded by Rufinus, who was the friend and contemporary of S. Jerome, A.D. 345-410, is as follows :—

"Credo in Deum Patrem omnipotentem, invisibilem et impassibilem :

Et in Christum Jesum unicum Filium ejus Dominum nostrum ; qui natus est de Spiritu Sancto ex Maria Virgine ; crucifixus sub Pontio Pilato

Y

testimony is given by S. Augustine, with respect to the Creed of the Church of North Africa at about the same period, in his discourse delivered, A.D. 393, upon " Faith and the Creed." [1]

et sepultus, descendit in inferna ; tertia die resurrexit a mortuis ; ascendit in cœlos, sedet ad dexteram Patris ; inde venturus est judicare vivos et mortuos.

Et in Spiritum sanctum, sanctam Ecclesiam [catholicam], remissionem peccatorum, hujus carnis resurrectionem."

[1] Cap. 1. " Est autem fides Catholica in symbolo nota fidelibus, memoriæque mandata, quantum res passa est brevitate sermonis ; ut incipientibus atque lactentibus eis, qui in Christo renati sunt, et nondum Scripturarum divinarum diligentissima et spiritali tractatione atque cognitione roboratis, paucis verbis credendum constitueretur quod proficientibus . . . multis verbis exponendo esset perficiendum."

Cap. 2. " Conati sunt enim quidem persuadere Deum patrem non esse omnipotentem." He goes on to argue that because we believe in God as Almighty, therefore we must believe that there is no creature which was not created by Him.

Cap. 3. " Credimus etiam in Jesum Christum filium Dei Patris unigenitum unicum Deum nostrum," &c. ;

Cap. 4. He goes on to argue that though with respect to the Son of God, as the Only-Begotten, it could not be said that He was, or that He will be, but only that He is ; yet for our salvation He became connected with time, and thus we believe " in eum Dei filium qui natus est per Spiritum Sanctum ex Virgine Maria."

Cap. 5. " Credimus in eum qui sub Pontio Pilato crucifixus est et sepultus. (Addendum enim erat judicis nomen propter temporum cognitionem)." " Credimus etiam tertio die resurrexisse a mortuis."

Cap. 6. " Credimus in cœlum ascendisse," &c.

Cap. 7. " Credimus etiam quod sedet ad dexteram Dei patris. (Ad dexteram ergo intelligendum est dictum esse in summâ beatitudine)."

Cap. 8. " Unde venturum convenientissimo tempore, et judicaturum vivos et mortuos."

Cap. 9. Contains a description of the Blessed Trinity, in connection with the belief in the Holy Ghost.

Cap. 10. " Credimus et Sanctam Ecclesiam, utique Catholicam ; nam et hæretici et schismatici congregationes suas ecclesias vocant." " Credimus et remissionem peccatorum." " Credimus et carnis resurrectionem, qua

But whilst the Creed of Rufinus is the earliest Latin version of the Western Creed in full, there is no doubt that a yet earlier version of the same Creed has been preserved in Greek by Epiphanius. He records, *circa* A.D. 376, that Marcellus, after being deposed from the bishopric of Ancyra, A.D. 336, betook himself to Italy, and wrote to Pope Julius (A.D. 337-352), expressing his desire that those who accused him of heresy should be brought to Rome, and meet him face to face, and adding a version of the Apostles Creed as he had received it, which Epiphanius proceeds to give in Greek. In many respects this version agrees with the Creed expounded by S. Augustine, for it omits the words, " Maker of heaven and earth," " dead," " Catholic," which seem to have been omitted in the Church of North Africa ; but it contains the words, " life everlasting," which were generally wanting in the Western Creed.[1] A similar Greek version is also found in Anglo-Saxon characters in the Psalter of King Æthelstan, which probably belongs to the ninth century.[2]

corporis resurrectione facta a temporis conditione liberati eterna vita ineffabili charitate atque stabilitate sine corruptione perfruemur."—S. August. de Fide et Symb., tom. iii., p. 61.

[1] Epiphanius, adv. Hæres. Hæresis, lxxii., vol. i., p. 836 ; Bingham, Antiq., Book x., chap. iv., sect. 12.

[2] Suicer, " Thesaurus," under the word Σύμβολον. There is no doubt that the ordinary Latin form of the Apostles Creed was in use at this time in the Anglo-Saxon Church. For in the Anglo-Saxon Ritual of Durham, of the ninth century, which is interlined with a Saxon version of the Latin, under the *Capitulæ ad Primam*, we find—

" Credo in Deum Patrem omnipotentem creatorem cœli.

Carnis resurrectionem in vitam æternam. Amen."

The reading *in vitam* is a curious one, but it is twice repeated in this book. It may be regarded as an illustration of the late admission of the words " vitam æternam " into the Western Creed.—Rituale Eccles. Dunelm.,

There is no doubt that variations continued to prevail in the Creed for many centuries in the Western Churches. Some truths were considered to be implied which were afterwards more clearly expressed. For instance, the words " Life everlasting " were very generally omitted. They occur in the form of Confession which may be gathered out of the works of Cyprian in the third century, but they are not generally found until a much later date.[1] Similarly, the words " suffered," " dead," " descended into hell," " Catholic," " Communion of Saints," [2] are referred to by writers and preachers as intended to be understood or implied in other words of the Creed long before they were universally adopted in the Creed itself; and these expressions were not finally fixed until the general assent of Christendom decided upon the form which seemed to be best suited to supply all that was needed. Consequently it is possible that when the variations in the Creeds used by different Churches, or at different periods, are brought prominently into notice, an importance appears to belong to them which they do not really possess. In practice such variations are passed over without notice. The different Churches meant the

pp. 166, 181. The same reading is found in Sacrament. Gallic.—Muratori, vol. ii., p. 968.

[1] Page 319.

[2] The expression " Communion of Saints " occurs in Sermo de Tempore, 181, amongst the doubtful works of S. Augustine, tom. x., p. 687. It is used also by Eusebius Gallicanus, *circa* A.D. 550.—" Prayer Book with Commentary," published by S.P.C.K. It is first found in a Creed in the Sacrament. Gallican.—Muratori, vol. ii., p. 831 ; but in the explanation of the Creed which follows, this clause is omitted. It occurs also in Missale Gallic. vetus, both in the Creed and in the explanation.—Muratori, vol. ii., p. 711-713. See Pearson on the Creed, for ancient and modern explanations of it.

same, if they did not express themselves always in the same words, for variations are found in different copies of the Creed, even in the same Service Books. For instance, in the Gallican Missals several forms of Creed occur, which vary considerably.[1] And even in the Book of Common Prayer three different versions of the Apostles Creed are found, yet the differences between them are recognized by 'few.[2] In the same way the changes of words which were made in the course of ages in this Creed, as revealed in the writings of the ancients, may be regarded as of little moment. The faith itself was the same, though the words of the Creed may have differed.

THE APOSTLES CREED as finally adopted.

"Credo in Deum Patrem Omnipotentem creatorem cœli et terræ.

Et in Jesum Christum Filium ejus unicum, Dominum nostrum. Qui conceptus est de Spiritu Sancto: natus ex Maria Virgine: passus sub Pontio Pilato: crucifixus, mortuus et sepultus: descendit ad inferos: tertia die resurrexit a mortuis: ascendit ad cœlos: sedet ad dexteram Dei Patris omnipotentis: inde venturus judicare vivos et mortuos.

Credo in Spiritum Sanctum, sanctam Ecclesiam Catholicam, sanctorum communionem, remissionem peccatorum, carnis resurrectionem, vitam æternam. Amen."

---

[1] The *Missale Gallicanum vetus* contains two forms, in one of which the word *Victor* is inserted after "ascendit." In *Sacramentarium Gallicanum* the Creed occurs with the variations, *unigenitum* sempiternum for "unicum," the omission of " qui," and the use of the accusatives *conceptum, natum*, &c. *Inferna* also is commonly found for " inferos," and *sedit* for " sedet."— Muratori, vol. ii., pp. 710-722, 830, 851, 967.

[2] In the Baptismal Version the words begotten, *again at the end of the world*, after death are added ; the words *from the dead* are omitted ; and these variations occur, *went down* for " descended," *at* for " on," *remission* for " forgiveness," *flesh* for " body." In the Catechism *at* is used for " on."

Section II.—*The Nicene Creed.*

It is evident that from the earliest times the Eastern form of Creed differed from the Western, and that it was variously worded in different Churches and at different times to meet the various heresies by which the East was distracted. The earliest form of Eastern Creed is found in the works of Irenæus, who carried with him from Smyrna to Gaul the faith in which he had been brought up. He became bishop of Lyons A.D. 177, and his words prove that such forms as that which he records had long been in regular use in the Church of Christ.[1] He says :—

" The Church, though dispersed over all the world, received from the Apostles and their disciples the faith in One God the Father Almighty, Maker of Heaven, and earth, and seas, and of all things in them ; and in one Christ Jesus, the Son of God, who was incarnate for our salvation ; and in the Holy Ghost, who preached by the prophets the dispensations (of God), and the Advents, and the Birth of a Virgin, and the Passion, and the Resurrection from the dead, and the bodily ascension into Heaven of His Beloved Son Christ Jesus our Lord, and His coming again from Heaven in the glory of the Father to sum up all things in Himself, and to raise the flesh of all mankind . . . . and that every tongue should confess to Him, and that He should give just judgment upon all."

Irenæus then goes on to declare that this faith was the same in all the world, and that men professed, kept,

---

[1] Irenæus, adv. Heres., lib. i., cap. 2, 3 ; see Bingham, Antiq., book x., chap. iv., 1.

and preached it as with one heart and voice, so that " the Churches in Germany had no other faith or tradition than those in Iberia or among the Celtæ, or in the East, or in Egypt, or in Libya, or in the middle parts of the earth." But whilst the faith was one and the same, many different specimens of Creeds are found, which belonged to different Churches of the East. So numerous were these Creeds, that in the one Patriarchate of Antioch three forms were in use, viz., the Creed of Antioch, the Creed of Cæsarea, and the Creed of Jerusalem. Amongst these numerous Creeds that which is mentioned by Eusebius, the Church historian, Bishop of Cæsarea in Palestine, A.D. 315-340, is the most important, because it seems to have been taken as the model for the Nicene Creed. He wrote to the people of Cæsarea, stating that he had recited their Creed at the commencement of the Council, and that after it had been received with general approval, the Emperor Constantine advised that it should be adopted by the Council, with the single addition of the word ὁμοούσιος, " of one substance with." It was commended to the assembly of the Fathers in the following words : " As we have received from the bishops who were before us, and in our first catechism, and at our baptism ; and as we have learned from Holy Scripture ; and as we have believed and taught during our priesthood and episcopate ; even so we believe to this day, and put forth our faith before you, in these words :—

Creed of Cæsarea.

We believe in one God the Father Almighty, Maker of all things visible and invisible ;

And in one Lord Jesus Christ, the Word of God, God of

God, Light of Light, Life of Life, the only-begotten Son, the first-born of every creature, begotten of God the Father before all worlds; by whom also all things were made; who for our salvation was incarnate, and dwelt among men, and suffered, and the third day He rose again, and ascended to the Father, and He shall come again to judge the quick and the dead.

We believe also in one Holy Ghost." [1]

Since Eusebius was born A.D. 264, we may conclude that this Creed had existed, as it was thus recited, from the middle of the third century at the latest. The Council evidently accepted it as the basis on which their Creed was formed, though other alterations, besides the addition suggested by the emperor, were inserted (as Eusebius felt it necessary to explain to the people of Cæsarea) by the decision of the assembled Fathers. [2] The result of the Council of Nicæa appeared in the following Creed :—

The Nicene Creed.

" We believe in one God the Father Almighty, maker of all things visible and invisible.

And in one Lord Jesus Christ, the Son of God, begotten of the Father, only-begotten (that is of the substance of the Father) God of God, Light of Light, very God of very God, begotten not made, of one substance with the Father, by whom all things were made, both the things in heaven and the things in earth; who for us men and for our salvation came down, and was incarnate, and was made man; He

---

[1] Socrates, Hist. Eccles., lib. i., cap. viii.—Bingham, Antiq., book x., chap. iv., 9.

[2] The Epistle of Eusebius ad Eccles. Cæsar. is preserved by Socrates Hist. Eccles., lib. i., cap. viii.

suffered, and the third day He rose again, He ascended into heaven, and He shall come to judge the quick and the dead. And in the Holy Ghost.

And those who say, 'there was a time when He was not, and before He was begotten He was not, and that He was made out of nothing;' or who assert that the Son of God is of another substance or essence, mutable or changeable, the holy Catholic and Apostolic Church anathematizes them."

A comparison of this Creed with that which has been traditionally received as the Nicene Creed, shows that many changes were introduced before it was finally adopted for general use. It remains to consider how this form was settled. The common explanation has been that it was remodelled at the Council of Constantinople, A.D. 381, when the clauses respecting the Holy Ghost were added, and that in consequence it has been frequently spoken of as " the Constantinopolitan Creed." But two reasons may be urged against this conclusion, either of which is fatal to it. No discussion of the Creed is found amongst the proceedings of the Council of Constantinople, and the Creed as it is now accepted was in use many years before the Council was held.

It is evident that the Creed of the Council of Nicæa was drawn up for the special purpose of condemning a certain form of error put forth by Arius, and it is reasonable to suppose that Churches which were not specially interested in his heresy would not feel it to be necessary to alter the form of Creed to which they had been accustomed. At all events, the Catechetical Lectures of Cyril, which were delivered at Jerusalem A.D. 347, prove that some of the special phrases of the Creed of the Council of Nicæa had not been adopted in the

Creed of Jerusalem at that date. Yet at the same time it appears that in many respects our present form of Creed is even more closely allied to the Creed which Cyril expounds than to the Creed of the Council of Nicæa. This will be seen on comparing the two.

Creed of Jerusalem.

"We believe in one God the Father Almighty, maker of heaven and earth, and of all things visible and invisible;

And in one Lord Jesus Christ, the only-begotten Son of God, begotten of His Father very God before all worlds, by whom all things were made; who was incarnate and was made man, and was crucified and was buried; and the third day He rose again and ascended into heaven, and sat on the right hand of the Father; and He shall come in glory to judge the quick and the dead; whose kingdom shall have no end.

And in one Holy Ghost, the Comforter, who spake in the prophets. And in one baptism of repentance for the remission of sins: and in one holy Catholic Church; and in the resurrection of the flesh; and in the life everlasting."

There are, moreover, other expressions which are used in these Lectures in such a way as to show that Cyril considered them to be implied in the words of the Creed, though not then belonging to it, as for instance, " God of God," " Light of Light," " according to the Scriptures." [1] So that it can be seen that the way

---

[1] Almost every word which now occurs in the Creed is put prominently forward in these Lectures. For instance, Ὑιὸς τοῦ πατρὸς ὅμοιος τῷ γεγεννηκότι, ζωὴ ἐκ ζωῆς γεγεννημένη, καὶ φῶς ἐκ φωτὸς . . . . καὶ θεὸς ἐκ θεοῦ.—Cyril, Catech. Lect. XI., p. 94; cf. p. 100. Παραδεχόμεθα λόγον ἐνανθρωπήσαντα κατὰ ἀλήθειαν οὐκ ἐκ θελήματος ἀνδρὸς . . . . ἀλλ᾿ ἐκ παρθένου καὶ πνεύματος ἁγίου.—Lect. XII., p. 105. Τίνος ἕνεκεν

was prepared for such additions. It should be noticed also that the occurrence of the clauses relating to the Holy Ghost proves that they were in use in a Creed which was regarded in A.D. 347 as the old traditional Creed of Jerusalem, and therefore probably belonged to an age anterior to the Council of Nicæa. Further evidence is derived from a work of Epiphanius, which appeared some years before the date of the Council of Constantinople. Herein two forms of Creed are recorded as used in baptism; one which corresponds almost exactly with our present so-called Nicene Creed, and which he states was in use until A.D. 373, and another, with many additions, which is described as having been introduced after that date in consequence of the Apollinarian heresy. Since Epiphanius was a native of Judæa, and was called from a monastery there to the bishopric of Cyprus, A.D. 367, there is little doubt that the earlier of these two forms was either the Creed then in use in Jerusalem, or was founded upon it.[1]

It is not precisely known how this Creed obtained the sanction of the name of " The Constantinopolitan Creed," since it does not appear amongst the acts of the Council of Constantinople, A.D. 381.[2] But there is no reasonable

κατέβη ὁ Ἰησοῦς ;—*Ibid*, p. 106. Ἡ ἐξ οὐρανῶν κατάβασις.—*Ibid*, p. 107. Τὸν ἐλθόντα ἐπὶ σωτηρίᾳ.—*Ibid*, p. 110. Lecture XIII. contains frequent mention of *Pilate*, and discussion περὶ τοῦ πάθους. In Lecture XIV. Cyril quotes and discusses 1 Cor. xv. 5, κατὰ τὰς γραφάς, p. 141. And in Lecture XVIII., after the words εἰς σαρκὸς ἀνάστασιν, he adds τοῦτ' ἐστὶ τὴν τῶν νεκρῶν, p. 223.

[1] Epiphanius, Anchoratus, cap. cxx., tom. ii., p. 122. All the above forms of Creed are given in Bingham, Antiq., book x., chap. iv. The texts may be found also in Suicer, " Thesaurus," under the word Σύμβολον.

[2] In Labbe's Concilia, Council of Constantinople, A.D. 381, the Creed is added after the Canons, but without authority, since there is no reference to

doubt but that it was accepted by the assembled Fathers, for it occurs together with the Nicene Confession in the acts of the Council of Chalcedon, A.D. 451, and it is there described as " The *Symbolum* of the One Hundred and fifty Fathers," *i.e.*, of the Council of Constantinople.[1] Having thus received the authority of a General Council, this Creed spread not only in the East, but throughout the whole of the Western Church under the form of various versions, having been translated by different hands for the Roman, Gallican, Spanish, and Celtic Churches, and appearing under the name sometimes of the Constantinopolitan, but more generally of the Nicene Creed.[2]

At first no variation from the Greek form of words appeared.[3] But in course of time two additions were made ; they appeared first in the Spanish version, and

it in the Canons themselves. It is omitted in Beverege's Councils. The history of this Creed has been most ably worked out by Professor Hort, " Two Dissertations," pp. 73-97, so as to leave little room for doubt that its acceptance may be traced to the influence of Cyril, who was one of the foremost members of this Council.

[1] Labbe, Council of Chalced·n, A.D. 451, tom. iv., pp. 342, 563, gives the *Symbolum* of the Three hundred and eighteen Fathers (Nicene), and the *Symbolum* of the One hundred and fifty Fathers (Constantinople).

[2] In the Third Council of Toledo, A.D. 589, Canon 2 (Labbe, tom. v., p. 1009), it was ordained that " throughout all the Churches of Hispania or Gallæcia the symbol of the faith according to the form of the Council of Oriental Churches at Constantinople, that is, of the one hundred and fifty bishops, should be recited." But Isidore, Bishop of Seville, A.D. 603-636, mentions it as " The Nicene Symbol," or as " The symbol put forth by the conference of the three hundred and eighteen holy Fathers at the Synod of Nicæa."—Isidore, de Eccles. Offic., lib. i., cap. xvi. And it has been commonly handed down in the Western Churches under this name.

[3] Evidence of this may be found in the Latin version of the Sacramentary of Gelasius, and in the Stowe Missal of the Celtic Church.

by degrees spread throughout the world. One of them, "God of God," *Deum de Deo,* has been accepted without contention ; the other, " and the Son," *Filioque,* has been one of the causes of the unending schism between East and West.[1]

In the following tables the reader will be able to follow the gradual formation of the Creed, first in the Greek, and then in the Latin versions. In the first table the Nicene Confession is traced from the more ancient form used in the Church of Cæsarea ; and then the Constantinopolitan Confession is traced from the more ancient form used in the Church of Jerusalem, and the difference between the two can be readily noted. In the second table four Latin versions are given : 1, the form which accompanies the Greek version in the Gelasian Sacramentary, representing a very early translation, used probably in some Gallican Church in the eighth century ; 2, the form in use in the Celtic Church of the ninth century ; 3, the Spanish version of the Mozarabic Breviary and Missal ; 4, the form which was finally adopted by the Roman Church and throughout the West.

[1] These additions appear in the records (apparently spurious) of the Spanish Council of Braga, A.D. 411. The Bishop Pancratianus expresses the belief of the assembled Fathers in various sentences, to which the others assent ; and these words occur, " Credo in unum Verbum genitum ab ipso Patre ante tempora, Deum ex Deo vero, &c." " Credo in Spiritum Sanctum procedentem a Patre et verbo," &c. The first undisputed appearance of the words is in the version of the Creed put forth by the Third Council of Toledo, A.D. 589, and hence they appear in the Mozarabic Missal and Breviary.—Labbe, Concilia, Bracarense Concilium, tom. ii., p. 1508 ; Third Toledo, tom. v., p. 1001 ; Mozar. Missal, fol. 6 ; Brev. Gothicum, p. 945. But in both cases the expressions which have been generally accepted differ from the words here used, " deum ex deo," and " et filio."

CREED OF CÆSARÆA.[1]	NICENE CREED.[2]

Πιστεύομεν εἰς ἕνα θεὸν πατέρα παντο-
κράτορα,

τὸν τῶν ἁπάντων ὁρατῶν τε καὶ ἀοράτων ποιητήν.
Καὶ εἰς ἕνα κύριον Ἰησοῦν Χριστόν,
τὸν τοῦ θεοῦ λόγον,

θεὸν ἐκ θεοῦ,
φῶς ἐκ φωτός
ζωὴν ἐκ ζωῆς,
υἱὸν μονογενῆ,
πρωτότοκον πάσης κτίσεως,
πρὸ πάντων τῶν αἰώνων ἐκ τοῦ θεοῦ
πατρὸς γεγεννημένον,
δι' οὗ καὶ ἐγένετο τὰ πάντα·
τὸν διὰ τὴν ἡμετέραν σωτηρίαν σαρκωθέντα,

καὶ ἐν ἀνθρώποις πολιτευσάμενον,
καὶ παθόντα,

καὶ ἀναστάντα τῇ τρίτῃ ἡμέρᾳ,

καὶ ἀνελθόντα πρὸς τὸν πατέρα,

καὶ ἥξοντα πάλιν κρῖναι ζῶντας καὶ
νεκρούς.

Πιστεύομεν καὶ εἰς ἓν πνεῦμα ἅγιον.

Πιστεύομεν εἰς ἕνα θεὸν πατέρα παντο-
κράτορα,

πάντων ὁρατῶν τε καὶ ἀοράτων ποιητήν.

Καὶ εἰς ἕνα κύριον Ἰησοῦν Χριστόν,
τὸν υἱὸν τοῦ θεοῦ,
γεννηθέντα ἐκ τοῦ πατρὸς μονογενῆ
(τοῦτ' ἐστὶν ἐκ τῆς οὐσίας τοῦ πατρός)
θεὸν ἐκ θεοῦ,
φῶς ἐκ φωτός,

θεὸν ἀληθινὸν ἐκ θεοῦ ἀληθινοῦ,
γεννηθέντα οὐ ποιηθέντα,
ὁμοούσιον τῷ πατρί,

δι' οὗ τὰ πάντα ἐγένετο,
τά τε ἐν τῷ οὐρανῷ καὶ τὰ ἐν τῇ γῇ·
τὸν δι' ἡμᾶς τοὺς ἀνθρώπους καὶ διὰ
τὴν ἡμετέραν σωτηρίαν κατελθόντα
καὶ σαρκωθέντα,

καὶ ἐνανθρωπήσαντα,
παθόντα,

καὶ ἀναστάντα τῇ τρίτῃ ἡμέρᾳ,

ἀνελθόντα εἰς τοὺς οὐρανούς,

ἐρχόμενον κρῖναι ζῶντας καὶ νεκρούς.

Καὶ εἰς τὸ ἅγιον πνεῦμα.
Τοὺς δὲ λέγοντας Ἦν ποτε ὅτε οὐκ ἦν
καὶ πρὶν γεννηθῆναι οὐκ ἦν, καὶ ὅτι Ἐξ
οὐκ ὄντων ἐγένετο, ἢ ἐξ ἑτέρας ὑποσ-
τάσεως ἢ οὐσίας φάσκοντας εἶναι τρεπ-
τὸν ἢ ἀλλοιωτὸν τὸν υἱὸν τοῦ θεοῦ,
ἀναθεματίζει ἡ ἁγία καθολικὴ καὶ ἀποσ-
τολικὴ ἐκκλησία.

---

[1] The text is taken from Socrates, Hist. Eccles., lib. i., cap. viii.; it is quoted
with a few various readings by Suicer, "Thesaurus," under the word Σύμβολον.
[2] Suicer, *ut supra*.

CREED OF JERUSALEM.[3]	CONSTANTINOPOLITAN CREED.[4]
Πιστεύομεν εἰς ἕνα θεὸν πατέρα παντο-κράτορα, ποιητὴν οὐρανοῦ καὶ γῆς, ὁρατῶν τε πάντων καὶ ἀοράτων.	Πιστεύομεν εἰς ἕνα θεὸν πατέρα παντο-κράτορα, ' ποιητὴν οὐρανοῦ τε καὶ γῆς, ὁρατῶν τε πάντων καὶ ἀοράτων.
Καὶ εἰς ἕνα κύριον Ἰησοῦν Χριστόν, τὸν υἱὸν τοῦ θεοῦ τὸν μονογενῆ, τὸν ἐκ τοῦ πατρὸς γεννηθέντα	Καὶ εἰς ἕνα Κύριον Ἰησοῦν Χριστόν, τὸν υἱόν τοῦ θεοῦ τὸν μονογενῆ, τὸν ἐκ τοῦ πατρὸς γεννηθέντα πρὸ πάντων τῶν αἰώνων,
	φῶς ἐκ φωτὸς,
θεὸν ἀληθινὸν πρὸ πάντων τῶν αἰώνων,	θεὸν ἀληθινὸν ἐκ θεοῦ ἀληθινοῦ, γεννηθέντα οὐ ποιηθέντα, ὁμοούσιον τῷ πατρί,
δι' οὗ τὰ πάντα ἐγένετο· σαρκωθέντα	δι' οὗ τὰ πάντα ἐγένετο· τὸν δι' ἡμᾶς τοὺς ἀνθρώπους καὶ διὰ τὴν ἡμετέραν σωτηρίαν κατελθόντα ἐκ τῶν οὐρανῶν, καὶ σαρκωθέντα ἐκ πνεύματος ἁγίου καὶ Μαρίας τῆς παρθένου,
καὶ ἐνανθρωπήσαντα, σταυρωθέντα καὶ ταφέντα, καὶ ἀναστάντα τῇ τρίτῃ ἡμέρᾳ,	καὶ ἐνανθρωπήσαντα, σταυρωθέντα τε ὑπὲρ ἡμῶν ἐπὶ Ποντίου Πιλάτου, καὶ παθόντα, καὶ ταφέντα, καὶ ἀναστάντα τῇ τρίτῃ ἡμέρᾳ κατὰ τὰς γραφάς,
καὶ ἀνελθόντα εἰς τοὺς οὐρανούς, καὶ καθίσαντα ἐκ δεξιῶν τοῦ πατρός, καὶ ἐρχόμενον (ἐν δόξῃ) κρῖναι ζῶντας καὶ νεκρούς, οὗ τῆς βασιλείας οὐκ ἔσται τέλος. Καὶ εἰς ἓν ἅγιον πνεῦμα,	καὶ ἀνελθόντα εἰς τοὺς οὐρανούς, καὶ καθεζόμενον ἐκ δεξιῶν τοῦ πατρός, καὶ πάλιν ἐρχόμενον μετὰ δόξης κρῖναι ζῶντας καὶ νεκρούς, οὗ τῆς βασιλείας οὐκ ἔσται τέλος. Καὶ εἰς τὸ πνεῦμα τὸ ἅγιον τὸ κύριον καὶ τὸ ζωοποιόν,
τὸν παράκλητον,	τὸ ἐκ τοῦ πατρὸς ἐκπορευόμενον, τὸ σὺν πατρὶ καὶ υἱῷ συνπροσκυνού-μενον καὶ συνδοξαζόμενον,
τὸ λαλῆσαν ἐν τοῖς προφήταις. Καὶ εἰς ἓν βάπτισμα μετανοίας εἰς ἄφεσιν ἁμαρτιῶν· καὶ εἰς μίαν ἁγίαν καθολικὴν ἐκκλησίαν·	τὸ λαλῆσαν διὰ τῶν προφητῶν. Εἰς μίαν ἁγίαν καθολικὴν καὶ ἀποστο-λικὴν ἐκκλησίαν· ὁμολογοῦμεν ἓν βάπτισμα εἰς ἄφεσιν ἁμαρτιῶν·
καὶ εἰς σαρκὸς ἀνάστασιν· καὶ εἰς ζωὴν αἰώνιον.	προσδοκῶμεν ἀνάστασιν νεκρῶν, καὶ ζωὴν τοῦ μέλλοντος αἰῶνος. Ἀμήν.

[3] Deduced from the Lectures of Cyril; Bingham, Antiq., book x., chap. iv., 8.
[4] Labbe, Concilia, Council of Chalcedon, A.D. 451, tom. iv., p. 342; see also p. 563; Suicer, *ut supra*; Epiphanius, Anchoratus, cap. cxx., p. 122.

SYMBOLUM.	CREED OF THE CELTIC CHURCH.
Sacramentarium Gelasianum, VIII. Cent.[1]	*Stowe Missal, IX. Cent.*[2]
Credo in unum Deum, Patrem omnipotentem, factorem cœli et terræ, visibilium omnium et invisibilium.	Credo in unum Deum patrem omnipotentem, factorem cœli et terræ, uissiuilium omnium et insuilium :
Et in unum Dominum Jesum Christum, Filium Dei unigenitum, de Patre natum ante omnia sæcula :	Et in unum dominum nostrum ihesum christum, filium dei unigenitum, natum ex patre ante omnia sæcula :
lumen de lumine : Deum verum de Deo vero ; natum non factum : consubstantialem Patri : per quem omnia facta sunt :	lumen de lumine ; deum uerum de deo uero natum non factum, consubstantialem Patri, per quem omnia facta sunt.
Qui propter nos homines, et propter nostram salutem descendentem de cœlis ; et incarnatum de Spiritu Sancto et Maria Virgine, et humanatum : crucifixum etiam pro nobis sub Pontio Pilato, et passum, et sepultum ; et resurgentem tertia die secundum scripturas ; et ascendentem in cœlos, et sedentem ad dexteram Patris : et iterum venturum cum gloria judicare vivos et mortuos : cujus Regni non erit finis. Et in Spiritum Sanctum Dominum, et Vivificatorem : ex Patre procedentem : qui cum Patre et Filio simul adoratum, et conglorificatum ; qui locutus est per Prophetas. In Unam, Sanctam, Catholicam, et Apostolicam Ecclesiam. Confiteor unum Baptisma in remissionem peccatorum. Spero resurrectionem mortuorum,	Qui propter nos homines et propter nostram salutem discendit de cœlo, et incarnatus est de spiritu sancto et Maria uirgine ; et homo factus est ; crugifixus hautem pro nobis sub pontio pilato, passus et sepultus ; et resurrexit tertia die secundum scripturas, et ascendit in cœlos, et sedet ad dextram dei patris : et iterum uenturus cum gloria judicare uiuos et mortuos, cujus regni non erit finis. Et spiritum sanctum, dominum et uiuificatorem, ex patre procedentem, cum patre et filio coadorandum et conglorificandum, qui loqutus est per profetas ; Et unam sanctam æclesiam catholicam et apostolicam : Confeeor unum babtismum in remissionem peccatorum : spero resurrextionem mortuorum
et vitam futuri sæculi. Amen.	et uitam futuri sæculi. Amen.

---

[1] Muratori, Liturg. Rom. vetus, vol. i., p. 541. This version accompanies a corresponding Greek Creed in Roman letters.

[2] F. E. Warren, Liturgy and Ritual of the Celtic Church, p. 231.

SYMBOLUM APOSTOLORUM.

Mozarabic form.[3]

Credimus in unum Deum Patrem omni-potentem, Factorem cœli et terræ, visi-bilium omnium et invisibilium condi-torem.[4]
Et in unum Dominum *nostrum* Jesum Christum, Filium Dei unigenitum,
et ex Patre natum ante omnia sæcula,
Deum ex Deo ;
Lumen ex lumine ; Deum verum ex Deo vero :
Natum non factum (Homousion Patri : hoc est, ejusdem cum Patre substan-tiæ :) per quem omnia facta sunt quæ in cœlo, et quæ in terra :
Qui propter nos homines, et propter nostram salutem descendit *de cœlis,*
Et incarnatus est de Spiritu Sancto, ex Maria Virgine :
et homo factus *est.*
Passus (est) sub *Pontio* Pilato : Se-pultus :
Tertia die resurrexit.

Ascendit *ad* (in) cœlos : sedet ad dex-teram *Dei* Patris *omnipotentis*
Inde (Iterum) venturus *est* (in gloria) judicare vivos et mortuos :
Cujus regni non erit finis.
(Credimus) et in Spiritum Sanctum, Do-minum (et) vivificatorem, *et* ex Patre et Filio procedentem.
Cum Patre et Filio adorandum et con-glorificandum : qui locutus *est* per prophetas.
Et (In) unam *sanctam* catholicam *et* (atque) Apostolicam Ecclesiam.
Confitemur unum baptisma in remis-sionem peccatorum.
Exspectamus resurrectionem mor-tuorum,
Et vitam *venturi*(futuri) sæculi. Amen.

SYMBOLUM CONSTANTINOPOLITANUM, VEL NICÆNUM.

Roman form.

Credo in unum Deum Patrem omnipo-tentem, factorem cœli et terræ, visibi-lium omnium et invisibilium.

Et in unum Dominum Jesum Christum, Filium Dei unigenitum.
Et ex Patre natum ante omnia sæcula.
Deum de Deo :
Lumen de Lumine : Deum verum de Deo vero.
Genitum non factum, consubstantialem Patri : per quem omnia facta sunt.

Qui propter nos homines, et propter nostram salutem descendit de cœlis.
Et incarnatus est de Spiritu Sancto ex Maria virgine :
Et homo factus est.
Crucifixus etiam pro nobis sub Pontio Pilato : passus et sepultus est.
Et resurrexit tertia die secundum Scripturas.
Et ascendit in cœlum : sedet ad dex-teram Patris.
Et iterum venturus est cum gloria judicare vivos et mortuos :
Cujus regni non erit finis.
Et in Spiritum Sanctum Dominum et vivificantem : qui ex Patre Filioque procedit.
Qui cum Patre et Filio simul adoratur et conglorificatur : qui locutus est per prophetas.
Et unam Sanctam Catholicam et Apostolicam Ecclesiam.
Confiteor unum baptisma in remis-sionem peccatorum.
Et exspecto resurrectionem mortuo-rum.
Et vitam venturi seculi. Amen.

---

[3] Labbe, Concilia, Third Toledo, A.D. 589, tom. v., p. 1001. Words in *italics* are found in Mozarabic Missal, fol. 6, but omitted in Labbe ; words in brackets are given in Labbe, but omitted in the Missal ; see also Brev. Goth. ordo Primæ, p. 945.
[4] Cf. Creed of Antioch, τὸν τῶν ὅλων δημιουργόν τε καὶ ποιητήν.—Soc., II. E., ii., c. x.

Z

Section III.—*Quicunque Vult.*

In addition to the Apostles and Nicene Creeds, there is another form of words in which Christians of the Western Churches have been accustomed to express the faith in acts of worship. It is commonly called "The Athanasian Creed," but more strictly speaking it is a hymn or psalm concerning the Holy Trinity.[1] It is now generally agreed that it was named after Athanasius, not because he was the author of it, but because the faith which it sets forth and guards is that faith which he so well defended in the contest against Arius. There is much uncertainty about its date and author, but it is generally supposed to have been drawn up in France at an early date, possibly during the fifth century. Its purpose evidently was to guard the faithful against the various forms of error which had been introduced into Christianity, and with which they might be brought in contact. It is found in psalters of the eighth century, and from France its use spread to England apparently about that period.[2] But it is evident that it was not known to Isidore, Bishop of Seville, A.D. 603-636. For whilst he refers to a rule of faith in addition to the Nicene and the Apostles Creeds, he uses words which

[1] The title, "The Creed of S. Athanasius," was not added until the last review of the Book of Common Prayer. It was commonly headed, "Symbolum Sancti Athanasii," in mediæval breviaries. But in the First Prayer Book of 1549 it was described merely as "this Confession of our Christian Faith. *Quicunque vult*, &c." And this was continued in the successive editions until 1662, when the words, "commonly called the Creed of Saint Athanasius," were inserted.

[2] Ommanney, "The S.P.C.K. and the Creed of Saint Athanasius," p. 37.

show that this included various matters of Catholic tradition, in addition to the explanation of the belief in the Trinity; and "Quicunque Vult" is not found in the Mozarabic or Spanish Service Books which were revised by him.[1]

SECTION IV.—*The use of the Creeds in Acts of Worship.*

For several centuries the public use of the Creed seems to have been confined to the profession of Christianity and to the Service of Holy Baptism. It was solemnly delivered and taught to the catechumens after they had gone through a course of preparation such as we find in the Catechetical Lectures of S. Cyril, but it was not otherwise used in the public services. The use of the Creed in baptism is frequently described in early writings. In the Apostolic Constitutions directions are

[1] Isidore, de Eccles. Officiis, lib. i., cap. 16, *De Symbolo Nicæno ;* cap. 22, *De Symbolo, i.e.,* the Apostles Creed ; cap. 23, *De Regula fidei.* " Hæc est autem post Apostolórum symbolum certissima fides, quam doctores nostri tradiderunt, ut profiteamur Patrem et Filium et Spiritum Sanctum unius esse essentiæ, ejusdemque potestatis et sempiternitatis unum Deum invisibilem, ita ut singulis personarum proprietate servata, nec substantialiter Trinitas dividi, nec personaliter debeat omnino confundi." He then goes on to explain about creation; about marriage; that baptism must not be repeated ; about the unity and peace of the Church ; and that temporal goods are not common; ending thus : " Hæc est Catholicæ traditionis et fidei vera integritas de qua si unum quodlibet respuatur tota fidei credulitas amittitur." From which it appears that though " Quicunque vult " was unknown to him, a somewhat similar form of explanation of the Christian faith was in use in his days.

For the Latin original of *Quicunque vult,* see Ommanney, " Early History of the Athanasian Creed," Appendix, p. 403 ; Bishop Harold Browne, " Exposition of the Articles," p. 229.

given for the instruction of the catechumens in the various subjects which a Christian ought to know, after which the person to be baptized is called upon to renounce Satan and express his adherence to Christ, and declare his belief in a form of words in general agreement with the Eastern model.[1]

Similarly, in the Roman Church an examination of the candidates for Holy Baptism was made with great care and many prayers during Lent; after which they were admitted to baptism on the Wednesday before Easter, as follows: first of all the names of the candidates were written down; then they were called into Church, and arranged, the males on the right, the females on the left; then prayer was made for them, and salt was blessed and given to them; then the exorcism followed, wherein prayer was offered that God would send to them His good angel, and the devil was summoned to depart from them. The ceremony named " the opening of the ears " followed, in which, after the word *Ephphatha* had been solemnly pronounced, an explanation of the four Holy Gospels was given, and portions from each were read. Then the Creed was repeated with a brief explanation.[2]

Such services in connection with the testing of the

---

[1] Apost. Constit., lib. vii., 39-41.

[2] A rubric at the end of the Gelasian Canon directs that notice should be given to the people beforehand: " Posthæc commonenda est plebs pro jejuniis . . . sive pro Scrutiniis, vel aurium apertione." The services on the Third Sunday in Lent referred to those who were about to bring their children to be baptized, the following words being added: " *Infra Canonem.* Memento Domine famulorum famularumque tuarum; qui electos tuos suscepturi sunt ad sanctam gratiam Baptismi tui . . ." Mention of those about to be baptized was again made on the Fourth and Fifth Sundays in Lent, and on the following Wednesday the services named *Scrutinia* were held.—Muratori, vol. i., p. 698; pp. 521, 526, 529.

candidates for baptism are found in various ancient missals, though nowhere so fully as in the Sacramentary of Gelasius; and it is evident from these services that there was much diversity of practice in early times respecting the Creed which was used on this occasion in the Western Church. In the earliest " Ordo Romanus," belonging, it is supposed, to the early part of the seventh century, the Apostles Creed is apparently appointed to be said. Similarly, in " Missale Gallicanum vetus," a Gallican missal of the eighth, or possibly the seventh century, the Apostles Creed is provided; and the same is found in a missal of the monastery of Gellone, *circa* A.D. 800, from the library of S. Germains.[1] But from the Sacramentary of Gelasius we learn that at some period between the fifth and eighth century the Creed which was used in baptism was the Nicene Creed, and this was repeated first in Greek and then in Latin to the candidates. And in other Service Books of France and Germany, previous to the tenth century, the same Creed was used.[2]

At the same time, whilst Churches differed as to the

[1] The meaning of the words in the Ordo Romanus is not quite clear: " Hac expleta ambulet sacerdos in circuitum, imposita manu super capita eorum, dicat tantum excelsa voce, *Credo in Deum*. Vertit se ad feminas et facit similiter."—Muratori, vol. ii., pp. 997; see also pp. 710, 721. But if the whole of the Apostles Creed was not repeated, it is evident that the service was intended to lead the thoughts of the catechumens to it. For the Gellone Missal, see Martene, lib. i., cap. i., art. xii., ordo 2.

[2] It is not certain that the Sacramentary of Gelasius describes the custom of the Roman Church; it is more probable that this was a peculiarity belonging to some Church of Gaul to which this particular MS. of the Gelasian Sacramentary belonged.—Muratori, vol. i., p. 540. See also Martene, lib. i., cap. i., art. xii., ordo 3, Pontifical of the Church of Poictiers, *circa* A.D. 900; ordo 4, MS. from the monastery of Werth, in Munster, &c.

Creed which was repeated to the candidates for baptism, the interrogatories which were put to them were universally founded on the same model, if not in exactly the same words, and followed the form of the Apostles Creed. It should be understood that the interrogatories were distinct from the services connected with the hearing and reciting of the Creed, which took place during the " Scrutiny," or previous preparation for baptism, and generally on a previous day. At the time of the baptism the questions were asked after this general form :—

" Credis in Deum Patrem Omnipotentem ? *Answer.* Credo.

Credis et in Jesum Christum Filium ejus unicum Dominum nostrum, natum et passum ? *Answer.* Credo.

Credis et in Spiritum Sanctum, Sanctam Ecclesiam catholicam, remissionem peccatorum, carnis resurrectionem ? *Answer.* Credo." [1]

But in some Churches the whole of the Apostles Creed was thus repeated under the form of three questions, and in the course of the Middle Ages the words " Vitam æternam " were added in all Churches.[2]

In later times the Apostles Creed was universally used in the Western Church as the Baptismal Creed. According to the Roman Use it is repeated with the Godparents at the beginning of the Service for the Baptism of Infants, and in the Baptism of Adults it is repeated by the bishop with the person to be baptized.[3] The me-

---

[1] Martene, lib. i., cap. i., art. xviii., ordo 4, 5, &c.

[2] *Ibid.*, ordo 6, 7, &c. In Sacramentarium Gallicanum the whole Creed is so repeated, with the variation, " carnis resurrectionem, vitam habere post mortem, in gloriam Christi resurgere."—*Ibid.*, ordo 3 ; Muratori, vol. ii., p. 851.

[3] Pontificale Romanum, 1818.

diæval Use of Sarum was the same, with the exception that the last interrogatory was worded thus, " et vitam æternam post mortem ? " which has been continued in our English form.[1] The ancient Celtic use was also similar.[2]

The Creed which was entrusted to Christian people with so much solemnity at the time of their baptism was stored up in their memories for continual use. But for many centuries the ordinary daily use of the Creed seems to have been confined to private repetition. For instance, in the Mozarabic Missal, in the service of Palm Sunday, on which day the Creed was delivered in the Spanish Church to those about to be baptized, an address was provided, taken from a sermon to catechumens by S. Augustine, in which the people were exhorted to use it daily, " before going to sleep, and before starting to their work," with a caution expressing the objection which was felt to its being committed to writing. After which it was solemnly repeated by all three times.[3]

The use of the Creed in the Liturgy can be traced back as far as the fifth century. But it is not known when it was first introduced. Probably it was the custom to recite it occasionally long before it formed part of the fixed service, and there is no doubt that its

[1] Maskell, Monum. Ritual., vol. i., pp. 12, 22, Office for Public Baptism of Infants.

[2] F. E. Warren, Liturgy and Ritual of Celtic Church.

[3] Mozar. Missal, folio 151 : " Charissimi, accipite regulam fidei, quod Symbolum dicitur. Et cum acceperitis in corde scribite, et quotidie apud vosmet ipsos dicite. Antequam dormiatis ; antequam procedatis vestro symbolo vos munite. Symbolum nemo scribit, ut legi possit. Sed ad recensendum ne forte deleat oblivio quod non tradidit lectio, sit vobis codex vestra memoria." Cf. S. Augustine, ad Catechumenos, lib. i., cap. i., tom. ix., p. 291.

regular use was ordained at different periods in different Churches. In the Church of Antioch it was first ordered to be used *at every service* by Peter the Fuller, who was Bishop of Antioch *circa* A.D. 471 ; and it began to be used in a similar manner at Constantinople, A.D. 511, where " it had been previously used only on the occasions when the bishop explained, and delivered it to those about to be baptized."[1] The example was followed in the Spanish Church in the course of the same century. For it was decreed by the Third Council of Toledo, A.D. 589, that the Constantinopolitan Creed should be recited immediately after the Consecration, before the Lord's Prayer ; and it is found in this position in the Mozarabic Missal.[2] It is mentioned also by Isidore, Bishop of Hispalis (Seville), A.D. 603-636, as the Creed "put forth at the Nicene Synod ; " and he says, " it is for this reason proclaimed by the people with general confession in all churches, because it tramples upon all impious errors and blasphemies of perverted faith."[3] From which it is evident that its regular use was introduced into the Liturgy in Spain in consequence of the recent prevalence of heresies there.

It is uncertain when the Creed was introduced into the Roman Liturgy. It is stated by Bingham that it was not so used in the Roman Church until A.D. 1014.[4] But there seems to be some mistake in this statement, since directions for its use in its present position after

[1] Martene, lib. i., cap. iv., art. v., 9 ; Bingham, Antiq., book x., chap. iv., 17.

[2] Labbe's Concilia, Third Council of Toledo, Canon 2, tom. v., p. 1009. See above, p. 332.

[3] Isidore, de Eccles. Offic., lib. i., cap. xvi.

[4] Bingham, Antiq., book x., chap. iv., sect. 17.

the Gospel are found in the second *Ordo Romanus*, which belongs to a very much earlier date, probably the seventh or eighth century.[1] And the author of the ancient exposition of the Mass named "Gemma Animæ," states that Pope Damasus, A.D. 366-384, first gave directions that it should be sung at the Mass.[2] Pope Damasus is known to have been a zealous defender of orthodoxy against the Arians, but there are difficulties in accepting this statement as correct. Possibly this tradition and the directions in the *Ordo Romanus* referred to the occasional use of the Creed. For it is evident that it was not in regular use in the days of Pope Gregory the Great, since the opening rubric of the earliest copy of his Sacramentary does not allude to it. Such occasional use of the Creed may have been allowed at that time to drop out altogether, so that its re-introduction into the Roman Liturgy in the eleventh century appeared to be a new addition to the service.

It is interesting to us as English Churchmen to find that the Celtic Church had adopted the use of the Nicene Creed long before this date, for it is found, without the *filioque* clause, in the Stowe Missal which is assigned to the ninth century.[3] It stands there in a similar position as in our English Service, only separated from the Gospel by certain collects.

---

[1] "Post lectum evangelium, candelæ in suo loco extinguuntur, et ab Episcopo *Credo in unum Deum* cantatur; et thuribula per altaria portantur et postea ad nares hominum feruntur et per manum ad os trahitur."—Muratori, vol. ii., p. 1023. In a note Muratori states that this passage has not been interpolated, though some have thought so.

[2] "*Credo in unum Deum* Constantinopolitana Synodus composuit; sed Damasus Papa ad Missam cantari instituit."—Gemma Animæ, lib. i., cap. 88.

[3] F. E. Warren, Liturgy and Ritual of the Celtic Church, p. 231.

At what date the Creed was introduced into the daily " Hour " Services cannot be stated with certainty. The regular use of a Creed belongs to the Service of Prime in · the Western Church, which is known to have been introduced in the time of Cassian, A.D. 390-440;[1] and in ancient examples of this Office the Apostles Creed appears amongst the *Preces*. It occurs again in a similar position in the Office of Compline. In many copies *Quicunque Vult* also occurs a little before it in the Office of Prime, having been in daily use in some Churches in addition to the Apostles Creed.[2]

In the Mozarabic Breviary, which in many particulars resembles the Eastern forms of service, the Nicene Creed is found in a similar position. It is ordered to be used after *Te Deum laudamus* and *Gloria in excelsis Deo* upon Sundays and Festivals in the Office of Prime, and it is headed " Symbolum Apostolorum."[3] But since Isidore makes no mention of Prime in his treatise upon the Offices of the Church it appears probable that this service was added in the seventh century or later.

In the Eastern Church the Nicene Creed is used in the Midnight or Mattin Service, and again in Compline.[4]

The use of the Creed as part of the preparation prefixed to the various " Hour " Services in the Western Church was an addition made after the eleventh century.[5]

---

[1] Page 121.

[2] Martene, de antiq. Eccles. rit., lib. iv., cap. viii., 3; de antiq. Monach. rit., lib. i., cap. iv., 13; Amalarius, de Eccles. Offic., lib. iv., cap. ii.; Rituale Eccles. Dunelm., pp. 166, 181. See above, pp. 135, 142, 259.

[3] Breviarium Gothicum, Horæ Canon. ordo Primæ, p. 945.

[4] Neale, Holy Eastern Church, Introd., vol. ii.

[5] Page 124. Martene, de Antiq. Monach. Rit., lib. i., cap. ii., 32, 33.

LIST OF WORKS REFERRED TO.

Alcuin. Opera. Migne's Patrol., tom. ci.

Amalarius. (See Speculum antiquæ Devotionis.)

Anecdotes of Archbishop Cranmer, by Ralf Morice. Camden Soc.

Athanasius. Opera. 2 vols. (Ex offic. Commelin.) 1600.

Augustine. Opera. 10 vols. Paris, 1614.

Beverege. Synodicon. Oxon, 1672.

Bingham. Antiquities of the Christian Church. 9 vols. 1838.

Bona. Rerum Liturgicarum libri duo. Rome, 1671.

Breviarium ad usum Sarum. Edited by Proctor and Wordsworth. Cantab. 1882.

—— Gothicum. See Mozarabic.

—— Romanum. Revised by Cardinal Quignon. 2nd edition. Rome, 1537.

—— Romanum. Mechlin, 1848.

Bryennius. Doctrine of the Twelve Apostles. Constantinople, 1883.

Bucer, Martin. Scripta Anglicana. Basil, 1577.

—— Defensio Deliberationis Hermanni. Basle, 1618.

Burnet. History of the Reformation. 6 vols. Oxon, 1829.

Canones Concilii Provincialis Coloniensis: cum Enchiridion Hermanni Archiepiscopi. Colon. 1538.

Cassian. Opera. Migne's Patrol. tom. xlix., l.

Chambers, J. D. Divine Worship in England in the Thirteenth and Fourteenth Cent. London, 1877.

Chrysostom, S. John. Opera. Græcè. 8 vols. Eton, 1612.

—— Opera. Latinè. 5 vols. Paris, 1536.

—— Liturgia, Latinè. Venice, 1644.

Collier. Eccles. Hist. 9 vols. 1840.

Cotelerius. Patres Apostolici. 2 vols. Amsterd. 1724.

Cyprian. Opera. Oxon, 1682.

Cyril of Jerusalem. Opera. Græcè et Latinè, by Prevotius. Paris, 1631.

—— Catechetical Lectures. Oxon, 1838.

Dionysius Areopagita. Latinè. Paris, 1515.

—— Græcè. Migne's Patrol., tom. iii.

Epiphanius. Opera. 2 vols. Paris, 1622.

Gemma Animæ. In Bibliotheca Patrum. 10 vols. Paris, 1644.

Graduale ad usum Sarum. Paris, 1532.

Greek Liturgies. Edited by Dr. C. A. Swainson. Cantab. 1884.

Gregory the Great. Opera. 4 vols. Antwerp, 1615.

Herman. Simplex ac Pia Deliberatio. Bonn, 1535.

—— A simple and religious Consultation. London, 1548.

—— Enchiridion. (See Canon. Concil. Prov. Colon.)

Hittorpius. De divinis Officiis. Colon. 1568.

Isidorus Hispalensis. De Officiis ecclesiasticis. Lipsiæ, 1534.

Justin Martyr. Apologiæ. Bonn, 1860.

Labbe. Concilia. 14 vols. Paris, 1671.

Lay Folks Mass Book. Edited by Canon Simmons. Early English Text Society.

Leofric Missal. Edited by F. E. Warren. Oxon, 1883.

Mabillon. De Liturgia Gallicana. Paris, 1685.

Martene. De antiquis Ecclesiæ ritibus. 2 vols. Bassani, 1788.

—— De antiquis Monachorum ritibus. Bassani, 1788.

Menard. Divi Gregorii liber Sacramentorum. Paris, 1642.

Mozarabic Missal. MSS. of tenth century. (British Museum Addit. 30,844-6.)

—— Toledo, 1500.

Mozarabic Missal. Migne's Patrol., tom. lxxxv.

—— Breviary. Migne's Patrol., tom. lxxxvi.

Muratori. Liturgia Romana vetus. 2 vols. Venet. 1748.

Pontifical of Egbert. Surtees Society.

Pontificale Romanum. 1818.

Prideaux. Connection of Old and New Testaments. 2 vols. 1718.

Processionale ad usum Sarum. 1544.

Rituale Ecclesiæ Dunelmensis. Surtees Society.

Rufinus. Expositio in Symbolum. Appendix to Cyprian's works. Oxon, 1682.

Sarum Missal. London, 1520.

—— Edited by F. H. Dickinson. 1884.

—— in English. Church Press Company.

Schleusner. Lexicon Vet. et Novi Test. Glasgow, 1822.

Speculum antiquæ devotionis. Edited by Joh. Cochlæus. Mogunt. 1549.

Stillingfleet. Antiquities of British Churches. Oxon, 1842.

Stowe Missal. In "Liturgy and Ritual of Celtic Church." By F. E. Warren.

Strype. Memorials of Cranmer. 2 vols. Oxon, 1840.

Suicer. Thesaurus Ecclesiasticus. 2 vols. 1682.

Sylloge Confessionum. Oxon, 1827.

Tertullianus. Opera. Migne's Patrol., tom. i., ii.

Wulafridus Strabo. In Bibliotheca Patrum. 10 vols. Paris, 1644.

INDEX.